The Lapita Peoples

General Editors
Peter Bellwood and Ian Glover

Each book in this series is devoted to a people (or group of associated peoples) from the vast area of the world extending from Hawaii in the north to Tasmania in the south and from Fiji in the east to Thailand in the west. The books, written by historians, anthropologists and archaeologists from all over the world, are both scholarly and accessible. In many cases the volumes are the only available account of their subject.

Already published

The People of Bali
*Angela Hobart, Urs Ramseyer
and Albert Leeman*

The Peoples of Borneo
Victor T. King

The Lapita Peoples
Patrick Vinton Kirch

The Khmers
I. W. Mabbett and David Chandler

The Bugis
Christian Pelras

In preparation

The Maoris
Atholl Anderson

The Malays
*A. C. Milner and
Jane Drakard*

The Fijians
*Nicholas Thomas and
Victoria Luker*

The Peoples of the Lesser Sundas
James L. Fox

The Melanesians
Matthew Spriggs

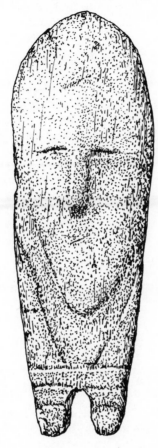

Frontispiece. Small anthropomorphic image carved from porpoise bone, excavated from the Talepakemalai Lapita site, Mussau Islands. (Drawing by Margaret Davidson)

THE LAPITA PEOPLES
Ancestors of the Oceanic World

Patrick Vinton Kirch

BLACKWELL *Publishers*

First published 1997
Reprinted 1999

Blackwell Publishers Inc
350 Main Street
Malden, Massachusetts 02148, USA

Blackwell Publishers Ltd
108 Cowley Road
Oxford OX4 1JF, UK

Library of Congress Cataloging in Publication Data
Kirch, Patrick Vinton.
    The Lapita peoples : ancestors of the oceanic world / Patrick Vinton Kirch.
        p. cm. — (The Peoples of South–East Asia and the Pacific)
    Includes bibliographical references and index.
    ISBN 1–55786–112–9. — ISBN 1–57718–036–4 (pbk.)
        1. Lapita culture. 2. Man, Prehistoric—Oceania. 3. Pottery, Prehistoric—Oceania. 4. Commerce, Prehistoric—Oceania.
    5. Excavations (Archaeology)—Oceania. 6. Oceania—Antiquities.
    I. Title. II. Series.
    GN871.K57   1996   96–8287
    995—dc20   CIP

British Library Cataloguing in Publication Data
A CIP catalogue record for this book is available from the British Library

Typeset in 11 on 12 ½ pt Sabon
by Graphicraft Typesetters Limited, Hong Kong
Printed and bound in Great Britain by MPG Books Ltd, Bodmin, Cornwall

This book is printed on acid-free paper

For
Roger C. Green
*Whose Myriad Contributions Have Enabled
Current Syntheses of Pacific Prehistory*

Figures

Maps

Tables

Preface

The Pacific Ocean spans virtually one third of the earth's surface. Scattered across the face of this watery world like so many celestial bodies are the islands and archipelagoes of Oceania. Traditionally, geographers and anthropologists classified the peoples who inhabited these islands into three main groups: Melanesians, Micronesians, and Polynesians. More recently, we have come to recognize the highly artificial nature of this taxonomy which runs roughshod over the history of origins and relationships of these varied peoples and cultures. A more historically-meaningful grouping of Pacific islanders derives from a linguistic perspective, dividing them into two fundamental groups: the Austronesians and the Non-Austronesians (a grouping that includes both Papuan and Australian languages). The Austronesians – or perhaps, more precisely, those peoples who speak Austronesian languages – are distributed throughout island Southeast Asia and along the north and east coasts of New Guinea, and out into the expanse of the central and marginal Pacific. Archaeological and linguistic research alike has recently converged on an understanding that the Austronesians, originating perhaps in the south China-Taiwan area some 6,000 years ago, underwent an unprecedented diaspora over the next several millennia, ultimately to span the distance between Madagascar in the west and Easter Island in the east.

This Austronesian diaspora began to encompass the islands of the Pacific Ocean proper about 3,500 years ago, with the eastwards movement of people out of island Southeast Asia and along the northern fringe of New Guinea into the Bismarck

Archipelago. Linguistically, this movement was marked by (or resulted in) a number of innovations in speech and vocabulary, such that a distinct subgroup of Austronesian languages can be defined: *Proto Oceanic*. Speakers of this Proto Oceanic language rapidly expanded and dispersed throughout a sizable area of the southwest Pacific, and ultimately their descendants discovered and populated the most remote islands and archipelagoes in the eastern Pacific. With the notable exceptions of Palau and the Marianas in western Micronesia, and of most of interior New Guinea and a few small pockets in the Bismarck Archipelago and Solomon Islands, all of the indigenous peoples of the areas classically called Melanesia, Micronesia, and Polynesia speak *Oceanic* languages.

Used in the sense described above, the Oceanic cultures of the Pacific span a vast geographic area ranging from New Guinea and its neighboring islands in the west, to Hawai'i, Easter Island, and New Zealand in the northern, eastern, and southern Pacific. Traditionally, the Oceanic peoples spoke at least 450 distinctive but related languages and had as many cultures, and prior to the decimation resulting from European-introduced diseases and firearms, their aggregate population numbered at least 1,230,000 people, and probably more (the estimate is from Oliver 1989:28). Oceanic societies are remarkably differentiated in various aspects of kinship, social organization, political structure, and religion, and yet they share a great many systemic cultural patterns (in other words, they are a wonderful instance of "variations within a theme").

This book is about the origins of these Oceanic-speaking peoples and cultures. One of the most important advances in Pacific islands archaeology in the 1960s and 1970s was the discovery that an early, well-attested archaeological horizon which came to be called Lapita, had once spanned the long-standing ethnographic divide between Polynesia and Melanesia. As investigations of Lapita archaeology proceeded – and the chronology of this horizon was traced gradually back into the islands skirting the Bismarck Sea – its importance for Oceanic origins was increasingly recognized. A majority of prehistorians and historical linguists have now come to regard Lapita as the archaeological manifestation of those peoples who spoke Proto Oceanic and its immediate daughter languages. Lapita – which spans a time period between about 3,600 and 2,000 years ago, and is distributed in space from the Bismarcks to New Caledonia and eastwards to Samoa and Tonga – has come to be recognized as the ancestral cultural stock from which the modern diversity of Oceanic-speaking peoples and cultures ultimately arose.

My own involvement with Lapita research now spans almost three decades. I first heard of Lapita around 1966 as a young student associated with the Bishop Museum in Honolulu, when the finds from recent excavations of Lapita sites in Tonga, Yanuca, and Île des Pins were sparking a re-thinking of long-held ideas concerning Polynesian origins, and of the relationships between Polynesia and Melanesia in antiquity. While preparing to partake in my first expedition to the South Pacific – as assistant to Bishop Museum zoologist Yoshio Kondo in his studies of the archaic Pacific land snail family Partulidae – I was advised by Roger Green to keep an eye open for possible Lapita pottery sites in our field area, the Loyalty Islands of southern Melanesia. (I did find sites during that 1968 field trip, but none with the characteristic dentate-stamped Lapita pottery.)

Roger Green himself soon embarked on an ambitious archaeological program in the southeastern Solomon Islands, jointly directed with Douglas Yen, with a central aim of investigating Lapita sites. Before commencing my graduate studies at Yale, Yen extended an invitation to accompany him on the second field season of the Southeast Solomons Project, in 1971. While en route to the remote Polynesian Outlier of Anuta, the aging British High Commissioner's ship *Belama* on which we sailed stopped briefly in the Reef Islands, allowing a visit to the Nenumbo site which Green had discovered and tested the previous year. The village headman guided us to Roger's excavations, and I was able examine first-hand the reddish-brown sherds covered with fine dentate-stamped and incised designs that littered the site's surface in large numbers. On Anuta, my excavations at the deeply stratified An-6 site produced plain ware sherds dating to 900 BC, overlapping in time with classic Lapita assemblages. These finds raised questions of the relationship between the Anutan plain ware and the elaborately decorated Lapita pottery, which are only now being answered.

Throughout the 1970s I was engaged in wrestling with matters pertaining to Lapita. During fieldwork for my Yale doctoral dissertation in 1974, I discovered and excavated the Late Eastern Lapita pottery site of Tavai, on Futuna Island in Western Polynesia. Dating to about 250 BC, the Tavai site is one of several Western Polynesian sites linking early Lapita assemblages to later Polynesian Plain Ware, through a millennium-long sequence of ceramic change. This critical linkage underlies our modern conception of the Polynesian cultures of the eastern Pacific as ultimately descended from the makers of Lapita pottery. Two years later, on the northern Tongan outlier of Niuatoputapu, I excavated the early Lapita occupation at Lolokoka. On Niuatoputapu, through seven months of survey and excavation, we were able to construct a prehistoric sequence that began with the earliest settlement of the island, at Lolokoka, and continued though Late Eastern Lapita and Polynesian Plain Ware assemblages, to classic aceramic "Polynesian" sites in the past two thousand years. Shortly after completing the Tongan work, Doug Yen and I returned to the Solomon Islands, where we were engaged for two years in an intensive study of anthropologically-famous Tikopia. As in the earlier Anutan work, our excavations demonstrated settlement of the island by about 900 BC, with the earliest deposits characterized primarily by plain ware, although in this case classic dentate-stamped Lapita sherds were also uncovered. The Anutan and Tikopian materials convinced me that we needed to pay greater attention to the plain ware components of Lapita ceramic assemblages.

After the Tikopian expeditions my research diverged from Lapita to other matters, yet the questions surrounding Lapita expansion into the southwestern Pacific were never far from my thoughts. Thus in 1983, when Jim Allen approached several archaeologists at the Pacific Science Congress in New Zealand to propose a major inter-institutional program in Lapita archaeology, I eagerly agreed to collaborate. Over large jugs of watery beer at Cook's Bar in Dunedin, Jim outlined his concept of a coordinated survey and excavation program in the Bismarck Archipelago of Papua New Guinea. By 1985, the Lapita Homeland Project was a funded reality, and I had accepted the task of investigating Lapita sites reported from the Mussau Islands, on the northerly rim of the Bismarck island arc.

In August 1985, the expedition's ship *Dick Smith Explorer*

took Pru Gaffey, Sally Brockwell, and me on a stormy passage from Kavieng to Mussau. That we would find Lapita was not in question, since prior tests by Brian Egloff had confirmed the presence of at least one large site on the off-lying coral islet of Eloaua. Nonetheless, what we were to uncover during the next weeks exceeded my wildest expectations. At Talepakemalai, a unique geomorphological sequence of shoreline progradation had buried and preserved the remains of a former stilt-house village, which stood over the Eloaua tidal flats some 3,600 years ago. Preserved wooden posts and the seeds and nuts of economically-important plants were recovered along with ex-quisitely decorated Lapita vessels, shell beads and armrings, fish-hooks, abundant obsidian flakes, and many other artifacts and faunal materials. Here was not only the oldest Lapita site yet discovered, but one so rich in cultural materials that it greatly expanded the possibilities for understanding Lapita settlements, economy, exchange, and society. A major research effort was called for and in 1986 and 1988 I returned to Eloaua with students and colleagues for additional excavations, not only at Talepakemalai but at several other Lapita and post-Lapita sites. Some of the results of these three expeditions have been pub-lished in a series of preliminary papers, and the final monograph on our project gradually nears completion.

Through the efforts of the Lapita Homeland Project and other recent research, knowledge of Lapita has expanded tre-mendously over the past decade. Social anthropologists, geo-graphers, natural scientists, historians, linguists, and many others are keen to know what Pacific archaeologists presently think about Lapita, for our findings often have bearing on their own research. Yet these colleagues cannot be expect to pour through site reports written in the specialized jargon of contemporary archaeology. They deserve a synthesis – no less grounded in the painstakingly extracted field and laboratory data – freed of the usual barriers erected by academic culture with its theor-etical and paradigmatic posturing. Such was the opportunity presented when the editors of Blackwell's Peoples of Southeast Asia and the Pacific series invited me to contribute this book. I hope that their patience through the several years that it has taken to write this work are adequately rewarded.

Acknowledgments

I would like to thank the editors, Ian Glover and – especially – Peter Bellwood, for their invitation to write a book for this series, even though it was not the book they initially requested! John Davey, of Blackwell Publishers, has been an extraordinarily patient and understanding editor. So many colleagues, students, and associates have been involved in my Lapita research over the years that it is impossible to thank or acknowledge them all. I must, however, mention Doug Yen, with whom I shared fieldwork experiences in the eastern Solomon Islands, and who taught me much about Pacific ethnobotany. Jim Allen invited my participation in the 1985 Lapita Homeland Project, which led to my excavations at the Talepakemalai site. I would also like to acknowledge the substantial support of the U.S. National Science Foundation, whose Anthropology Program funded the majority of my field investigations of Lapita sites, through a series of grants between 1974 and 1990. In these politically-conservative days when research funding is increasingly threatened, I can only be grateful to have been an active young fieldworker in the decades of the seventies and eighties. It also gives me much pleasure to acknowledge the loving support of my wife, Thérèse Babineau, who has unfailingly encouraged me in my research and writing projects. Thérèse also lent material support to this project by taking many of the fine photographs of Lapita artifacts that grace the following chapters.

The following colleagues graciously read one or more chapters of the draft manuscript: Jim Allen, Peter Bellwood, Jonathan Friedlaender, Roger Green, Rosemary Joyce, Andrew Pawley,

Sue Serjeantson, and Matthew Spriggs. Their critical comments were most helpful in the final stage of revising the manuscript. Mark Hall provided assistance with the calibration of radiocarbon dates using the OXCAL program.

Finally, I pay homage on two accounts to Roger C. Green. Intellectually, Roger has done more than anyone else to put Lapita on the map of world prehistory, and the present book would quite literally have been impossible to write without his outstanding contributions to the field. And on the personal side, Roger has been a mentor, friend, and colleague to whom I owe more than I can ever repay. My dedication of this book to him is a slight advance against that debt.

1

Introduction

Beaches are beginnings and endings. They are the frontiers and boundaries of islands.

I think history is more likely to be born on beaches, marginal spaces in between land and sea. Anyway this is where I would take you, to beaches where everything is relativised a little, turned around, where tradition is as much invented as handed down, where otherness is both a new discovery and a reflection of something old.

Greg Dening, *Mr Bligh's Bad Language*

In the middle centuries of the second millennium BC, the beaches of the Bismarck Archipelago in western Melanesia witnessed a remarkable scene. Piercing the arc of the western horizon, well-crafted sea-going canoes brought an exotic cargo to these coral sand and mangrove-rimmed shores, baking under an equatorial sun. This cargo was not material, though the canoes certainly carried the impedimenta of a people intent on establishing permanent outposts on unknown islands. The cargo I speak of was transported in the minds of those voyagers, encoded in *culture* and in *language*. On those beaches, seafaring strangers who spoke an Austronesian language encountered indigenous people of the land, distant descendants of much earlier migrations into the Pleistocene super-continent of Sahul. The indigenous "land people" (for it seems that they were more at home in the "bush" than at sea) spoke diverse Papuan languages,[1] and carried in their heads other kinds of culture, other world views. On these tropical shores – in this liminal space between land and sea – a meeting of peoples and cultures would transform

the face of Melanesia, and in due course precipitate one of the
greatest migratory feats of human history: the human conquest
of the vast eastern Pacific. Societies that nineteenth-century
European voyagers were to classify as "Polynesian," as well as
the eastern "Micronesian" peoples of the Caroline and Marshall
Islands, all trace their genesis to a common history in the Bismarck Archipelago and adjacent regions of Near Oceania[2] in
the second millennium BC. Indeed, this history has profound
implications for long-standing anthropological concepts, such
as the explanatory value of the classic tripartite division of the
Oceanic world into Melanesia, Polynesia, and Micronesia.

On these Melanesian shores in the second millennium BC, no
scribes or chroniclers penned accounts for distant generations of
historians or anthropologists to ponder. Yet the sands of these
beaches – beaches with names like Talepakemalai, Etakosarai,
and Apalo – entomb another kind of historical text. In patterned
scatters of potsherds from which stylized faces stare coldly
with a semiotic virtuosity we can sense yet not translate (plate
1.1), in the half-rotted bases of wooden stilt houses preserved
below the water table, in obsidian artifacts traded hundreds of
kilometers beyond their sources, in the bones of fish, turtles,
and pigs served up in feasts of unknown import, in the seed
cases of coconuts, tropical almonds and other plants that
sustained life, these beaches hold a record of an encounter
between stranger and native 3,500 years ago. From this archaeological record – this patterned material "text" – we may hope
to read a history of what transpired on those shores. The sites
and artifacts dating to this critical period in Melanesian prehistory have come to be called *Lapita*, after the name of a beach
on the western coast of New Caledonia, where typical dentate-
stamped pottery was excavated in the early 1950s.

The translation of the Lapita archaeological "text" into social
and cultural history is a complex matter. Archaeological fieldwork in Melanesia commenced in earnest just three decades
ago, and much of the material on which this book is based
has been excavated only within the past nine years. In such a
youthful enterprise, interpretations are bound to change rapidly, and disagreement among scholars must be expected. What
I have written here will provoke debate – if not outright disagreement – among some of my colleagues. This state of affairs

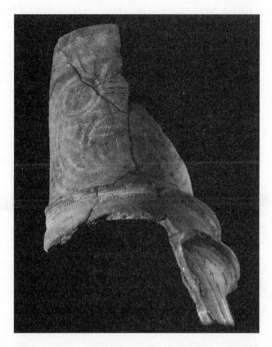

Plate 1.1   *Portion of a large ceramic cylinder-stand excavated at
the Talepakemalai site, Mussau Islands. The central motif is a
stylized human face nested within a more abstract frieze.
(Photo by Thérèse Babineau)*

recommends caution, yet it also promotes intellectual exhilaration. This is an exciting time in Melanesian archaeology and prehistory, as our knowledge and understanding seem to increase by leaps and bounds on a yearly basis. In this spirit, I offer here my reading of these archaeological texts, of what I think they may tell us about an essential *conjoncture* on those Melanesian beaches so long ago.

The Southwest Pacific

The area of concern to us in this study of the Lapita peoples is the southwest Pacific, extending from New Guinea and the Bismarck Archipelago in the west, through the large island-arcs of the Solomons and Vanuatu (formerly, New Hebrides) to New Caledonia in the south, and as far east as Fiji, Tonga, and Samoa (map 1.1). In classic geographical terms, this region includes both Melanesia and some western island groups within Polynesia (Samoa and Tonga). For reasons that will become clear in this book, these older geographic divisions sometimes hinder our understanding of the archaeological record and of historical process. A more useful distinction, which I will use repeatedly, is between *Near Oceania* and *Remote Oceania* (Green 1991a). Near Oceania encompasses New Guinea, the Bismarcks, and the Solomons, a region that is biogeographically rich in comparsion with Remote Oceania.[3] The latter consists of those islands and archipelagoes to the north, east, and south of the heavy line shown in map 1.1. Not only is Remote Oceania more depauperate in its terrestrial flora and fauna than Near Oceania, but on current evidence its islands knew no human footprints until the advent of the Lapita peoples. Near Oceania, on the other hand, was settled by hunting-and-gathering populations at least 40,000 years ago.

The southwest Pacific region encompasses a remarkable diversity of island types and landforms.[4] The larger archipelagoes from the Bismarcks to Fiji are primarily of andesitic island-arc formation, at the boundary between the Pacific Plate and the complex mosaic of sub-plates underlying the Melanesian region.[5] These large islands are geologically old and often deeply weathered. Prior to human advent, they were cloaked in dense rainforest vegetation. At the eastern end of the Lapita region, the Samoan and Tongan archipelagoes present somewhat contrasting island formations. Most of the Tongan islands are of the *makatea* type, consisting of elevated reef limestones on submerged volcanic pinnacles. Samoa, much younger than the other groups, consists of mid-plate volcanic islands (of "hot spot" origin) built up by successive lava flows emanating from a magma plume that periodically pierced the thin Pacific Plate.

For the most part, this is a tropical world (although New Caledonia extends into the subtropics). The islands were covered in rainforests notable for their high diversity of plant species, and the soils and rainfall regimes of these islands were conducive to cultivating tropical root, tuber, and tree crops. Moreover, the oceans surrounding these archipelagoes supported

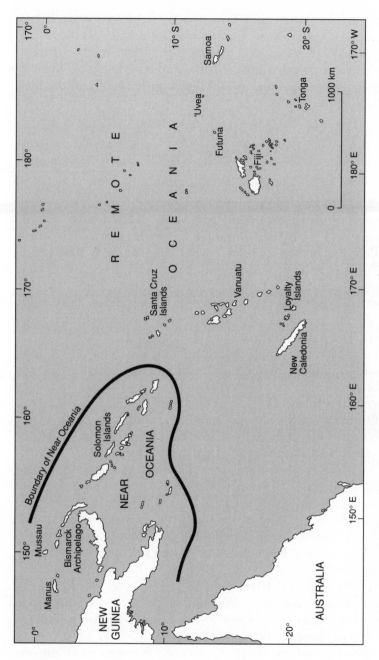

Map 1.1 Islands and Archipelagoes of the Southwest Pacific; the solid black line separates Near Oceania and Remote Oceania.

a rich marine fauna and flora, part of the vast Indo-Pacific biogeographic province.[6] Coral grows luxuriantly in these seas, and extensive reefs and lagoons enshroud the island coastlines, habitats for a diverse range of fishes and invertebrates. Not surprisingly, such resources would figure prominently in the lives of the Lapita peoples.

Discovering Lapita[7]

The initial discovery of archaeological remains that would in time come to be classified under the rubric "Lapita" was serendipitous, resulting from a different kind of encounter between stranger and native. In the opening decade of the twentieth century, Father Otto Meyer crossed the beach at Rakival on the small island of Watom off the northeastern tip of New Britain, to establish a Catholic mission station. After a tropical storm exposed some curiously-decorated potsherds, Meyer dug around the buildings of his little settlement, revealing more sherds. The priest thought these might provide evidence of ancient contacts with South America, though he qualified his opinion with a humble disclaimer: "I, poor hermit, what do I know of these scientific questions which are still so perplexing, even for you, the scientists, by the Grace of God?" (Meyer, trans. in Anson 1983:283). Meyer sent some sherds to Paris, where they were duly cataloged into the collections of the Musée de l'Homme, and then forgotten for forty years.

W. C. McKern, a young American anthropologist dispatched to the Western Polynesian island of Tongatapu in 1920 with the Bernice P. Bishop Museum's Bayard Dominick Expedition, excavated several "kitchen middens" from which he recovered 1,587 potsherds, some bearing delicate, dentate-stamped motifs. Had McKern been aware of Meyer's Watom Island finds, he might have pushed Oceanic prehistory over the narrow interpretive divide that held the field back until after World War II. Instead, unable to directly date his Tongan pottery (radiocarbon dating lay a quarter century in the future), McKern assumed that it was merely a variant of late-prehistoric Fijian ceramics, and therefore of no great significance for understanding the origins of Polynesian culture (McKern 1929:122).[8]

*Plate 1.2   Professor E. W. Gifford the University of California,
Berkeley, excavating with Fijian assistants in 1947.
(Courtesy of the P. A. Hearst Museum)*

The full import of identically-decorated pottery in Watom,
New Caledonia, and Tonga – bridging the anthropological abyss
between Melanesia and Polynesia[9] – was not recognized until
the late 1940s. New discoveries of pottery on the Île des Pins
(off the southern tip of New Caledonia) prompted Avias to
finally make the comparative link with the Watom Island sherds
forgotten in the Paris storerooms of the Musée de l'Homme.
Meanwhile E. W. Gifford, professor of ethnology at the University of California at Berkeley (plate 1.2), launched the first
of three ground-breaking archaeological expeditions, to Fiji
in 1947, followed by work in New Caledonia and Yap in the
early 1950s.[10] Gifford (who ironically had been McKern's
co-fieldworker during the 1920 Bayard Dominick Expedition
to Tonga) foresaw that resolving the long-standing issues of
Polynesian origins would require new archaeological evidence.

It was during his second expedition, at a beach site on the Koné Peninsula of New Caledonia called by the local people "Lapita," that Gifford recovered a large collection of potsherds, finely decorated in a style nearly identical to the earlier discoveries from Tonga and Watom. More importantly, Gifford obtained charcoal for direct dating by the radiocarbon method, then newly invented by Willard Libby of the University of Chicago. The new ^{14}C dates from Lapita (Site 13), coming in at 2,800 ± 350 and 2,435 ± 400 years BP,[11] exceeded anything anticipated by Pacific scholars. It was Gifford who finally assembled the disparate bits of evidence which had gradually accumulated since Father Meyer's long-forgotten report. Gifford's synthesis demonstrated that nearly three thousand years ago a common pottery style was distributed from Watom and New Caledonia to Fiji and Tonga, spanning the ethnographic divide between Melanesia and Polynesia. Moreover, Gifford recognized resemblances between these "Lapita" finds and pottery excavated by the Dutch archaeologist van Stein Callenfels at a site along the Karama River in Sulawesi (van Heekeren 1972).[12] Though he not did live to appreciate the stimulus created by his pioneering archaeological work, Gifford had revolutionized anthropological thinking about Pacific prehistory.

The 1950s and 1960s were heady times in Pacific archaeology. With the realization that the Pacific Islands indeed possessed a deep archaeological record, and bolstered by the ability of radiocarbon dating to provide an "absolute" time scale, major field programs were launched in various island groups. Appointed in 1955 to the first academic archaeology post in New Zealand at the University of Auckland, Jack Golson took up the Lapita challenge. Following six years of new excavations in Tonga, Samoa, and New Caledonia, Golson (1961) argued for unambiguous connections between the Lapita pottery assemblages of these and other islands: "We can propose for the S. W. Pacific some early community of culture linking New Caledonia, Tonga, and Samoa, antedating the 'Melanesian' cultures of the first and ancestral to the historic Western Polynesian cultures of the other two. This community is expressed in terms of variants of the same pottery tradition" (Golson 1961:176). Here was a bold claim indeed: that the ethnographically known cultures of Polynesia could be traced directly back to those people who had made Lapita pottery, and whose geographic distribution had at one time, at least, extended right across Melanesia.

From a new institutional base at the Australian National University, to which he had moved in 1961, Golson dispatched several students to investigate variation in Lapita assemblages over time and space. Jim Specht went to Watom to re-excavate Meyer's original site, while Colin Smart dug in New Caledonia, and Jens Poulsen tackled the complex sequence of Tongatapu (Specht 1968; Poulsen 1968, 1987).[13] In Fiji, work by Lawrence and Helen Birks in the Sigatoka sand dunes and at the Yanuca rockshelter, as well as by Elizabeth Shaw at the eroding coastal site of Natunuku, helped to clarify stages in the sequence of Lapita pottery use in the Fiji Islands (Birks 1973; Birks and Birks 1967; Shaw 1975). Drawing upon these diverse studies, Golson (1971) wrote a seminal paper for a 1969 Wenner-Gren Foundation sponsored Sigatoka Conference, in which he argued that all of these pottery assemblages, from Watom eastwards to Tonga and Samoa, could be encompassed within an archaeological *ceramic series*.[14] Although the striking similarities in the pottery – characterized by its distinctive dentate-stamped decorative technique – allowed Golson and others to define this prehistoric complex, he was painfully aware that as a *culture*, Lapita remained largely undefined. This problem of fleshing out a prehistoric "cultural complex" from the chronological framework provided by the pottery became the central problem of Lapita research in the 1970s and 1980s.

Despite the work at Watom and in New Caledonia, the majority of Pacific field research and excavation up until 1970 had focused on Polynesia, rather than on Melanesia. Since it appeared that the early Lapita sites in Fiji and Tonga (at the western "gateway" to Polynesia) had been settled by peoples migrating eastwards, the next logical step was to target the Solomon Islands for a major research program. In 1971, when Roger Green and Douglas Yen launched the Southeast Solomon Islands project,[15] this geographically key set of islands was archaeological *terra incognita*. While Green had predicted that Lapita sites would be found in the eastern Solomons, he was nonetheless "more than a little excited" to find that his prediction was confirmed by the reality of two sites in the Reef-Santa

Cruz Islands.[16] Reflecting then-current methodological debates among prehistoric archaeologists, Green applied new approaches and techniques in his excavation of these Lapita sites, with the goal of learning more about the cultural context within which the classic pottery had been made and used. "My own efforts were . . . directed at recovering details of the size of the settlements, the post holes of former buildings, pits, fireplaces and ovens, any refuse which reflected the economy, and the sources of the various materials used in the artefacts." Using the new settlement and economic data from his own and others' excavations, Green offered a newly expanded synthesis of Lapita as a *cultural complex*. Rather than merely defining Lapita on the basis of pottery styles, Green saw the "Lapita cultural complex" as based on a sophisticated horticultural-fishing economy, with fairly large villages occupying beaches and offshore islets, and using a broad range of distinctive material culture including various kinds of stone, shell, and bone implements.[17]

Another major advance, contributed by Sidney Mead, at Green's urging, was the formal deconstruction of the complex Lapita pottery design system into a series of design elements and motifs, enabling systematic and quantitative comparisons between pottery assemblages (Mead et al. 1975).[18] Armed with this comparative tool, Green was able to demonstrate that the Lapita ceramic series first defined by Golson could be subdivided into Western and Eastern Lapita components. The earliest Western Lapita sites, exemplified by the Reef-Santa Cruz Islands excavations, also contained obsidian flakes deriving from one or more sources in the Bismarck Archipelago, some 2,000 km to the west (Ambrose and Green 1972). This startling discovery not only revealed that the makers of Lapita pottery had been involved in long-distance voyaging and trading, but pointed once again to the west as the area in which a putative "Lapita homeland" would have to be sought.

Influenced by these important discoveries in the Solomon Islands, Green proposed that the "original Lapita adaptation was to an area with a complex continental island environment," which he placed in "the New Britain-New Ireland area." However, except for Specht's re-excavations at Watom (Specht 1968), and some minor test pits at a Lapita site on Mussau,[19] the vast region encompassed by the arc of the Bismarck Archipelago was almost unexplored from an archaeological standpoint. How then to test Green's hypothesis of a western Melanesian "homeland" for Lapita? Jim Allen put the question to several archaeologists (including the author) during the 15th Pacific Science Congress in Dunedin, New Zealand in 1983. His plan, soon after implemented by the international Lapita Homeland Project, was bold: working as lone researchers in the traditional fashion, it might take decades before sufficient new sites were discovered and excavated. Allen proposed that an international research consortium be formed to tackle the Bismarck Archipelago as an integrated whole, with separate but closely collaborating field teams targeting key areas within the vast circle of islands. In 1985 the plan was put into action as fifteen teams, aided by the expedition vessel *Dick Smith Explorer* and centralized logistics, surveyed and dug sites in Manus, Mussau, New Ireland, Watom, the Duke of Yorks, Nissan, and at several localities on New Britain.[20] The results were stunning: seventeen new Lapita sites were discovered, including waterlogged deposits with preserved stilt-house posts and plant remains in Mussau and the Arawe Islands. Moreover, excavations in rockshelters and caves on New Ireland suddenly thrust the prehistory of the Bismarcks right back into the Pleistocene, with basal radiocarbon dates older than 30,000 years BP.

Inspired by these results, work at several localities in the Bismarcks continued thorough the 1980s, even as renewed investigations of Lapita sites have begun in New Caledonia and in Western Polynesia.[21] In the two decades since Roger Green defined the "Lapita cultural complex" our knowledge of this major phase in Oceanic prehistory has expanded exponentially. Much new data have yet to be fully published, but the time has come for a new synthesis, as much to inspire the next phase of research as to take stock of what we have learned.

What is Lapita?

It took several decades for archaeologists to recognize that the potsherds recovered by Father Meyer on Watom were somehow related to those dug out of the Tongan kitchen middens by McKern, separated by a geographic distance of more than

*Plate 1.3   This dentate-stamped potsherd from the Talepakemalai
site, Mussau Islands, displays a classic Lapita motif, made by
repetitive application of a limited number of dentate-stamps.
(Photo by Thérèse Babineau)*

4,000 km. Long-held assumptions concerning the different origins of Melanesian and Polynesian peoples, as well as the lack
of direct dating prior to Libby's invention of the radiocarbon
method, were in part responsible. This recognition of an early
and widespread culture bridging Melanesia and Polynesia –
when it was first put forward tentatively by Gifford and later
with more sophistication by Golson – was based on the remarkable *stylistic similarities* in the decorative techniques and
specific design motifs found on Lapita pottery. Golson (1971:67)
credits Gifford for this insight, "since at that time there was
nothing to go by apart from decorative technique." As can be
seen from the pottery vessel in plate 1.3, the dominant feature of
the Lapita style is the repetitive combination of sets of dentate
or "toothed" stamps pressed into the clay prior to firing. These
stamps were applied in a regular and highly consistent manner,

usually in bands or zones encircling the upper parts of pots, largely on the exterior but in some cases including the rims and extending into the interior surfaces. The patterned manner in which the stamped "design elements" were combined to form particular motifs, and with which the motifs were then applied across vessel surfaces, is so consistent that Sidney Mead and others have subsequently been able to write "grammatical rules" underlying the decorative system (this is considered in more detail in chapter 5). This highly patterned, elaborate yet consistent system of ceramic design permits us to associate assemblages of excavated potsherds from many sites spanning a large part of the western Pacific into an "archaeological culture."

Fundamentally, "Lapita" is an *archaeological construct* based – as are many prehistoric "cultures" throughout the world – on stylistic similarities in pottery. In the parlance of classic culture-historical archaeologists, the various Lapita pottery assemblages display aspects of both a *horizon* (relatedness across space at the same time period), and of *tradition* (a sequence of temporal changes). Indeed, it became increasingly evident as archaeological study of Lapita pottery progressed that an early, widespread initial Lapita horizon had given rise to several regional traditions in different parts of Melanesia and Western Polynesia. This variation in time and space is best described as a *ceramic series*, a concept developed by the Caribbean archaeologists Irving Rouse and Jose Cruxent (1963) for a very similar kind of archaeological distribution.

In his initial efforts to define Lapita, Golson realized that such ceramic comparisons, no matter how detailed and rigorous, were an insufficient basis for understanding the complex historical and cultural implications posed by the wide geographic distribution of these related assemblages. He thus turned to other associated artifact forms, including stone adzes and shell objects in order to advance "the frame of reference of Lapita from a distinctive style of ceramic decoration to a culture complex" (Golson 1971:73). While Golson's early efforts were frustrated by the dearth of well-excavated materials, Green took up the problem more successfully, based on the expanded information from the southeastern Solomon Islands and other sites. In his now-classic synthesis of Lapita written for Jesse Jennings's *Prehistory of Polynesia* volume, Green (1979a:34) argued that while the characteristic pottery "provided the most obvious traits used to identify the cultural complex, a better understanding can be achieved if other aspects of the complex are summarized without reference to the pottery." For Green, these "other aspects" included the following features:

- Lapita settlements were "internally differentiated, self-sufficient villages occupied by sedentary populations." Moreover, these settlements consistently occupied coastal situations, either on beach terraces opposite reef passages, or on small offshore islands.
- The Lapita economy integrated the gathering of shell-fish and the taking of fish from lagoons and reefs, with animal husbandry of pigs and fowl, and with horticulture.
- Interaction between Lapita communities was indicated by a range of non-local materials such as obsidian, chert, pottery, and oven-stones found at most sites. From these materials, Green inferred the presence of "a network of reciprocal exchanges between related communities that maintained frequent contact."
- Finally, the Lapita cultural complex exhibited a "full range of portable artifacts typical of many Oceanic assemblages," including stone adzes, shell adzes, flake tools of obsidian and chert, shell scrapers and peelers, anvils, polishers, slingstones, shell rings, bracelet units, beads, discs, needles, awls, tattooing chisels, shell fish-hooks, net sinkers, and other items.

In short, while the highly distinctive pottery is unquestionably the key element permitting the recognition of a prehistoric cultural complex, the definition of that complex and what it enailed can be extended to other realms. These go well beyond the confines of material culture, to encompass settlement patterns and spatial arrangements, the subsistence economy, and even social interactions between distant communities. In the chapters that follow, we shall see to what extent Green's definition of the Lapita cultural complex has been supported, amplified, and in some cases modified by the latest archaeological investigations.

Lapita and the Oceanic-Speaking Peoples

That the people who made and used Lapita pottery were also the speakers of languages within a primary branch of the Austronesian language family, is a proposition increasingly supported by a diversity of archaeological and linguistic evidence. The Austronesian family today comprises about 1,200 modern languages (Tryon 1995), and its speakers are distributed from Madagascar to Easter Island.[22] The greatest diversity of Austronesian languages is found in island Southeast Asia and Melanesia, and its probable homeland (i.e., where Proto Austronesian was originally spoken) may have been the island of Taiwan. Beginning around 4–3,000 BC Austronesian groups began a major expansion into the tropical archipelagoes of island Southeast Asia (Bellwood 1995), and certainly had reached the western borders of what we call "Melanesia" by about 1,500 BC. As typically happens when a linguistic group expands and colonizes new territory, differentiation within the group occurs, due to network breaking (isolation) and distance, and to innovation in the now separated daughter communities. Thus by 1,500 BC, the Austronesian speakers were already differentiated into a significant number of daughter languages, in some regions probably arrayed geographically as a complex network of dialect chains. One of the new Austronesian subgroups – situated in the area around southern Halmahera and Cenderawasih Bay in northwest New Guinea – then expanded eastwards along the New Guinea coast into the Bismarck Archipelago. This movement and the distance-isolation and subsequent linguistic innovations resulting from it, gave rise to the *Oceanic* subgroup of Austronesian languages.

In chapter 4 I will review the detailed evidence and arguments that have convinced many prehistorians that the speakers of Proto Oceanic language and the makers of Lapita pottery were one and the same.[23] As we shall also see (in chapter 3), these people continued to expand eastwards into the southwest Pacific, leading to the rapid differentiation of Oceanic languages. Ultimately, descendants of the Proto Oceanic speakers who first moved into the Bismarck Archipelago about 1,500 BC would discover and colonize the farthest reaches of Remote Oceania,

including the far-flung islands of Polynesia and the archipelagoes of central and eastern Micronesia.

The position I take in this book – and which I argue for in
detail in chapter 4 – is that the Lapita peoples were the ancestors of those modern Pacific islander populations who speak
Oceanic languages. The vast region within which the Oceanic
languages are today distributed is shown in map 1.2, which
also indicates the extent of Lapita archaeological sites. Linguists
Andrew Pawley and Malcolm Ross have this to say regarding
the distribution of the Oceanic languages:

> The region covered by "Oceania" in this context is the Pacific
> east of a line drawn from north to south and dividing Chamorro
> (Mariana Islands) and Belau (formerly Palau) from the rest of
> Micronesia and crossing the north coast of Irian Jaya at 138°E
> longitude. This means that the seam between Oceanic and its
> closest Austronesian relatives is in the west of New Guinea be-
> tween the Bird's Head and the Sarmi Coast. The Oceanic sub-
> group includes the Austronesian languages of all of Melanesia
> except the extreme west of New Guinea, all of Polynesia and
> most of Micronesia. Apart from languages brought by coloni-
> alism, languages of Oceania which are *not* Austronesian are
> found only in New Guinea and nearby archipelagoes [see chap-
> ter 4, this volume]. These are the so-called non-Austronesian or
> "Papuan" languages of many of the peoples of New Guinea
> and some island peoples as far east as Savo in the Solomon
> Islands (and a probable outlier area in the Reef Islands). (Pawley
> and Ross 1995:43–4)

Throughout this book I explicitly use the terms *Oceanic* and
Oceania in this linguistic sense.

Even though I argue that the peoples who made and used
Lapita pottery spoke Oceanic languages, it is important that
we do not confuse or conflate archaeological and linguistic
concepts. It is a long-standing (although sometimes overlooked)
tenet of anthropology that biology, language, and culture are
independent entities, even though they often co-vary in patterned ways. Thus, we must not simply assume at the outset
that the makers and users of Lapita pottery conformed to linguistic and biological entities; rather, this is a hypothesis to be
carefully tested. Indeed, there are strong reasons for arguing
that the Lapita peoples were a dynamic group who recruited

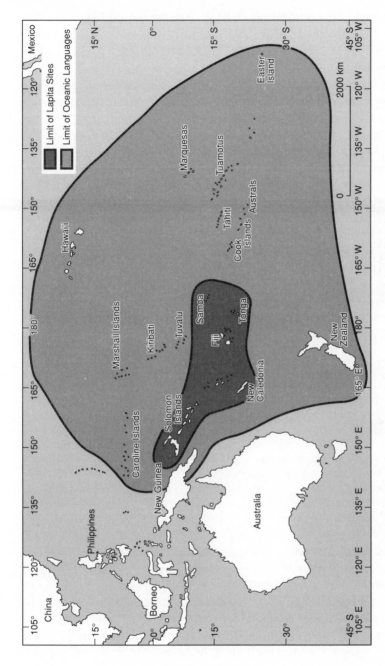

Map 1.2 *Distribution of historically-known peoples speaking languages of the Oceanic subgroup of Austronesian, and the presently-documented geographic limits of the Lapita cultural complex.*

a diversity of populations (biological entities) and speech communities into their sphere over the millennium or so that Lapita existed as an archaeologically-identifiable entity. Depending upon what point in time and in what specific archipelago or island group we are specifying, certain Lapita people are likely to have been different – in speech and/or physical appearance – from their relatives in other places or at other times. It is for this reason that we must speak of Lapita *peoples*, not people, and Lapita *societies*, not society.[24]

Despite this important caveat, I regard Oceania (in the sense defined above) as a coherent and meaningful unit for historical study, and Lapita as the archaeological manifestation of its earliest stages. A few years ago, Roger Green and I asserted the case for understanding the Polynesian peoples as a *phylogenetic unit*, an ethnolinguistic entity whose history of divergence and differentiation (and in some instances convergence) could be unraveled through the combined methods of historical anthropology (Kirch and Green 1987).[25] Recently, Bellwood et al. (1995:3–4) have extended our approach to the Austronesians as a whole. To quote them:

> Basically, the idea of phylogenetic relationship revolves around derivation from a common source, in cultural terms identifiable through shared patterns of language and society, in biological terms identifiable through shared configurations of the gene pool. Phylogenetic units, whether defined culturally or biologically, are subject to divergence or radiation of their internal elements through the operation of processes such as population fission with subsequent geographical separation, founder or bottleneck effects, selective adaptations to differing or changing environments, and the effects of contact with external societies. (1995:3–4)

In my view, Oceania (as a subgroup of the Austronesian world) constitutes just such a phylogenetic unit. Of course, this does not mean that it was some kind of closed, "hermetically-sealed" entity. Like all human groups and societies, the speakers of Oceanic languages comprised an "open system," and their interactions with non-Oceanic peoples at times played critical roles in changing their own biological, linguistic, and cultural history.

This was especially so in the early stages of Oceanic history, in the region we call Near Oceania (see chapters 2 and 3).

Reflections on Time and Space

A main criticism leveled at an older school of culture history by the "New Archaeologists" of the 1960s and 1970s was that in defining and describing prehistoric cultures, the culture historians often were trapped by an essentialist paradigm. Each culture, period, or phase was carefully described in terms of its typical or modal characteristics, but because insufficient attention was paid to temporal and spatial variability, the *dynamics* of culture change were lacking. Thus change – whether this was viewed as evolutionary or transformational – was compressed to the boundaries separating cultural periods in the time-space charts of prehistory texts. It is important that we do not fall into such a potential trap when treating something as large and complex as Lapita.

The category "Lapita" encompasses both a large geographic region and a considerable span of time: some 4,300 km from Mussau to Samoa, and between ten to fifteen centuries, a period equivalent to roughly 75 human generations. While there is sufficient continuity and shared similarity to classify a range of archaeological sites and their assemblages found throughout this space-time envelope under a single rubric such as "Lapita," there is also significant variability. Working largely on the evidence of decorative designs on Lapita pottery, archaeologists have subdivided the Lapita world into three main geographic provinces: Far Western Lapita (the Bismarcks region), Western Lapita (the Solomons to New Caledonia), and Eastern Lapita (the Fiji, Tonga, Samoa region); I will argue also for a Southern Lapita province. Temporal subdivisions have also been proposed for some areas, as in the Eastern Lapita region where a sequence of ceramic change from Early Eastern Lapita, through Late Eastern Lapita, to Polynesian Plain Ware has been outlined. More will be said of these terms and their implications in later chapters. For the present, it is sufficient to stress that the archaeological record encompassed by the term "Lapita" displays both geographic and temporal variation. Only by sensitive exploration of this variation can we write a history of Lapita that is dynamic, reflecting the continued adaptation of people to new islands, new challenges, changing social alignments, and upstart political aspirations.

At the same time, the realities of writing a general synthesis such as this book impose constraints on how much variation and change can meaningfully be treated without loosing the reader in a morass of detail. My chosen path is to privilege three Lapita sites: Talepakemalai (Mussau), Nenumbo (Reef Islands), and Lolokoka (Niuatoputapu). Although I will also draw upon data recovered from many other Lapita localities and excavations, these three sites will be used repeatedly to exemplify changing aspects of Lapita culture. My decision to focus on these three sites is based on several considerations. First, they span the geographic range of Lapita distribution, from the Bismarck Archipelago, to the eastern Solomon Islands, to Western Polynesia. In this regard, they encompass some of the major changes that transformed Lapita culture over the course of its dispersal throughout the western Pacific. Talepakemalai exemplifies the earliest known phase of Lapita in the Bismarcks "homeland" (the Far Western Lapita region), Nenumbo is typical of early expansion to the far reaches of the Solomon Islands (Western Lapita), while Lolokoka was settled by colonists who voyaged into what is today known as Polynesia (Eastern Lapita). These three sites are also among the most intensively excavated and thoroughly studied Lapita sites: Nenumbo was dug by Roger Green over several field seasons from 1970 to 1978 using a carefully planned sampling strategy, while Lolokoka (investigated in 1976) and Talepakemalai (excavated from 1985–8) were both projects directed by the author.

My decision to privilege the evidence from these three sites should not be misunderstood to mean that the range of variation or the complexities inherent in Lapita archaeology can be wholly subsumed or encompassed by this limited sample. Talepakemalai, Nenumbo, and Lolokoka are *representative* of the range of variation found in Lapita settlement patterns, pottery assemblages, and faunal remains in space and time, but it would be facile to think that they englobe the diversity inherent in more than a hundred known Lapita sites.

The Significance of Lapita for Oceanic Anthropology

The term "Lapita" has at least two referents to Pacific anthropologists. First, it refers to a set of archaeological sites and the assemblages excavated from them, characterized in part by a specific kind of pottery. In a more general sense, Lapita also refers to a *historical construct*, itself the reflections of certain theories regarding the origin and dispersals of those people who today speak Oceanic languages. In both senses, Lapita represents phenomena of a unique sort within the Pacific Island realm. In space, Lapita sites span a greater geographic range than any comparable entity before or after. More importantly, this distribution crosses with impunity the lines or boundaries drawn so carefully by nineteenth-century explorers between perceived ethnographic or cultural regions in the Pacific (i.e., the older Melanesia, Polynesia, Micronesia distinction). Arguably the "foundation culture" for most of the island cultures and societies found today in island Melanesia, Polynesia, and central-eastern Micronesia, Lapita forces us to re-think the most basic concepts in Oceanic anthropology.

The archaeological record of Lapita sites provides empirical documentation of a crucial period in the making of modern Oceania, a millennium during which seafaring and horticultural peoples occupied coastal sectors of Near Oceania, then expanded dramatically into previously-uninhabited lands north, east, and south. Careful comparison of this archaeological record with the evidence of historical linguistics and human biology allows us to understand more fully the implications of this diaspora. The Lapita expansion was nothing less than the initial diversification and differentiation of the Oceanic cultures. The process would not be fully completed until perhaps AD 1,000, but it would be carried out by the direct descendants of the early Lapita people, as they explored and settled the most remote islands of Polynesia and central-eastern Micronesia.

In short, the modern ethnographic map of Oceania – including the mosaic of languages and the patterns of human biological variation – is the Lapita legacy. Anthropological understanding of the tremendous cultural variation to be found within the boundaries of the Oceanic world requires the historical perspective accorded by a study of Lapita prehistory and archaeology.

2

Old Melanesia

The lowering clouds and humid air threatened an equatorial cloud-burst as the four-wheel drive pick-up crawled along a slippery clay track through plantations freshly carved out of the New Ireland rainforest. Jim Allen, the organizing force behind the 1985 Lapita Homeland Project then in its first month of fieldwork, had met me two hours earlier at Kavieng airstrip where I had arrived on the pre-dawn flight from Port Moresby en route to investigate Lapita occupations in the remote Mussau Islands. Jim and his co-diggers had invited me for a diversion to see their excavations in the Panakiwuk rockshelter. Nestled in a doline in the central, uplifted limestone spine of New Ireland, Panakiwuk's earth floor was yielding startling finds that hinted at major revisions in our understanding of the prehistory of Near Oceania (plate 2.1).

The threatened rain began falling torrentially as Jim pulled the truck off the narrow track, and we began slogging our way up a steep slope through uncut rainforest at the base of the island's central spine. Half an hour later – thoroughly soaked and perspiring in the ninety-degree heat – we emerged at the lip of the doline where an overhanging limestone cliff had sheltered small groups of people in the distant past. There had not yet been time to submit charcoal or bone samples for radiocarbon dating, and Jim could only speculate that the simple flaked stone tools recovered from the deeper layers might predate the Holocene-Pleistocene boundary some 10,000 years ago. As we discussed the exposed stratigraphy, checked the sieving screens for small scraps of rodent bone, and examined the

Plate 2.1   View of the Panakiwuk Rockshelter, a Pleistocene
habitation site situated in the interior mountains of New Ireland.
(Photo courtesy of Jim Allen)

chert and obsidian flakes, our conversation was charged with excitement. Up until 1985, no truly Pleistocene sites were known beyond the large island of New Guinea, although a rockshelter tested by Jim Specht of the Australian Museum in the interior of New Britain had provided a basal radiocarbon date right at the Holocene-Pleistocene boundary (Specht et al. 1981).[1] Our conversations continued well into the night at the Mangai Village field camp as we poured over the bones, shell midden, and stone flakes by the light of a kerosene lamp, our imaginations lubricated by the whisky I had brought from Port Moresby. It was clear that Melanesian prehistory was going to be substantially rewritten.

When we all met again a year later – in the comfort of an air-conditioned seminar room at The Australian Museum in Sydney – it would be to hear the startling results not only of the Panakiwuk excavations for which the radiocarbon samples now gave an age of 15,000 years for the earliest occupation, but from several other sites on New Ireland. The Balof 2 shelter had produced a sequence similar to that at Panakiwuk, while the Matenbek rockshelter went back 20,430 ± 180 years BP. But no one had quite expected the date of 33,300 ± 550 years BP from Matenkupkum, essentially as old as anything then known from the entire Australasian region! The 1985 Lapita Homeland Project had, in a single field season, tripled the known time span for human occupation in island Melanesia (Allen, et al. 1989). Bolstered by continued excavations at these and other sites, archaeologists have had to rethink their concepts of Melanesian prehistory. The early colonization of the Bismarck Archipelago and Solomon Islands more than thirty thousand years ago has implications for our understanding of the Lapita phenomenon as well, for it was the descendants of these first voyagers across the Vitiaz Straits and beyond who would become the indigenous occupants of "Old Melanesia."[2]

Sahul

Alfred Russel Wallace, famed explorer of the Malay Archipelago and co-discoverer along with Darwin of the theory of natural selection, was one of the first biogeographers systematically to describe and enumerate the remarkable biological differences between the islands of Southeast Asia and the Australia-New Guinea region. In *Island Life*, Wallace observed that "the great feature of the Australian region is the almost total absence of all the forms of terrestrial mammalia which abound in the rest of the world, their place being supplied by a great variety of Marsupials" (1895:46–8). (The boundary separating these regions as drawn by Wallace – which runs between Kalimantan and Sulawesi, and between Bali and Lombok – is today known as Wallace's Line.) This disjunct faunal distribution is all the more intruiging – and thus puzzled nineteenth-century zoologists – because the Southeast Asian archipelagoes are so close to Australia and New Guinea.[3] Wallace was one of the first scientists to realize that the answer to this biogeographic conundrum would be found beneath the tropical seas surrounding these lands, as modern oceanography began to reveal "the depth and contour of the ocean-bed, since this affords an important clue to the former existence of now-submerged lands, uniting islands to continents" (Wallace 1895:9).

Great strides have been made since Wallace's day in our understanding of these "now-submerged lands," thanks not only to detailed submarine cartography, but to advances in our knowledge of paleoclimates and sea-level changes during the Pleistocene. It is now well established that New Guinea, Australia, and Tasmania, along with some smaller islands, were all linked as a single land mass at several periods in the past (map 2.1), a phantom continent baptized with the name *Sahul*.[4] The shared marsupial fauna that Wallace observed for New Guinea and Australia, as well as many floral similarities, are thus explained by this common history that extends in time back to the primordial Gondwana.[5] Biogeographically speaking, Near Oceania is an integral part of Sahul.

The complex cycles of transgression and regression of the seas that alternately sundered or rejoined the components of Sahul are tracked by sea-level curves which have been painstakingly reconstructed through isotopic studies of deep-sea cores, and by radiometric dating of emerged reefs, such as the remarkable sequence from the Huon Peninsula of New Guinea.[6] The greatest expanse of Sahul in relatively recent times occurred at about 18,000 years ago at the height of the last glacial

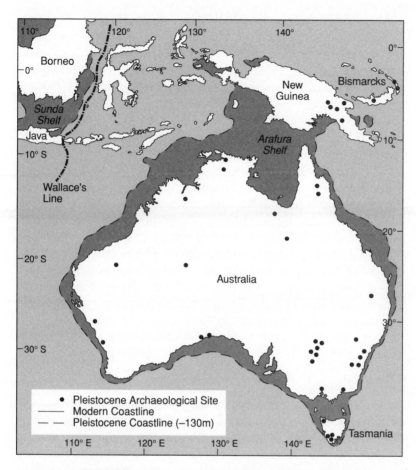

*Map 2.1   The Pleistocene super-continent of Sahul, defined by the
submarine 130 m contour, at times connected New Guinea,
Australia, and Tasmania, while the islands of the Bismarcks and
Solomons were always separated by deep submarine trenches.
Symbols show the locations of some major Pleistocene sites.*

maximum, when sea levels fell more than 100 m, matching a
similar period of glacial expansion about 140,000 years ago.
Surprisingly, however, the arrival of humans into Sahul seems
not to have coincided with either of these lowest sea-levels, but
most likely sometime during the interval between 40–60,000
years ago, a period of substantial fluctuation with coastlines
about 50 m lower than today.

Although it was only a little more than 30 years ago that John Mulvaney reported the first radiocarbon date of Pleistocene age from an Australian site (Kenniff Cave), archaeological knowledge of Sahul during the Pleistocene has expanded exponentially. In a recent overview of the geographic and temporal structure of the Pleistocene archaeological record, Mike Smith and Nancy Sharp report 154 sites from the Sahul region.[7] Geographically, these range from Tasmania in the temperate south to the islands of the Bismarck Archipelago in the equatorial north, out into the Solomons chain, and across the breadth of the Australian continent. Equally notable, this vast geographic distribution extends back in time to the earliest sites more than 35,000 years ago, suggesting that the human colonizers of Sahul pushed rapidly to the margins of that world.[8]

Dating the initial entry of humans into Sahul has been a controversial matter, in part due to the problems associated with radiocarbon dating of samples with true (chronological) ages greater than 30,000 years. Some archaeologists (e.g., Allen 1994) maintain that the available radiocarbon dates (which now run to more than 1,100 dates from 149 sites) indicate colonization at about 35,000 years BP. Others have argued that there is a radiocarbon dating "barrier" created by the problem of old samples being swamped out by background radiation and sample contamination, and that alternative dating methods must be used to resolve the issue. Thermoluminescence dating from a northern Australian site has been used to argue that humans entered Sahul at least 50,000 years ago, an estimate that may find some support in the dating of waisted axes from the Huon Peninsula at between 40–60,000 BP.[9] Most recently, however, Allen and Holdaway (1995) argue that disparities between suites of archaeological and geological radiocarbon dates from Pleistocene contexts show a real base age for Sahul sites at about 40,000 years ago.[10] Whether the well-established date of ca. 40,000 years for the entry of humans into Sahul will ultimately be pushed back farther in time thus remains to be seen.

Whatever date may ultimately be decided upon, what were the most likely points of entry into Sahul? A close consideration of the geography of *Wallacea* (the island region between Sahul and the former Pleistocene land mass of Sunda) suggests two probable routes.[11] The first would have utilized as major steppingstones the large island of Sulawesi, and thence on to Peleng and Sula; thereafter one could have moved on to what is now the "Bird's Head" of New Guinea (in Irian Jaya) via a northern route involving Halmahera, or via a southern route involving Buru and Seram. The second major route would have followed the chain of inter-visible islands east of Java, beginning with Bali and moving successively through Lombok, Sumbawa, Flores, and Alor, to Timor. At Timor, one could have crossed directly onto Sahul (a water crossing of slightly less than 90 km), or alternatively, continued to follow the chain of small islands from Leti to Tanimbar, coming ashore on Sahul just south of what are now the Aru Islands. The essential point is that several routes were possible, all involving a succession of over-water crossings in the range from 10–100 km between largely inter-visible islands. Most likely all of these routes saw gradual movement of humans eastwards into Sahul, since it is likely that more than one colonization "event" was involved. Moreover, some simple form of watercraft was surely necessary; simple bamboo or mangrove rafts, bark canoes, or dugouts are all possibilities. These issues of entry routes and watercraft are matters of speculation, for they are currently beyond the possibilities of archaeology to disclose. One thing is certain, however: early modern humans were fully capable of traversing Wallacea, which had for millions of years previously formed such a barrier to the dispersal of plants and animals.

Near Oceania

Whatever the initial route or routes of entry into Sahul, it is increasingly clear that people rapidly explored this geographically diverse new continent throughout its length and breath. One of the oldest known sites from Sahul is at the Huon Peninsula on the northeastern coast of New Guinea (map 2.2). From uplifted beach terraces dated to between 40–60,000 years ago, Les Groube and his associates recovered split-cobble "waisted axes" of unknown function.[12] From the Huon terraces it is possible to see the large, rainforest cloaked island of New Britain looming across the Vitiaz Strait. A deep submarine trench separates New Britain and New Guinea, and the

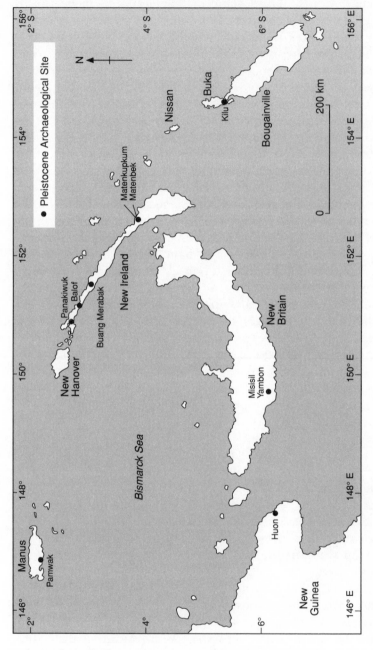

Map 2.2 The north coast of New Guinea and adjacent islands of the Bismarck Archipelago and northern Solomons, showing the locations of important Pleistocene and early Holocene sites.

two land masses were never joined by a land bridge in the
Pleistocene. But to the early human explorers of Sahul, whose
ancestors had already crossed similar water gaps between Sunda
and Sahul (and who were at home along coasts and water-
ways) such water gaps did not pose a formidable barrier. New
Britain was visible from New Guinea and beckoned; and, from
the northern tip of New Britain, New Ireland would likewise
entice people across the narrow straits, with the Duke of York
Islands providing convenient "stepping stones." Before losing
sight of New Britain's high mountain ranges, voyagers eastwards would have been able to see Buka and Bougainville, at
the northwestern terminus of the Solomon Islands. Between
New Britain and Bougainville, the smaller islands of Nissan
(Green Is.) and Feni reduced inter-island crossings to only 50–
60 km (Wickler and Spriggs 1988:705).

These inter-visible archipelagoes of the Bismarck and Solomon chains along with New Guinea comprise the region of
Near Oceania.[13] Because water gaps always separated the islands of Near Oceania from Sahul, they are marked by dramatic reductions in biotic diversity. For example, the 265 species
of birds recorded from the coasts of New Guinea immediately
falls to some 80 species across the Vitiaz Strait on New Britain.
According to Roger Green (1991a:494), "the Bismarcks have
only one bandicoot, one wallaby, and two species of phalanger,
one cassowary, and four genera of rats. The Solomons have one
phalanger, three genera of rats, several snakes, [and] 9 genera
of frogs" among the non-volant terrestrial fauna; there are also
a number of fruit bats.[14] Thus, although the water barriers
between these largely inter-visible islands did not pose serious
challenges to would-be human colonists, these gaps had acted
as effective barriers to plant and animal dispersals, resulting in
a significant degree of biotic impoverishment. This depauperate
biota greatly restricted the range of potential food sources for
human colonists dependent upon a hunting-and-gathering mode
of subsistence. Only in the reefs and seas of Near Oceania
were natural resources not significantly reduced, for the Bismarck Archipelago is incredibly rich in the diversity of fish,
mollusks, echinoderms, crustacea, seaweeds, and other edible
life that thrive on reefs and in lagoons (Stoddart 1992). The
Bismarcks and Solomons are home to more than 90 families of

marine shorefishes, including thousands of species. (In contrast, Fiji has about 50 families, and the Society Islands only 30.) Indeed, there are indications that these coastal marine resources were very likely essential to the survival strategies of the earliest human colonists.

And colonize they did, as the newly-excavated evidence from several sites in Near Oceania demonstrates. In the interior of New Britain, open occupations buried under later tephra falls at Yombon date as early as 35,000 years BP (Pavlides and Gosden 1994). The oldest dates for Pleistocene colonization of New Ireland come from the Buang Merabak and Matenkupkum sites, which have been radiocarbon dated to roughly 33–32,000 years BP and earlier (Gosden and Robertson 1991; Allen et al. 1989; J. Allen, personal communication, 1995). The Kilu rockshelter on Buka Island, dated to about 28,000 years BP, firmly establishes that humans had crossed into at least the northern part of the Solomon Islands by that time (Wickler and Spriggs 1988), when many of the central Solomon Islands were joined due to lowered sea levels. Other rockshelters on New Ireland – including Matenbek (ca. 20,000 years BP), Panakiwuk (ca. 15,000 years BP), and Balof 2 (ca. 14,000 years BP) – and the Misisil cave in the interior of New Britain (ca. 11,000 years BP) are beginning to fill in the sequence of later Pleistocene occupation.[15] And on Manus Island to the east of New Ireland – the colonization of which required a water crossing of at least 200 km – late Pleistocene occupation by 12,000 years BP or earlier is indicated by the Pamwak rockshelter.[16]

Archaeological samples from the oldest of these sites are still so limited that it is difficult to say much concerning this early period in Near Oceania without succumbing to speculation. Artifacts are limited to simple core and flake tools of amorphous or "expedient" forms, made out of locally available siliceous and volcanic stones (figure 2.1). The faunal materials include terrestrial species such as birds, bats, lizards, snakes, and rats, but also significant quantities of marine shellfish, such as large *Turbo* mollusks that frequent fringing reefs, and some inshore fish. Jim Allen, drawing upon the evidence from Matenkupkum, suggests that fishing in this early period did not involve specialized technology or "deliberate pursuit" of prey. "Fortuitous accidental or deliberate trapping or spearing

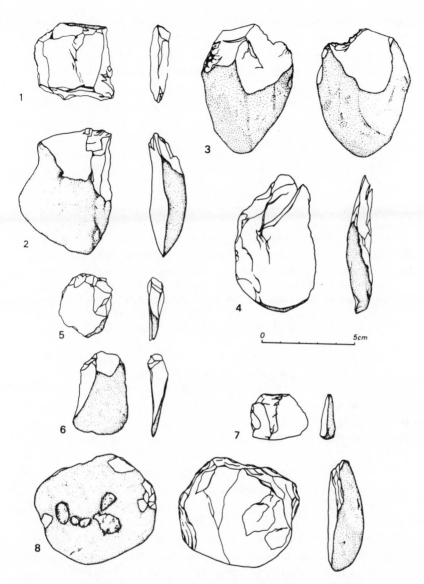

Figure 2.1 Stone tools from the Matenkupkum site, dating in age from 12,000–32,000 years BP. (After Allen et al. 1989)

on reefs on outgoing tides would account for the evidence to hand" (Allen 1993:144). Rather, the main emphasis in this marine adaptation was on 'the reef itself, with shellfish and echinoderms the most common food remains."

Chris Gosden, who has worked with the materials from the Matenkupkum rockshelter, has ventured some hypotheses on this remote period:

> It seems that we are dealing with small numbers of people who may well have moved over large areas. They used their seafaring abilities to move between dispersed resources and could thus be labeled maritime hunters and gatherers. Movement would also have been necessitated by small group numbers. It is unlikely that any group was biologically or socially self-sufficient. They therefore had to keep up contact with others on a regular basis. It may be that our usual notion of socially bounded groups is inappropriate to a situation such as this one. People may have been not just physically, but also socially, mobile. In any case, people lived in a spatially extensive world with a few dispersed social contacts. It is a world without any ethnographic parallel and it lasted for over 10,000 years. (1993:133)

The Pleistocene-Holocene Transition in Near Oceania

After more than ten millennia of this "world without ethnographic parallel" several significant changes began to take place in Near Oceania, commencing around 18–20,000 years ago. In the New Ireland site of Matenbek, obsidian flakes first appear in the sequence at this time, a noteworthy find given that the obsidian source lies on New Britain in the area of Talasea. This is about 350 km by straight-line distance, and presumably considerably longer by its actual path of human transport. Moreover, that transport had to involve at least the sea crossing between New Britain and New Ireland, if not longer distances by sea along the island coasts (a more efficient means of transport, assuming available voyaging technology, about which we admittedly remain ignorant). By the terminal Pleistocene and early Holocene, obsidian from Talasea regularly occurs in all of the New Ireland sites, suggesting an exchange network between social groups occupying New Britain and New Ireland.[17]

A second major innovation in the Bismarck Archipelago sites at ca. 18–20,000 years ago is the first appearance of bones of the Gray Cuscus (*Phalanger orientalis*), an arboreal marsupial. Averaging about 75–90 cm in length including its prehensile tail, the Gray Cuscus is a slow-moving animal with soft thick fur, a largely nocturnal vegetarian at home in the canopies either of climax forest or second growth.[18] Various species of *Phalanger* are "widely kept as pets and for food throughout Melanesia," but *P. orientalis* may have been particularly suited to translocation by people, "because it is the only species of *Phalanger* known to have twins regularly" (Flannery and White 1991:108). The apparently deliberate introduction of the Gray Cuscus from the island of New Guinea into the Bismarck Archipelago (and eventually into the Solomons) may be one of the earliest archaeologically documented instances anywhere in the world of human efforts to modify their environments through improvement of "natural" food resources.

Gosden has summarized the import of these two innovations – the movement of obsidian and of the Gray Cuscus – by noting that "instead of moving people to resources, resources were [now] moved to people" (1993:133). He sees this as a signal of a changed attitude of people towards the environment and its constraints. Whereas earlier generations of colonists in Near Oceania had moved about the landscape drawing their subsistence and other needs from what was locally available, the beginnings of a new strategy are now evident. "People did not passively suffer the problems of island life but developed strategies to overcome them and these strategies date back well into the Pleistocene."

Both of these developments obviously imply some increased frequency of over-water and between-island movement of people – and by extension – perhaps some technological improvements in watercraft. Of course, we have as yet no direct evidence of what the watercraft of these late Pleistocene people might have comprised, although rafts, bark canoes, and dugouts are all likely possibilities.[19] Geoffrey Irwin, who has made an in-depth study of Pacific voyaging and colonization,[20] suggests that the region encompassing the Bismarck Archipelago and the Solomons is a natural "voyaging nursery," in which gradual improvements in watercraft and voyaging skills were

encouraged. This region encompasses a band of shelter between the northern and southern tropical cyclone belts. Moreover, "seasonal and predictable changes" in wind and current
direction would have facilitated simple return voyaging between
these largely inter-visible islands. During the southern summer
(January), for example, the prevailing winds and currents would
favor voyages from the Bismarcks into the Solomons, with a
return readily possible in the southern winter (July).

If these changes are only minimally reflected in the evidence
from Matenbek at 18–20,000 years ago, they become much
clearer in the terminal Pleistocene and early Holocene deposits
at Panakiwuk, Balof, Pamwak, Misisil and other sites. Another
translocated marsupial (*Thylogale brunii*) appears in the Balof
cave sequence by about 7,000 years ago, while the quantities
of transported obsidian generally increase. The terminal
Pleistocene-early Holocene was also a time of significant environmental change, brought on by global warming at the end of
the last glacial maximum. Such climatic changes as might have
occured in Near Oceania, such as a shift in the position of the
inter-tropical convergence zone (ITCZ) and in rainfall patterns or
cyclones, are not as yet well documented. One well-understood
environmental change, however, is that of post-glacial rise in
sea level, from a low stand of about 130 m below present, to
the more-or-less modern level about 6,000 years ago. This
rapid rise in sea level precipitated by glacial melting would
have drowned familiar coastlines and necessitated continued
shifts inland in settlement pattern. Transgressive coasts, however, would also have favored the growth of coral reefs, cre-
ating conditions of rich marine life in turn stimulating the
development of maritime exploitation strategies.

Of potentially greatest import is the as yet sparse but provocative evidence for early steps toward plant domestication
and cultivation around the time of the Pleistocene-Holocene
boundary. Evidence that the peoples of New Guinea and Near
Oceania were independently developing horticulture[21] at this
time period is especially significant in relation to the subsistence economy that emerged in the early Lapita period (see
chapter 7). Ethnobotanists have long recognized that New
Guinea and the immediately adjacent islands of Near Oceania
were well within the vast Indo-Oceanic "foyer" of tropical

plant domestications. Jacques Barrau, who more than anyone advanced the modern field of ethnobotany in the Pacific,[22] recognized that such important crops as sugar cane (*Saccharum officinarum*) and the *Australimusa* or *fe'i* bananas (which have upright fruit stalks and orange-red flesh), as well as such lesser-known domesticates as *Pueraria lobata* and *Cordyline fruticosum*, were most likely brought under cultivation in the New Guinea region. Their evidence was classically botanical, based on the distribution of the wild relatives or ancestors of the domesticated plants, and on inference regarding the most probable area of initial human exploitation and genetic manipulation. In recent years a more intensive collaboration between archaeologists and paleoethnobotanists such as Douglas Yen[23] has produced a tentative historical sequence for horticultural origins in Near Oceania.

Of pivotal importance in this emerging picture of the development of horticulture in Near Oceania is the Kuk site, situated in the New Guinea Highlands, and extensively excavated by Jack Golson and his associates over the past two decades.[24] In this Wahgi Valley swamp, six distinct phases of artificial drainage and agronomic modifications have been revealed, and radiocarbon dates span the period from 9,000 to 250 years ago. Of special relevance to the question of *origins*, however, is the oldest Phase 1 which is dated to the early Holocene. The unquestionably artificial modifications of the swamp floor exposed in Golson's excavations for this period consist of "small basins and interconnecting runnels which can admit and circulate water, as well as dispose of its excess" (1990:145). Unfortunately, no plant macrofossils or pollen were recovered at Kuk that might directly indicate which early domesticates were being planted or tended in these features. Golson believes that these earliest systems "represent mixed gardening with the intercropping of different plant species and allowance for their varying soil and moisture requirements."

Among the plants which may have been cultivated in the Kuk swamp floor at 9,000 BP, we must count the strong possibility of taro, *Colocasia esculenta*, one of the most important crop plants underlying indigenous Oceanic agricultures today. While taro was long thought to be domesticated in southeast Asia and dispersed to Oceania through the early migrations of

agricultural peoples, recent research now suggests that it may
have been independently domesticated in New Guinea, possibly including the Near Oceanic archipelagoes, with some claims
for early dates.[25] Wild *Colocasia* is distributed throughout the
tropical parts of Sahul,[26] and recent karotype analysis raises
the distinct possibility of a New Guinea or Sahul domestication.[27] Two other aroid cultigens of some importance to later
Pacific agricultural complexes, the giant *Cyrtosperma chamissonis* swamp taro, and *Alocasia macrorrhiza* also have natural
distribution ranges spanning the Near Oceanic region, and are
likely possibilities for early Holocene domestication. *Cyrtosperma*, a lowland swamp aroid which is not known in the
island southeast Asian region to the east, may have come under
the scrutiny of late Pleistocene or early Holocene occupants of
the Bismarcks and coastal New Guinea region. Indeed, microscopic plant residues identified from the surfaces of obsidian
and shell tools from the Balof 2 rockshelter included starch
grains consistent with the processing of *Cyrtosperma* or *Alocasia*
tubers.[28]

In addition to the tuberous plants such as taro, archaeobotanical evidence is accumulating for early Holocene experimentation with a number of fruit and nut-bearing trees in
Near Oceania. Ethnobotanically, the Melanesian islands are
notable for their highly developed arboriculture, including not
only such well-known tree crops as coconut (*Cocos nucifera*)
and breadfruit (*Artocarpus altilis*), but a wide range of other
taxa.[29] Of special interest is the *Canarium* almond, a large,
handsome tree bearing hard-shelled nuts, the woody endocarps
of which preserve well in archaeological deposits especially if
they become carbonized through burning. Yen reports domesticated *Canarium salomonense* remains from a Sepik River site
excavated by Paul Gorecki, dated to the late Pleistocene, as
evidence for a mainland New Guinea locus for the domestication of this important tree crop (Yen 1991a:82–86, figures 4–
6). "Wild" *Canarium* was recovered at the Panakiwuk site in
New Ireland at an 8,000 BP level, and *Canarium* nuts of unknown status are also reported from the Pamwak site on Manus
Island in mid-Holocene contexts.[30] As we will see in chapter 7,
a fully developed tree crop complex including *Canarium* and
many other species is well evidenced for the earliest Lapita

sites in the Bismarck Archipelago. Combined with the emerging indications from the late Pleistocene-early Holocene sites just mentioned, it seems likely that the initial experimentation with, and domestication of, these plants began in the Near Oceanic region some 10,000 or more years ago.

Near Oceania at 2,000 BC

Unfortunately, the mid-Holocene period after about 7–8,000 years ago remains scarcely evidenced in the archaeological record thus far recovered for Near Oceania. Rockshelter sites such as Balof and Panakiwuk were abandoned at this time, not to be re-occupied until the last two thousand years. This abandonment of the rockshelters is itself an intriguing phenomenon, as it hints at a change in settlement patterns, just possibly associated with the developing horticultural and arboricultural subsistence adaptations described above. Until open sites dating to this critical period are discovered and excavated, this interpretation remains highly speculative. A few sites, however, such as Lolmo Cave in the Arawe Islands (Gosden et al. 1994) have yielded limited archaeological samples of the period immediately preceding the appearance of Lapita, that is from about 5,000 to 3,500 years ago. These sites give us a glimpse of the world of the Bismarck Archipelago and Solomon Islands on the eve of those fateful encounters at Talepakemalai, Apalo and other beaches, encounters that would rapidly transform the world of Old Melanesia.

It seems fairly certain that the peoples of Near Oceania in the millennium or so immediately preceding the advent of Lapita had evolved a subsistence economy in which domesticated plants – especially tree crops and some tuber crops such as *Cyrtosperma* and probably *Colocasia* taro – played an important role.[31] At the Dongan Village along the Lower Ramu River on northern New Guinea, Nick Araho and Pam Swadling of the Papua New Guinea National Museum discovered a midden deposit dated to about 5,800 years BP, covered by some three meters of later alluvial deposits.[32] The water-logged midden yielded well-preserved plant remains, including the seeds or nuts of a number of important tree crops (*Canarium, Pangium,*

Parinarium, Pometia, Aleurites and others). Of particular interest is the discovery of betel nut (*Areca catechu*) husk, suggesting that this important stimulant plant was already domesticated and in use by the mid-Holocene.[33] On Nissan Island between the Bismarck and Solomon archipelagoes, Spriggs (1991a:232–3, 237) reports a number of important tree crops present in his Halika Phase, which immediately precedes Lapita. These crops include three species of *Canarium* (*C. indicum, C. harveyi,* and *C. salomonense*), and such nut and fruit crops as *Sterculia, Terminalia,* and *Pangium*. Also represented is the sago palm (*Metroxylon* sp.), whose pith yields an edible starch which can be stored. This agricultural economy continued to be augmented, however, by hunting of the islands' terrestrial fauna, including marsupials, fruit bats, lizards, rats, and birds, as in preceding millennia. Fishing and shellfish gathering also continued to provide a significant contribution to the diet of these people, and there are indications that fishing technologies had become more sophisticated than those possessed by their Pleistocene ancestors. In particular, there is limited evidence for simple *Trochus*-shell fishhooks of one-piece (rotating) form, which would have provided access to deeper water fish off the reef edge and in lagoons.

The kind of mixed-strategy subsistence adaptation that seems to have become widespread throughout Near Oceania by 2,000 BC has been well described by David Roe, based on excavations at the Vatuluma Tavuro rockshelter site on Guadalcanal in the Solomon Islands:

> The initial occupation layer at Vatuluma Tavuro contains evidence for the exploitation of relatively undisturbed and undeveloped forest and the collection of molluscan foods from fresh and brackish water environments. The bone material is largely restricted to primary forest taxa and especially the endemic *Uromys* rats and the arboreal skink, *Corucia zebrata*. Plant macrofossils are restricted to small fragments of *Canarium* nutshell. (1992:95)

The limited archaeological samples as yet available for the immediately pre-Lapita period in Near Oceania also hint at other important technological adaptations, especially in the use of shell. A number of sites, including Pamwak in Manus, Lolmo in the Arawes, the Halika Phase sites on Nissan Island, and the Vatuluma Posovi rockshelter on Guadalcanal have all produced small numbers of worked shell artifacts. Among the artifact types represented are simple, edge-ground adzes of *Tridacna* clam shell, arm rings of *Trochus* shell (in the Solomon Is. sites only), and rough-outs for simple fishhooks, finished one-piece fishhooks of *Trochus* (in Lolmo), and a simple cone-shell bead. Edge-ground adzes of stone also make their appearance in these assemblages. Bone working, however, has not thus far been evidenced.

Our knowledge of this pre-Lapita world of Near Oceania is still very incomplete. For example, most of our evidence thus far comes from a few rockshelters which are not likely to have been the primary habitations of these people. Open sites, which are likely to have been relatively small and not marked by the presence of pottery are exceedingly difficult to locate in the dense rainforest-covered landscape of Near Oceania. It does seem likely, however, that the offshore islets – soon to become the principal foci of large Lapita villages – were not much frequented in the older Near Oceanic settlement pattern.

How, then, might we sum up this world of Old Melanesia on the threshold of the cultural 'revolution' that we have come to call Lapita? Through the successive lifespans of more than 1,700 human generations since humans first crossed the Vitiaz Straits from Sahul into the island world of Near Oceania, a unique adaptation to an island way of life had gradually developed. Change and innovation were slow at first, but increased in tempo and momentum as the Pleistocene glacial maximum ended and the rising seas of the Holocene encroached on island shores. While some vestiges of Pleistocene lifeways remained – in the hunting-and-gathering of forest resources, for example – important new modes of social and economic life had developed. Long-distance, inter-island contacts became important with the exchange of obsidian, the transport of animals, and – we can only presume – social exchanges as well. Various wild forest resources, especially nut- and fruit-bearing trees and tuber-bearing aroids were gradually brought into domestication as a unique tropical Oceanic mode of agricultural developed. Millennia of familiarity with coasts, reefs, and lagoons also led to increased knowledge of the sea's resources and of how to capture these. Despite these marine innovations, however, the overall orientation of Old Melanesia appears to have been more to the land, to the 'bush.'

I have endeavored to keep closely to the archaeological evidence in developing a dynamic portrait of the slowly evolving material world of "everyday life" in Near Oceania. Of the complex social, political, aesthetic, or spiritual aspects of life in this region we know essentially nothing, and it will take many more seasons of hard and careful fieldwork with sites as yet undiscovered before the shreds of evidence from which to tease such patterns may emerge. Given the long spans of time involved, the numbers of islands and their size, and the distances between them, it is reasonable to suppose that substantial cultural and linguistic diversity had already arisen in Old Melanesia; biological diversity among the human inhabitants of the islands is also a reasonable supposition. These aspects of language and human biology will be addressed further in chapter 4, following a consideration of the evidence for Lapita origins and dispersals.

3

The Lapita Dispersal

By the opening of the second millennium BC the cultural land-scape of Old Melanesia had become a diverse mosaic, the product of thousands of years of genetic, cultural, and linguistic changes among the descendants of successive peoples who migrated into this tropical island region during the Pleistocene. Change was gradual at first, but the tempo increased substantially in the early Holocene. It would be foolish to suppose that these post-Pleistocene transformations took place within a "closed system," in splendid isolation. More likely, the boundaries of Near Oceania were porous, with genetic and cultural flows between the populations of New Guinea and the Bismarck Archipelago, and between those of New Guinea and island Southeast Asia to the west. Indeed, the archaeological record of eastern Indonesia and the Philippines – although still incompletely documented – reveals that similar cultural transformations (such as experimentation with plant domestication, and the development of new stone and shell tool technologies) were occurring in this vast island realm during the early to mid Holocene.[1] Some of these developments were certainly transferred from island to island, presumably through complex networks of interacting populations. Pigs, for example, may have been introduced into New Guinea as early as 5,000 years ago, when they first appear in the archaeological record of Highlands sites.[2] Despite the fact that Near Oceania was not a closed system, and that cultural and genetic flows obviously extended across Wallacea, there is no evidence for any substantial, and distinctively different, population incursions into Near Oceania

until the mid-second millennium BC. Then – seemingly quite
abruptly – the face of Old Melanesia was forever transformed
with the appearance of the Lapita cultural complex. As I argue
below and in chapter 4, the Lapita phenomenon must be understood in terms of the movement into the Bismarck Archipelago
of a group (or related groups) of people who were both genetically and linguistically distinct from the autochthonous populations they encountered. What would emerge from the complex
interactions – genetic, linguistic, and cultural – between these
immigrant and indigene groups is the archaeological phenomenon we call "Lapita" and its legacy, which is nothing less than
the modern ethnographic map of Oceania.

Homelands and "Fast Trains"

In the 1980s academic discussions of Lapita origins became
polarized between two models or viewpoints; unfortunately,
neither provides a compelling account of the archaeological (not
to mention genetic or linguistic) evidence. However, in their very
oversimplification these models provide a useful starting point
for discussing Lapita origins. The first model has been dubbed
the "Express Train to Polynesia" (ETP) theory, while the second
might be called the "Indigenous Melanesian Origins" (IMO)
theory. I shall briefly discuss each in turn.

The "Express Train" or ETP theory represents the more
orthodox anthropological perspective, and has been around in
one or another versions at least since E. W. Gifford's recognition that the dentate-stamped pottery he had excavated at Lapita
in New Caledonia (along with that from Fiji and Watom) bore
strong resemblances to certain Neolithic assemblages from
eastern Indonesia.[3] The modern version of the ETP theory is
most closely associated with Peter Bellwood, who has articu-
lated his view of Lapita in several books and articles.[4] In es-
sence, Bellwood argues that Lapita must be regarded as the
archaeological record of a significant population intrusion of
Austronesian-speaking peoples into Near Oceania. In his words,

> the Lapita Culture is the record of a number of highly mobile
> groups of sea-borne colonists and explorers, who expanded

very rapidly through Melanesia in the mid-late second millennium BC, and on into Polynesia, whose present inhabitants are almost certainly their direct descendants. The Lapita Culture is therefore intricately involved in the question of Polynesian origins. The Lapita potters were quite possibly the first pottery-making Austronesians to enter Melanesia. (Bellwood 1979:244)

It is important to note that Bellwood did *not* say that the Lapita culture was ancestral *only* to the modern Polynesians, even though it has sometimes been implied by detractors to the ETP model that this was the case. Moreover, the term "express train" was never actually used by Bellwood or other archaeologists who have argued that Lapita has a Southeast Asian island origin (e.g., Kirch 1987, 1988b, Spriggs 1984, 1991a, in press), although it was the title of a short essay by the biogeographer Jared Diamond in an attempt to synthesize recent results from the Lapita Homeland Project.[5] In fact, the metaphor of an "express train" is quite inappropriate, because it implies that such a train *passed through* Melanesia en route to Polynesia, without stopping. In Bellwood's view, the train would also have stopped at various points throughout Melanesia to drop off boxcars full of colonists![6]

The opposing IMO model was put forward by Jim Allen (1984), in part as a stimulus to participants in the Lapita Homeland Project then being launched. Allen drew upon suggestions initially made by Roger Green that "the original Lapita adaptation was to an area with a complex continental environment, which possessed a wide range of resources that related communities could assemble through exchange," a region that Green thought most probably to have been the "New Britain-New Ireland area" (1979a:45). Although he admitted that the "ultimate derivation" of pottery technology in Melanesia was probably from the west, Allen argued that the Lapita style was an indigenous development in the Bismarck Archipelago, as were other key aspects of the Lapita culture. Drawing upon a range of data, Allen concluded that:

> the concept of pottery, canoes and horticulture coming simultaneous from the west, as the cultural baggage of Austronesians *passing through*, is not substantiated. . . . What is evident in the data from the Bismarcks is that a sufficient time period elapsed

to allow for a local cohesive social and economic universe to have developed, one that could receive technologies from outside its immediate region, as well as develop internal technologies; and that could subsequently bring them together in such a way as to lead to both the Lapita expression and the later development of the Bismarck region. (1984:194, emphasis added)

While Allen left open the question of assessing the relative contributions of these external and internal technologies, others have advocated a more extreme view of the IMO model in which there is "no need to believe in migrations at all" (White et al. 1988:416).[7] In this view, Lapita is wholly an indigenous development out of earlier social and economic configurations in the Bismarcks, with the acquisition of pottery being the only contribution from the west. Unfortunately, the IMO model utterly fails to explain or account for the linguistic map of Oceania, with Austronesian languages spread from Indonesia and Taiwan through coastal Near Oceania and on to Remote Oceania, or the patterns of biological variation, matters that will be discussed at greater length in chapter 4.

While the ETP and IMO theories of Lapita origins as originally formulated sparked useful debate, each leaves critical aspects of the archaeological, linguistic, and biological records of Oceania unexplained. A more sophisticated model was required, one that incorporated aspects of both the ETP and the IMO theories. Roger Green has proposed the label "Triple-I" for such a model, standing for the terms "Intrusion/Innovation/ Integration" (Green 1991b:298). Green's model recognizes that some aspects of Lapita must be accounted for by *intrusion*, the movement of people and their culture into the Bismarck Archipelago, where existing populations were then integrated into a new cultural pattern which itself underwent certain *innovations*.[8] In this book I have chosen another – perhaps more literary – model, invoking Greg Dening's metaphor of "the beach," of sustained encounters between immigrant and indigenous peoples out of which a new cultural synthesis emerged.[9] In either case, we must account not only for the archaeological record of Lapita – with the sudden appearance in the midsecond millennium BC not only of elaborate pottery, but of new settlement patterns, economic systems, and regional exchange networks – but also for the linguistic and human biological patterns of Near and Remote Oceania. In this chapter, I focus largely on the archaeological evidence for Lapita, its geographic and temporal limits, and its transformations in Polynesia and Micronesia. In chapter 4, I turn to the correspondences between this archaeological record and the evidence of historical linguistics and human biology (both ancient and modern), returning finally to a further consideration of Lapita origins. I ask the reader's indulgence, but the issues are complex and it is essential that the independent strands of archaeological, linguistic, and biological evidence be given their separate due.

Archaeological Precursors to Lapita in Island Southeast Asia

Reminding ourselves that the "Lapita cultural complex" is fundamentally an archaeological construction (see chapter 1), we note that it is defined first and foremost by its distinctive ceramics. However, a large number of other technological traits are also characteristic of Lapita, including adzes in stone and shell, a wide variety of marine shell artifacts (pendants, beads, armbands, rings, and fishhooks), and substantial settlements incorporating houses on stilts. The economic base of Lapita is also defined archaeologically as incorporating fishing and marine exploitation along with horticulture (based on a root and tree crop complex) and animal husbandry (of pigs, dogs, and fowl). In assessing Lapita origins from an archaeological perspective, the first step must be a careful comparison of these traits with archaeological assemblages immediately pre-dating Lapita, both in the Bismarck Archipelago and in islands to the west. While some aspects of this Lapita complex are indeed represented in mid-Holocene archaeological assemblages in the Bismarcks as discussed in chapter 2 (such as limited shell artifact technology and tree-cropping), other key elements are absent, especially the pottery and the permanent village or hamlet settlement pattern. When we turn to the neighboring Southeast Asian island region (including Taiwan, the Philippines, Sulawesi, and Halmahera), however, we find that virtually all of the archaeologically-defining features of Lapita developed and spread through those islands over roughly a one-thousand year period, beginning around 3,000 BC on Taiwan, and extending as far as Halmahera by about 1,600 BC.[10] Peter Bellwood (1985, 1992, 1995) has convincingly argued that the spread of this ceramic complex represents the expansion of early Austronesian-speaking populations out of Taiwan and across insular Southeast Asia, in time giving rise to Lapita (map 3.1).

The oldest sites occur on the island of Taiwan, where they are known as the Ta-p'en-k'eng Culture, possibly representing an early stage of Austronesian cultural development.[11] The Ta-p'en-k'eng Culture is succeeded on Taiwan by a diverse group of archaeological assemblages, typically marked by "fine red ware" pottery, dating to between 2,400–1,900 BC. These assemblages (including the Suo-kang and Nan-kang sites in the P'eng-hu Islands [Tsang 1992], and O-Luan-Pi at the southern tip of Taiwan [Li 1983]) exhibit a ceramic complex with bowls or dishes supported on pedestal feet and with large globular jars with everted rims. More striking are the associated artifacts such as net sinkers, polishing stones, pitted cobbles (probably nut-cracking hammers), fishhooks in both bone and *Turbo* shell, and *Conus*-shell rings, all forms that are reflected in later Lapita assemblages.

Similar Neolithic assemblages are present in the Philippine archipelago south of Taiwan by about 2,500 BC. At the Lal-lo and Magapit sites in the Cagayan Valley of Luzon Island,[12] the pottery (again, with pedestal-supported bowls, as well as everted-rim jars) carries fine, dentate-stamped decoration similar to (although not identical with) Lapita. At the Duyong Cave site in Palawan (R. B. Fox 1970), a burial dated to ca. 3,000 BC was associated with *Tridacna* clam-shell adzes and perforated *Conus*-shell ornaments, forms again typical of the later Lapita complex. And on Sanga Sanga Island in the Sulu archipelago, red-slipped pottery decorated with lime-infilled stamped designs, is also associated with *Tridacna* adzes (Spoehr 1973:184–91).

On Sabah island, in northeastern Borneo, the Bukit Tengkorak and Madai sites excavated by Bellwood (ed. 1988; Bellwood and Koon 1989) yielded red-slipped pottery dated about 1,000 BC. Small quantities of flaked obsidian in Bukit Tengkorak came from the Talasea source on New Britain, the principal obsidian source of the Lapita exchange network (see chapter

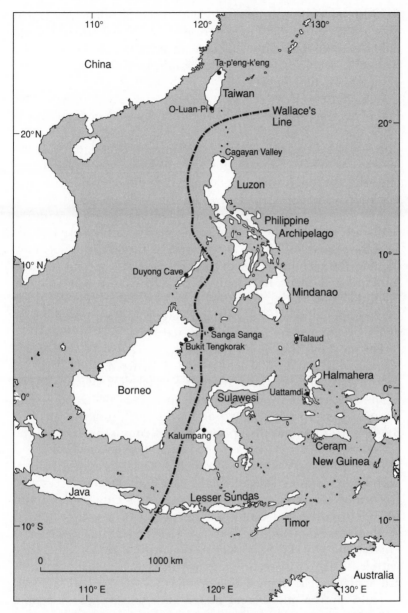

Map 3.1 The archipelagoes of island Southeast Asia, showing
some of the key sites containing archaeological assemblages
associated with the mid-to-late Holocene expansion of the
Austronesian-speaking peoples.

8). Although the stratum from which the obsidian was dated falls at the end of the Lapita period (ca. 2,700–2,300 BP), these flakes demonstrate actual movement of materials between the Bismarck Archipelago and island Southeast Asian communities, a significant find indeed.

Immediately west of New Guinea are the Sulawesi and Halmahera archipelagoes (the region known biogeographically as Wallacea), and it is from these islands that the founding populations of early Lapita communities would most likely have come. These large islands are still little explored archaeologically, although some six decades ago pioneering archaeologist P. V. van Stein Callenfels found the Kalumpang site on the Karama River, containing incised and impressed pottery (figure 3.1) with remarkable parallels to Lapita (van Heekeren 1972: 185–9, plates 96–101). These stylistic similarities not only include the techniques of decoration, but specific motifs and human-face designs. In Minahasa and the Talaud Islands, other Neolithic sites dating to about 2,500 BC have been identified by Peter Bellwood (1976), with red-slipped pottery assemblages again dominated by jars with everted rims, and by bowls.

The most exciting recent finds with respect to possible Lapita "homelands" in the Wallacea region come from the Halmahera group, especially at the Uattamdi Rockshelter site on Kayoa Island, excavated by Geoff Irwin and Peter Bellwood.[13] The deposits in this shelter, dated on marine shell (uncalibrated) to 3,440 ± 100 BP (and thus probably contemporaneous with the earliest known Lapita sites in the Bismarcks), yielded plain and red-slipped pottery virtually identical in vessel form to that from such Lapita sites as Talepakemalai and Etakosarai in Mussau.[14] Decorated ceramics, however, are mostly lacking at Uattamdi. Most intriguing, the Uattamdi site produced a wide range of shell artifacts, including disc beads, bracelets/rings, scrapers, knives, and worked pearl shell, along with a ground stone adz with lenticular cross-section (a known Lapita form), all of which are artifact styles typical of Lapita.

Thus, by the mid-second millennium BC, groups of people using ceramics and shell tools, with an agriculturally-based economy, were well established throughout the area known biogeographically as Wallacea. The ceramic assemblages are in all respects highly similar to Lapita pottery, with calcareous

Figure 3.1   Incised and stamped potsherds from the Kalumpang
site, Karama River, Sulawesi, excavated by van Stein Callenfels in
1933. (After van Heekeren 1972)

sand temper, paddle-and-anvil construction, red slip, incision, and in some cases the use of stamped decorations and lime-infilling. Vessel forms included large globular jars with everted rims, and open bowls supported on pedestals or ring-feet, both forms also characteristic of the earliest Lapita pottery. Only the specific decorative motifs that define Lapita are lacking in the Southeast Asian ceramic assemblages. Thus, while aspects of the *decorative style* of Lapita pottery seem to have been an innovation within Near Oceania, the Lapita ceramic complex as a whole is unquestionably an extension of the later Neolithic Southeast Asian ceramic series represented by such sites as Lallo, Kalumpang, Talaud, and Uattamdi.

The Southeast Asian archaeological antecedents of Lapita include far more than pottery. The complex shell technology, including *Conus*-shell rings and discs, *Tridacna*-shell adzes, *Trochus*-shell fishhooks, and other objects is well attested. So is an economy based on horticulture (including some tree crops) and animal husbandry (with pigs, dogs, and probably fowl), as well as fishing. Moreover, settlement patterns included large village sites, with some suggestion of houses on stilts. In sum, most of the key archaeological parameters that define the Lapita complex had been developed in the islands west of New Guinea and the Bismarcks during the two millennia or so prior to the appearance of Lapita. It was from this island Southeast Asian "hearth" that Austronesian-speaking colonists expanded eastwards into the seas of Old Melanesia, where their encounters with indigenous peoples "on the beach" would give rise to what we call Lapita.

Space: Defining the Boundaries of the Lapita World

The first task an archaeologist faces in defining a prehistoric "culture" is to define its limits in space and time. To qualify as a "Lapita" site, a given archaeological assemblage must possess – at a minimum – a ceramic component decorated with the definitive dentate-stamped style (see chapter 5). In 1988 Terry Hunt and I cataloged all known sites meeting this minimal definition, a total of 79 sites of which 82 percent were "open" sites (primarily beach midden sites) with a few rockshelters or caves.[15] Since then, several new sites have been discovered or reported, bringing the total to approximately one hundred sites. Not all of these have been fully reported, however, and indeed only slightly more than half have been excavated or tested, with perhaps one third of the sites adequately published. Most of the newer discoveries are in the Bismarck Archipelago, the result of the Lapita Homeland Project (Gosden et al. 1989; Allen and Gosden, eds 1991). In the appendix, I provide a gazetteer and brief descriptions of the most important of these sites, particularly those which have been excavated or studied in more than a cursory fashion.

Geographically, Lapita sites are distributed over a vast expanse of the southwestern Pacific, from the Bismarck Archipelago in the west to Samoa in the east, and as far south as New Caledonia and the Île des Pins (map 3.2). The distance – "as the frigate bird flies" – between Manus and Samoa is 4,300 km, slightly more than the distance between New York and San Francisco.

Within this vast region, Lapita sites are well represented in all island groups with one notable exception: the Solomon Islands. On Buka Island at the western end of the Solomon chain, Stephen Wickler (1990:145–8) discovered Lapita pottery scatters on reef flats, evidently the eroded remnants of stilt-house villages. At the eastern extremity of the Solomons, in the Reef-Santa Cruz Islands, at least 14 Lapita sites are known. The large intervening islands stretching between Bougainville and San Cristobal, however, are currently a Lapita void.[16] Whether this gap is an artifact of incomplete archaeological survey (the main Solomon Islands have been quite neglected archaeologically) or a real break in the chain of Lapita sites remains an unresolved question. It is possible that Lapita colonists simply skirted these large islands, which were already populated (Roe 1992, 1993).[17] However, the presence in Lapita sites of the Reef-Santa Cruz Islands of chert flake tools quarried on Ulawa Island in the main Solomons, and of other materials from Nggela and Guadalcanal, indicates that there were certainly contacts with peoples in the central Solomons.[18] Roe (1993:185), who failed to find ceramic evidence for Lapita on Guadalcanal despite a 6,400-year long sequence revealed in

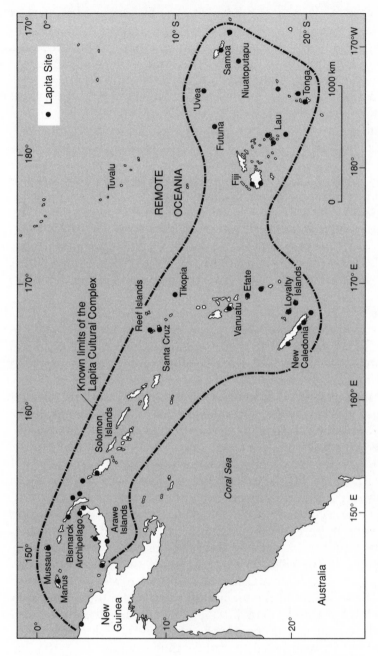

Map 3.2   Distribution of Lapita sites in the Southwestern Pacific region.

cave and rockshelter deposits, leaves the question open; ultimately, the problem will not be resolved until more intensive
fieldwork is carried throughout the main Solomon Islands.[19]

What of the outer limits of the Lapita distribution; are these
securely established through archaeological survey? For the east,
the answer appears to be affirmative, with the Tonga-Samoa
archipelagoes marking the furthest eastwards advance of the
Lapita dispersal.[20] In the west, however, the boundaries of
Lapita remain "fuzzy." A handful of Lapita-style sherds are
known from the Manus Islands, and there is a surface find
reported from Aitape on the north coast of New Guinea. Substantial open sites with well-documented assemblages, however,
are presently confined to an arc of islands including Mussau,
Watom, the Duke of Yorks, and New Britain in the Bismarcks
chain. Is this indeed the "Lapita homeland" in which the distinctive dentate-stamped decorative style was first used in a potting
tradition clearly imported from island Southeast Asia? Or, are
we still missing critical links in a chain extending between
Gebe, Halmahera, and the Bismarcks? Again, the answer must
await further field exploration, because the long coast of New
Guinea between the mouth of the Sepik River and the "Bird's
Head" of New Guinea in Irian Jaya (about 1,250 km in straight-
line distance) remains archaeological *terra incognita*, as do
numerous small islands off the coast (such as Wuvulu and the
Schouten Islands). Whether or not sites containing Lapita style
pottery do eventually turn up in this intervening region, it is
certain that explorations there will reveal important intermediate
links in the chain of dispersal of Austronesian-speaking, pottery-
making peoples in the mid-second millennium BC.

One other "fuzzy boundary" of the Lapita distribution de-
serves comment: the region south of New Britain, along the tip
of Papua (Collingwood Bay) and out into the Massim region
(including the Trobriand Islands and the D'Entrecasteaux group).
Archaeological sequences for this region presently extend back
in time about 2,000 years, post-dating Lapita.[21] The earliest
ceramic assemblages along the Papua coast, however, appear
to have been derived from Lapita, and at Collingwood Bay,
Brian Egloff reports the isolated find of a typically Lapita-like
pedestalled bowl (figure 3.2). Moreover, Roger Green has demonstrated that at least one flake of obsidian in his Reef Island

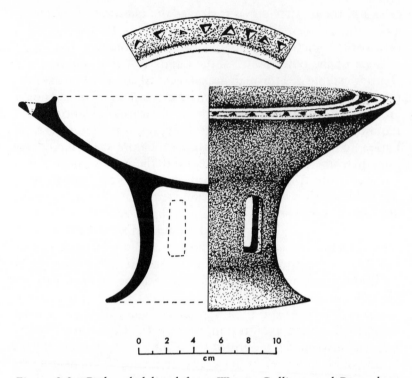

Figure 3.2   Pedestaled bowl from Wawa, Collingwood Bay, along the Papuan coast, in a typical Lapita style. (After Egloff 1971)

site came from the D'Entrecasteaux Islands, proving at least some contact between Lapita communities and the Massim area (Green and Bird 1989). These are tantalizing hints that when Papua and the Massim are more intensively explored they may yet prove to contain Lapita sites.

   In sum, as presently defined on the basis on archaeological surveys, the Lapita world began in the Bismarck Archipelago in the west, and extended through the island arcs of the Solomons and Vanuatu, down to New Caledonia in the south. It also reached across the 850 km wide ocean gap between the Santa Cruz Islands and Fiji, to encompass the Fiji, Lau, Tonga, and Samoa archipelagoes, as well as several smaller islands ('Uvea, Futuna, and probably Rotuma). Two key points must be underscored regarding this geographic distribution. First, it encompasses both Near Oceania in the west, a region that had been long settled by humans since the late Pleistocene, and Remote Oceania to the east, a pristine island world that seemingly had not felt human footsteps prior to those of the Lapita potters. Second, from the traditional viewpoint of the cultural anthropologist or ethnographer, the Lapita world crosses the long-established boundary separating "Melanesia" from "Polynesia." The archaeological discovery of Lapita – as an historical entity that cross-cuts and indeed *integrates* these regions – requires that we continue to rethink some of the long-standing anthropological assumptions about the cultural history of Oceania.

Time: Calibrating the Rate of Dispersal

Having defined the spatial boundaries of Lapita, what can be said of the temporal dimensions of this world – when did it commence, how rapid was its spread eastwards into Remote Oceania, and when did it either cease to exist or transform into something different? Archaeologists construct their chronological frameworks in two main ways, which they generally refer to as *relative* and *absolute* dating. Relative dating sequences are constructed through the systematic comparison and correlation of stylistic changes in material culture (most often in ceramics, given the highly "plastic" nature of this material). The relative sequencing of Lapita sites through comparison of changes in vessel form and motif composition has been important in working out local sequences in various areas, such as the Reef-Santa Cruz Islands and in Western Polynesia, and will be discussed further in chapter 5. In order to position archaeological assemblages in "absolute" time, however, it is necessary to apply one or more of the chronometric methods developed largely since 1950, such as radiocarbon, thermoluminescence (TL), or dendrochronology. There have been a few attempts to use TL dating on Lapita pottery, but the most important method for establishing the age of Lapita sites has been radiocarbon (^{14}C) dating.

In 1979, Roger Green made the first attempt to outline a Lapita chronology based on 26 "reliable" ^{14}C dates from 17 sites (Green 1979a:32–4, table 2.1). Green observed that "statistical comparisons between the earliest estimates for sites in Santa Cruz, Malo, Fiji, and Tongatapu reveal no significant difference in their ages." This apparent absence of "any trend to Lapita settlement" was the first indication that the dispersal of people making Lapita style pottery must have been rapid indeed. Green was left to conclude "simply that Lapita sites as a cultural horizon date from between 1,600 and 500 BC." As general "bracketing" dates for the Lapita cultural complex, Green's estimate still stands. However, significant advances have recently been made in the radiocarbon dating of Lapita sites, particularly as the corpus of ^{14}C dates has expanded through the efforts of the Lapita Homeland Project and other research. While confirming that the Lapita dispersal was fast paced, they now allow us to detect a distinct west-to-east temporal trend.

By 1988, the radiocarbon corpus from Lapita sites had expanded to 78 dated samples, which Terry Hunt and I calibrated to "calendrical" years using the newly-available calibration curves developed by Minze Stuiver and others (Kirch and Hunt 1988a, 1988b).[22] This expanded sample again indicated that Lapita populations had moved from the Bismarcks to Tonga over a short time period, beginning about 1,500 or 1,600 BC, with beachheads established throughout the whole extent of the "Lapita world" by no more than about three centuries later.[23] Most recently, Matthew Spriggs (1990a) has compiled a suite of no less than 213 radiocarbon dates from Lapita sites, and from sites with closely related ceramic traditions, again paying close attention to issues of calibration and sample reliability. These studies now allow us to begin to detect the actual chronology of Lapita dispersal out of the Bismarck archipelago and on to the islands of Remote Oceania, and thus to calibrate the dispersal rate.[24] Figure 3.3 shows the distribution of calibrated radiocarbon ages for the earliest sites in four geographic subregions of Lapita: Far Western, Western, Southern, and Eastern. The earliest reliable radiocarbon age determinations (upon which the graphs in Figure 3.3 are based), are given in Table 3.1.

The earliest known Lapita sites appear in the Bismarck Archipelago between about 1,550–1,400 BC; these include the Talepakemalai site in Mussau, and probably also sites in the Arawe Islands off the coast of New Britain, as well as on Nissan Island.[25] A phase of rapid eastwards expansion out of the

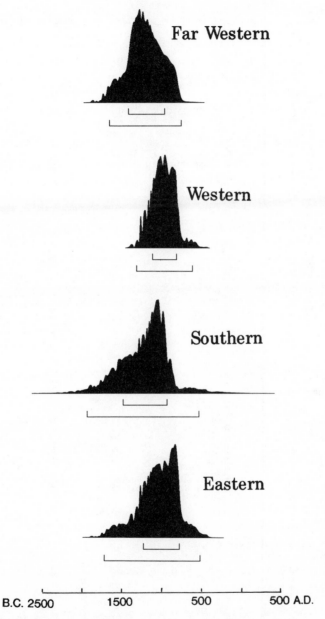

Figure 3.3 Probability distributions of combined radiocarbon age determinations from four Lapita regions, as determined by the OXCAL radiocarbon calibration program. The horizontal bars under each distribution indicate the one and two standard deviation error ranges.

Table 3.1 Selected radiocarbon ages for initial Lapita occupations in four geographic regions

Island	Site	Laboratory number	Conventional radiocarbon age (BP)	Sample type[a]
Far Western region				
Mussau	Talepakemalai	ANU-5080	3260 ± 90	C
	Talepakemalai	B-20452	3050 ± 70	W
	EHB	ANU-5088	3470 ± 90	S
	EHB	ANU-5089	3380 ± 90	S
Arawe	Lolmo	B-26644	3530 ± 70	S
	Magekur	B-27946	3200 ± 70	S
Watom	SAC	ANU-5339	3490 ± 80	S
Nissan	Yomining	ANU-5228	3350 ± 80	S
Western region				
Nendo	SZ-8	SUA-111	3140 ± 70	S
Reef Islands	Nenumbo (RF-2)	Pooled Mean of 4 Dates	2838 ± 54	C
Tikopia	Kiki (TK-4)	UCR-964	2680 ± 90	C
Anuta	AN-6	I-6275	2830 ± 90	C
Malo	NHMa-8	ANU-1135	3150 ± 70	S
Aneityum	Anawau	ANU-2421	2890 ± 60	P

	Site	Lab no.	Date (BP)	Material[a]
Southern region				
New Caledonia	Tiwi	B-44650	3240 ± 220	C
	Naia (55)	ANU-96	3165 ± 120	C
	Naia (56)	ANU-259	2855 ± 95	C
	Nessadiou	UW-471	2875 ± 115	C
	Lapita (13B)	B-61955	2850 ± 50	C
	Lapita (13)	M-341	2800 ± 350	C
	Vatcha	ANU-262	2855 ± 165	C
Eastern region				
Viti Levu, Fiji	Natunuku	GaK-1218	3240 ± 100	C
		NZ-7864	2750 ± 30	S
		GaK-1226	2980 ± 90	C
Naigani, Fiji	Yanuca	NZ-5616	3152 ± 50	S
	Naigani	NZ-5615	3142 ± 50	S
Lakeba, Fiji	Qaranipuqa	NZ-4594	2876 ± 70	C
	Wakea	NZ-4807	2701 ± 120	C
Tongatapu	To-2	ANU-541	3090 ± 95	S
	To-1	K-904	3180 ± 100	S
Lifuka, Ha'apai	Holopeka	CAMS-12918	2800 ± 70	C
Ha'apai	Pukotala	CAMS-7148	2870 ± 60	C
Foa, Ha'apai	Faleloa	CAMS-7145	2940 ± 60	C
Upolu, Samoa	Mulifanua	NZ-1958	3251 ± 155	S
Ofu, Samoa	To'aga	B-35601	2950 ± 110	C

[a] C, charcoal; W, wood; S, marine shell; P, peat.

Bismarck Archipelago appears to have commenced some 2–300 years later. Lapita sites were certainly established in the Santa Cruz group east of the main Solomon Islands (the Western region) by 1,100 BC, although there is reason to believe that the initial colonization sites in this area may not yet be adequately dated. The open-ocean gap between the Santa Cruz Islands and the Fiji, Tonga, and Samoa Islands to the east seems to have been crossed at virtually the same time. Indeed, the radiocarbon corpus from this Eastern Lapita area supports a colonization date as early as 1,200 BC.[26] This suggests that once the Lapita expansion out of the Bismarck Archipelago had commenced, it moved extremely rapidly as far as the Fiji and Western Polynesian islands. At the same time, other groups of Lapita people were exploring southwards through the Vanuatu archipelago and beyond to the large island of New Caledonia. A settlement date for New Caledonia by at least 1,000 BC is well supported on the current radiocarbon evidence.

In sum, a temporal cline extending from the Bismarck archipelago south to New Caledonia and east to the Fiji-Tonga-Samoa region marks the path of the Lapita diaspora, a phase of population expansion occurring in no less than three and no more than five centuries. The total straight-line geographic distance involved is about 4,500 km, so that the "average" rate of dispersal or population movement was on the order of 9–15 km per year. Naturally, in an island world dispersal would not have taken place 1 km at a time, but rather in "jumps" of varying distance. It may be more insightful, therefore, to think of this dispersal in terms of human generations. If each successive generation had a reproduction span of about 20 years, then the Lapita diaspora required somewhere between 15 and 25 generations to accomplish. This suggests that, again on "average," each successive generation moved eastwards or southwards somewhere between 180 and 300 km.

At the rates of dispersal indicated by radiocarbon date analysis, the Lapita diaspora was one of the most rapid of such events known in world history. By way of comparison, we may consider the dispersal of Neolithic peoples and agricultural technology from the ancient Near East across Europe, a process that has also been subjected to radiocarbon calibration.[27] The European agricultural diffusion – one of the greatest diasporas of the Old World – took place at an average rate of about 1 km per year, or 20 km per generation. Thus the Lapita dispersal was literally an order of magnitude more rapid. Certainly, one factor underlying such a high dispersal rate was the difference between a continental land surface and the island landscape of the southwest Pacific. Nonetheless, such a high rate of spread raises important issues of how this was accomplished in *demographic* terms, especially given that beyond the Solomon Islands, Lapita populations were moving into an unpopulated realm.

Population ecologists sometimes draw a theoretical distinction between species which have high reproductive rates, referred to as "*r*-selected," and those with low reproductive rates, known as "K-selected."[28] Demographic anthropologists have applied this *r*-K model to different human populations as well, noting that human reproductive strategies (including cultural birth control mechanisms) vary substantially in environments depending upon the human population density.[29] In "open" environments where human population density (and thus pressure on resources) is low, reproductive rates tend to be high, but may shift toward reduced rates when the landscape becomes densely packed. Such shifts have been noted, for example, in Hawai'i and other Polynesian islands between the period of initial human settlement and later time periods when large and dense populations had become established. In the case of Lapita, it is clear that we are dealing with a situation of a high reproductive strategy ("*r*-selected"), in which the continued availability of new, and unpopulated, islands just beyond the eastern frontier of the Lapita dispersal front put no "brakes" on population growth. Indeed, one can suggest that in order for the Lapita "express train" to keep moving eastwards and southwards, it was essential to have a high rate of population growth, to populate the new landfalls (recalling that the "train" left "boxcars" all along its path). This demographic situation raises some very intriguing questions regarding the human biological aspects of Lapita, which we will revisit in chapter 4.

Some Speculations on Motive

What impelled or propelled the Lapita people to expand their world so rapidly from the islands of Near Oceania into the vast expanses of the central and eastern Pacific? The question of motive – of why? – is impossible for prehistorians to answer definitively, yet it is perhaps the most compelling. We cannot resist wondering what could have been in the minds of these people to inspire successive generations to leave one island home to seek a new life on undiscovered lands beyond the horizon. While the question is not amenable to definitive "scientific" resolution, we can make some informed speculations about motive.

As David Anthony suggests in a review of migration theories in archaeology, the conditions favoring migration are generally thought to be of either "push" or "pull" varieties, the former consisting of negative stresses in the homeland area, and the latter of positive attractions in the area being migrated to (Anthony 1990:899). Probably the most frequently suggested "push" underlying diasporas is that of "population pressure" in the homeland area. In the case of Lapita, the initial movement of Austronesian-speaking peoples out of island southeast Asia into the Bismarcks might have been prompted by such demographic considerations, but there is no proof of this. Moreover, the expansion of Lapita populations beyond the Bismarcks can hardly be explained in such population-density terms, because there is no evidence that the large islands of New Britain or New Ireland were at all densely settled in the second millennium BC. Indeed, the opposite appears to be case, that these islands had large tracts covered in primary rainforest, and were only sparsely occupied, at least in their interior regions. It may be, nonetheless, that the Lapita people had a strong preference for clusters of offshore islets with extensive reef-lagoon habitats – such as the Mussau Islands or the Arawe group – in which case highly local population densities could have contributed each generation or two to the search for new clusters of marine resource-rich offshore islets to colonize.

What of possible "pull" factors that may have attracted Austronesian speakers to voyage beyond Halmahera and along the northern coasts of New Guinea, to establish new settlements in the Bismarcks? One distinct possibility is that these maritime people were in search of trading opportunities, looking for new resources to exploit. As we shall see in chapter 8, a key aspect of Lapita was long-distance movement of a variety of materials and artifacts over considerable distances. The discovery – in archaeological contexts on Borneo in southeast Asia – of obsidian flakes which originated at Talasea on New Britain (Bellwood and Koon 1989), demonstrates that at least some materials moved between the island southeast Asian "homeland" islands and the Bismarcks.[30] Ethnologist Ward Goodenough has proposed that the remarkable expansion of Austronesian-speaking peoples throughout Southeast Asia and the Pacific was in part due to developing "economic or commercial interests . . . fostered by some developing center of wealth and population on the Asian mainland that provided a growing demand for products from abroad" (1982:52–3). Goodenough suggests that an expanding trade in the region of the South China Sea in such items as rattan, resins, woods, feathers, turtle shell and so forth "would have provided the impetus needed for overseas exploration and settlement." It may well be that the initial expansion of Austronesian-speakers into the Bismarcks was stimulated by just such economic interests as Goodenough proposes.[31]

Continued expansion of Lapita people beyond the Solomon Islands, and into Remote Oceania, however, is unlikely to have been driven by a search for new trading opportunities. The distances were simply too great, and moreover these new landfalls in Vanuatu, New Caledonia, Fiji, Tonga, and Samoa were virgin islands previously unpopulated by humans. We must assume that other attractions "pulled" these Lapita voyagers farther and farther out into Oceanic "outer space." One possibility lies in the social organization of the Lapita people themselves, which seems to have incorporated a birth-order based ranking system in which first-born sons inherited rights to the ancestral house and its estate.[32] In such societies, junior siblings frequently adopt a strategy of seeking new lands to settle where they can found their own "house" and lineage, assuring their own offspring access to quality resources. Among the Polynesian peoples who were the direct descendants of Lapita colonizers in the Tonga-Samoa region (see below), rivalries between senior and junior members of a group are commonly cited in oral traditions as a major incentive behind voyages of discovery. In these sagas, it is usually the younger brother who leaves the home island to sail over the horizon in search of a new land where his line can be established as foremost. For example, "Maui-of-a-thousand-tricks," one of the greatest of the Polynesian culture heroes and reputed navigator and discoverer of new archipelagoes (which he pulled up from the sea with his magic fishhook) was in most versions a rebellious junior brother.[33] It is entirely plausible that similar structural tensions within Lapita social groups contributed to the eastwards expansion in a quest for new islands to settle.

In sum, the Lapita diaspora will not adequately be explained in the simple terms of single causes. More likely there were complex sets of both homeland stresses and attractions of new lands that fueled this expansion, and moreover the mix of specific "push" and "pull" factors doubtless changed over time. The circumstances that led to the initial movement of Austronesian speakers into the Bismarcks were unlikely to have been the same motivations that led their descendants several generations later to brave the 850 km open ocean crossing from the Santa Cruz Islands to Fiji. We can only guess what emotions of hope and trepidation, excitement and nostalgia, accompanied each canoe load of voyagers as they re-enacted once again the history of their ancestors.

Eastern Lapita and Polynesian Origins

In Pacific anthropology, no single issue has inspired more debate and argument – ranging from the scholarly to the sublimely ludicrous – than the "problem of Polynesian origins." Theories of Polynesian origins and migrations began to be formally stated with the late eighteenth-century European explorers (among whom Captain James Cook had a remarkably modern fix on the matter, recognizing linguistic connections between Polynesian and "Malay" languages), and continued unceasingly throughout the nineteenth century. Serious anthropological investigations of the issue began in the 1920s, with an emphasis on systematic ethnographic comparisons and an unfortunate neglect of archaeological evidence. During this pre-World War II period of intensive study of Polynesian ethnography a rather romantic notion of Polynesian migrations in large "fleets" out of Asia held sway, epitomized in the classic synthesis of Sir Peter Buck, appropriately titled *Vikings of the Sunrise*.[34] Such studies tended to assume that the time depth of Polynesian occupation had been short, and that there had been little *in situ* cultural change. Rather, Polynesian culture had developed elsewhere (most theorists looked to Asia, although a few cast their gaze towards the Americas) and had been carried to the islands fully formed.

Only with the advent of stratigraphic archaeology in the Pacific Islands in the late 1940s and early 1950s, accompanied by the invention of radiocarbon dating and hence the ability to determine the "absolute" (that is, calendric rather than relative) chronology of human settlement, did the long-held diffusionist paradigm of Polynesian origins begin to break down. We need not recount in detail the sequence of archaeological discoveries in various Polynesian islands (as well as in Melanesia to the west) that led to a complete rethinking of Polynesian origins by the early 1970s. Suffice it to say that the appearance of Lapita pottery in the earliest settlement sites in Tonga, Samoa, and Fiji, all dating to the end of the second millennium BC, was recognized as being of fundamental significance to Polynesian origins.[35] In a classic article, "Tonga, Lapita Pottery, and Polynesian Origins," Les Groube drew upon the emerging archaeological sequences of Fiji and Western Polynesia to argue that the Lapita colonization of this region was the critical founding event underlying Polynesian origins:

> There seems little reason to doubt that, by the end of the twelfth century BC, people with Lapita pottery had penetrated into the region we now call Polynesia. In all probability, at this early date, the Fijian and Tongan Lapita populations were a closely related cultural community, the perfect candidate for (in linguistic terms), the pre-Polynesian (East-Oceanic) speech community. The subsequent isolation following separation led to the linguistic innovations which separate the Polynesian and Fijian languages. (1971:306)

Thus, as Groube summed up the converging evidence of both archaeology and historical linguistics, "the Polynesians . . . did not strictly come from anywhere: they *became* Polynesians and the location of their becoming was Tonga" (1971:313).

Groube's pinpointing of the Polynesian "homeland" to Tonga reflected the lack of decorated Lapita pottery in Samoa at the time of this synthesis. A few years later, the discovery of the

submerged Mulifanua Lapita site under a reef flat off Upolu
Island revealed that the early "pre-Polynesian" community had
encompassed *both* Tonga and Samoa. Indeed, archaeological
work throughout the Western Polynesian region has now shown
that Lapita sites were widely distributed on all of the major
islands in this region, including not only Tongatapu and the
main Samoan group, but also the Ha'apai Islands, Vava'u,
Niuatoputapu, Futuna, and 'Uvea, and throughout the main
Fiji and Lau archipelagoes.[36] The pottery assemblages from
these early Lapita sites share a number of characteristics both in
vessel form and in details of decorative motifs (see chapter 5),
which allow us to define a distinctive "Eastern Lapita" ceramic
tradition.

Thanks to intensive archaeological study on most of the
main islands of Western Polynesia, the early Eastern Lapita
assemblages of these islands are linked in unbroken cultural
sequences spanning about one millennium, with later assemblages that can be identified as Ancestral Polynesian.[37] In terms
of the pottery sequences, gradual and continuous change from
classic, dentate-stamped Early Eastern Lapita through a Late
Eastern Lapita phase (in which decoration declines markedly,
and certain vessel forms are dropped), to a terminal Polynesian
Plain Ware phase is well attested (see chapter 5). The manufacture and use of pottery was finally abandoned in Polynesia
early in the first millennium AD for reasons that are not entirely clear. Pottery is only one of many artifact classes signaling
the gradual development of a varied but distinctive Ancestral
Polynesian culture out of its immediate Eastern Lapita ancestor.[38] Similar changes are evident in the stone adz kit, in various shell and bone tools, as well as in settlement patterns and
subsistence systems.

Thus in Western Polynesia the "end" of Lapita is the "beginning" of Polynesian culture. Eastern Lapita was gradually
transformed through processes of cultural change and adaptation to new island environments to something recognizably
different, yet retaining many of the ancestral cultural patterns.
In terms of formal archaeological taxonomy, we cease to label
the ceramic and artifact assemblages found in the Western
Polynesian region after about 500 BC as "Lapita," and now
label them "Polynesian" (the pottery specifically is labeled

"Polynesian Plain Ware"). It cannot be over-emphasized, however, that this terminological framework is a heuristic, classificatory device of the archaeologist, a necessary convenience for dealing with excavated artifact assemblages spanning more than one thousand years. In reality there was *continuity* – genetically, culturally, and linguistically – between the Lapita pottery makers who first discovered and colonized these archipelagoes toward the end of the first millennium BC, and their descendants who would come to be known to the European world as Polynesians.[39]

That the Polynesian cultures owe their origins to one group of Lapita people who expanded eastwards beyond the Santa Cruz Islands and into Remote Oceania is of fundamental importance not only for understanding Polynesian history, but for what it tells us of Lapita itself. Because the Polynesians are *direct descendants* of at least one group of Lapita people, it is possible to construct certain arguments regarding the language and culture, as well as the human biology, of this early Eastern Lapita group. Naturally, one cannot simply project back contemporary Polynesian traits across some three millennia to construct a portrait of Lapita, for that would be to naively deny the many changes that occurred subsequently in the various Polynesian cultures as they differentiated over time. But through carefully controlled comparative work using the independent evidence of historical linguistics and archaeology, as well as comparative ethnography, it is possible to make plausible inferences regarding Eastern Lapita. One of the most important of these inferences is that this Eastern Lapita group spoke an Austronesian language, and more specifically a language that the linguists would reconstruct under the label "Proto-Central Pacific." I will return to this matter in more detail in chapter 4, to explore how linguistic analysis together with archaeology enables a more robust reconstruction of Lapita.

Regional Differentiation: Far Western, Western, Southern, and Eastern Lapita

As we have seen, the Lapita people spread over a remarkably large expanse of the southwestern Pacific during the course of only a few centuries. Throughout much of the early part of this dispersal, contacts between newly-founded settlements and homeland communities were maintained through regular voyaging contacts and are archaeologically attested by material evidence for exchange between such groups (see chapter 8). Yet as this expansion continued, it was inevitable that there would be a decline in the frequency of contact between settlements across such a vast array of islands. Moreover, certain natural geographic "breaks" such as the 380 km water gap between the Solomon Islands and the Santa Cruz group, and the even wider 850 km gap separating Santa Cruz from Fiji, would tend to inhibit regular voyaging, and hence would lead to decreased and infrequent communication between Lapita communities. As such network-breaking began to occur, with groups of more closely-related and interacting communities forming *regional* social systems, a process of differentiation began. Because all of these regional networks shared a common cultural legacy, they are archaeologically recognizable as falling within the Lapita "tradition," but each displays aspects of local variation. Chris Gosden (1992b:25) has remarked of Lapita "that it bespeaks a tremendous sense of tradition combined with enormous diversity and dynamism," a phenomenon he labels "dynamic traditionalism." In Gosden's words:

> During the Lapita period people keep up a considerable pace of change, exploring and settling new areas and restructuring the bounds of the world in which they live. At the same time they also maintain solid central threads which give some constant shape and stability to life over hundreds and thousands of years. To stay in motion and yet maintain balance was the problem facing the Lapita social system. (1992b:25)

As our knowledge of archaeological variability within the larger Lapita tradition has increased, it has become feasible to recognize and delimit several regional sub-traditions, each of which probably represented to some degree a network of social interactions persisting over a considerable period of time. In his classic synthesis of Lapita, Roger Green was the first to formally distinguish "separate style areas" based on the formal analysis of decorative motifs on pottery (see chapter 5):

Analyses of the decorative systems through time reveals . . .
differences between the western and eastern Lapita sequences.
In western sequences such as those from the Reef-Santa Cruz
island group, there is an indication of some impoverishment of
the local design system through time. . . . In the New Hebrides
[Vanuatu] there are fewer vessel forms, and incising becomes
the main decorative technique. By contrast, in the eastern Lapita
sequences of Fiji, Tonga, and Samoa, the more elaborate and
highly decorated vessel forms disappear during the second half
of the sequence, and by the end only simple bowls and globular
jar shape with little or no decoration remain. It seems that in
the one case continued exchange of pots, as well as other items,
provided a high degree of continuity and integration within the
western Lapita exchange system. In the other cases isolation
from this network resulted not only in a drift away from the
original system, but also, in eastern Lapita, in a quite separate
line of ceramic simplification. (Green 1979a:43–4)

At the time Green proposed this distinction between "western" and "eastern" Lapita little was known of sites and assemblages in the Bismarck Archipelago, and his sample of "western"
materials was drawn primarily from the newly excavated Reef-
Santa Cruz Island sites. Later, when Dimitri Anson extended
the analysis of ceramic style to pottery assemblages such as
Eloaua (ECA), Watom, and Ambitle in the Bismarcks, it became necessary to distinguish a "far western" Lapita province
in distinction to the western group centered around the Reef-
Santa Cruz and northern Vanuatu sites.[40] Similarly, it appears
that there was also regional differentiation of those Lapita
communities that ventured further south down the Melanesian
arc into the large island of New Caledonia and its near neighbors
(Îles des Pins and the Loyalty group), and that this should be
formally designated "southern Lapita." At the present time,
then, there is sufficient archaeological evidence to distinguish
four regional sub-traditions or "provinces" within Lapita:[41]

Far Western Lapita. The Far Western province encompasses
the Bismarck Archipelago and islands as far east as Buka, and
includes the earliest known Lapita sites, dating to about 1,500
BC. Indeed, on present evidence this is the immediate homeland of the Lapita tradition. Moreover, even after the eastwards
expansion of Lapita commenced, communities within the Far
Western province continued to maintain regular exchange

relationships, so that various cultural innovations occurring within this region were shared. There thus appears to have been considerable regional continuity within the Far Western province for as long as one millennium.

Western Lapita. Were the term not already in widespread use, "western" might better have been labeled "central," for this cluster of Lapita sites focuses on the Reef-Santa Cruz and neighboring islands, and on the northern Vanuatu archipelago. As we have seen, communities in this region were evidently the first to cross the boundary between Near and Remote Oceania, that is they were the first to venture into previously uninhabited lands. The first Western Lapita communities were established by about 1,200 BC, but did not all become immediately isolated or disengaged from the Far Western homeland.[42] Rather, as Green's extensive work on the importation of obsidian, chert, and other materials into several Reef Islands sites has shown, there were continued and regular long-distance voyaging contacts between the Western and Far Western provinces that persisted for at least several centuries. These exchange contacts will be discussed at greater length in chapter 8.

Southern Lapita. At present we know relatively little of the archaeology and prehistory of the southern part of Vanuatu, so that the absence of Lapita sites there may simply be a reflection of incomplete sampling. However, at least 25 sites containing dentate-stamped Lapita pottery have now been recorded in the Loyalty Islands and New Caledonia (including the Île de Pins; see Sand 1994:271–2), and it seems important to distinguish these as a distinct Southern Lapita province. The prehistory of New Caledonia has been subject to vigorous debates on several crucial issues ever since Gifford and Shutler published the results of their pioneering archaeological excavations carried out in 1952.[43] Among these is the mtter of whether New Caledonia was settled by a non-ceramic using people prior to Lapita. The main evidence in support of this hypothesis consists of a number of tumuli which Roger Green has convincingly argued were incubation nests of the extinct giant megapode-like bird *Sylviornis neocaledoniae*.[44] While the possibility of a pre-Lapita population cannot be definitively ruled out, there is at present no direct archaeological evidence in support of it, and we must assume that the first human occupation of this biogeographically fascinating large island was by one or more groups of Lapita people.

Understanding the Southern Lapita province in New Caledonia and the Loyalties is further complicated, however, by an important degree of ceramic variation within this region. While many sites, such as the type site of "Lapita" itself (Gifford and Shutler's Site 13 at Koné on the western coast), contain large quantities of classic, dentate-stamped Lapita pottery, others have yielded only small quantities of Lapita sherds. Moreover, a significant number of sites dating to the same time period (ca. 1,200–200 BC) are marked by the presence of plain ware jars only, these being distinctively marked on their surfaces with carved-paddle impressions. This carved-paddle impressed pottery has been called Podtanéan, and some scholars regard it as a cultural tradition distinct from Lapita.[45] However, it is noteworthy that the dominant vessel form of Podtanéan pottery is also typical of Lapita plain ware assemblages elsewhere, and that paddle-impressing is also known within the larger Lapita tradition, especially in Fiji and Western Polynesia.[46] Exactly what the Lapita-Podtanéan ceramic variation in New Caledonia represents in terms of social systems or cultural traditions during the first millennium BC remains, in my view, open to further discussion (see Chapter 5). I consider it likely that these two ceramic "traditions" represent the rapid development of some kind of social or "ethnic" differentiation on the island – in which pottery had a key symbolic role – among groups of people who were culturally of the same origin. Certainly these are intriguing questions that will continue to be hotly debated for some time to come, and will only be resolved through continued field and laboratory studies in New Caledonia.

Eastern Lapita. Finally, the Eastern Lapita province encompasses the Fijian, Tongan, and Samoan archipelagoes along with several isolated islands in that region such as Futuna, 'Uvea, and Niuatoputapu. As we have already seen, this region was settled by 1,200–1,100 BC, and due to the great ocean distance between Santa Cruz and Fiji, quickly became isolated. However, within the Eastern Lapita province inter-community exchange and interaction networks continued for some time, as evidenced by the movement of obsidian (from Tafahi Island), chert, adzes, and other materials.[47] Eventually these networks began to break at critical points, especially between Fiji on the west, and Tonga-Samoa on the east. The descendants of those Lapita settlers in the Tonga-Samoa alignment would by 500 BC become sufficiently differentiated that we now label them with the new term "Polynesian."

Lapita and Micronesian Settlement

We have seen that at the eastern terminus of their dispersal the Lapita people discovered the Tongan and Samoan archipelagoes and other islands in their vicinity; the descendants of these colonizers would in time become the Polynesians, whose offspring subsequently voyaged to the most marginal lands of the eastern Pacific, including Easter Island. We have also seen that other groups of Lapita people settled the eastern Melanesian archipelagoes of Vanuatu, New Caledonia, and Fiji, giving rise to the varied local cultures of those regions. What then of Micronesia, the vast western Pacific region north of the equator, dominated by coral atolls but also dotted here and there with a few high volcanic islands such as Truk, Pohnpei, and Kosrae? What role, if any, did the Lapita dispersal play in the initial human settlement of these islands?

To answer this question, it is crucial to note that although the category "Micronesia" is of long-standing in ethnology, it masks significant cultural and linguistic diversity by combining two groups of island cultures which in reality had rather separate histories. In the western part of Micronesia are the Palau and Marianas archipelagoes, whose indigenous inhabitants speak Palauan and Chamorro, languages which while Austronesian are not Oceanic, but part of the Western Malayo-Polynesian branch (which includes the Philippine Islands languages). In contrast, the languages spoken by people throughout the Caroline Islands (including Truk, Pohnpei, and Kosrae) and the Marshall Islands belong to the *Oceanic* subgroup of Austronesian, as do the Austronesian languages of Melanesia and of Polynesia. The historical linguistic evidence thus strongly suggests two distinct origins and histories for the languages spoken in Micronesia, those in the west having an ancestry directly from island Southeast Asia (specifically the Philippines region), and those in the central and eastern region having a common history with the Oceanic languages of the Melanesian and Polynesian areas.[48] (The linguistic history of the Oceanic languages is discussed in more detail in chapter 4.)

Archaeological research in various Micronesian island groups has now independently confirmed this culture-historical division of the region into two parts.[49] In western Micronesia, population movements out of the Philippine Islands region up through Palau and the Marianas probably began by at least 3,500 BP, if not earlier (Bonhomme and Craib 1987; Masse 1990; Rainbird 1994). The oldest known sites in the Marianas group have yielded large quantities of well-made earthenware with a fine red slip (known as Marianas Red Ware), along with low frequencies of a decorated ware with stamped or impressed designs filled in with lime. These lime-filled, impressed sherds are nearly identical with pottery from the Sanga Sanga site in the Sulu archipelago of the Philippines.[50] Although further field-work both in Palau and the Philippines (and in such critical "steppingstone" islands as Sonsoral and Tobi) will be necessary to refine this picture, the archaeological evidence to date seems to link the history of western Micronesia to that of the Philippine region in island southeast Asia, thus independently reinforcing the linguistic interpretation.

For the central and eastern Micronesian islands the emerging archaeological evidence for initial human settlement suggests a different historical sequence, one closely linked with the later Lapita settlements of the Bismarck and Solomon Islands. Unlike Palau, the Marianas, and Yap in western Micronesia where pottery was being made and used in recent times, the central and eastern Micronesian islands lacked ceramics at the time of European contact, and none was known archaeologically. In the late 1970s, however, a partly submerged coastal site at Fefan, Truk, was discovered bearing significant quantities of a sand-tempered mostly plain earthenware (some sherds were decorated by notching along the rim). Associated with this pottery was an impressive range of shell artifacts, including adzes, chisels, scrapers, discs, pendants, rings, and probable fishhook fragments manufactured from *Tridacna*, *Conus*, *Cassis*, and other shell taxa. The Fefan shell technology bears striking resemblances to that of Lapita sites such as Talepakemalai in the Bismarcks, while the Fefan pottery is highly similar to late Lapita ceramic assemblages found from the Bismarcks westwards as far as the Reef-Santa Cruz Islands.[51] Radiocarbon dates from the Fefan site put the date of occupation at about 2,000 years ago.

Recent archaeological excavations on Pohnpei Island (particularly at the famous megalithic site of Nan Madol) and on Kosrae Island have also revealed sand-tempered plain ware ceramics dating to the final few centuries of the first millennium BC. At Nan Madol, the initial occupations were probably on stilt houses built over the reef, a settlement pattern associated with the earliest Lapita people (Bath and Athens 1990:280; see chapter 6). While there are some stylistic differences between the Truk, Pohnpei, and Kosrae pottery assemblages, all are similar in their technology of manufacture (sand-tempered, low-fired, paddle-and-anvil produced), in vessel forms (dominated by globular pots with restricted orifices and flaring rims), and in the restriction of decoration (where present) to notching or crenellating of the rim. These are the same features that characterize the late Lapita pottery assemblages found in the Bismarck and eastern Solomon Islands at this time period (ca. 500 BC to the first few centuries of the Christian era). Stephen Athens has recently summed up the emerging evidence from Truk, Pohnpei, and Kosrae as follows:

> Regarding the origins of the Pohnpeian settlers and, perhaps, those of Truk and Kosrae, it appears that the best case can be made for a linkage with the late Lapita Plain Ware pottery tradition. The chronology is consistent: it begins after 500 BC. The pottery vessel shapes and decorative techniques are consistent: simple globular pots and bowls with perhaps some rim notching or punctation. Also, its location is consistent: late Lapita Plain Ware pottery is found in the southeast Solomon and New Hebrides [Vanuatu] Islands where linguistic data suggest the homeland for nuclear Micronesians is located. . . . Based on the above inferences, it appears likely that the settlement of at least central Micronesia occurred as a result of separate landings on the various islands by people of the late Lapita Plain Ware tradition who came directly from various locations in the southeast Solomon and New Hebrides [Vanuatu] Islands. (Athens 1990a:29)[52]

Thus the initial expansion of humans into central and eastern Micronesia appears to have been by Lapita people in the last few centuries of the first millennium BC. On the high volcanic islands such as Truk, Pohnpei, and Kosrae where potting clay was available, they continued to practice their ceramic arts, although these would later decline and be abandoned as they were in Polynesia. As people moved off the high islands and colonized the neighboring coral atolls, they faced a new set of environmental and ecological challenges, including a complete lack of clay and stone resources.[53] However, the sophisticated shell manufacturing technology (as well as marine exploitation subsistence strategies) which was a part of their cultural legacy from Lapita ancestors, readily enabled these adaptations to atoll conditions.

The "End" of Lapita

By the opening of the first millennium BC, the Lapita peoples had expanded their world to encompass the entire southwestern Pacific region, including a great many islands and archipelagoes in which they were the first humans to set foot. Although their descendants would later undertake the final stage in Oceanic settlement with the discovery and colonization of both eastern Micronesia and eastern Polynesia, as we have just seen, these events would not commence for another millennium (at the end of the first millennium BC). Having established communities throughout Melanesia from the Bismarcks to New Caledonia and Fiji, and on into what we now call Western Polynesia (Samoa and Tonga), the Lapita diaspora seems to have "run out of steam" at the beginning of the first millennium BC. Rather than continued dispersal and expansion, a complex (and regionally varied) process of "settling in" seems to have occurred, leading to several different local transformations.[54]

In strictly archaeological terms, Lapita comes to an end between the middle and the end of the first millennium BC throughout its entire range of distribution. By this we mean that its distinctive and defining material-culture signature – dentate-stamped pottery carrying a formal design system – disappears from the archaeological record at this time. But it is also abundantly clear that in most local archaeological sequences there is continuity between Lapita and those archaeological assemblages that immediately succeed it. For example, in Samoa and Tonga there is continuity on into a phase marked by Polynesian Plain Ware pottery.[55] In other areas such as the Mussau Islands, Buka, and Watom, the dominant dentate-stamped decorated wares increasingly are replaced by ceramics decorated with incised and appliqué designs, but often continuing many of the original Lapita motifs. Given the overwhelming archaeological evidence for continuity, it is clear that the "end" of Lapita was simply a change in one aspect of material culture – ceramics – albeit an aspect of key significance to archaeologists.

But surely ceramics were not the only aspects of culture that underwent change as the now widely dispersed Lapita communities settled in to their diverse island homes. Indeed, a variety of processes and conditions influenced and directed change throughout the Lapita world. In Near Oceania, where the first Austronesian-speaking immigrants had established their beach-heads, interaction with indigenous populations continued to result in complex cultural, linguistic, and genetic exchanges. In Remote Oceania, increased distances between pioneering Lapita communities led to decreased communication, inevitably leading to differentiation over time. Originally wide-spread exchange or trade networks also gradually contracted over time, becoming locally specialized (see chapter 8). Moreover, as populations grew on individual islands there were increased adaptations to local environmental opportunities and challenges, such as inland settlement and agricultural intensification. Through these and other processes, the Lapita people underwent varied cultural, linguistic, and even biological transformations in the different islands and archipelagoes that their ancestors had settled. By the mid-to-late first millennium BC these transformations had led to sufficient differentiation and diversification such that a "uniform" or archaeologically distinctive "Lapita cultural complex" is no longer evident across the archaeological landscape of the southwestern Pacific. But the "end" of Lapita was a beginning: its legacy would be cultural map of Oceania as known to modern anthropology.

4

Lapita in Linguistic and Biological Perspective

The preceding chapter reviewed the evidence for Lapita as a regionally-varied set of archaeological assemblages, with origins in island Southeast Asia and a period of rapid expansion eastwards into Remote Oceania. Since Lapita is an archaeological construct, it was important to stick closely to the material evidence of sites bearing classic dentate-stamped pottery, sites which can be fitted into a temporal framework through extensive radiocarbon dates. In reconstructing the cultural history of the southwest Pacific, however, material remains are not the sole form of historical evidence. I now turn to two other approaches and lines of evidence available to the historical anthropologist: those of historical linguistics and human biology. These fields differ from archaeology in that their data are largely synchronic, consisting of the *contemporary* patterns of variation in the modern languages spoken by various peoples of a region, and in the genetic variability in those populations.[1] Nonetheless, such patterns of variation encode and reflect a *history* which is accessible through formal methods of analysis and comparison.[2] In linguistics, the "genetic comparative method" has a well-established record of yielding historical reconstructions of divergence and change within families of genetically-related languages.[3] With recent advancements in human genetics (such as the sequencing of mitochondrial DNA from various modern as well as ancient human populations), biological anthropologists have also taken renewed interest in the historical implications of their data. Moreover, some scholars have recognized that by applying systematic comparisons between the independent data sets generated by historical linguistics and human biology, powerful hypotheses regarding the recent history of human population dispersals may be advanced.[4] This is certainly the case in the southwestern Pacific, for when the Lapita archaeological evidence is compared with the culture-historical hypotheses generated by linguistic and biological patterns of variation, a coherent and rich historical reconstruction emerges.[5] I begin first with the linguistic evidence, from which a strong argument can be advanced that the Lapita people were speakers of a single discrete branch of the Austronesian language family. The second part of this chapter then turns to the human biological evidence for a "genetic trail" of population intrusion and expansion into Near and Remote Oceania.

The Linguistic Map of Oceania: Austronesian and Papuan

Linguistic comparisons have played an important role in the intellectual history of scholarly debates on the origins of Pacific peoples. Captain James Cook and other late eighteenth-century explorers were impressed by the evident similarity and historical relationships between the far-flung islands of the Polynesian "Nation," taking this as proof of a common origin. Later, in the mid-nineteenth century, philologist Horatio Hale of the US Exploring Expedition marshaled a substantial set of linguistic evidence (using a surprisingly modern and sophisticated approach) to propose a theory linking Polynesian origins to the "Malaisian race" of island Southeast Asia, with Fiji as an intermediate "staging area" on the putative route of migrations (see Howard 1967:49–52). Indeed, that languages as widely dispersed as Madagascar, Indonesia, and Polynesia all belonged to a single *Austronesian* language family had been suggested as early as 1708. It was not until the 1930s, however, that the German linguist Otto Dempwolff (drawing upon a host of lexicons, grammars, and dictionaries that had by then been compiled, often by missionaries) systematically applied the fully modern comparative method to Austronesian languages, resulting in a massive three-volume study of historical phonology, and in the reconstruction of more than two thousand Proto Austronesian root lexemes.[6] Dempwolff (1934, 1937, 1938) firmly established the Austronesian language family, providing the basis for all future linguistic work on this group. Moreover, Dempwolff's reconstruction of the phonological history of Austronesian, based on a representative sample of the entire language family, led him to recognize the existence of what is now called the *Oceanic* subgroup. The scope and sophistication of linguistic research on Austronesian languages has increased dramatically in the past few decades, thanks to such scholars as Bruce Biggs, Robert Blust, Ross Clark, Otto Dahl, Isidore Dyen, Paul Geraghty, George Grace, Andrew Pawley, Malcolm Ross, David Zorc, and others.[7] Although debate on aspects of Austronesian historical linguistics is vigorous, there is general agreement concerning many key issues such as the general outlines of the Austronesian "family tree."

The Austronesian languages have a remarkable distribution, from Madagascar off the east African coast, to remote Easter Island in the southeastern Pacific Ocean. However, the majority of Austronesian languages are concentrated in a more circumscribed region, namely the islands of Southeast Asia and Oceania. However, most of the large island of New Guinea is excluded from this distribution map, with Austronesian languages confined to certain coastal areas. Australia also falls wholly outside the Austronesian realm. The most recent linguistic surveys indicate that there are between 1,000–1,200 modern Austronesian languages, which as Pawley and Ross (1993:429) observe makes this "the world's largest well-established language family."

The internal subgrouping of these one thousand or more modern languages has also been the focus of considerable recent linguistic work, especially by Robert Blust (1985), whose widely-accepted subgrouping is shown in figure 4.1. That the several Formosan languages spoken by indigenous (non-Chinese) populations on Taiwan Island form one or more first-order subgroups is significant, for this is strong evidence that Taiwan may have been (or been part of) the original Austronesian "homeland." The extra-Formosan languages all form another first-order branch called Malayo-Polynesian by Blust. Malayo-Polynesian itself branches into several major subgroups along

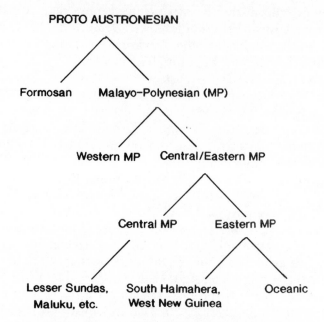

PROTO AUSTRONESIAN

Formosan   Malayo–Polynesian (MP)

Western MP   Central/Eastern MP

Central MP   Eastern MP

Lesser Sundas,   South Halmahera,   Oceanic
Maluku, etc.   West New Guinea

*Figure 4.1   Subgrouping of the Austronesian languages, according
to Robert Blust. (After Pawley and Ross 1993)*

a west-to-east geographic axis. As Peter Bellwood and others
have argued, this geographic cline to the subgrouping of Malayo-
Polynesian is plausibly the outcome of a process of geographic
expansion of the early Austronesian speakers between perhaps
4,000 and 2,000 BC (Bellwood 1995).

What is most significant from the perspective of Lapita culture history is that *all* of the Austronesian languages east of
Cenderawasih Bay on New Guinea fall into a single high-order
subgroup of Malayo-Polynesian, called *Oceanic*. (The most
closely related languages are those immediately to the west, in
the Halmahera Islands and on the western tip of New Guinea.)
This large subgroup thus contains all of the modern languages
spoken within the area of the Lapita diaspora, and also on into
the areas settled by Lapita descendants in Polynesia and Micronesia (with the exception of the western Micronesian languages
of Palauan, Chamorro, and possibly Yapese). This Oceanic subgroup is well attested by a significant number of lexical inno-

vations, and is widely accepted by most linguistics. As Pawley and Ross point out, "the Oceanic hypothesis . . . has powerful implications for Pacific culture history. If all Austronesian languages of the southwest and Central Pacific derive from a single linguistic interstage exclusive of the rest of the family, the implication is that there was a single effective Austronesian colonization of this area" (1993:433).

But the Austronesian language family does not exclusively dominate the map of the southwestern Pacific, because the large island of New Guinea as well as a few localites within Near Oceania and in the Moluccas contain languages wholly unrelated and classed as Non-Austronesian or Papuan. The Papuan languages number about 750, which as linguist William Foley observes, makes "New Guinea and its environs the linguistically most complex area in the world" (1986:3; see also Wurm 1982). Unlike the Austronesian languages which were recognized long ago to form a single family and which have become one of the best-studied groups through the application of the comparative method, the Papuan languages are still poorly documented. Serious linguistic documentation of Papuan languages began early in this century (e.g., Ray 1926), and received a major boost from the activities of the Summer Institute of Linguistics beginning in the 1950s. Still, of the 750 known Papuan languages, perhaps only 50 are reasonably well documented through published lexicons or grammars.

Again in contrast to the Austronesian situation, the Papuan languages do not form a single coherent language family with demonstrated genetic (i.e., historical) relationships. Rather, there are probably as many as 12 distinct Papuan language families![8] Further research will probably demonstrate historical linkages among some of these, so that the number of families will in time probably be collapsed to a lesser number of "super-families." Nonetheless, the degree of linguistic diversity within Papuan cannot be underestimated. Foley (1986:8–9) gives three main reasons for this extreme diversity: (1) "First, a time depth of 40,000 years for human habitation in New Guinea would allow ample time for the natural processes of language change and diversification to produce a great plethora of languages." (2) The difficult, highly dissected terrain of New Guinea "poses some genuine barriers to human social interactions and would certainly favor, rather than inhibit, linguistic diversity." And, (3) certain cultural attitudes and aspects of Papuan social organization favor the maintenance of high linguistic diversity. It has been proposed that the Papuan languages of New Guinea and the Australian languages share a common origin, although this hypothesis has yet to be convincingly demonstrated through the use of the comparative method. As Foley comments:

> fifty thousand years is a very long time, and if the present-day populations in the Sahul region descend directly from this period, then the extreme linguistic diversity found here, especially in New Guinea, finds a ready historical explanation. Furthermore, if the split between Australian language groups and Papuan languages dates from a period anywhere approaching this date, then certainly all traces of an earlier unity would have been long obliterated. (1986:270)

Nonetheless, the hypothesis of an historical connection between the Papuan and Australian languages seems plausible, and indeed Foley has marshaled a limited set of cognates between certain New Guinea highlands languages and those of Australia.

As can be seen in map 4.1, the Papuan languages are highly concentrated on the island of New Guinea, and particularly in the interior parts of the island, with only a few scattered outliers. To the west of New Guinea, there are a few Papuan languages in the northern part of the Halmahera group, while in the Bismarck Archipelago there is one Papuan language on New Ireland and three Papuan languages on New Britain. Much of the southern part of Bougainville Island is occupied by one other Papuan language (Buin).[9] The other parts of the Halmahera group and islands clustered around the western tip of New Guinea, as well as the rest of the Bismarck and Solomon Islands (i.e., island Near Oceania) are occupied by speakers of Austronesian languages. Likewise, Austronesian speakers inhabit a number of coastal sectors of New Guinea, such as around Collingwood Bay, at the eastern tip of Papua, and along the southern coast of Papua.

This distribution pattern readily suggests an historical scenario: given the extreme linguistic diversity of Papuan languages, it is certain that they have been in place in New Guinea and the adjacent islands of Near Oceania for a very long time.[10]

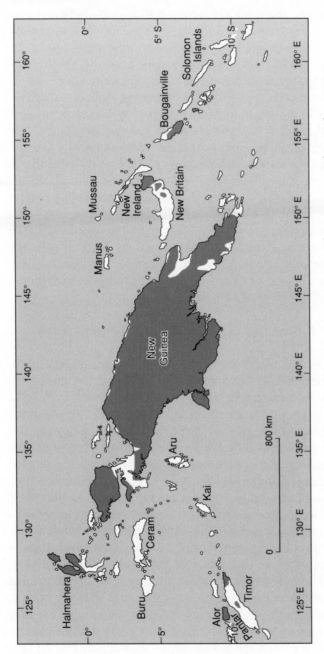

Map 4.1   Distribution of the Papuan (Non-Austronesian) languages. (After Foley 1986)

In contrast, the demonstrated relationships between the Austronesian languages and the reconstruction of a time-depth for Proto Austronesian of perhaps 5–6,000 years make it clear that these languages are more recent arrivals. Moreover, all of the Austronesian languages east of Cenderawasih Bay belong to the single Oceanic subgroup. It seems probable, then, that the modern linguistic map of this region is the result of a lengthy period of in-situ diversification of Papuan languages, followed by the more recent intrusion of the Austronesian speakers. Moreover, these Austronesian speakers all belonged to a single unified subgroup, Proto Oceanic, which rapidly spread throughout the Melanesian island region, but did not deeply penetrate the large island of New Guinea. It is possible that until about 5–4,000 years ago, the entire Near Oceanic region was occupied exclusively by Papuan language speakers, and that the few disjunct Papuan languages remaining in the Bismarcks and Solomons are mere remnants of this original pattern.

Establishing the Lapita-Austronesian Linkage

The only reasonable explanation for the geographic pattern of Austronesian languages across Near Oceania would be through a major and relatively late intrusion of a fairly uniform group of Austronesian language speakers (given that the languages throughout this region are all of the Oceanic subgroup, these intruders would presumably have been Proto Oceanic speakers). If we turn to the archaeological record in search of an appropriate cultural horizon that could be equated with this linguistic intrusion, it can only be the Lapita cultural complex. Both the approximate time, and the degree and extent of geographic distribution are correct: that is, during the second millennium BC, and geographically concentrated along coasts and island archipelagoes of Near Oceania. No other archaeologically-attested cultural complex even remotely meets these critical criteria. Prehistorians, however, are often skeptical of making linkages between archaeological cultures and proto-languages (or linguistic "inter-stages" as Proto Oceanic is properly defined), even when the evidence for such a link appears to be straight-forward. In part this stems from a long history of methodological abuse in the correlation of Indo-European languages and archaeological cultures of Eurasia (often with racist overtones, as during the Nazi regime), a debate that continues today.

However, establishing a robust linkage between the Lapita cultural complex and the Oceanic subgroup of Austronesian languages can be accomplished more readily than in the Indo-European case, and on additional evidential grounds than merely the geographic analysis presented above, as strong as that evidence is. In an important paper published over two decades ago, Pawley and Green (1973) laid out several principles for the correlation of linguistic and archaeological sequences in the Pacific. They termed "the language of the first well-established population in an island region the foundation language," and the first cultural tradition to become established the foundation culture; later arrivals are termed intrusive or invading languages and cultures. They then went on to propose that "under the conditions obtaining in the Pacific in pre-contact times, the foundation language of a remote island group could not be replaced by an intrusive language," defining "remote" as an island isolated by at least 450 km of open ocean (Pawley and Green 1973:38–9). This situation applies to all of Polynesia and much of Micronesia, areas that have exclusively Oceanic languages, and indeed, particular low-order subgroups within Oceanic.

Pawley and Green further suggested two additional principles which are the key to linking Lapita as an archaeological complex with Oceanic languages:

> For a given island group, the foundation language can be equated with the foundation culture in the archaeological sequence, provided that the latter is well established and widely distributed throughout the group.... If the archaeological sequence in a remote island group is continuous, i.e., if one tradition has not replaced another at some stage, then the foundation language is ancestral to the present language or subgroup spoken in that region. (1973:41)

Because these conditions and principles apply throughout much of Remote Oceania, they allow us to directly link Lapita as the foundation culture with a specific subgroup of Oceanic as the foundation language. The case of Eastern Lapita is paradigmatic:

the contiguous archipelagoes of Fiji, Tonga, and Samoa were all settled within one or two centuries at the close of the first millennium BC by Lapita populations. Direct continuity in archaeological sequences is well documented for both Tonga and Samoa, and for Fiji (although in the latter case there is evidence for some later cultural intrusion, but not replacement). The languages spoken throughout these islands today are all closely related, and can be traced back to an Oceanic subgroup or interstage called Proto Central Pacific. In short, the hypothesis that the Eastern Lapita people were speakers of Proto Central Pacific is uncontested. Similar linkages can be established for other parts of Remote Oceania where Lapita groups clearly provided the founding cultural traditions, and where various branches of Oceanic languages were also the founding languages. Such is the case for Nuclear Micronesian in the Carolines-Marshall archipelagoes, for Vanuatu, and for New Caledonia. In aggregate, they provide a very sound case for correlating the archaeologically-attested Lapita culture with earlier interstages of Oceanic languages.

Lapita and Proto Oceanic

The problem becomes more complicated in Near Oceania because in this region Lapita was not the foundation culture, nor are Oceanic languages the foundation languages. Indeed, both Lapita and Oceanic are arguably *intrusive*. Two decades ago, these complications in Near Oceania made Pawley and Green hesitant to propose a direct correlation between Lapita and Oceanic, even though this appeared to be the most parsimonious hypothesis.[11] A decade later, however, advances both in the subgrouping of Oceanic and in archaeological knowledge of Lapita sites in Near Oceania had eliminated their original hesitancy. While cautioning that "the spread of Oceanic need not have been carried out exclusively by Lapita potters," they nonetheless seemed convinced that "the latter were the spearhead of an Oceanic expansion into Remote Oceania" (Pawley and Green 1984:142). Continued archaeological and linguistic research has now made the case for a tight correlation between

Lapita and Oceanic even stronger. As Pawley and Ross explain in their synthesis of Austronesian historical linguistics:

> The initial [Austronesian] expansion in Oceania was the work of sailing people who appear to have moved quickly. For at least the first few centuries after the Lapita expansion, some degree of contact was often maintained between settlements along island chains extending up to 600 km. . . .
>
> This swift spread of Lapita culture across Island Melanesia and into western Polynesia, following a perhaps 400 year period of earlier development in the Bismarck Archipelago, is consistent with the pattern of Oceanic subgrouping. . . . The subgrouping indicates a period of Oceanic unity, most likely in western Melanesia, where Oceanic has its immediate external relatives, followed by the breakup of Proto Oceanic into a number of widely dispersed subgroups that are either coordinate or close to coordinate.
>
> A long period of common development apart from the rest of Oceanic, perhaps on the order of a thousand years, is indicated by the phonological, grammatical, and lexical innovations of the Polynesian group. The archaeological record shows a correspondingly long pause between the Lapita horizon in western Polynesia and the settlement of eastern Polynesia. (Pawley and Ross 1993:445–6)

Pawley and Ross' position is not wholly without its detractors, although it is accepted by the majority of specialists in Oceanic historical linguists as well as archaeologists active in the field today. My own view is that the correlation of the early Lapita phase with Proto Oceanic, and of the subsequent Lapita dispersal with the spread and later the break-up of Proto Oceanic speech community, is an extremely robust hypothesis – indeed, the only explanation which makes consistent sense of *both* the linguistic and archaeological evidenced amassed to date.[12]

The Breakup of Proto Oceanic and the Lapita Dispersal

Recent advances in our understanding of the internal relationships among the Oceanic languages – especially their subgrouping – provide further insights into the processes of rapid population expansion and subsequent differentiation during the Lapita period. As linguists began to focus on the subgrouping of the Oceanic branch of Austronesian languages,[13] they were initially puzzled in that they could find no evident deep, tree-like structure which would indicate a typical branching pattern resulting from an A $\Rightarrow$ B $\Rightarrow$ C island settlement sequence, with subsequent isolation and linguistic separation. Rather, a somewhat "flat" tree (a "spreading bush" if you prefer) appeared to best suit the Oceanic evidence, with the exception of the clearly-marked Central-Pacific subgroup and its Fijian, Rotuman, and Polynesian branches. It was this flat subgrouping that required a model of the rapid dispersal of the Proto Oceanic speakers (Pawley 1981).

Subsequent work by Malcolm Ross (1988) has identified three large high-order subgroups or "clusters" of Oceanic within the Bismarcks-Solomons region: these are the North New Guinea cluster, the Papuan Tip cluster, and the Meso-Melanesian cluster, the geographic distributions of which are shown in map 4.2.[14] The languages of Manus (Admiralty Islands) form another distinct group, with which the Mussau Island languages may possibly cluster. This now gives a family tree or subgrouping model for the Oceanic languages as shown in figure 4.2. This model has several important culture-historical implications that correlate well with the archaeological evidence for Lapita. First, it shows that the most likely "primary dispersal center" for Oceanic lay in western Melanesia, specifically around the Bismarck Sea. Furthermore, the subgrouping model indicates "a rapid dispersal of Oceanic-speaking peoples from northwestern Melanesia across southern Melanesia and into the Central Pacific following the breakup of Proto Oceanic" (Pawley and Ross 1993:441).

Rather than a classic branching, or tree-like model for the gradual differentiation of Oceanic languages due to island-to-island settlement followed by isolation and language change, what is required is a model of an initially widespread *dialect network* or *dialect chain*, over which innovations continued to be transmitted for some period.[15] This initial network clearly extended over a considerable distance, probably encompassing not only the Bismarcks but the Melanesian archipelagoes to the east and south. Such a dialect chain correlates precisely

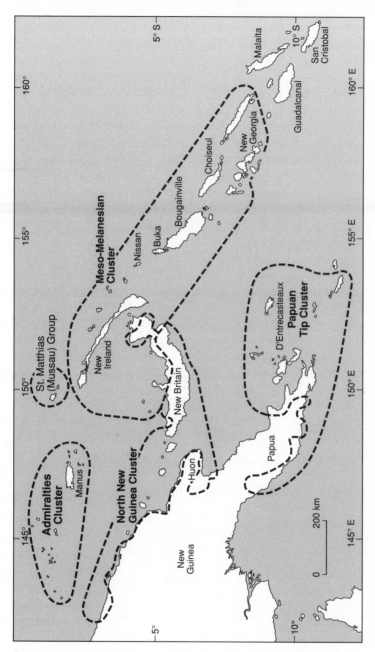

Map 4.2   *The four main clusters of Oceanic languages in the Near Oceanic region. (After Ross 1988)*

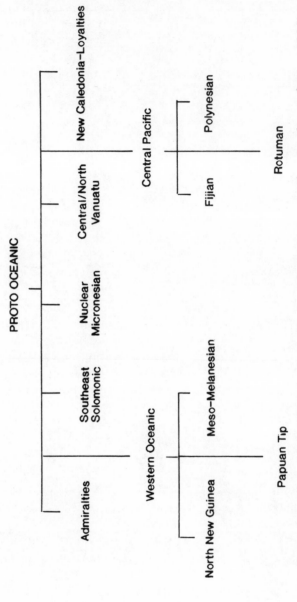

Figure 4.2 A partial subgrouping of the Oceanic languages. (After Pawley and Ross 1993)

with the archaeological evidence for a Lapita exchange network with regular voyaging contacts between communities over several centuries following initial colonization (see chapter 8). However, the Central Pacific subgroup indicates a sudden linguistic split, which again fits with the archaeological evidence for a lack of significant voyaging contacts between Western and Eastern Lapita groups once the Fiji-Tonga-Samoa area had been discovered and settled – again, the 850 km wide ocean gap was presumably too great. The high-order subgroups of Western Oceanic identified by Ross each appear to "derive from an old dialect network" (Pawley and Ross 1993:439), and archaeological evidence suggests that these clusters coincide with increasingly regionalized and specialized trading or exchange networks that began to develop toward the end of the Lapita period, ca. 500 BC (see chapter 8).

In sum, the breakup of Proto Oceanic and its subsequent diversification into several high-order subgroups reflects a process of: (1) initially rapid population expansion; (2) maintenance of a dialect chain within the Melanesian region for some time; (3) a sudden splitting-off of the Central Pacific (and later, Nuclear Micronesian) group; (4) subsequent breaking of the initially widespred dialect chain into a number of regional networks; and (5) further differentiation within local regions. This linguistic history for the Oceanic branch of Austronesian correlates extremely well with the emergent archaeological evidence for a rapid dispersal of Lapita people out of a Bismarck Archipelago "homeland," the continuance of long-distance exchange-trade interactions for some time, a discrete disjunction with the settlement of the Eastern Lapita region (Fiji-Tonga-Samoa), and finally with the gradual differentiation of Lapita into regional and increasingly specialized networks toward the end of the first millennium BC.

The pre-Oceanic speakers who moved rapidly into the Bismarck Archipelago around 1,500 BC found the region already peopled by speakers of Papuan or Non-Austronesian languages. Most archaeologists would agree that the later Lapita cultural complex was in certain respects a "fusion" arising out of the interaction between these two sets of peoples (see chapter 3). We should therefore also expect that for those Oceanic speakers who remained in the Near Oceanic region (the Bismarcks-

Solomons) there would be substantial linguistic effects derived from these complex interaction patterns. This is indeed the case, and the resulting lexical diversity of the Oceanic languages within the Melanesian region had led earlier generations of linguists to propose several explanatory theories. Some, such as S. H. Ray (1926) and A. Capell (1943), regarded the "Melanesian" languages as hybrids, which developed through a process of pidginization resulting in languages that had an Austronesian superstrate and a Papuan substrate (see also Wurm 1967:27).[16] While most linguists now reject this "hybrid" theory, it is nonetheless clear that Oceanic languages in the Melanesian region have been substantially influenced by contact with Papuan speakers, and that considerable "structural and lexical diversity of languages" has been the end result (Pawley and Ross 1993:435).[17] In contrast, the Central Pacific languages including those of Polynesia were carried into Remote Oceania by their ancestral speakers before significant influence due to prolonged contact with Papuan speakers could occur.

Contacts between Austronesian and Papuan speakers in Near Oceania also had significant impacts on the Papuan languages. Most notably, Papuan languages which must originally have been spoken throughout this region were largely replaced on the islands, leaving a major disjunct set on Bougainville Island, and isolated enclaves on New Britain, New Ireland, and elsewhere in the Solomons. Where Papuan languages were not replaced, they often borrowed extensively from neighboring Austronesian speech communities. Foley speculates that "the intrusive Austronesian population may have possessed technological superiority over the indigenous Papuan groups in a number of areas, suggesting that borrowing from the prestige population in both language and culture would occur. This has, in fact, occurred extensively, especially in the vocabulary" (Foley 1986:281).[18]

This model for the spread and eventual diversification of the Oceanic languages – and its close correlation with the archaeological evidence for Lapita – is now widely accepted by many historical linguists and prehistorians; nonetheless, a minority of scholars still demur. Perhaps the most outspoken is John Terrell, who vigorously opposes the idea that Lapita can be interpreted in terms of either "ethnic" or "linguistic" criteria.

Rather, Terrell (1989:625) would have us believe that Lapita is nothing more than "a trade ware in Melanesia." In earlier writings, Terrell made it clear that he discounted the validity of most historical linguistic research in the Pacific, maintaining that both the Austronesian and Papuan languages "may be of common origin," and that Near Oceania was their common homeland (Terrell 1981:250; 1986:42–64). This is an extreme position, one that no contemporary linguists countenance. More recently, Terrell and Robert Welsch have analyzed a large museum collection of artifacts from the north coast of New Guinea, in order to assess the degree to which style differences between material objects are correlated with language or geographic distance (Welsch et al. 1992). One implicit aim of their project has been to call into question the association between Lapita and Proto Oceanic, or indeed *any* linguistic unit. In presenting their results, Terrell and his associates claimed that geographic distance was a far better predictor of material culture similarity. Repeating a "well-known anthropological fact" that "there is no necessary correlation between race and language, or between culture and language," they then argue, using a less than convincing analogy, that Lapita cannot be correlated with Austronesian-language speakers (1992:592).[19]

It turns out, however, that things are not quite as Terrell and his associates would have us believe. In several reanalyses of the same data set, Carmella Moore and A. Kimball Romney have now shown, first, that the statistical methods used by the Terrell team were not the most appropriate measures of analysis, and second, that when better statistical measures are applied, "language and distance account for almost identical amounts of variation among material culture assemblages" (Moore and Romney 1994:387).[20] This conclusion comes as no surprise to anyone who has thought about this matter, for it is entirely predictable that given the kind of subgrouping structure for Oceanic discussed earlier, geographic distance and degree of linguistic relatedness are not independent variables. Rather, distance and language can expected to be strongly correlated, as the reanalysis by Moore and Romney proved.[21] Thus, "if the North coast New Guinea data [of Terrell et al.] has any bearing on the Lapita problem," it is certainly *not* to rule out "a strong role for language as part of the Lapita cultural tradition"

(Roberts et al., in press, manuscript p. 17). Terrell is right to caution that language and culture need not *necessarily* be correlated; often, however, they are, and the Lapita-Oceanic case is certainly one such example.

Lexical Reconstruction and Lapita Prehistory

Establishing the historical linkage between Lapita as an archaeological complex and the linguistic interstage of Proto Oceanic, and determining that the regional differentiation and transformation of Lapita corresponds well with a network-breaking model for diversification of the Oceanic languages, are in themselves important advances in our understanding of southwest Pacific culture history. These steps – which required the use of the genetic comparative method to produce a robust subgrouping model and the application of certain principles for the linking of archaeological cultures and proto-languages – are, however, not the end point of linguistic contributions to prehistory. Rather, they enable the historical anthropologist to reconstruct more fully the culture, society, and daily life of those people who spoke Proto Oceanic and its later daughter languages. This is made possible through the use of "lexical reconstruction,"[22] in which a set of reconstructed "words" (lexemes) and the probable meanings (semantic values) of those words are defined for a particular proto-language. In many instances, such lexical reconstructions may refer to material objects whose use by speakers of the proto-language can be independently verified through archaeological evidence. Such is the case with Proto Oceanic *kuron meaning "pottery vessel." Of much greater interest are aspects of ancient life and culture that are either poorly attested archaeologically or wholly absent from the archaeological record, such as terms referring to kinship and social organization, to categories of the natural world (not only the names of plants and animals, but to seasons and weather), and to ritual and belief. Lexical reconstruction opens a window on what the *Annales* historians call *mentalités*, or what anthropologists refer to as the shared "culture" of a group of people as it was encoded in language and speech.[23]

Unfortunately, some archaeologists – not understanding the methods of historical linguistics – have looked suspiciously at the reconstructions put forward by their linguistic colleagues, preferring to ignore or discount their relevance to cultural history. But as Andrew Pawley and Malcolm Ross observe, "this attitude is no more excusable than that of a linguist who would ignore ^{14}C dates for artifact assemblages because he does not understand how such dates are arrived at or who would discount the relative dating of assemblages in any archaeological sites on the suspicion that worms, humans or earthquakes have disturbed the layers" (1995:49). Principles for the reconstruction of a set of words or lexemes in a proto-language – based on an established subgrouping model and on demonstrated regular sound correspondences between the various daughter languages that provide the cognate reflexes on which reconstruction is based – are well established. Such work over the past few decades has now led to the recovery of a Proto Oceanic lexicon with more than 2,000 lexemes; similar lexicons have also been developed for lower-order subgroups within Oceanic, including Proto Polynesian (3,500 items) and Proto Micronesian (1,300 items).[24] But building such lexicons containing reconstructed morphemes is only part of the work of lexical reconstruction; determining the probable meanings of these words – *semantic reconstruction* – is also required, and this problem has until recently received less formal methodological consideration. In a seminal paper on Proto Austronesian "house" terms, Robert Blust called attention to the necessity for a formal method of semantic reconstruction that applied the Saussurian principle of *contrast*:

> At least since Saussure it has been widely accepted that meaning is defined by contrast, and that contrast becomes clear only where the full semantic extension of a term is known. No less than the linguist, then, the anthropologist should be concerned with the question "What was the probable meaning of protomorpheme 'X'?", not with the question "What was the protomorpheme which probably meant 'X'?". (Blust 1987:85)

In practice, this requires that for any reconstructed word the historical anthropologist or linguist must carefully examine the full range of meanings associated with the various modern reflexes, in daughter languages from which the word was reconstructed. This requires going beyond mere dictionary glosses, which are often notoriously brief or incomplete, and drawing upon more detailed ethnographic sources.[25] Fortunately, several historical linguists and prehistorians in the Oceanic field have taken such a methodological requirement seriously, and are now engaged in the work of building extensive lexicons for Proto Oceanic and other related language interstages. The payoff will be a marvelously detailed picture of the *mentalités* and daily life of ancient Pacific peoples.[26]

Lexical reconstruction (of the sort just described, involving sophisticated semantic reconstruction) opens up endless possibilities to extend our knowledge of the lifeways of prehistoric peoples. In the case of the Lapita peoples, having established a firm basis for correlating Lapita with Proto Oceanic, we are able to cross-check and extend our archaeologically-based reconstructions with lexical reconstructions. For example, consider the issue of Lapita voyaging. In chapter 3 the archaeological evidence for very fast dispersal of the Lapita peoples over a vast sector of the Pacific was described. Surely such a diaspora required a well-developed maritime technology and knowledge of the ocean. Lapita peoples were able not only to make open-ocean crossings of up to 850 km (e.g., between the Reef-Santa Cruz Islands, or Vanuatu, and Fiji), but regularly maintained contact between communities on islands some distance apart (witnessed by the continuous importation of exotic materials, such as obsidian; see chapter 8). But archaeology is thus far relatively mute on the nature of this maritime technology, which presumably involved canoes made of perishable materials that have not been preserved in Lapita sites.

Here lexical reconstruction is capable of extending the picture sketched out in the archaeological evidence for dispersal and inter-island contact and exchange. Andrew and Medina Pawley have reconstructed an extensive set of Proto Malayo-Polynesian and Proto Oceanic terms associated with canoes and sailing (Pawley and Pawley 1994).[27] Some form of vessel is indicated by Proto Oceanic **waga*, but what type of vessel might this have been? Additional reconstructed terms help to narrow the possibilities: **layaR* indicates that a sail was used, and the presence of outriggers was amply indicated by **saman* (outrigger), *kiajo (outrigger boom), and *patoto (sticks connecting outrigger and boom). The presence of carved, projecting headboards – possibly decorated with human or animal figures – is indicated by the term *ijuŋ. One can begin to visualize from these terms an early form of the classic Oceanic outrigger canoe with mat sail. Some large canoes may have carried platforms (*patar) over the hull and outrigger, or between double-hulls. Moreover, additional terms refer to a topstrake or washstrake (*[q]oRa), cross-seats or ribs (*soka[r]), to caulking (*njema), to paddles (*pose), and to steering or steering paddles (*quliŋ). Bailing was obviously necessary (*lima[s]), and cargo (*rujan) was carried aboard, doubtless including the pottery vessels, obsidian, and other materials that archaeologists identify from their excavations.

This linguistically-derived portrait of complex, outrigger sailing-canoe technology can be further tested against the comparative ethnographic information available on canoes throughout the Austronesian world.[28] As Adrian Horridge observes, the common technological basis of all Austronesian canoes – and thus arguably an ancient feature – is the "lashed-lug construction technique, in which projecting perforated lugs are left in the dug-out base of the hull and on the additional planks which are sewn on to its sides" (1995:138). These additional planks generally include washstrakes (for greater freeboard), and separate stem and stern pieces. This hull and its attached outrigger were propelled by a triangular sail (usually made of woven *Pandanus* mats) that tilts on its point, much like a modern windsurfer. Once developed, this technology was remarkably conservative, although additional innovations were made in Oceania (such as the perfection of the double-hulled canoe in Polynesia, and the asymmetric hull of central Micronesia).

In sum, when the full arsenal of techniques available to the historical anthropologist – archaeological evidence, lexical reconstruction, and comparative ethnography (the "triangulation approach"[29]) – are brought to bear, our resulting understanding of the past becomes ever so richer than that which can be achieved by any single approach. In the chapters to follow, I draw upon these methods to augment the basic picture of Lapita as evidenced by archaeological materials, even though I always privilege archaeology as the starting point from which our reconstruction of the Lapita people and their world must begin.

Human Biological Diversity in Oceania

If the evidence of historical linguistics tells us that Austronesian-speaking peoples intruded into what had previously been an exclusively Papuan world prior to the second millennium BC, it seems reasonable that we should be able to test this hypothesis on the independent evidence of human biology. A major linguistic intrusion of the sort represented by the Oceanic languages is unlikely to have resulted from language replacement alone; the actual movement and spread of *populations* of Austronesian speakers is required. The evidence, of course, must be sought largely in the contemporary patterns of morphological (phenotypic) and genetic variation among the people of the Pacific, and the challenge is to properly infer the historical processes that produced the modern human biological "map" of this region. We must not lose sight of the fundamental problem that – as paleontologist George Gaylord Simpson once put it – "one cannot be one's own ancestor." Populations (like languages) undergo continual change and it is a mistake to think that the ancestral Lapita population is still represented by some unchanged group of modern Pacific people (such as the Polynesians). It is entirely conceivable, however, that some groups have undergone relatively less gene flow and change as a result of isolation, although in such isolated (and usually small sized) populations genetic drift and the "founder effect" may also have had their impact. Of course, in rare instances where skeletal remains have been archaeologically excavated from Lapita sites it is possible to look directly at *some* Lapita "ancestors." The latest techniques of extraction and amplification of ancient DNA even make it possible to analyze the genomic composition of these remains, as will be described below. However, only a handful of Lapita sites have yielded human remains, and to generalize about all "Lapita people" from the bones of the perhaps twelve individuals represented would be akin to describing the human biological variation of San Francisco based on a non-random sample of twelve people at three Market Street subway stations! Until many more Lapita skeletal remains have been recovered,[30] the most important evidence for historical inference will therefore have to come from our knowledge of human biological diversity in modern Oceania.

Early twentieth-century physical anthropologists expended inordinate amounts of time collecting huge runs of both metric and non-metric (discrete) observations ranging from cranial dimensions and stature to skin color and hair texture, from a large number of living Pacific populations, as well as from skeletal remains obtained (often by dubious means) from burial caves and other sepulchral sites. Unfortunately, lacking the theoretical foundations provided by modern population genetics (as well as hampered by inappropriate statistical methods and an absence of the yet-to-be-invented computer), these scholars followed a taxonomic approach which pigeon-holed different groups into a small series of "races."[31] From the beginning, however, it was clear to most investigators that the tremendous variability displayed by Pacific islanders defied any simplistic taxonomy.[32] Categorizing the peoples inhabiting Melanesia as "Oceanic Negroids," or subdividing them into coastal "Melanesian" and interior "Papuan" races[33] not only did no justice to the region's human biological diversity, but also yielded no meaningful insights into historical process.

Fortunately, much of the data collected by these pioneers is amenable to reanalysis and interpretation from a modern biological perspective.[34] Biological anthropologists such as William Howells, Michael Pietrusewsky, C. Loring Brace, and Christy Turner II have applied sophisticated multivariate statistical analyses to various morphological data sets (using both metric and non-metric traits) in order to assess the "similarity" or "distance" between the sampled populations.[35] One of the most comprehensive of these studies, by Howells (1970), utilized seven metrical characters for 151 Pacific region populations. The resulting similarity dendrogram grouped these populations into twelve main clusters, with four principal branches. The most distant branch comprised populations in Australia along with some Melanesian groups (New Caledonia and Loyalty Islands, Nakanai of New Britain). A second branch lumped together all of the Polynesian populations, along with Fiji, Tanna in Vanuatu, and southern New Caledonia. The third branch consisted of various coastal populations in Melanesia (New Guinea, Bougainville, Solomon Islands, Vanuatu) along with Micronesian groups (Carolines and Marshalls). Finally, the fourth branch was a cluster focused largely on New Guinea and including various interior populations, along with other groups dispersed throughout the Bismarck Archipelago, Solomons, and Vanuatu (and the western Micronesian populations of Palau, Yap, and the Marianas). What do such studies of morphological variability in the Pacific tell us? Above all else, that there is no such thing as a typical "Melanesian" population; indeed, the term "Melanesian" is clearly meaningless in a biological sense. What stands out strikingly is the tremendous diversity within the geographic region called Melanesia.[36] Moreover, in contrast, the tight clustering of the Polynesian populations speaks to their being a distinct and well-defined (phenotypically homogeneous) group.[37]

Recently, Michael Pietrusewsky (1983) applied a similar multivariate analysis to data sets of 28 cranial measurements from some 38 populations including groups in the circum-Pacific margins as well as Oceania proper. While the clustering pattern is complex, several important observations emerge. First, the discrete and tight clustering of Polynesian populations is unambiguous. It is highly significant that the groups most similar to the Polynesians are not found in geographically-adjacent Melanesia, but with a set of island Southeast and mainland Asian populations (e.g., Borneo-Celebes, Java, the Sulu Archipelago, China, and Japan). Populations sampled from the geographic region of Melanesia, however, comprise a major branch of their own which then links most closely with another large branch of Australian and Tasmanian populations.

Similar results have also been obtained through studies of tooth size variation in Pacific populations, and from multivariate analysis of craniofacial variation.[38] While these are only a sample of many such studies of the phenotypic variation among Pacific islanders (and space precludes a more extensive review here), they are representative. They allow us to abandon forever older notions of a few distinct "races," and to look at the range of diversity in terms of relative similarity and distance. Among the deductions that can be drawn from these patterns of diversity, Howells (1973:48–9) notes the following: (1) that while various Melanesian and Australian groups share some characters in common, "they are not a continuous or single population;" (2) that Melanesian groups display "great genetic diversity;" (3) that the Polynesians are well-defined with limited genetic variation; (4) that Micronesian groups are variable "having some Polynesian resemblances but interdigitating with Melanesia to a considerable extent;" and (5) that "Micronesia and Polynesia have a basically east Asiatic affiliation."

These deductions in turn pose certain hypotheses for the history of human populations in the Pacific. The evident connections between certain Australian and Melanesian groups is strongly suggestive of common ancestry, but at the same time their great genetic diversity speaks of long periods of separation and divergence. Now that archaeology has set the "clock" for the human occupation of Sahul at 40,000 years or more, the genetic diversity of Near Oceania is explicable in *evolutionary* time. The opposite, of course, is true for Polynesia (and to a lesser extent, Micronesia) where the homogeneity of the various island populations indicates a common ancestry with a relatively short time depth. Moreover, the affinities between Polynesian and Asiatic groups strongly suggest that Polynesian origins cannot have been derived solely through a process of drift or selection from ancestors in Near Oceania alone. Rather – in parallel with the evidence of historical linguistics – some substantial movement or intrusion of people from Southeast Asia into the Pacific in relatively recent times is strongly indicated. As we shall see, this intrusion is reflected not only in geographic patterns of morphological variability, but in a "genetic trail" encoded in the chromosomes, protein structures, and blood groups of Pacific peoples.

The Genetic Trail

Until relatively recently, biological anthropologists had to rely largely upon morphological variation among populations in order to assess degrees of relatedness, and thus to infer historical process. Modern statistical methods have allowed much of the old data to be meaningfully reworked, as discussed above, but these are still *phenotypic expressions* of genetic variation, and thus subject to numerous influences from environmental factors (such as differences in climate, nutrition, cultural practices, etc.). Since about 1960, however, tremendous advances have been made in understanding human genetic variation through the study of various polymorphic systems, such as blood groups, lymphocyte antigens (HLA), and immunoglobulins, and most recently through sequencing of DNA chains, the basic structural code of life itself.[39] Of course, these new genetic data are like the older anthropometric data in being derived primarily from *living* populations, and the same cautions of historical inference from synchronic patterns of variation apply. However, when ancient skeletal materials are excavated, it is sometimes possible to extract and sequence DNA from these samples (through the technique of PCR [polymerase chain reaction] "amplification" of DNA fragments); as more prehistoric skeletal remains are recovered and analyzed, this will become an increasingly important data source.

A thorough review of the newly-acquired knowledge of genetic variation among Pacific region populations is beyond my scope, but is fortunately provided in several recent volumes.[40] Reviewing a substantial body of work on HLA genes and antigens, biologist Sue Serjeantson (1989:162–3, figure 3.3) finds that a phylogenetic analysis yields four main groups or clusters: "Australoid, non-Austronesian Melanesian, island Melanesian, and Polynesian." She draws several significant conclusions from these analyses. First, that the "populations of Australia and the Papua New Guinean Highlands have a common ancestry of great antiquity," a finding not surprising in light of the classic studies of morphological variation. In contrast to the New Guinea Highlands, the coastal populations of New Guinea share highly similar HLA distributions with populations in island Melanesia. Moreover, while there is a shared "substratum of HLA features found in Australians and Papua New Guinean Highlanders . . . these have been overlaid with Austronesian elements." In other words, it is in coastal New Guinea and island Melanesia – *the Lapita corridor* – that the "genetic trail" makes its appearance. The HLA evidence reveals further insights, moreover, in that (1) the Micronesians and Polynesians share only a limited number of HLA similarities; and (2) "although the early Austronesian voyagers left genetic influences in coastal and island Melanesia, they did not carry Melanesian elements into eastern Polynesia." This suggests that the founding populations in Polynesia (who we would correlate with the Early Eastern Lapita settlements) were few in number and subject to a genetic "bottleneck" effect. Furthermore, their immediate ancestors had not spent sufficient time in island Melanesia to have acquired a significant HLA genetic component through inter-marriage and gene flow.

The HLA patterns are substantially matched by evidence from hemoglobin and globin gene variants, based on extensive research by A. V. S. Hill and colleagues (Hill et al. 1989:275–7; Hill et al. 1985). These data indicate that the Polynesians are a basically "Mongoloid population," but that there has been indisputable contact with populations in Melanesia. Such contact is most conclusively indicated by the presence of a unique $-\alpha^{3.7}$ III thalassaemia deletion, associated with the presence of malaria, in both island Melanesia and Polynesia (but absent in Southeast Asia). The possible role of malaria in the genetic history of Oceanic populations will be discussed further below. In terms of population origins, however, it is worth quoting, in full, Hill's scenario:

> the Polynesians [were] from an originally small population that moved from somewhere in island South-east Asia to the Bismarck Archipelago about 4–5,000 years ago. The small size of the population would have allowed the new $-\alpha^{3.7}$III mutation to rapidly reach polymorphic frequency. Subsequently, some of these Austronesian-speaking, Lapita pottery-making people moved south-east to the rest of island Melanesia. During this time some mixing with Papuan-speaking populations led to the assimilation of some of their genetic markers but not of their language. Then, some 3,500 years ago a section of this population moved east to Fiji to subsequently colonize Polynesia. (Hill et al. 1989:276)

Geneticists Cavalli-Sforza, Menozzi, and Piazza (1994:362–67) come to essentially the same conclusions based on a phylogenetic and principal-components analysis of genetic distances between some 31 of the better-studied Pacific populations. Noting that Micronesian populations share a greater Melanesian genetic component than do Polynesians, these authors suggest that this might be explained by Micronesian ancestors being "the first settlers from Southeast Asia in northern Melanesia," followed later by Polynesian ancestors. In light of what we know from archaeological evidence of both Polynesian and Micronesian settlement chronologies (see chapter 3), however, an alternative explanation seems more plausible. This is that the ancestors of *both* the central Micronesian and Polynesian groups came from the same pool, notably Proto Oceanic speakers out of island Southeast Asia. However, while the Polynesian founding group moved quickly out of Near Oceania and eastwards into the Fiji-Tonga-Samoa region prior to substantial genetic exchange (although picking up the $-\alpha^{3.7}$III deletion), the central Micronesian ancestors did not move north out of island Melanesia until a thousand years later (ca. 2,000 BP). They thus acquired a much greater genetic component from the indigenous Papuan-speaking populations of Near Oceania.

Probably the most important potential contributions of genetic studies to the problem of the origins and relationships of Oceanic populations will come from analysis of DNA, both mitochondrial and nuclear. At the present time, such work is still in its early stages and the number of sampled populations is too small to assess broad geographic patterns. However, it is worth reporting that recent work on mtDNA (mitochondrral DNA) by Rebecca Cann and associates has shown that at least three distinct maternal lineages contributed to the founding Polynesian group (Lum et al. in press). One of these clades (Haplotype 1) possesses a 9-base pair deletion in Region V which is shared between Polynesians and Asian populations, indicative again of a Southeast Asian origin (Hertzberg et al. 1989; see also Hagelberg and Clegg 1993). However, one of the two other less frequently represented clades (Haplotype 2) appears to match lineages found in island Melanesia, and conforms with the evidence of the $-\alpha^{3.7}$III thalassaemia deletion mentioned earlier. As the Cann team reports, "Haplotype 2 may represent an ancestral, Lapita haplotype derived from admixture with island Melanesia."

Let us attempt to put the matter in more direct human terms. Since mitochondrial DNA is transmitted only from the mother, these recent findings suggest that the founding Eastern Lapita populations (i.e., the Polynesian ancestors) included women of both Southeast Asian *and* island Melanesian ancestry. Perhaps nothing could be a stronger indication that "the Lapita peoples" were biologically dynamic, resulting from a population originating in island Southeast Asia and migrating into the Bismarck Archipelago, where recruitment of and intermarriage with indigenous people took place. "The beach" was more than a meeting place of cultures.

Above all, what is most gratifying about the recent genetic studies of Pacific peoples is the strong convergence between the scenario indicated by genetics, and that reconstructed by the historical linguists. These two fields – working with wholly independent data sets – have produced historical narratives both requiring a relatively recent intrusion of people into the long-settled region of Near Oceania. They are also wholly consistent with the archaeological evidence for the rapid appearance and expansion of the Lapita complex between 1,500–500 BC. Moreover, "the extreme view of Terrell [1986] and White et al. [1988] that Polynesians evolved entirely from Melanesian stock must be incorrect," in the light of the genetic evidence, as Serjeantson and Hill assert (1989:287).

"Some Lapita People"

The biological evidence reviewed thus far has come from modern human populations, some of whom are surely the descendants of Lapita peoples but who are nonetheless removed in time more than two thousand years from these ancestors. In a few rare instances, however, Lapita sites have yielded the physical remains of their inhabitants, providing a glimpse – albeit highly limited – of their skeletal morphology and genetic makeup. Because the samples recovered to date are so limited – and are from generally late Lapita contexts – we must be extremely cautious in generalizing too much from them. Nonetheless, they provide the opportunity to examine "some Lapita people."

That more Lapita skeletal remains have not been excavated is due to the general absence of burials in Lapita sites. In the earliest known Lapita sites human remains occur only as isolated fragments – for example the partial mandible, humerus,

*Plate 4.1   Excavations at the Reber-Rakival Lapita site on
Watom Island exposed several burials in shallow pits,
next to a stone alignment, possibly the edge of a house.
(Photo courtesy of R. C. Green and D. Anson)*

other fragments, and teeth from the Talepakemalai site in
Mussau (Kirch et al. 1989). It is possible that in these earliest
Lapita stilt houses in the Bismarck Archipelago (see chapter 6),
ancestral human remains were curated in bundles in the rafters
or other special sectors of the house, as is the pattern in some
Austronesian societies today. Only one Lapita site in the Bismarcks has yielded *in situ* burials, this being the SAC site on
Watom Island excavated by Roger Green and Dimitri Anson in
1985 (Green et al. 1989). Here eight adults and a two-year old
child were interred in flexed positions, close together in shallow pits, with their heads oriented towards the west. A rock
wall and post molds adjacent to the burials might suggest that
these bodies were interred under the floor of a house, although
this is uncertain (plate 4.1). These eight adults and one child
are the largest single sample of Lapita people yet recovered by
archaeology but, unfortunately, they date to the terminal end

of the Lapita period in the Bismarck Archipelago. The excavators indicate a date of between 500 and 100 BC, which is some thousand or more years after the beginning of the Lapita phase in this region. Thus the Watom population is likely to have been influenced by gene flow from indigenous Near Oceanic populations, and cannot be taken as representative of the earliest migrants into this area.

Outside of the Bismarcks or Far Western Lapita region, the only skeletal remains that have been recovered and analyzed are from Fiji and Tonga in the Eastern Lapita region. These include a partially complete skeleton of an adult male from the Natunuku site in Fiji, fragmentary remains of two people from Lakeba Island in Fiji, and a partial skeleton from Tongatapu.[41] Unfortunately, the most complete of these – the Natunuku skeleton – has recently been re-dated to AD 29–243, and thus post-dates the Lapita period in Fiji (Davidson and Leach 1993:102–3). Thus, like the Watom materials, it must be used cautiously as a possible descendant representative of the earliest Lapita colonists in this region.

Given these caveats, what have analyses of these few actual remains of Lapita people suggested about their biological identities? The highly fragmentary nature of the early Mussau remains restricts the possible observations or analyses, but the dental patterns hint at closer relationships with Southeast Asian populations than with those of Melanesia (Kirch et al. 1989:74–5). The later Watom population, on the other hand, displays many traits that are close to those of modern island Melanesian populations. Turner, for example, found "the dentitions of the two Watom crania . . . more similar to teeth from New Britain than to teeth of recent Thai or late prehistoric Hawaiians" (1989:296). Extensive univariate as well as multivariate analyses by Pietrusewsky (1989a, 1994) indicate that the Watom people do not closely cluster with either modern Polynesians or island Melanesians, a finding that might be anticipated for a population that was in the early stages of genetic change due to inter-breeding between immigrant Southeast Asian and indigenous Near Oceanic clades.[42]

In the first effort to date to extract and sequence ancient DNA from Pacific archaeological materials, Erica Hagelberg and John Clegg (1993) managed to isolate mitochondrial DNA from samples provided to them from Watom and Natunuku, as well as from several skeletal remains of somewhat later age.[43] In particular, these geneticists attempted to see if the characteristic 9-base pair deletion occurring in high frequency among modern Polynesian and Asian populations (but absent in island Melanesia) was present in these samples. While the deletion was detected in Polynesian remains of later age, it was lacking in the Watom and Natunuku samples. This absence is not surprising, given the late Lapita age of these materials and the likelihood that the individuals whose DNA was sequenced were descendants of mixed Southeast Asian and indigenous Near Oceanic parentage. While it is highly encouraging that ancient DNA can now be extracted and sequenced from human skeletal remains, a far more extensive sample of individuals – and particularly those from earlier dated contexts – will be essential before this powerful new tool of human genetics will be able to add its contribution to Pacific history.

Malaria

Prehistoric population movements – and demographic history in general – were at times significantly influenced by environmental factors, one of which was disease. The identification of diseases in prehistory, however, and the assessment of their role and impact on local or regional populations can be a tricky matter. For the islands of Remote Oceania, the increased distances which restricted the frequency of communication and interaction, plus low population numbers, prevented the spread of many of the infectious diseases of the Old World, leading to well-documented and horrifying consequences when such diseases as measles and smallpox were eventually introduced following initial European contact. In Near Oceania, the situation appears to have been quite different, and a number of tropical diseases have long been endemic in northern Australia, New Guinea, and the Bismarck-Solomons region. Among these is malaria, a debilitating and often fatal disease resulting from infection by one or more of three species of *Plasmodium* (*P. vivax*, *P. malariae*, and *P. falciparum* are present in Near

Oceania), transmitted in the blood through an intermediary *Anopheles* mosquito host. Groube makes a strong case that given the natural distribution of *Anopheles* mosquitoes in Sahul, the presence of vast lowland swamps, and certain etiological conditions favoring transmission, that "it would be incredible, considering the proximity of Southeast Asia (the possible homeland of *P. vivax*), if this parasite was not introduced before the end of the Pleistocene" (1993:169). Indeed, human populations in this area evolved a number of genetic responses to malaria as a result of intense selection pressure, including the $-\alpha^{3.7}$III thalassaemia deletion mentioned earlier. It is not certain, however, whether all species of *Plasmodium* have been present in Near Oceania for the same length of time, and there is a possibility at least that the highly virulent *P. falciparum* was a later arrival.

The possible relationship between malaria and human population movements in Near Oceania has intrigued scholars for some time. The great Austronesian linguist Otto Dempwolff (1937:193–4), for example, thought that the original Non-Austronesian speaking inhabitants of Melanesia possessed a strong resistance to malaria, something the Proto Oceanic speakers lacked when they began to migrate into this region. As Pawley and Ross summarize his argument:

> Proto Oceanic speakers were in contact with such people, intermarried with them and were influenced by them linguistically. Oceanic speakers then spread out over Melanesia and such contacts were repeated. In places where malaria was rife, the malaria-resistant genes of the darker, frizzy-haired people dominated. In places free of malaria, such as Polynesia, the original gene pool of the Oceanic-speaking colonists was better preserved. (Pawley and Ross 1993:433)

Some validity to Dempwolff's hypothesis is provided by the discovery of genetic resistance to malaria among Near Oceanic populations, such as the $-\alpha^{3.7}$III thalassaemia deletion, which was picked up by some Lapita groups quickly enough to be carried on into Polynesia, even though the absence of the disease in Remote Oceania meant that it no longer conferred a selective advantage.

Recently, Jeff Clark and Kevin Kelly (Kelly 1990; Clark and

Kelly 1993) have argued for a converse scenario, that the Austronesian-speaking populations who moved into Near Oceania in the second millennium BC carried in their genes their own malarial resistance, and may even have been responsible for the introduction of the disease.[44] Their theory is based on the presence of a Gm haplotype (also conferring resistance to malaria) among Southeast Asian as well as Austronesian-speaking peoples in Near Oceania, but absent among interior or highland peoples in Melanesia. Clark and Kelly are uncertain whether malaria was actually an Austronesian introduction, but note that if this was indeed the case, "then the Austronesian-speaking populations that moved into the region would have been at a distinct advantage relative to Non-Austronesian speakers, who would soon find the coastal lowlands to be decidedly unhealthy environments" (Clark and Kelly 1993:621).

As will be discussed in greater length in chapter 6, the earliest Lapita settlements in the Bismarck Archipelago seem to have been primarily clusters of stilt or pole-supported houses situated on reef flats or small sand cays off the coasts of the main islands. This is a settlement pattern that is also present ethnographically through parts of island Melanesia today, and which some ethnographers have explicitly noted is an adaptation to mosquito-infested lowland terrain. Walter Ivens, for example, notes that the "artificial island" settlements off Malaita Island in the Solomons are free from malarial mosquitoes due to the distance from the shore (Ivens 1930:122–3). I observed a similar situation first-hand at Taumako Island in the Santa Cruz group in the 1970s, where the entire population is concentrated on an artificially-constructed islet village on the reef flat, thereby avoiding the dense (and ferociously-biting) mosquito populations on the main island.[45] It may well be that the early Lapita stilt-house settlement pattern was in part an explicit strategy for mosquito avoidance. Indeed, it is noteworthy that this pattern was evidently abandoned in favor of settlements directly on beach ridges once the Lapita dispersal expanded beyond Near Oceania into Remote Oceania, the latter being largely devoid of malaria. Geneticists Sue Serjeantson and X. Gao also comment on the pattern of offshore island settlement, and believe that this is because "early Austronesians may have arrived in Melanesia to find a malarious region inhabited by peoples comparatively well adapted to the environment. For many Austronesians, it may have been prudent to continue east" (Serjeantson and Gao 1995:169).

Clearly, a great deal more research will be necessary before the question of malaria in Near Oceanic prehistory is resolved, but one possible scenario can be suggested. Following Groube's suggestion, forms of the disease were indeed present from Pleistocene times (*P. vivax* and *P. malariae*), accounting for the evolution of the thalassemias and other forms of resistance among Papuan speakers. However, the more virulent *P. falciparum* may have been carried with the Proto Oceanic speakers who had their own forms of Gm resistance. Thus the implications for the Lapita people would be a combination of the theories of Dempwolff and of Clark and Kelly. Only further research will tell, but malaria in Near Oceania surely had an important role to play in the history of human settlement of this region.

On "What Lapita Is and Isn't"

As Lapita studies expanded following the initial realization that a widespread ceramic horizon had at one time crossed the ethnographic-divide separating Polynesia from Melanesia – and as numerous new sites were discovered and their assemblages wrested from the ancient beach sands – the intellectual terrain has become increasingly defined, problematized, and even sharply contested. A little more than a decade ago, Jim Allen (1984) provoked a substantial intellectual exchange with his proposal that the Lapita cultural complex may have had its origins not in a population movement out of island Southeast Asia (as maintained by Bellwood [1979], Green [1979a], Kirch [1984] and others), but rather was wholly indigenous to the Bismarck Archipelago, developing out of earlier cultural forms that could be traced at least back to the end of the Pleistocene.

The 1985 Lapita Homeland Project was explicitly designed to test Allen's challenge to the orthdox model that the Lapita cultural complex was closely associated with (if not entirely the result of) a population expansion out of island Southeast Asia, an expansion that many scholars correlated with the diaspora of Austronesian-speaking peoples. While the alternative model of exclusively indigenous "Melanesian" origins for Lapita has continued to be voiced by a small minority (e.g., White et al. 1988), most researchers concur that the Lapita Homeland Project results generally strengthen the notion that Lapita represents the rapid appearance of something quite new and distinctive on the archaeological landscape of the Bismarck Archipelago in the mid-second millennium BC. Moreover, these results reinforce the associations between Lapita and an Austronesian expansion (Green 1991b; Kirch 1995, in press; Spriggs 1991, 1995). At the same time, it has been necessary to build some measure of internal dynamism into our models of Lapita, recognizing that interaction, interchange, and adoption of ideas and technology between intrusive populations and indigenous occupants of Near Oceania was an important aspect of the Lapita phenomenon (Green 1991b). But not all prehistorians concur, and recently some have been quite strident in their assertions about "what Lapita is and isn't." The detailed evidence to rebut their assertions has been presented above. Here I will speak to some of the larger epistemological issues and cultural implications.

John Terrell is among those most sharply critical of any prehistorical construction of Lapita in terms of an expansion of Austronesian-speaking peoples into the Pacific region. In a commentary that closed a special section of the journal *Antiquity*, dealing primarily with new results from the Lapita Homeland Project, Terrell began by referring to "this [surely his] growing distrust of linguistics as currently practised by most Pacific linguists" (1989:624). Dismissing decades of rigorous and careful linguistic work on Oceanic languages and their historical relationships with a few comparisons to the old, racially-charged arguments about the Indo-Europeans, Terrell proceeded to dismiss language from the realm of prehistory by quoting Colin Renfrew to the effect that "the notion of ethnicity cannot properly be used as the fundamental organizing principle for the prehistoric past" (1989:625; the quote is from Renfrew [1988:438]). Evidently Terrell does not understand the aims, methods, or assumptions of historical linguistics, or how linguistic and archaeological data have been constructively used as independent lines of evidence to test and cross-check various historical models and narratives in the Pacific.

Apparently Terrell is not completely alone in his "distrust" of linguistics. In an article as remarkable for its theoretical naievété as for its ignorance of Pacific historical linguistics (not to mention human biological variation), Anita Smith (1995:374) claims that "it is unlikely that the linguistic construct [of Oceanic prehistory] can be traced archaeologically." Although she references not one of the careful and robust linguistic works of scholars from Dempwolff to Blust to Pawley and Ross, she nonetheless asserts that "archaeological evidence is not capable of supporting or refuting linguistic models." Smith's attitude is precisely that bemoaned by Pawley and Ross (1995:48) when they refer to prehistorians who "find the methods of historical linguistics so arcane . . . that they prefer to ignore or discount the reconstructions as irrelevant to prehistory." While archaeological and linguistic data are unquestionably quite different in nature, and thus require different and appropriate methods of investigation, both yield robust historical narratives and reconstructions. As *independent* sources of information on past events and historical processes, archaeology and historical linguistics most certainly are capable of helping to support or refute models constructed by the other. At least as far back as Chamberlain's classic tract on the "method of multiple working hypotheses", the importance of bringing multiple lines of evidence to bear on the testing of alternative hypotheses or models has been a cornerstone of scientific method, and continues to be recognized as such by contemporary philosophers of science.

What we are discussing here is not merely an arcane academic debate, a squabbling among scholars of little relevance to the larger world. Terrell, Smith, and others leave themselves exposed to the critique that they are practicing a rarified but nonetheless insidious academic form of neocolonialism, in which modern Oceanic cultures and peoples are denied their archaeological legacy and with it their cultural history. In insisting that Lapita sites and artifacts can *never* be correlated with specific ethno-linguistic categories (such as Proto Oceanic), these prehistorians exercise their own form of academic hegemony over these material witnesses of the Oceanic past. Excluded from being the cultural patrimony of modern Oceanic peoples, Lapita becomes strictly an academic "object."

The Lapita Peoples: A Holistic Perspective

In chapter 3, I systematically examined the archaeological evidence for Lapita as a complex of assemblages with a discrete distribution in space and time. Here, I have canvassed the independent evidence from historical linguistics and biological anthropology allowing us to assess the strength of certain hypotheses that extend the construction of Lapita beyond the narrow realm of ceramics or material culture. In my view – and indeed that of many culture historians working in the southwest Pacific today – the convergences between the independently-derived data sets of archaeology, linguistics, and human biology are remarkably clear and robust, making a compelling case for the correlation of Lapita sites with a significant population intrusion of Austronesian-speakers in the second millennium BC. We therefore come back to the question, who were "the Lapita peoples?" The answer, we find, depends in part on at what time and in what place one is referring to, for Lapita was a dynamic phenomenon, the result of a constantly changing interaction between immigrant Austronesian-speakers from island Southeast Asia and indigenous Papuan-speaking peoples already resident in the Bismarck Archipelago. Some descendants of the earliest Lapita people – those whose ancestors moved relatively rapidly through Near Oceania on into the Fiji-Samoa-Tonga region – would later become the Polynesians. Others – descendants of those who continued to reside in Near Oceania and whose ancestors thus continued the process of genetic exchange (and linguistic borrowing) – would become the modern inhabitants of island Melanesia.

Barely a decade ago, in a book that sought to question many prevailing views of Oceanic prehistory, John Terrell wrote: "For a hundred years, scholars have told us that the prehistory of the Pacific Islanders can be divided into two phases. First there were the Papuan-speaking aborigines. Then came the Austronesian-speaking migrants. But what are we to think of such a portrait of the past?" (1986:63). Terrell's answer was clear: such portraits were antiquated holdovers of the nineteenth century. While Terrell is to be credited with forcing us to reassess fundamental assumptions and methodological approaches, the mounting pace of research in archaeology, historical linguistics, and human biology has only reinforced the long-standing "portrait," while of course, adding immensely to our understanding of its subtle complexities. Perhaps our academic predecessors – scholars such as Rivers, Codrington, Dempwolff, and more recently Gifford, Grace, or Howells, with a wealth of experience accumulated often through intensive fieldwork – were not so naive as Terrell thinks, despite the fact that they appear from our "modern" perspective to have worked within less sophisticated theoretical paradigms. We continue to grapple with the same difficulties of reconstructing the past from the complex patterns and evidence of the present, but our task is sometimes made easier in that we stand on the shoulders of giants, and the accumulated knowledge they have passed down to us.

5

Lapita Pottery and the
"Community of Culture"

In 1961, Jack Golson assayed the newly won results of stratigraphic excavations in Tonga, Samoa, Fiji, and New Caledonia, which had for the first time in Pacific archaeology produced
deep pottery sequences. Initial application of Libby's revolu-
tionary radiocarbon dating technique demonstrated that these
sequences spanned a "real" time depth of two to three thousand
years. Moreover, at the base of the Tongan, Fijian, and New
Caledonian sequences (and – as would later be demonstrated
– in Samoa as well) Golson noted a remarkably similar kind
of pottery, characterized by highly distinctive motifs typically
executed with small, toothed (or "dentate") stamps. What
particularly impressed Golson on reviewing this evidence was
that the early pottery style showed no regard for the long-
standing ethnological divide between Melanesia and Polynesia,
a boundary deeply entrenched in anthropological thought about
the Pacific. Cautiously pointing to the need for further excavations to verify the initial results, Golson nonetheless boldly
proposed that this ceramic style signaled "some early community of culture linking New Caledonia, Tonga, and Samoa,
antedating . . . the 'Melanesian' cultures of the first and ancestral to the historic Western Polynesian cultures of the other
two" (Golson 1961:176). Echoing remarks made a few years
earlier by E. W. Gifford regarding finds from Site 13 (the
Lapita "type locality") in New Caledonia, Golson drew attention to the obvious similarities between this early ceramic style
and pottery known from sites farther to the west, at Watom
Island in the Bismarcks and even at Kalumpang in Sulawesi. A

decade later, "Lapita" had become well established in the Pacific archaeological literature as a highly distinctive ceramic style, the name of Gifford's New Caledonian Site 13 being extended to include all assemblages of this style.

Pottery is of more than just historical interest for Lapita prehistory, for it remains the primary defining artifact class of the cultural complex. It behooves us, then, to take a closer look at these ceramics which have in recent years been subjected to a diversity of technical and formal analyses. As with other aspects of the Lapita "cultural complex," we shall see that considerable variation exists over space and time within the range of pottery assemblages classified as Lapita. At the same time, there is sufficient cohesiveness in manufacture technique, vessel form, and decorative style that there is usually remarkably little debate as to whether a given archaeological assemblage should be included under the Lapita rubric.[1] Indeed, one of the truly striking aspects of Lapita ceramics – to anyone who has spent even a little time examining collections from several geographically dispersed sites – is the obvious relationships between the decorative motifs, all reflecting an elaborate and sophisticated design system. That sites separated by thousands of kilometers all contain pottery with motifs sharing the same formal "grammar," and obviously produced within a common semiotic tradition, remains the strongest evidence for Golson's "community of culture."

The Lapita Ceramic Series: An Overview

Before examining in detail the grammar of Lapita ceramic design, let us briefly canvas the ceramic complex, in part to dispel several persistent misconceptions. Ignoring for the moment the geographic and temporal variability within the Lapita ceramic series, what are some of the characteristic features of this pottery? I begin with some aspects of its manufacture, moving then to vessel forms, and finally to techniques of decoration.

Lapita pottery would be defined technically as *earthenware*, because it was low fired, often yielding incompletely-oxidized interiors (and thus giving a "sandwich filling" appearance when freshly-broken sherd edges are examined). Experimental re-firing of sherds from the Talepakemalai site indicates that much of the pottery was fired at temperates as low as 5–600°C, and that temperatures of 800°C were probably never exceeded.[2] No evidence for kilns has ever been uncovered, and it is likely that vessels were fired using open fires with fast-burning, hot fuels such as coconut shells. This kind of firing is still practiced by indigenous potters in Fiji and elsewhere in the Pacific.[3] The pottery is handmade, without the aid of a wheel. Sand of various kinds was frequently mixed with the clay as temper; both calcareous sands of marine origin (beach sands) and volcaniclastic sands (occurring in rivers, or as placer deposits on beaches) were used. After hand-forming (both slab and ring building techniques are evidenced), vessel walls were commonly thinned using a paddle-and-anvil technique, leaving telltale anvil impressions on the inside surfaces of globular jars. The paddles were at times carved in a series of parallel "ribs," leaving distinctive paddle impressions on the exteriors of the larger, otherwise plain jars. The exterior surfaces of most vessels, however, were typically smoothed and burnished, and sometimes a thin slip of red clay was applied. After firing, Lapita vessels typically took on a reddish brown to brown color.

A substantial range of vessel forms and shapes (as well as sizes) is encompassed by the Lapita ceramic series, although no single assemblage includes all of these. Moreover, decoration was applied to certain distinctive shapes, whereas other shapes were usually left plain. Later on I will review the specific vessel forms and decorative associations found at representative sites. For the present we may simply note that the main decorated shapes include bowls (both simple bowls and carinated bowls), bowls supported on pedestal feet (found mostly in the earliest Far Western assemblages, see plates 5.1 and 5.2), flat-bottomed dishes, and carinated jars with flaring rims. Undecorated or plain vessel shapes are typically large globular jars with restricted necks and flaring rims, and sometimes also bowls.

Clearly, these different vessel shapes must have had specific and differing functions. This aspect of Lapita pottery has been little studied, however, and more research on residues, surface wear patterns, and so forth would be useful in interpreting function and use.[4] In general, however, Lapita pottery was not used directly over cooking fires, for neither exterior fire

Plate 5.1   Portion of a ceramic pedestal base or ring-foot from the Talepakemalai site, Mussau Islands, illustrating the use of dentate-stamping and carving. The design was originally in-filled with white lime. (Photo by Thérèse Babineau)

Plate 5.2   Portion of a ceramic pedestal base or ring-foot from the Talepakemalai site, Mussau Islands, with triangular-shaped cut-outs, and decorated with relatively thick-tined dentate-stamps. (Photo by Thérèse Babineau)

smudging nor interior carbonaceous residues are commonly evidenced.[5] (See chapter 7 for a discussion of Lapita foods and cooking methods.) Rather, the bowls and dishes are designed as serving vessels, although precisely what was presented in these remains a matter of speculation. The large, typically plain globular jars on the other hand were more likely storage containers. These would have functioned well for storing liquids (such as water) or other substances; similar jars were used in historic times in parts of Melanesia for storing sago flour.

Lexical reconstructions of Proto Oceanic vocabulary associated with pots and pottery making inform us about some of the terms used by the Lapita people to refer to these ceramic objects (Pawley and Ross 1995, table 5). The generic term for pot in Proto Oceanic was *kuron, and a large pot (quite likely the large globular jars) was called *b^wa ŋa. Lids or covers are suggested by the term *tupa(n), and indeed, there are indications in some Lapita sherd assemblages of ceramic lids. There are also a number of terms relating to the manufacture of pottery, including words for clay (*raRo[q]), for a paddle to beat the clay and thin vessel walls (*buli), and for the coiling method (*pilit).

Discussions of Lapita pottery have usually emphasized the decorated component (not surprisingly, as this carries the greatest stylistic "information" of interest to the archaeologist), but all Lapita assemblages include *both* decorated and plain wares. Indeed, plain ware makes up the greatest part of Lapita assemblages from a quantitative perspective. Moreover, the higher frequencies of decorated sherds occur in the earlier sites, and there is a marked trend toward diminished decoration over time.

Lapita potters used several *techniques* to decorate vessel surfaces, the most distinctive being the application of several kinds of small, toothed or "dentate" stamps to the clay surface before drying and firing (plate 5.3). After firing, the tiny depressions created by the teeth were often filled in by the application of a paste of white coral lime, which had the effect of making the delicate designs stand out in sharp contrast against the reddish-brown clay. These dentate stamps include both linear and curved shapes of varied lengths, and there are also round stamps. The tools themselves have never been recovered

*Plate 5.3   Potsherd from a flaring-sided bowl, excavated at the
Talepakemalai site, Mussau Islands. The surface of this vessel
was decorated with both rectilinear and curvilinear motifs,
executed using the dentate-stamped technique.
(Photo by Thérèse Babineau)*

archaeologically, and it is presumed that they were made of
some perishable material, most likely wood or bamboo. A
replicated set of tools made from hardwood by a student of
Roger Green's successfully imitated the decorative result on
experimental pottery. It cannot be overstressed, however, that
dentate-stamping was not the only technique used, and that
incising (drawing a line in the clay surface with a sharp tool)
is also fairly common.[6] Indeed, both dentate-stamping and incising are sometimes found together on a single vessel. Another
technique evidenced especially in the early Far Western assemblages is carving or sculpting the clay surface, both along rim
edges and on vessel walls. The pedestal bases that supported
some early Far Western Lapita bowls have triangular cut-outs
piercing the walls. Other techniques, such as modeling, and
rocker-stamping with the naturally-serrated edge of a bivalve
are more rarely seen. I stress the point that several decorative

techniques were used because – as we shall see below – the remarkable similarities in Lapita pottery assemblages are not due to the techniques applied, *but to the motifs and their grammar of recombination*, regardless of which technique was used to create them.[7]

While certain aspects of manufacture, vessel form, and decoration pertain to Lapita pottery as a whole, there is substantial variation between specific ceramic assemblages excavated from sites in different archipelagoes and dating to different phases within the millennium-long Lapita period. More than a quarter-century ago Golson recognized that "Lapita ware partakes of the features of both the *horizon* and *tradition* of American archaeological writing."[8] That is, a recognizable Lapita style has both synchronic representation over a wide geographic area, as well as persistence through time. The temporal changes vary regionally, so that it is perhaps more accurate to speak of a number of regional traditions which all developed out of an early horizon. Archaeologists term such collective regional traditions a *ceramic series*.[9] Based on a careful, quantitative analysis of shared and unique decorative motifs, Roger Green (1978, 1979a) demonstrated the existence of a set of common, widespread motifs defining an early horizon, as well as distinctive Western Lapita and Eastern Lapita motif sets, the latter indicating regional traditions (figure 5.1). To this it has been possible to add a Far Western tradition centered on the Bismarck Archipelago, and a Southern tradition encompassing New Caledonia and adjacent islands.[10] The earliest assemblages within all of these traditions continue to share a common core set of motifs (Green's "early widespread motifs"), while later sites reflect local innovations that remain confined to specific regions. In order to understand more fully how such continuities and innovations in Lapita design can be traced through analysis of archaeological assemblages, we need to examine the formal structure of the design system.

The Grammar of Lapita Design

Anyone who spends time working closely with a collection of decorated Lapita sherds comes to appreciate that the designs

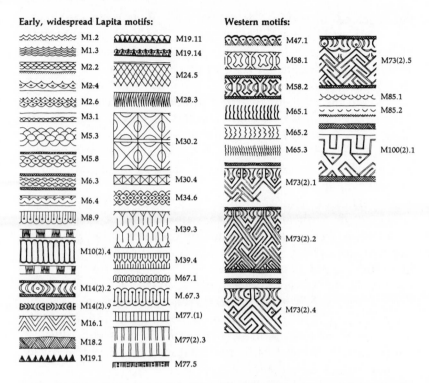

Figure 5.1 Selection of early, widespread Lapita motifs, and of certain motifs typical of the Western Lapita province. (After Green 1979a)

stampd as well as incised into the vessel surfaces are highly regular, structured, and repeated. One quickly senses that the potters who applied these designs worked within a framework of explicit rules for the creation and application of motifs. Not only is the range of motifs restricted (given the possible range of geometric forms that might have been created given the tools and techniques used), but the combination of motifs and their placement on vessel surfaces are also highly constrained. There can be little doubt that the Lapita potters had a well-developed cognitive model of this design system, which they transmitted from one generation to the next; special linguistic terms for design elements and motifs were probably a part of this *emic* artistic code. Unfortunately, this emic code is not accessible to us, even though its transformed successors arguably persist today in certain Melanesian and Polynesian mobiliary art forms such as wood carving and barkcloth decoration.[11] However, it is possible to apply formal methods of structural analysis to the designs on Lapita potsherds in order to generate an *etic* model or code which can replicate the inventory of motifs and the rules for their recombination on vessel surfaces. That is, although we may never know what was in the minds of those potters and design-makers, we can understand in a more formal or structural sense their system of art and design, and use this as a tool for tracing the history of Lapita pottery in time and space.

The major breakthrough in the analysis of the Lapita design system came with Sidney Mead's application of a structural approach based on an explicit analogy with one kind of formal linguistic analysis.[12] Mead had previously used this approach in a study of Polynesian adz hafting patterns, and was encouraged by Roger Green to tackle the problem of Lapita pottery designs.[13] Mead's working principle required him to go "beyond a mere listing of elements and motifs to a structural approach in which an attempt is made to reveal the steps and rules by which patterns were constructed" (Mead et al. 1975:19). Mead set out certain key assumptions and terms:

> It is assumed that the decoration applied by potters to their pottery consists not of elements haphazardly arranged but rather of elements arranged in a systematic manner. The decorative systems may be broken down into three main parts: a set of techniques by which design elements can be given visual form; an inventory of design elements and units; and a set of design processes which may be couched in the form of rules. All three parts yield data which are susceptible to comparison for the purpose of inferring cultural relationships. (Mead et al. 1975:20)

The formal system which Mead developed makes use of the following fundamental categories: *Design Elements* – these are the "building blocks" of the Lapita design system, and consist mostly of individual dentate-stamped units (i.e., each design unit was produced by the application of a specific tool), although they can also be produced by incising or – in the case of three-dimension units – through modeling or carving. There are a limited number of design elements from which all motifs and

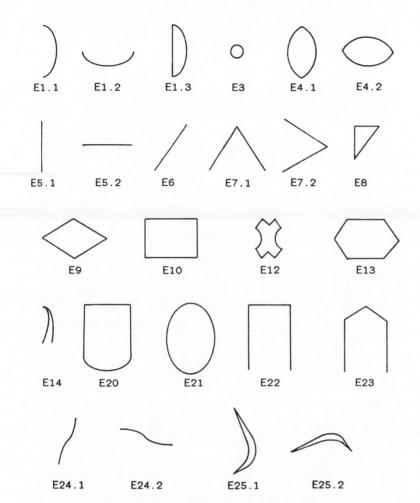

E1.1	E1.2	E1.3	E3	E4.1	E4.2

E5.1	E5.2	E6	E7.1	E7.2	E8

E9	E10	E12	E13

E14	E20	E21	E22	E23

E24.1	E24.2	E25.1 E25.2

Figure 5.2 Basic design elements from which the array of Lapita decorative motifs was constructed. (After Sharp 1988)

patterns are produced; the most common of these are shown in figure 5.2. *Motifs* – motifs are more complex units created by some combination of one or more design elements according to a set of process rules. Motifs themselves then generally recur in repeated patterns across the surface of a vessel. Mead recognized that there are frequently minor variants of the same motif, resulting from the addition or subtraction of some detail,

Motif 8.1

Figure 5.3   Lapita motif M8.1; see text for the process rule associated with this motif.

and he terms these *alloforms* of the same motif. *Zone Markers* – motifs were not applied randomly to vessel surfaces but rather in specific zones, generally running horizontally around a vessel circumference. These zones are delineated by zone markers such as dentate-stamped or incised lines, or a band of superimposed dentate-stamps. *Design Field* – the combination of motifs in specified zones makes up the total design field of a vessel, and these two follow regular patterns. The major design field in Lapita pottery is the exterior surface bounded by the rim at the top and by the base, or by an inflection or carination in the vessel surface, at the bottom. Minor design fields include the flat rim lip, and a narrow zone just inside the rim on some bowls and vessels with flaring rims.

The *process rules* for constructing a particular pattern were also formally specified by Mead, as in the following example:

$$P = M8.1 \rightarrow ConR/E\text{-}W/CLS.$$

Here the pattern (P) is generated by a continuous (Con) transverse or east-west (E-W) repetition of motif alloform M8.1 such that coalescence (CLS) occurs at the junction of each motif unit. The pattern is illustrated in figure 5.3.

As specified by Mead, the key to setting out a process rule was the following:

$$P = /1/2/ \rightarrow /3/4/5.$$

The specific design element or motif is specified in slot 1, while slot 2 specifies the process to be applied to 1. The third slot

Motif 17.1

Figure 5.4   Lapita motif M17.1; see text for the process rule associated with this motif.

identifies the "major pattern-making process" (such as continuous repetition, or arrangement in a half-drop mesh), while slot 4 identifies the direction of repetition (transverse, vertical, or multi-directional). The fifth slot identifies any secondary process applied (such as interlocking, superposition, mirror-imaging, etc.). A more complex process rule might, for example, be written:

$$P = M17.1 \text{ (rep)} + MR/M17.1 \rightarrow DisR/E\text{-}W.$$

This pattern is illustrated in figure 5.4.

The formal analytical system designed by Mead is thus based on a structural linguistic model. The role of the *phoneme* in a language – the minimal structural unit – is analogous to that of the design element. Similarly, the motif and the *morpheme* are analogous as the minimal segments of signification or meaning. Note that a much larger number of motifs or morphemes can be constructed from a minimal number of design elements or phonemes. The linguistic analogy goes further, in that the recombination of motifs follows a set of process rules which constitute the "grammar" or rules of syntax for the design system. Mead was concerned only to write the formal process rules applied to motifs, although he recognized that similar rules could be specified for the generation of motifs and their allomorphs. This more tedious task was later undertaken by Nancy Sharp (1988) at my urging, who demonstrated the analytical clarity that stems from such an exercise.

The nonspecialist may be forgiven for thinking at this point that we are engaged in a highly arcane exercise, of little general interest. In point of fact, an explicit, replicable, and controlled framework for analysis of Lapita ceramic design provides a critical avenue for understanding the historical relationships between Lapita communities in space and time. First of all, the demonstration that all Lapita ceramic assemblages share a common structure (despite differences in specific motif content) lends substantial support to Golson's hypothesis that we are dealing with the archaeological reflection of a "community of culture." If Lapita pottery was merely a "trade ware" for example, we would expect that the design fields on distant assemblages would not exhibit the same shared process rules. Even though the design system gradually changed and underwent transformations as Lapita potters and their descendants expanded throughout the southwestern Pacific, the underlying structural patterns were highly persistent, as would be expected for a *culturally-encoded* artistic system. Archaeologists have long recognized that "pots" do not always equate with "people," and that potting techniques and even designs can be borrowed or diffused across linguistic and cultural boundaries. When such borrowing or diffusion takes place, however, it is usually individual elements that are selected and then recombined in new patterns or structural codes. This is clearly not the case with Lapita, where the entire complex design system (including the core set of design elements, common motifs, and process rules) is replicated from site to site. Such structural consistency can only reflect a shared, ancestral tradition.

Mead's formal system also permits archaeologists to undertake detailed comparisons between the pottery assemblages recovered from individual sites. A number of archaeologists have extended Mead's initial application of the system (to pottery from Yanuca and Natunuku in Fiji) to additional site assemblages in Tonga, Samoa, the Reef Islands, and New Caledonia.[14] A formal catalog of more than 120 Lapita motifs has been generated through this work, and Green (1978, 1979a) was able to show that these include a core set of early, widespread motifs, as well as sets of motif innovations that developed later in specific regions. A statistical analysis of shared motifs further permitted Green to demonstrate that the Western and Eastern Lapita provinces could be formally described with regard to style differences. Recent work stemming from the Lapita Homeland Project has also made it clear that it will be possible to define the specific content of a Far Western Lapita style, although the formal work of design analysis remains to be carried out.

Not all archaeologists working with Lapita pottery have followed the formal system developed by Mead. This is unfortunate, because it has hindered the comparison of pottery assemblages between different regions, and created some ambiguity in the assessment of similarity or difference between sites. Dimitri Anson, for example, used a cumbersome motif trait list in his study of the Far Western style province (Anson 1983, 1986). More recently, a group of French archaeologists working in New Caledonia have developed an alternative formal system based on the rhythm and sequence of application of several forms of dentate-stamped tool (Siorat 1990, 1992). Their method works well for the description of zone markers and simple motifs, but fails to produce rigorous formal descriptions of more complex motifs. However, their analysis has yielded some additional insights into the technical processes used by Lapita design-makers. By paying close attention to details of overlap between tool impressions, J. Siorat was able to ascertain that "the successive bands of motifs were made starting from the top, as the impressions left by the tools of the lower motif always overlapped the traces of the preceding tool." Work also proceeded from left to right, as "the impression of a tool was always superimposed on the impression to its left" (Siorat 1990:61). These technical details reinforce our understanding that the creation of a design field on a Lapita vessel was a highly structured process, which not only followed certain rules but which had to be executed in a particular sequence of steps.

In his seminal monograph, Mead made the important observation that the decorative system of the Lapita potters could have existed independently of the ceramic artifacts to which it was applied. "The design elements used on Sigatoka pottery were not necessarily applied only to ceramics but could have been applied to textiles, woodcarving and tattooing as well" (Mead et al. 1975:20). Tattooing is a widespread Austronesian practice that was probably used by the Lapita people as well (tattooing needles or combs have been excavated from Eastern Lapita sites), and indeed there is reason to think that there was a link between tattooing and dentate stamping (see discussion below). Barkcloth made from processing and beating the inner bark of several species of plants is of considerable antiquity in the Austronesian-speaking world, and was almost certainly a part of Lapita material culture.

Roger Green (1979b) took up Mead's proposition regarding the Lapita decorative system in relation to other decorated media by examining the case for persistence of this system into later, ethnographically-documented designs on Polynesian barkcloth and in tattooing. "Accepting that there are deep structures indicative of continuous cultural transmission it was also possible to propose that both the rules for the production of the designs in tattooing and on barkcloth and the design motifs used in these media ethnographically still exhibited numerous parallels with those of the Lapita design system" (Green 1990: 38). His analysis showed that of 130 Lapita motifs, no less than 52 could be identified in Polynesian barkcloth and tattooing patterns. Moreover, other structural aspects of the Lapita design system have also been retained, such as the use of formal zones defined by zone markers. This is especially evident in Western Polynesian barkcloth, where motifs are repeated in transverse rectangular grids. Indeed, in an early comparative study of Polynesian "decorative designs," written long before any knowledge of Lapita culture or its historical significance, Ruth Greiner had written: "The fact that most of the angular geometric designs of Polynesia are also present in Melanesian art, leads to the supposition that Polynesian art is not a thing apart from all other art but that it is a part of an underlying Oceanic art or culture which is characterized by this same angular geometric feature and that this art was carried by the Polynesian people to the farthest outposts of Oceania" (1923:99). What Greiner had glimpsed – but lacked the tools of modern archaeology to interpret – was the artistic legacy of the Lapita people as it continues to be expressed in mobiliary art throughout the Oceanic world.

Anthropomorphic Representations and their Transformation

With the accumulated knowledge derived from many excavations ranging from the Bismarck Archipelago to Tonga, we now know that the Lapita design system underwent successive transformations over time and space. In the Eastern Lapita region, these transformations produced a series of localized design clusters, all of which were simplified in comparison with the chronologically-antecedent design system represented by early Far Western Lapita assemblages, such as Talepakemalai in Mussau. The temporally later Eastern Lapita design clusters – having been the first to have been excavated in reasonably large samples – were those investigated by Mead et al. (1975) in their pioneering analysis of design structure. From one point of view, it is perhaps fortunate that Mead and his associates first tackled these later and structurally less complex assemblages. Working out the analytical procedures and grammatical structure of Lapita design was made considerably easier by virtue of the simplified nature of the Eastern Lapita design clusters. However, one unintended consequence of this quirk of research history is that Mead (and those who were to use his method) saw the design corpus as purely geometric and abstract, lacking evident *representations* of aspects of the Lapita world. When Green shifted the main locus of Lapita field research away from the Fiji-Western Polynesian region into the Southeast Solomons, he began to discover among his decorated ceramic sherds, various depictions of human faces (e.g., Green 1979a, figure 2.1). Such anthropomorphic representations (which included part of a modeled human figurine as well [Green 1979b, figure 2]) hinted that the iconic content of Lapita ceramic design may have been more complex and layered than at first suspected.

My own excavations at Talepakemalai, beginning in 1985, yielded many anthropomorphic face designs, ranging from finely executed motifs with eyes, nose, arms, digits, and a kind of "headdress" all clearly depicted, to more simplified versions (plate 5.4). The latter frequently appear as repetitive strings of stylized eye-and-nose combinations, or merely as repeated, highly stylized individual eyes or noses (plate 5.5). As I began to work with the large ceramic collections from our first two excavation seasons at Mussau, it became apparent that the *majority* of the decorated sherds came from vessels with one or more human face icons. Moreover, it seemed possible to arrange the various design variants in a chronological sequence,

Plate 5.4   Potsherd from a flaring-sided bowl, excavated at the Talepakemalai site, Mussau Islands. The human face motif here is fairly simplified, with almond-shaped eyes and the classically-elongated nose, but lacking a mouth or headdress.
(Photo by Thérèse Babineau)

with the most elaborate anthropomorphic motifs occurring early in the sequence, and the more stylized, geometric transformations of these motifs (allomorphs) occurring later in time. In short, adopting the terminology of Leroi-Gourhan (1982), one could detect a transformational sequence from *synthetic figurative* to *geometric figurative* states.[15] On my way to Mussau for the final excavation season in 1988, I gave a seminar at the University of Papua New Guinea in which I outlined this tentative model of the Lapita design system as being essentilly focused on the representation of human faces. At approximately the same time, but working independently, Matthew Spriggs came to much the same conclusion based on a comparison of

Plate 5.5   A bowl rimsherd excavated at the Talepakemalai site, Mussau Islands. Here the anthropomorphic face motif has been iconically simplified to a row of almond-shaped eyes inter-connected by geometric patterns. (Photo by Thérèse Babineau)

published design data from a number of Far Western, Western, and Southern Lapita ceramic assemblages (Spriggs 1990a, 1993c). Moreover, Douglas Newton (1988), inspired by Green's publication of the face motif from his Nenumbo site, explored the wider connections between Lapita anthropomorphic repre-sentations and other face motifs in Austronesian and Non-Austronesian speaking cultures of Melanesia and Southeast Asia. Newton boldly claimed that "the addition of a rich Austronesian component to the earlier populations of the Western Pacific was enormously fertilizing to the cultural frameworks and the arts which expressed them. The Lapita culture roused echoes in the arts of Melanesia which have reverberated to the present day" (1988:23).

Spriggs (1990a, 1993c) finds two main classes of face designs, which he terms *double-face* and *single-face* designs, with several variants within each class. The double-face designs, of which Green's well-published Nenumbo sherd is a good example, consists of a somewhat naturalistic face (with eyes and nose) nested within a larger, complex, curvilinear tableaux that incorporates a more stylized pair of eyes below the main face. Moreover, flanking the faces are paired emblems which Spriggs has labeled "earplugs or ear ornaments," although this function is not unambiguously established. The magnificent design so painstakingly stamped and carved into the surface of a large "cylinder stand" from Talepakemalai (figure 5.5) is one of the finest examples of a double-face design yet excavated. Double-faced designs are known not only from Far Western contexts, such as at Mussau, but also from the Western and Southern sub-regions of Lapita.

The single-face designs, in their most elaborate versions, consist of a prominent nose (usually depicted by a cross-stamped band) flanked by almond-shaped eyes, and delineated on the top by horizontal eyebrows or brows; above the brow a series of vertical arrows or triangles may depict a headdress, while emblems or "earplugs" are also depicted to either side of the face. The Talepakemalai site also yielded a superb example of such a single-face design, shown here as figure 5.6. In this design, the cross-hached bands that define the nose and face curve out on both sides to become stylized arms, ending in narrow, triangular "digits." More striking, in this composition, are the two delicate figures that take the place of the "earplugs" (to use Spriggs' term): these consist of identical mirror-image creatures, with two heads springing from a single ovate body, bent arms tipped by three toes or fingers. These mythical zoomorphs seem unlikely to represent earplugs, but one can readily imagine them as tattoos on human cheeks.

Single-face designs are usually simpler than the elaborate motif illustrated in figure 5.6, and indeed, it is this class of anthropomorphic face designs which becomes increasingly stylized in assemblages which date slightly later in time, thus changing from synthetic figurative to geometric figurative. For example, published versions of single-face design transformations include the reconstructed vessel recovered by Hedrick from the

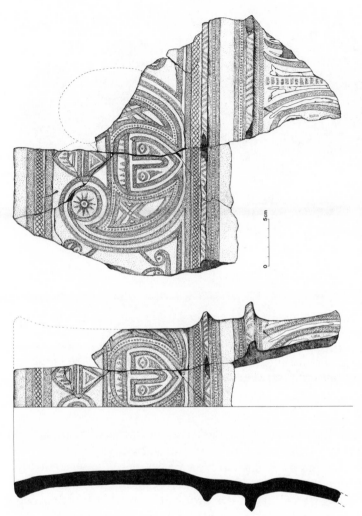

Figure 5.5 Drawing of the anthropomorphic designs on a large cylinder stand excavated at the Talepakemalai site, Mussau Islands. (Drawing by Margaret Davidson)

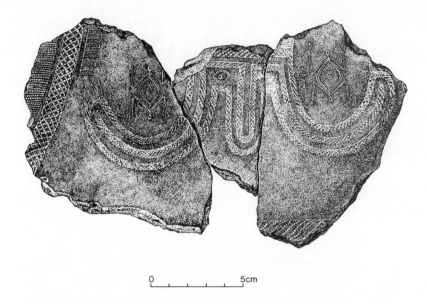

0   5cm

Figure 5.6   Drawing of an anthropomorphic face design on three potsherds excavated at the Talepakemalai site, Mussau Islands. Note the two-headed, four-limbed creatures on either side of the face, and the five digits at the ends of the arm-like extensions from the face. (Drawing by Margaret Davidson)

Paoancarai Lagoon at Malo, Vanuatu (see Spriggs 1993c, figure 2.12), shown here as figure 5.7, and a number of examples from Vatcha and other sites in New Caledonia. Likewise, highly stylized transformations of single-face designs, consisting of no more than repeated sets of eye motifs, can readily be identified in Early Eastern Lapita assemblages from Tonga and Fiji. Indeed, the Eastern Lapita designs have become so simplified that without knowing the longer history of iconic transformation from which they derive, one would classify them as purely geometric (as, indeed, was Mead's original interpretation). The Eastern Lapita design corpus no longer included motifs that would be unambiguously recognizable as a human face to the culturally non-informed viewer (such as an archaeologist). However, to the living participants in the design system (those cultural "insiders" who made and used the pottery) the abstract,

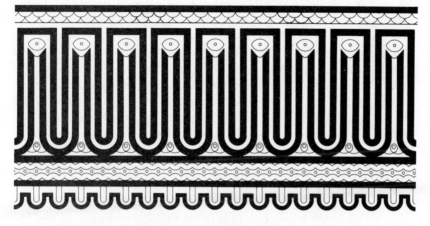

Figure 5.7 Schematic rendering of the highly stylized anthropomorphic face motif on a vessel excavated from Malo Island, Vanuatu. (Courtesy of Matthew Spriggs)

geometric motifs were presumably intended to symbolize persons, part of the shared knowledge passed down through successive generations.

In his analysis of "the changing face" of Lapita designs, Spriggs stresses the need for "a lot more contextual information than is usually provided in excavation reports" (1990b: 119). While being able to define a number of types and variants of double- and single-face designs, and developing a reasonable hypothesis that these types form a chronological sequence, Spriggs could not press the analysis further based on available published sources. For example, whether face designs are correlated with particular vessel forms is a key area requiring further exploration. In our Mussau project, we have been able to demonstrate that face designs are indeed confined to particular vessel forms. The early, most elaborate face motifs (such as the double-face design shown in figure 5.5) are found on large, open-ended ceramic objects that we label "cylinder stands,"[16] as well as on open bowls supported by pedestal feet or rings. Later in the sequence, single-faced designs are found on such bowls and on flat-bottomed, flaring sided dishes. It is significant that no face designs occur on smaller bowls or on the large, globular pots (most of which are plain, but some of which are decorated with incised motifs above a carination or inflection in the body). Thus anthropomorphs are present only on a restricted range of vessels, the forms of which seem best suited either for display or serving, but not for storage or cooking. Equally significant, these decorated vessels are not evenly distributed within the Talepakemalai site: rather, they are discretely associated with the stilt-houses that formerly stood over the shallow reef flats. On the adjacent beach terrace, contemporary deposits contain only the abundant sherds of large, undecorated globular jars with everted rims.

The only known example of a human face motif executed in a non-ceramic medium was also excavated from the deposits surrounding the stilt-house post bases at Talepakemalai. This is a small figurine of bone (see frontispiece), carefully carved in a synthetic geometric style with eyebrows (or, slit eyes) and nose well delineated. Gently curved lines beneath the nose might represent either a mouth, or simply the outline of the face. No torso or arms are depicted, but the figure tapers to two short legs with cross-grooves (it is likely that these served to attach the figurine to some kind of shaft). The bone is apparently from a cetacean or marine mammal, most likely a porpoise. The co-occurrence of this figurine with several ceramic vessels bearing elaborate face designs, and a substantial range of shell exchange valuables (see chapter 8) in this stilt-house over the Talepakemalai reef flat seems to hint that this structure was of particular social significance.

The elaborate and painstakingly-executed anthropomorphic designs found on early Far Western Lapita cylinder stands and pedestal-footed bowls must have occupied a significant role in the social life of the Lapita people. The time-consuming decoration of these vessels, requiring many hours of repetitive application of finely-carved dentate stamps, indicates that the manufacture of these vessels was labor-intensive, in turn suggesting a high value or "prestige" object. What role did such objects play in the daily negotiation and construction of Lapita society, just as all human societies use material culture to frame their social actions? Before we explore this question, a tentative hypothesis on the origin of the Lapita ceramic design system may be put forth, as this has implications for the possible social meaning of the decorated vessels.

Possible Origins of the Lapita Ceramic Style

In chapter 3 I reviewed the emerging archaeological record for island Southeast Asia during the period immediately preceding the appearance of Lapita in the Bismarck Archipelago. The Lapita ceramic complex seems to have developed out of an earthenware ceramic tradition that is well attested in sites dating to the third millennium BC in such archipelagoes as the Philippines, Sulawesi, and Halmahera. The techniques of manufacture as well as the range of vessel forms (large globular jars with everted rims, pedestal-supported bowls, as well as other bowl and dish forms) in such assemblages are entirely consistent with the second-millennium BC Lapita ceramic complex. What is distinctive about Lapita, however, is the particular dentate-stamped (and incised) *design system* which we have examined in some detail. While the earlier Southeast Asian ceramic assemblages include stamping and incising, as well as lime-infilling techniques, and while there are some striking similarities in motif (e.g., the Cagayan Valley assemblages in Luzon, see Aoyagi and Tanka [1985] and Aoyagi et al. [1986, 1991]), on present evidence it cannot be claimed that the Lapita design system has direct antecedents in island Southeast Asia. Rather, to most archaeologists who have studied the matter, it increasingly appears that the Lapita ceramic design system is a local development within the Bismarck Archipelago or immediately adjacent regions.[17] In short, while Lapita ceramics are arguably a continuation of earlier Southeast Asian traditions, they also reflect a phase of innovation in the complex decorations with which their surfaces were embellished.

What was the inspiration for this apparent efflorescence in ceramic decoration? Early Far Western Lapita design fields, as illustrated by the vessels from Talepakemalai shown in figures 5.5 and 5.6, are highly complex, both technically and semiotically. As we have seen, they are the product of a complex grammar of design, in which motifs are built up from sets of design elements through highly specific process rules. Was this elaborate system invented *de novo* for application to cylinder stands and pedestal-footed bowls? Or, is it conceivable that an extant design system already in use on other media now became transferred to pottery?

In a seminal paper on early Lapita art, Roger Green (1979b) argued that tattooing and barkcloth decoration were art forms that also existed in Lapita culture, and that many aspects of Lapita style (such as the use of zones, as well as specific motifs) could be traced through time to ethnographically-documented Polynesian tapa and tattooing designs. The numerous parallels both in rules for design production and in motifs, in tattooing, on barkcloth, and on Lapita pottery "were too striking and numerous to be explained by chance or through analogues resulting from coincidence" (Green 1990:38). While neither barkcloth nor human skin with tattoo designs has been preserved in Lapita period sites,[18] Green's hypothesis has considerable merit, and we can readily posit that the Lapita repertoire of mobiliary art encompassed the media of barkcloth and human skin, and probably also wood, as well as ceramics. Indeed, both tattooing and barkcloth manufacture are widespread Austronesian cultural practices. A term for tattooing can probably be reconstructed to Proto-Austronesian (Zorc 1994:561), while barkcloth technology is widespread through the Austronesian-speaking world (Kooijman 1972).

Starting from his argument that the design system displayed on Lapita ceramics was also in use in tattooing and barkcloth, Green (1985:220) further suggested a hypothesis for the origins of complex decoration on early Far Western Lapita ceramics. Briefly stated, around 1500 BC, Lapita artisans may have decided to extend the range of media on which their design system was expressed, to include ceramics. Moreover, I would posit that this extension was specifically *from tattooing to ceramics*, because the dominant technique used to decorate the clay was the same as that used in piercing the human skin. Oceanic tattoos are made by piercing the skin with small "chisels" (usually carved of bone or shell) which have rows of sharp, needle-like teeth. The row of punctures inflicted by a tattoo needle are virtually identical to the effect produced by applying a dentate-stamp to the leather-hard surface of a ceramic vessel. Furthermore, both the human body and a ceramic vessel are three-dimensional surfaces, so that process rules for zonation and joining of motifs are readily adaptable from one kind of surface to the other.

In short, I am suggesting that the complex design system

seen on early Far Western Lapita ceramics was not an innovation developed specifically for pottery, but rather the transference of an already highly-developed, pervasive art style to a new medium. But this hypothesis also raises a highly intriguing possibility: is it conceivable that in the minds of the Lapita potters, the vessels themselves were now being tattooed? It is essential here to remember that only a few specific kinds of ceramic shapes were so decorated: cylinder stands and pedestalled bowls, both objects intended for display and/or presentation. Furthermore, the dominant or central motif throughout the corpus of early Far Western ceramics is the *human face*, originally in a highly recognizable synthetic figurative style, and later transformed to a more conventionalized, geometric figurative style. We are compelled to ask: were these cylinder stands and pedestalled-bowls more than mere utilitarian objects? Were they in fact representations of human beings, living or dead, real or mythical?

There is precedent within the Austronesian-speaking world for treating pots as ancestral representations. Among the Paiwan "aborigines" of south-central Taiwan, "pots were personified and given sexual characteristics," while the "ancestors of certain families were born from the pots" (Chen 1968:122). Chiang (1992:105) relates an origin myth of the Parilaiyan Village people, in which a "noble girl" is born when sunlight strikes a pot. Among high-ranking Paiwan lineages, "male" and "female" pots were exchanged as part of the marriage contract, and these special ceramics were kept in special loci within the ancestral dwelling houses (Chiang, personal communication, 1992). Even more intriguing, the vessels themselves (which are globular, carinated jars with restricted, flaring rims) are decorated below the neck with bands of stamped designs, which the Paiwan refer to as tattooing of the pot! While it would be far-fetched to claim any direct, homologous connection between Paiwan and Lapita, this ethnographic example within the Austronesian sphere opens our imaginations to the possibility that certain kinds of Lapita ceramics may conceivably have been regarded as representations of human beings, particularly ancestors.

As we shall see in chapter 6, there are also reasons to think that the Lapita people organized themselves into social groups based on the *house*, as is the case in the majority of Austronesian-speaking societies today. A fundamental characteristic of "house societies" is the worship or ritual recognition of ancestors, who are often depicted iconically through anthropomorphic representations in which the face is central. In many ethnographically-documented Austronesian societies these representations are carved on house posts or other parts of the house structure. In her outstanding monograph on Austronesian houses, Roxana Waterson (1990) illustrates many examples of such face motifs, and the frequent iconic parallels with Lapita ceramic faces are too numerous to discount as mere coincidence. Common parallels are the strongly ovoid eyes and prominent nose (often to the total exclusion of a mouth), upraised arms, and "flame" headress motif (see, for example, Waterson 1990, figures 190–2 compared with figure 5.6 herein). It seems a reasonable hypothesis that both the Lapita anthropomorphic pottery, and the various carved representations of ancestors found in Austronesian house societies today, represent a common and old inheritance from early Austronesian social organization.

Pottery and Exchange

It may seem that in this discussion of Lapita decorated ceramics we have now climbed high on a "ladder of inference." However, there is empirical evidence that at least certain Lapita ceramic wares were of sufficient social value to be transported over considerable distances, as components of inter-community exchange networks. The topic of Lapita exchange has occupied archaeologists considerably over the past few years, and a more comprehensive consideration of their findings is given in chapter 8. Here I confine myself to a few relevant comments regarding the movement of decorated ceramics, drawing specifically from the results of our Mussau Project excavations.

Studies of the *temper*, or non-plastic inclusions[19] incorporated within the clay matrix or "fabric" of Lapita ceramics from various southwest Pacific sites, have yielded a number of examples of inter-island or inter-archipelago movements (see Dickinson and Shutler 1979, for a summary review). In our

Mussau Project, we addressed the question of ceramic origins not only by examining temper suites, but also through the application of energy-dispersive X-ray florescence analysis of the chemical composition of the clays themselves (Hunt 1989). With the aid of these analytical techniques, we have been able to demonstrate that much of the pottery excavated from Talepakemalai and other Mussau Lapita sites actually derived from a variety of locales. Perhaps the most striking result of these analyses was that a large part of the Mussau assemblages (perhaps as much as 90 percent) is of non-local origin. While some local Mussau clay was being utilized, as many as eleven other clay "sources" (compositional groups) were represented in our analyzed samples. Two of these have been provisionally determined to come from the Manus group (Admiralty Is.) to the west of Mussau; our lack of detailed geological knowledge for the Bismarck Archipelago does not permit us to tie down the source localities of the other clays.

We can now state with some certainty that the early Far Western Lapita ceramics were an essential part of a complex, multi-nodal exchange network that linked many Lapita communities. Of course, the mere transport and exchange of pottery need not imply that the ceramics were of high intrinsic value, "prestige goods" as it were. The Melanesian ethnographic record documents many examples of extensive trade in large quantities of utilitarian pottery, such as the pots traded by the Motu of southern Papua on their annual hiri voyages to the peoples of the Papuan Gulf region (Allen 1977; Frankel and Rhoads 1994), or the Mailu Island potting industry (Irwin 1985). Some of the pottery which was being moved between Lapita communities was probably just of the same sort of utilitarian value, especially in situations where the resources with which to manufacture pottery (clay and temper) were locally absent. However, it is reasonable to suppose that certain classes of ceramics – especially the highly labor-intensive decorated wares, bearing the anthropomorphic face designs, and which occur in specific depositional contexts in sites such as Talepakemalai – were indeed prestige items, possibly one focus of regular exchange voyages between Lapita groups. If such elaborated decorated cylinder stands and pedestalled bowls were iconic representations of house or lineage ancestors, they may well have been given as prestige gifts in marriage exchanges, or other kinds of social interactions. The question of exchange relationships between Lapita communities is indeed complex, and further discussion of the matter is best deferred to chapter 8, when the evidence of other kinds of artifacts, such as obsidian, can also be brought to bear. Suffice it to say that among the Lapita peoples, pottery was intimately bound up in their web of social relations, a key component of the material culture through which they constructed their daily life. Ceramics were an integral part of this "community of culture."

The Plain Wares

The decorated wares offer so many intriguing avenues for analysis and theoretical exploration, it is easy to lose sight of their relative significance within the large universe of Lapita ceramics. Actually, decorated potsherds rarely make up more than about ten percent of a Lapita pottery assemblage.[20] While the plain wares display a more restricted range of stylistic variation, they are nonetheless significant components of Lapita material culture, and deserve more careful scrutiny than has often been the case. Most plain ware in Lapita sites comes from a restricted range of vessel forms, primarily large, relatively thin-walled, globular "jars." These generally have restricted necks and everted, sometimes quite flaring, rims. Occasionally there is some minor decoration along the rim lip, in the form of fine parallel notches or incisions, or of finger-pinching. These large vessels were invariably made using the paddle-and-anvil thinning technique (as evidenced by anvil impressions on interior surfaces), and in many instances the paddles were evidently either ribbed, or wrapped in some coarse substance, producing shallow, parallel grooves or ribs on the exterior surface of the jar. In other cases, the exterior surfaces were smoothed by wiping and/or burnishing, and a thin red slip or wash was frequently applied. In addition to the jars, the plain ware includes open bowls, usually fairly small; these are much less common than the jars.

The importance of plain ware in the early Far Western Lapita assemblages is evident in Talepakemalai and the other Mussau

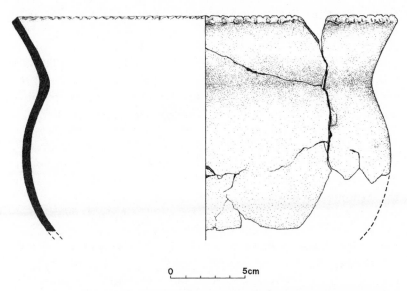

0   5cm

*Figure 5.8   Drawing of a plain ware vessel with notched rim,
excavated at the Talepakemalai site, Mussau Islands.
(Drawing by Margaret Davidson)*

Island sites. There the plain wares were, as just noted, in the
form of large globular jars with flaring rims, as shown in figure
5.8. A large percentage of these bear red slip, a characteristic
that relates them closely to identical pottery of contemporary
age in the Halmahera Island site of Uattamdi (see chapter 3).
In Talepakemalai, the red-slipped, plain pottery was heavily
concentrated on the beach terrace, whereas the decorated wares
were found in association with the offshore stilt houses (see
chapter 6). This suggests some clear functional (and perhaps
also social?) differences in the use of these two kinds of pottery.

We now have evidence of several instances where Lapita
groups abandoned the use of decorated, dentate-stamped ware
almost immediately after colonizing a new island, continuing
only to make and use plain ware. One well-documented case
is Tikopia, a small volcanic island in the Santa Cruz group of
the southeastern Solomons. The Kiki Site (TK-4) on Tikopia
was settled about 900 BC, perhaps two centuries after Lapita
people first colonized the main island of Nendö and the nearby

Reef Islands of the group (Kirch and Yen 1982:111–25, 312–4). The Kiki site ceramics included a handful of dentate-stamped sherds (Kirch and Yen 1982, figure 81), but 99 percent of the pottery was plain ware of typical Lapita type: globular jars with restricted necks and everted rims, and a few bowls. At the time that Tikopia was first colonized, its population must have been linked to the long-distance Lapita exchange network that connected communities in the Santa Cruz group with those in the Far Western "homeland" region (see chapter 8), because in the site's deposits we found such exotic items as obsidian from Talasea (New Britain), and chert and meta-volcanic adzes from the Solomons. It seems, however, that once the island was settled its occupants quickly became disengaged from these external networks. That they no longer continued to make or import decorated pottery may therefore be significant, since we know that the dentate-stamped pottery figured pominently in such exchange transactions. For the next eight centuries, the Tikopia people continued to manufacture plain ware pottery, using local clay and calcareous sand for temper.[21] Eventually they abandoned the local manufacture of pottery, although some ceramics were later imported to the island from the south, in Vanuatu.

A similar rapid loss of the dentate-stamped pottery, but continued use of plain ware, is evident in the archaeological sequence of Samoa, in the Eastern Lapita region. Only one site in Samoa containing substantial quantities of dentate-stamped ceramics has been found, the now-submerged Mulifanua site on 'Upolu Island (Green and Davidson 1974). Within a very short time after the Samoan Islands were colonized, the use of dentate-stamped ceramics ceased. In the deep, well-stratified To'aga site on Ofu Island, in the Manu'a group of eastern Samoa, we found thin, fine plain wares in deposits dated to as early as 1,100 BC, but no evidence of decorated wares (Kirch and Hunt, eds 1993). At To'aga use of plain wares continued for more than a millennium, with gradual change to a thick, coarse-tempered ware, until ceramics were finally abandoned altogether, around AD 3–400.

Nowhere has the problem of the relationship between Lapita decorated and plain wares been more controversial, or more confusing, than in New Caledonia. In their revision of the New

Caledonian cultural sequence based on an exhaustive reanalysis of the assemblages oiginally excavated by Gifford and Shutler (1956), Roger Green and J. S. Mitchell (1983) defined a ceramic style which they labeled Podtanéan (after site 14, on the Foué Peninsula). According to Green and Mitchell, Podtanéan pottery was characterized by ribbed-paddle impressing on otherwise plain vessels (largely globular jars with everted rims). While admitting that Podtanéan and Lapita pottery shared "some elements of vessel shape and incised motifs" (1983:61), they nonetheless felt that these were different and distinct ceramic complexes, with the implication that they were introduced to the island by different cultural groups. This introduction would have to have been simultaneous, however, for radiocarbon dates from sites with Lapita pottery, and those with the Podtanéan sherds, yielded contemporaneous ages.

It is the case, however, that paddle-impressing on plain ware jars is not confined to the so-called Podtanéan style of New Caledonia, and in fact is widely-attested as one aspect of other Lapita assemblages, in Fiji, Tonga, Futuna, 'Uvea, Niuatoputapu, and the eastern Solomon Islands. At the Yanuca Rockshelter in Fiji, for example, Hunt (1986) demonstrates the persistence of paddle-impressing from the Early Eastern Lapita phase through to later time periods, and in the Late Eastern Lapita site of Tavai, Futuna, parallel-ribbed paddle impressions were extremely common (Kirch 1981). That paddle-impressing on some plain ware vessels of the Lapita ceramic complex is widespread should immediately raise suspicions that the Podtanéan "style" of New Caledonia actually represents a wholly distinct ceramic series on the island.

Indeed, recent work by several French archaeologists[22] now overwhelmingly indicates that the paddle-impressed pottery which Green and Mitchell termed Podtanéan – and which is contemporary with dentate-stamped Lapita assemblages – does not represent a distinct ceramic or cultural tradition. Rather, it is simply the plain or non-dentate decorated component of New Caledonian Lapita. This conclusion is bolstered by the discovery of both dentate-stamped and paddle-impressed sherds *in the same site*, such as at Koné, Bourail, and Paita. Moreover, through careful petrographic study of temper inclusions in New Caledonian potsherds, Jean-Christophe Galipaud demonstrated that both kinds of pottery contain identical temper suites, and were thus made by the same potters (Galipaud 1988, 1989, 1990). Galipaud has renamed the Lapita phase of the New Caledonian cultural sequence the "Koné tradition" (1988:148).

It nonetheless remains the case that the spatial distribution of classic, dentate-stamped and the paddle-impressed types of pottery is usually distinct or separated within New Caledonian sites of the Koné period. As Galipaud reports, "in all Lapita sites, Paddle Impressed pottery is abundant near the Lapita-bearing location and is generally also found on nearby off-shore islands" (1990:140; see also Sand 1993b:126). This pattern strongly suggests that the two kinds of pottery had distinct patterns of use within these sites, and that "these two different types of pottery reflect different functions, i.e., social behavior." As Galipaud posits, the paddle-impressed ware is probably representing the "common pottery used for everyday life" whereas the dentate-stamped Lapita "was presumably linked with ritual performances" (1990:141).

The New Caledonian case is a poignant reminder of the danger of too narrowly equating ceramic styles with prehistoric cultures. It also underscores the point that the Lapita cultural complex must be defined not just by its "flashy" dentate-stamped decorated component but by its numerically more abundant plain wares, along with a wide range of non-ceramic aspects. Lapita societies were highly complex structures as reflected in the sophistication of their ceramics and how these formed part of their daily "habitus."[23]

Who Made the Lapita Pots?
Some Speculations on Gender

In their monumental study of the traditional pottery of Papua New Guinea, Patricia May and Margaret Tuckson (1982) drew attention to certain distribution patterns associated with female and male potting industries. They observed that "the paddle-and-anvil technique is used exclusively by a number of localized coastal and small island groups in which the potters are women. In the majority of cases these groups are Austronesian" (1982: 14, 24, map 3). Most of the paddle-and-anvil produced pots are round-bottomed, and utilitarian. In many of these coastal industries, the female-made pottery is extensively traded between communities and islands, and such trade is always controlled by men. In contrast are largely coil-made traditions in which the potters are more often men, situated in inland rather than coastal villages; frequently these are Papuan speakers. While some coil-made pottery is utilitarian, it also includes vessels made exclusively for ritual use.

Drawing upon the distributional data provided by May and Tuckson, augmented by other ethnographic sources, Yvonne Marshall (1985) developed an enthnographically-based gender model for ceramic production and use in Lapita times. Noting that the area of Lapita site distribution is also coastal and coincides to a large extent with the female-dominated industries seen today, and that extensive maritime trade was involved, Marshall put forward the reasonable hypothesis that as with the modern paddle-and-anvil traditions of Papua New Guinea, Lapita pottery was made exclusively by women. She also posits that the "industry was promoted by participation in a maritime trade and communications network operated by the men" (1985:224).

While Marshall's hypothesis is plausible, there are reasons to suspect that the Lapita situation may have been somewhat more complex than what holds among coastal Austronesian-speaking potters today. For one thing, the contemporary industries are almost exclusively focused on utilitarian wares, and lack elaborately-decorated, ritually-centered wares such as would have been the function of Lapita dentate-stamped pottery. Furthermore, there is strong evidence from many Lapita sites for discrete spatial distribution of the decorated and plain ware components, suggesting some kind of socially (particularly, gender) based distinction.

In analyzing the extensive collection of early Far Western Lapita ceramics from Talepakemalai, I was struck by differences in manufacture of the dentate-stamped, decorated vessels and of the plain wares. Whereas the latter are invariably thin, paddle-and-anvil finished, and well-fired, the decorated vessels are usually much thicker, often slab built, frequently low-fired, and in general exhibit less "skill" in the potting arts. The two kinds of wares seem, frankly, to have been constructed at the hands of two rather different groups of people, one highly proficient in technical expertise, the other exhibiting less technical control but obsessed with execution of the finely detailed stamped decoration.[24] Could these groups possibly have been the women and men, respectively? The hypothesis is tantalizing, for recall the possibility that the initiation of dentate-stamping on the surfaces of Lapita pots may have been inspired by a pre-existing art form expressed in tattooing. In the Polynesian societies descended from Eastern Lapita populations, tattooing is practiced exclusively by men (although both men and women's bodies are tattooed).

In short, I think there is sufficient evidence to elaborate Yvonne Marshall's original hypothesis, along the following lines: the Lapita plain wares were indeed manufactured by women, who used the paddle-and-anvil method and whose tradition placed great emphasis on technical control of the pottery-making process.[25] At some point early during the expansion of Austronesian-speakers into the Bismarck Archipelago, however, pottery intended strictly for ritual use began to be made by men who transferred the techniques and designs of tattooing to the surfaces of pots. The men were not concerned with technical competence, nor was this a necessity, for their vessels were not intended to withstand the stresses of everyday utilitarian use. Rather than mastering the more difficult paddle-and-anvil technique, they adopted simpler methods of slab building and coiling, producing thick-walled vessels. They were, however, obsessed with covering the surfaces of these ritual vessels with intricate and iconically-charged representations of human beings, most probably, their ancestors. Both these ritually-charged, decorated vessels and the more ubiquitous plain wares were transported between Lapita communities through long-distance exchange, but they moved in discrete pathways, the ritual vessels in ceremonial gift exchange, and the plain ware in commodity exchange ("trade"), especially in areas where clay or temper were not readily available locally. As external exchange networks gradually contracted and declined throughout the Lapita world (see chapter 8), the social value of ritual pottery declined, and was eventually abandoned. In many areas, however, the utilitarian female-produced plain wares continued to be of value, and have continued through until the present time. The scenario outlined above is, naturally, only a set of hypotheses which seem to me to make the best sense of several kinds of empirical evidence (e.g., the discrete spatial distribution of pottery in Lapita sites, the differential quality of manufacture of decorated and plain wares). I hope it may stimulate further research into the fascinating but difficult question of "who made the Lapita pots?"

Regional Variation in the Lapita Ceramic Series

As I emphasized at the beginning of this chapter, the Lapita *ceramic series* extends in space over several thousand kilometers, and in time persisted for more than a millennium. Considerable change in vessel form and manufacture technique, along with transformation of the decorative system, occurred as the Lapita potters dispersed and as their art was transmitted to successive generations. It would require a weighty monograph to describe and illustrate all of the local variants in time and space that collectively comprise the Lapita ceramic series.[26] In the following paragraphs, I attempt to review succinctly the chronology of ceramic change in three locales, as examples of the kinds of transformation and variation in Lapita ceramics. These summaries are based on some of the larger and more completely analyzed assemblages of Lapita pottery, from Talepakemalai, Nenumbo, and Lolokoka. The sites from which these ceramics were excavated will be discussed in chapter 6.

Far Western Lapita in the Mussau Islands

Excavations carried out under my direction at Talepakemalai (ECA), Etakosarai (ECB), Etapakengaroasa (EHB), Epakapaka (EKQ) and other sites in the Mussau Islands between 1985–8 yielded one of the largest collections of Lapita ceramics, including more than 50,000 sherds.[27] These assemblages span a time period beginning about 1,500 BC and continuing until possibly as late as 500 BC, thus providing a valuable record of local ceramic change within the Far Western Lapita region.

The earliest components in these Mussau sites are represented by the Etapakengaroasa site on Emananus Island, and by the Zone C deposits at Area B of the Talepakemalai site. In both of these contexts, the decorated wares are dominated by two forms: open bowls supported by pedestals (or "ring-feet"), and "cylinder stands." The pedestal or ring-feet frequently have triangular or rectangular cut-outs in them, and are also decorated (see plates 5.1 and 5.2). The decorative techniques include dentate-stamping (generally very finely executed, with small needle-like impressions), along with incising, and considerable use of carving or cut-outs. As far as can be ascertained, the dentate-stamped and carved designs were always filled in with white lime (although this has not always been preserved). There are many examples of human face designs, some of which have been illustrated above. Microprobe analysis of the clays used in these ceramics indicate that as many as 12 different sources were being used, so that the assemblage probably incorporates pottery manufactured in several different communities, and imported to clay-impoverished Mussau. In addition, these earliest assemblages also contain significant quantities of plain ware, almost exclusively comprised of thin-walled, large globular jars with strongly everted rims and narrow or constricted necks. These jars are generally calcareous sand tempered, and were treated with a thin red slip.[28]

An intermediate phase in the Mussau ceramic sequence is represented by Zone B at Area B, and by other deposits along several transect excavations in the Talepakemalai site, dating to between ca. 1,200–800 BC. A number of key changes are evident in these components, both in vessel forms and in decoration. The most common decorated vessel forms in the early phase – pedestalled bowls and cylinder stands – are now virtually absent, having been replaced with open bowls lacking feet, and with flat-bottomed dishes. While the general structure of the design system, including specific motifs, shows continuity from the earlier phase, there is a marked shift towards a more "open" style of dentate-stamping, in which the stamps themselves have larger and more widely spaced teeth. The use of incising also shows a significant increase in this phase. Microprobe analyses indicate that these ceramics derive from a decreased number of clay sources, perhaps numbering eight.

The large, plain ware jars continue to be represented, but many of these now bear notching along their rims, and some have incised decorations above a carination at the mid-line.

About 800 BC, and continuing to possibly as late as 500 BC, dramatic changes occurred in the Mussau ceramic assemblages. This later time phase is represented at Talepakemalai by the Area C component, and also by the more than 12,000 sherds from the Epakapaka (EKQ) site. By this time, the use of dentate-stamping had become rare, and most of the decorated sherds are incised. Moreover, the bowls and flat-bottomed dishes are also now largely absent, with the majority of sherds coming from large, thin-walled jars. Indeed, there is a significant reduction in vessel wall thickness, matched by an increase in vessel hardness, both indicating higher firing temperatures and better control over the manufacture process. The incised designs are now almost entirely geometric (chevrons, cross-hatchuring, etc.), and notched or crenellated rims are common. New decorative techniques also appear, although infrequently, such as nubbins, shell-edge stamping, and punctation.

Although our archaeological record for the Mussau Islands after about 500 BC is still incomplete, on current evidence there was a dramatic decline in the importing and use of pottery after this time. Later sites reveal very sporadic ceramics, some of which appear to have been imported from the Manus Islands to the west, where pottery continued to be manufactured until the historic period. In Mussau itself, ceramics were not made at the time of early European contact (Nevermann 1933).

Western Lapita in the Reef Islands

Roger Green's excavations at three Lapita sites in the Reef/Santa Cruz Islands (sites SZ-8, RF-2, and RF-6) yielded ceramic collections that have been more intensively studied than virtually any other collection of Lapita pottery.[29] As such, they provide the best known sequence of ceramic change within the Western Lapita region. On the basis of radiocarbon ages, and of statistical comparisons of ceramic decorative motifs and vessel forms, it is clear that the oldest of these three sites is Nanggu (SZ-8). A single radiocarbon date from Nanggu yielded an age of 3140 ± 70 BP (1048–876 cal BC). The Nenumbo site (RF-2) seems to be only slightly younger in age, with a pooled mean date from four radiocarbon ages of 2838 ± 54 BP (1187–926 cal BC).[30] The youngest site in this local sequence is undoubtedly Ngamanie (RF-6) which has a pooled mean date from two radiocarbon ages of 2495 ± 67 BP (791–431 cal BC), and may, therefore, be two or three centuries younger than Nenumbo.

Ceramics from the early Nanggu site display the greatest range of vessel forms, including several types unique to it. One of the latter is a ring-foot, the only example of a ring-footed vessel in the Western Lapita region. (This suggests that the use of ring- or pedestal-feet, common in early Far Western region ceramics, was already rare at the time that Nanggu was settled.) The range of vessel forms at Nenumbo is slightly reduced from that at Nanggu, but still considerably broader than at the late Ngamanie site (Parker 1981, table 19). In the Nenumbo collection, flat-bottomed dishes are quite common among the decorated types, again suggesting a connection with the later Far Western ceramics (such as at Zone B of the Talepakemalai site, see above).

Analysis of the decorated components from these three sites also exhibits a parallel sequence. Nanggu and Nenumbo share the greatest number of motifs in common, and these include certain motifs (such as anthropomorphic faces) with links back to early Far Western assemblages.[31] In general, there is a reduction in the complexity of the design system from the two earlier sites, compared to Ngamanie, with such features as complex curvilinear motifs confined to the earlier assemblages. Thus, as Green summarizes the Reef/Santa Cruz ceramic sequence, "the earliest site in this case exhibits the most complex ceramic assemblage in terms of vessel shape and associated elements of decorative design, and ... these have been simplified through time in this region" (1991c:199). As Green observes, this temporal pattern is consistent with a general "distance decay" from west to east in the whole Lapita ceramic system, "with each local region then exhibiting some loss of the more elaborately dentate decorated vessel shapes through time."

Eastern Lapita on Niuatoputapu Island

The general pattern of "distance decay" in the Lapita decorative system, and reduction in the complexity and variability of both vessel forms and decorative motifs over time within local sequences, is most strikingly evident in the Eastern Lapita region. Several local ceramic sequences within this region have now been reported in some detail, such as that for Tongatapu (Poulsen 1983, 1987), the Lakeba sequence reported by Best (1984), the Samoan ceramic sequence (Green and Davidson 1974; Kirch and Hunt, eds 1993), or that from the islands of Futuna and 'Uvea (Kirch 1981; Sand 1990). Although there are minor, local variations in each island group, these Eastern Lapita sequences all show essentially the same transformation from an Early Eastern Lapita phase marked by a broad range of vessel types and the use of classic dentate-stamped decoration, to a Late Eastern Lapita phase with a more restricted range of vessels and only rare use of dentate-stamping, to a Polynesian Plain Ware phase in which vessel forms are highly limited, and decoration virtually absent. This sequence is visually summarized in figure 5.9, where the reduction in the range of vessel forms can be clearly traced.

Excavations which I conducted in 1976 on the island of Niuatoputapu, a northern outlier of the Tongan Kingdom, produced more than 43,000 potsherds from 12 sites, providing an excellent case study of the Eastern Lapita ceramic sequence.[32] The earliest site in the Niuatoputapu island sequence is Lolokoka (NT-90), which will be described in greater detail in chapter 6. Here a wide range of vessel forms is represented, as seen in figure 5.10. These included several kinds of carinated bowls carrying dentate-stamped decorations, as well as plain ware bowls, jars, and large globular pots. Although dentate-stamping was used to decorate certain vessels at Lolokoka, the designs show nothing of the complexity present in the earlier Western or Far Western assemblages. There are no face motifs, and the designs are appear as relatively simple, and "open" geometric motifs.

Unlike the situation at the Far Western site of Talepakemalai, or at Nenumbo in the Santa Cruz Islands, where the importing

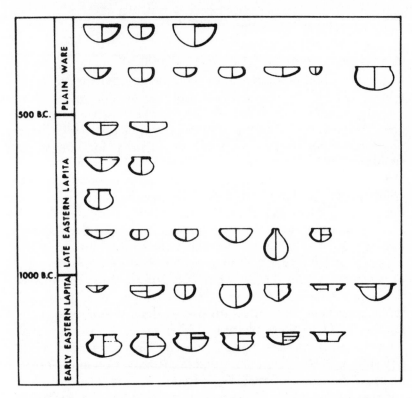

Figure 5.9   The Eastern Lapita ceramic sequence, showing changes in the main vessel forms over time. (After Green 1979a)

of pottery or the materials for its manufacture are well attested, it appears that the ceramics at Lolokoka were entirely of local manufacture. Studies of the paste and temper (Kirch 1988a:149–51) show no sign of the importing of ceramics that might have been manufactured in other island groups. Dickinson et al. (in press) have reached a similar conclusion regarding Lapita sites in the Ha'apai group of Tonga. Thus, it would appear that despite evidence from other kinds of material culture for continued external exchange relationships between Eastern Lapita communities (see chapter 8), ceramics were not a significant part of such exchanges.

Sites dating to the Late Eastern Lapita and Polynesian Plain Ware phases on Niuatoputapu (such as NT-100 and –93)

Figure 5.10   The range of reconstructed vessel forms represented in the ceramic assemblage excavated from the Early Eastern Lapita site of Lolokoka on Niuatoputapu Island. (Drawing by P. V. Kirch)

exhibit a greatly simplified range of vessel forms, primarily small bowls or cups, and large plain jars. The latter includes a variety with a narrow neck and handle, probably a water jar. Dentate-stamped decoration is entirely lacking, and the only decoration of vessels is the occasional notching of the flat rims of bowls or cups.

In the Eastern Lapita sequences, such as at Niuatoputapu and elsewhere, ceramic transformation occurred rapidly, with dentate-stamped decoration and the vessel forms carrying that decoration persisting for only a relatively short period (perhaps one or two centuries) after the region was colonized. Plain ware, however, continued to be manufactured and used for a long period, and was not completely abandoned in the Tongan and Samoan islands until around AD 400, perhaps later in some islands. In Fiji, of course, a ceramic tradition has continued until the present time, although this went through several subsequent stages of stylistic transformation.

The Loss of Pottery

Undoubtedly the most puzzling aspect of Lapita ceramics is the ultimate loss of pottery throughout so much of the Lapita world. Lapita ceramic sequences run backwards from what we have become accustomed to seeing in most parts of the world. Rather than a gradual improvement and refinement in the ceramic art, Lapita pottery starts out in the earliest sites being the most elaborate and complex, and gradually undergoes local sequences of reduction in the range of vessel forms and simplification in the design system. Finally, after a thousand years or so, the production of pottery in many islands settled by Lapita people ceases altogether, as it did in Mussau, the Reef-Santa Cruz Islands, and in Tonga and Samoa. (In some areas, of course, pottery production did continue, and the Mangaasi and related Naïa traditions of Vanuatu and New Caledonia arguably developed out of the older Lapita traditions.)

Why should something as useful as pottery drop out of the material culture inventory of not just one group of people, but of groups of people distributed throughout the southwestern Pacific? When put to students studying Pacific prehistory for the first time, the question almost invariably invokes a response that the natural resources for pottery making (clay, temper) surely must have been lacking, for the students find it hard to comprehend any other reason for abandoning such an important material item. Indeed, such an environmentally-determined explanation has been offered more than once; unfortunately, it simply will not do. Suitable potting clays and temper are found in all of the regions where pottery ceased to be made, and indeed, it can be shown that the local raw materials were known and used prior to the abandonment of ceramics.

An explanation for the loss of pottery must be situated outside of simple environmental factors and, indeed, most probably requires a model of changing social relations. In all of the sequences we have examined, it is the decorated pottery that is the first to change and undergo simplification. Keeping in mind that this decorated pottery played important roles in external exchange and probably also in house rituals involving ancestors, the transformation of Lapita decorated pottery must imply significant social changes. For one, we know that the external exchange networks underwent retraction, regionalization, and simplification over time (a topic covered in more detail in chapter 8). Thus the highly-valued position of decorated ceramics in early external exchange networks may have declined substantially over time, to the point where they became "proletarianized," or replaced by other kinds of exchange valuable (such as pigs, used in competitive feasting).

Changing external exchange networks are indeed the most likely explanation for the gradual decline and loss of the decorated component of Lapita pottery, but this does not necessarily explain the loss of the utilitarian plain wares. Why should these not have continued to be made and used? Indeed, they were manufactured for hundreds of years after decorated pottery had disappeared in the Eastern Lapita region, so it does seem that their *social* value was entirely different from the decorated wares. But eventually even these plain jars and pots were no longer part of the everyday material culture of Lapita people in various island groups. Why should this be so? There is no clear-cut answer, although we may speculate on possible reasons. One concerns the role of the plain wares in cooking. With its emphasis on the earth oven method of underground steaming, supplemented by roasting over open fires (see chapter 7), Lapita cuisine was not dependent upon the use of pottery.[33] Indeed, it is likely that ceramics always played a minor role in Lapita cookhouses, used mainly for storage of liquids, and perhaps also of dried sago flour. But liquids could just as readily be stored in other kinds of containers, especially the dried endocarps (shells) of coconuts, and in bowls carved out of various hardwoods. Boiling, too, can readily be performed by dropping heated stones (out of the earth oven) into heavy wooden bowls, so pots are not required for this function either. It is possible, then, that as the plain wares were marginal to Lapita cooking and cuisine they eventually ceased to be valued, and younger generations lost interest in learning the complex art of ceramic production from their elders. This is, of course, only a hypothetical scenario, but for the present it seems to offer the best explanation for a curious phenomenon indeed.

6

Between Land and Sea:
Houses, Settlements, and Society

"The beach" is more than a metaphor for the complex meeting and interaction among peoples and cultures along the arc of the Bismarck Sea in the second millennium BC. In a very real and material sense Lapita archaeology is about beaches, for these accumulations of coral sand and reef detritus comprise the geomorphological contexts for most Lapita sites.[1] On this fragile interface between land and sea the Lapita peoples constructed their pile dwellings and cookhouses, hauled up their canoes, processed and prepared the harvests of their gardens and the catches from their nets. Into these sands the sherds of their broken pots, the fishbones and empty shells left over from their feasts, and the dropped, misplaced, and discarded impedimenta of their lives gradually accumulated. Any attempt to write a history of Lapita culture and its everyday life must include a consideration of these beach sites: their location in relation to the surrounding island landscapes, both terrestrial and marine, their sizes, and their internal spatial arrangements of structural features, artifacts, and food refuse. From such evidence we gain knowledge of how these people interacted with and exploited their environments (that is, their ecological adaptations), as well as important clues regarding their social order as this was structured by the material world of houses and living spaces.

Sea Levels and Shorelines

In his 1979 synthesis of Lapita archaeology, Roger Green drew attention to a salient characteristic of Lapita sites, "their situation on raised coral platforms, marine terraces, and marine sand beaches from which the sea had fairly recently retreated" (1979a:32). Roughly 80 percent of all known Lapita sites are situated on geomorphologically similar environments: beach terraces constructed of unconsolidated calcareous sand and coral reef debris. These terraces are now typically situated between 2–4 m above present sea level, and thus are no longer active depositional environments. Frequently, as on Niuatoputapu Island (Tonga) or on Tikopia (southeast Solomons), these beach terraces containing Lapita deposits lie some distance inland of the modern shoreline and active beach ridge. Detailed studies of the geomorphology and lithology of these sand terraces reveal that they were deposited at periods when the sea was closer, and when relative sea level was somewhat higher.[2]

At the time his essay was written, geological understanding of Holocene sea levels in the southwestern Pacific was incomplete, and while Green could point to "first-order transgressions" (i.e., eustatically-controlled higher sea-level stands) in the period between 3,500–2,800 years BP as one causal factor for these elevated beach terraces containing Lapita pottery, he also noted the local importance of "tectonic uplift or tilting." Since 1979, a great deal of new geological and geomorphological information, along with many radiocarbon dates, have clarified the mid-to-late Holocene history of sea levels in the southwestern Pacific. The global rise of sea levels which commenced at the end of the Pleistocene Period about 10,000 years age continued in the Pacific region until about 4,000 years ago, when a high stand of between 1 and 1.5 m higher than the modern level was reached. This high stand cut solution notches in the coral escarpments of many upraised limestone islands, notches which provide important evidence of this period of higher relative sea level (plate 6.1). This high stand remained at approximately the same level for about two millennia and then fell by about 2,000 years ago – fairly rapidly by some indications – back to its modern level.[3] This eustatic sea-level fall often exposed coral reefs in front of beach terraces, subjecting the fragile coral formations to attack and erosion by the sea during cyclones and storm surges, and greatly increasing the influx of sand and coral debris into coastal sediment budgets. Consequently, many Pacific island beaches prograded rapidly in the period after 2,000 years BP. To be sure, the effects

Plate 6.1 A wave-cut notch in the upraised coral escarpment of one of the Mussau Islands. These notches were formed when the sea level was approximately 1–1.5 m higher than at present. (Photo by P. V. Kirch)

of local tectonics must also be considered in any individual case, and uplift or submergence due to such effects as point-loading of the crust or lithospheric flexure in some islands either amplified or offset the specific degree of progradation resulting from sea-level fall.[4]

This higher sea level between 4–2,000 years BP correlates closely with the period of Lapita dispersal through Melanesia and into Western Polynesia, and explains why so many Lapita sites are associated with elevated beach terraces. In some cases, as at Talepakemalai on Mussau (see below), rapid progradation of the shoreline after 2,000 years BP also led to the burial and preservation of stilt-house occupations which were originally situated over open reef flats. This higher sea level also has implications for the inshore marine environments that many Lapita communities exploited so heavily for fish and shellfish. On many islands – such as Mussau, the Arawe Islands, the Reef Islands, Tikopia, Tongatapu, Niuatoputapu, Futuna, and Ofu to name a few cases – the area of active coral reef and lagoon habitats during Lapita occupation was considerably more extensive and biotically productive than at present. For example, parts of the reef in Mussau which are sandy, tidally-exposed sea-grass flats today were subtidal coral "gardens" in the second millennium BC, supporting a much richer array of marine resources, including mollusks of all kinds, lobsters, crabs, seaweeds, eels, and the entire food chain of fish from herbivorous grazers to carnivores. There is no question that at the time of the rapid dispersal of Lapita peoples from western Melanesia into the previously-unoccupied islands of remote Oceania, the inshore marine environments of most Pacific Islands offered marvelous resource zones to these people who had developed highly sophisticated methods of fishing and gathering (see chapter 7).

Lapita Settlement Landscapes

The Melanesian beach is a "between-space," a transitional zone. Sitting on the crest of the beach berm of Eloaua Island, as I have so often done in the late afternoon, you gaze over the sea-grass covered reef flat in its tidally-changing modes, harboring a diversity of marine life providing a bountiful food source for those who know its micro-habitats. Just turning on your heel, the jungle looms overhead – its humid air rank with the smell of things rotting – and offers other resources: wood, leaves, and fibers for mats and baskets, and most important of all, the earth itself in which tuber, root, and tree crops are planted. Living out their lives on these beaches, the Lapita peoples had just such a dual outlook on their landscapes, and must have chosen the beach for their homesites precisely because they wished to live between these two worlds of land and sea.

From a careful study of the environmental settings of 28 Lapita sites, Dana Lepofsky (1988) discovered a number of traits common to Lapita settlements. First, all sites – even the few rockshelters and those that are some distance inland today – were originally on the coast at the time they were inhabited. Equally important, all sites were situated facing passages in the reef through which canoes could come and go. A majority of sites are also situated in areas where there is either a broad fringing reef, or a lagoon and barrier reef, or both. Access to the sea and its resources, while clearly significant, was not the only consideration in the choice of settlement location, for three-quarters of these settlements are also adjacent to identifiable fresh water sources (springs or streams), and every site has arable land with good soils within less than a one kilometer walk.

While some Lapita sites are located on the coasts of large, high islands (such as New Caledonia or Viti Levu) a significant number are also situated on small, offshore coral islets. This is particularly common in the Far Western and Western areas (the Bismarck Archipelago and in the eastern Solomon Islands). In the Mussau group, for example, three Lapita sites including the extensive Talepakemalai site lie on the offshore, partially-upraised coral limestone islands of Eloaua and Emananus, within easy canoe travel to the main high island of Mussau. Along the southwestern coast of New Britain, Gosden (1991a; Gosden and Webb 1994) has found several Lapita sites again sited on coral islets just off the coast. The same pattern is repeated in the Reef-Santa Cruz group of the eastern Solomons, as Roger Green discovered in the 1970s. The preference for such offshore islets may have several possible explanations, not necessarily exclusive. Certainly, the extensive reef flats and lagoons surrounding these islets provided vast and bountiful shellfish beds and fishing grounds. In the Bismarck Archipelago, a more important consideration may have been that the main high islands were already inhabited and territorially claimed, while the offshore islets were underutilized. A further consideration could have been the presence of mosquito-borne malaria, and a desire to avoid the thick swarms of mosquitoes in the humid jungle (see chapter 4). Once the Lapita dispersal proceeded beyond the eastern Solomons, however, this proclivity to settle offshore islets seems to have waned, and most settlements – while retaining their location on beaches – were positioned on the coasts of the main (and previously uninhabited) islands.

The Scale of Settlement: Villages to Hamlets

Having explored Lapita sites from the macroscopic viewpoint of their localization within larger island landscapes, I turn to the sites themselves. *Size* is one fundamental measure of an archaeological site, and a useful starting point. Some might naively assume that the size (in this case, specifically, the area in square meters) of an archaeological site is a straight forward matter to determine, and that basic data on site area would be readily available for all Lapita localities. Unfortunately, such is not the case. On many sites, dense rainforest obscures the extent of surface pottery and midden, while other sites have been reduced in size due to coastal erosion. In many of the earlier excavations, determination of site size was not an objective (the goals were instead usually limited excavation to obtain a stratigraphic sequence).

Reliable data on site area are available for 36 Lapita sites.[5] Although data from many sites are missing, the size range indicated has several important implications. Two-thirds of the sites are smaller than 5,000 m² in area, and comprise a discrete size cluster, while another eight sites (22 percent of the sample) fall in a cluster between 9–15,000 m². Finally, there are just three very large sites, especially the Talepakemalai site in Mussau that covers at least 82,000 m².

What do these size ranges imply for the kinds of former settlements they represent? We can gain a rough idea by thinking in terms of a typical ethnographically-documented Oceanic house as taking up something like 50 m² of floor space,[6] but also surrounded by at least another 500 m² of yard or open-air activity areas, since in these tropical societies much work takes place on open spaces surrounding the house. Thus, the smaller-sized Lapita settlements (ca. 500–5,000 m² in area) might have incorporated anywhere from one to about ten dwelling houses and associated open space with subsidiary structures (cookhouses, canoe sheds, racks, etc.). We might, then, characterize such settlements as *hamlets*, small clusters of a few houses inhabited by several household groups. The somewhat larger-sized site cluster (ca. 9–15,000 m² in area) might have incorporated anywhere from 15 up to perhaps 30 households, and would begin to approximate what we may call a *village*. An unusually large site such as Talepakemalai might conceivably have housed 150 or more households, but Lapita settlements of this scale were clearly few.

Three Lapita Communities

In their environmental settings and internal features, Lapita sites share much in common, including their highly characteristic emplacement on coastal terraces between land and sea. Yet within this overall patterning there is variability, and even minor differences can yield important clues about the practice of everyday life within Lapita communities. Summary statistics and diagrams – while essential to archaeological analysis – fail to transform these deposits of potsherds and broken tools into vivid historical reconstructions, as the homesteads of real people who structured their domestic spaces in distinctly cultural ways. To explore in a more particular and intimate fashion the commonly-shared, as well as unique, aspects of Lapita sites, I turn to three localities for a closer consideration. My choice was guided by three objectives: (1) to select sites spanning both far Western and Eastern Lapita examples; (2) to represent both large villages and smaller hamlets; and (3) to focus on sites where the excavators consciously sought to obtain information about the internal organization of space.[7]

Talepakemalai (Mussau Islands)

Eloaua Island, the largest of several upraised coral limestone islets encircling a small lagoon off the southern tip of Mussau, is the setting of the largest Lapita village yet discovered, Talepakemalai (figure 6.1).[8] In the indigenous Mussau language, Talepakemalai means "under the *malai* (*Spondias dulcis*) tree," invoking an imagined scene of houses shaded by the magnificent towering limbs of the *vi*-apple, one of the largest Melanesian fruit trees.[9] *Malai* trees certainly grew in the vicinity of the Lapita village founded here about 1,500 BC and occupied for nearly one thousand years, as testified by their spiny seeds recovered in large numbers from the Talepakemalai sediments (see chapter 7). But the Eloaua landscape has been dynamically transformed over the past 3,500 years, and only through careful geomorphological and paleoenvironmental studies can we reconstruct with some accuracy the setting of Talepakemalai when it was a thriving settlement.

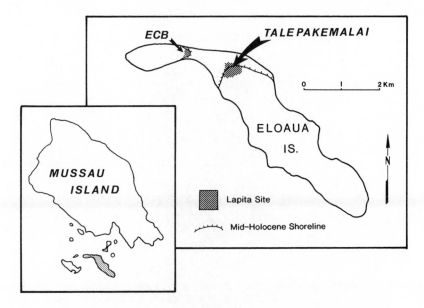

Figure 6.1 Plan of Eloaua Island with inset of the Mussau Islands, showing the position of the Talepakemalai site in relation to the mid-Holocene shoreline, and to site ECB.

The higher sea level at about 1,500 BC had separated Eloaua into two islands separated by a shallow, sand-covered reef flat about 1 km wide. The Talepakemalai settlement occupied both the beach terrace and the adjacent reef flat at the northwestern tip of the main island, while a much smaller Lapita community (a site called Etakosarai, see appendix) straddled a narrow arc of sand at the eastern tip of the smaller islet. The inhabitants of these two settlements looked across the open water of the reef flat at each other, and it is not difficult to envision canoes carrying food, artifacts, and "gossip" between these closely linked settlements.[10] When the Pacific Ocean fell to its modern level around 2,000 years ago, the Eloaua shoreline prograded rapidly and the two separated islets were eventually joined by a narrow neck of calcareous sand and coral debris, today cloaked in thick rainforest.

When I began excavations at Talepakemalai in 1985 during the Lapita Homeland Project, the site was thought to consist

Plate 6.2   The large cylinder stand (see figure 5.5) as originally exposed in excavations into the water-logged deposits at Area B, in the Talepakemalai site, Mussau Islands. (Photo by P. V. Kirch)

of a typically shallow cultural deposit, confined to an elevated beach terrace about 2 m above present sea level. A former shoreline could be traced as a distinct 1 m drop in the topography, and potsherds and shell midden were visible everywhere on this terrace inland of the old beach. In order to probe the exact limits of the pottery distribution in relation to the old shoreline, I excavated a series of test pits along systematic transects across this geomorphic feature. This transect included a test pit about 40 m north and seaward of where we had inferred the beach to have been situated at about 1,500 BC. Expecting at most a handful of water-rolled potsherds in this excavation well beyond the old beach, I was startled and initially puzzled when at a depth of about 50 cm we encountered a heavy concentration of beautifully-decorated Lapita sherds with no evidence of erosion (plate 6.2), along with large obsidian

Plate 6.3   The areal excavation of Area B, in the Talepakemalai site, at the conclusion of the 1986 field season. The dark objects protruding from the floor of the excavation are the anaerobically-preserved bases of wooden posts, which once supported a stilt-house over a shallow lagoon in this location. The white hoses were connected to pumps used to keep the excavation from flooding. (Photo by P. V. Kirch)

flakes, a drilled pig tusk pendant, two complete cone-shell rings, and other artifacts. This undisturbed deposit was associated with the upper limit of the island's brackish-water lens (technically referred to as the Ghyben-Herzberg aquifer). As we trowelled downwards into the waterlogged sands, bailing the brackish water with our buckets, the Lapita pottery and artifacts continued to a depth of a little more than 1 m below surface, where we encountered a concentration of branch coral fingers and rubble indicating the former reef flat. Over the next few weeks and in two subsequent field seasons, I expanded this excavation, and was rewarded with the discovery – for the first time in Lapita archaeology – of a settlement of stilt or pole-supported houses, constructed out over the reef flat. The water-logged, anaerobic conditions in the site had preserved the bases of the wooden posts, many still bearing the marks of adz blades on their sharpened tips (plate 6.3).

Through our excavation strategy of combining systematic transect test pits with larger areal exposures, we were able to reconstruct in broad terms the internal spatial structure of this large Lapita village, which in time covered some 82,000 m². Talepakemalai was divided into two main zones, one on the dry beach terrace, the other consisting of an alignment of stilt-house structures paralleling the beach between 10–50 m offshore.[11] While the large suite of radiocarbon dates indicates that both zones were occupied contemporaneously, they reveal highly distinctive architectural patterns as well as artifact assemblages. To begin with the beach terrace, the archaeological deposits here are shallow and have been thoroughly disturbed by centuries of yam gardening on the anthropogenically-enriched midden soils. Thus, such features as earth ovens or post molds that might once have indicated the presence of structures have been largely obliterated, and it is virtually impossible to say with any precision how the Lapita people organized this space. However, the beach-terrace middens yield almost exclusively plain ware pottery, primarily from large globular jars with narrow necks and strongly everted rims. These jars, some of which have a red-slip on the exterior, have relatively thin walls and would have been well suited either to cooking (boiling) or to storing liquids or even such materials as sago flour. The beach terrace deposits also yielded obsidian flakes, high densities of shell midden, and fishbone, but relatively few other kinds of portable artifacts except for rings of cone-shell, in various stages of manufacture.

In contrast, the zone of stilt-supported houses lying immediately offshore is marked by a deposit containing not only plain ware jars, but also a variety of beautifully decorated dentate-stamped ceramics, including open bowls supported on pedestals or ring-feet, cylinder stands, flat-bottomed dishes, and other forms. Clearly, whatever functions the elaborately-decorated pottery served, these were utilized in the spatial context of the off-shore stilt-houses, and not on the beach terrace. In addition to the pottery, the stilt-house zone excavations yielded a broad array of other kinds of portable artifacts including shell "ornaments" or exchange valuables of various types (shell rings, beads, pendants, etc.), adzes, abrading tools, vegetable peeling knives and scrapers, fishhooks and the debris from their manufacture, and even an exquisitely-carved human figure of porpoise bone (frontispiece).

Reconstructing the stilt-houses themselves is a difficult task, since all that remains as evidence of a once complex and elaborate world of houses poised above water is now a palimpsest of sherds and artifacts, along with the half-rotted bases of wooden posts and associated stakes, shell and bone midden, anaerobically-preserved seeds and other plants, and burned oven stones. In a 28 m² excavation (Area B) we exposed two sides of a large stilt-house dwelling, with 33 posts and stakes (with diameters ranging from 2–20 cm), but complete exposure of this structure was well beyond our project's means. Posts belonging to many other such structures were revealed by test pits spanning an area of at least 10,000 m². That these stilt-houses suspended over water contained earth ovens is indicated by the heavy density of burned coral oven stones which were tossed into the shallow waters around the houses after use. Such ovens continue to be used on raised structures in Mussau today, and are confined by rectangular earth-filled boxes set in the middle of the house floors. Some of the Eloaua villagers still construct and occupy over-water stilt houses, as shown in plate 6.4.

As revealed by the palimpsest of artifacts and midden that accumulated beneath these wooden structures, a wide variety of activities took place on the platforms suspended above the warm lagoon waters. Preparation and cooking of shellfish, fish, turtles, birds, porpoise, and occasional pigs as well as of a wide range of root, tuber, and tree crops certainly must have consumed substantial time and energy. Large quantities of debris and unfinished rejects in *Conus* and *Trochus* shell speak to hours spent in manufacturing rings, beads, and fishhooks from these shells, using coral abraders and probably aided by heated sticks and abrasive lianas. The obsidian flakes, along with those of chert, suggest fine wood-working. In addition to these commonplace and repeated aspects of everyday life, there were unquestionably periods of time devoted to events of a more symbolically and semiotically-charged nature. These socially significant events are archaeologically signaled by certain pottery vessels, especially open bowls supported on pedestals, and cylinder stands, both bearing intricately-wrought human face

*Plate 6.4   A modern stilt-house along the shore of Eloaua Island
gives some impression of what the Lapita stilt houses at
Talepakemalai may have looked like. The walls and roof are of
leaf thatch, and a narrow plank walkway connects the house to
the beach terrace. (Photo by P. V. Kirch)*

motifs. Microprobe analysis of the clays from which these pots
were made indicates that most of them had not been made
locally, but rather were imported from a number of other
Lapita communities within the Bismarck Archipelago.[12] Confronting the timeless gaze of an almond-eyed, long-nosed Lapita
face staring up from the curved surface of a 3,500-year old
Lapita plate, I have more than once lamented that we shall
never fully comprehend either the social matrix in which these
icons functioned, nor their rich symbolism.

The village at Talepakemalai spanned the lives of many generations of Lapita folk, perhaps as many as 40 generations if
one averages 20 years per generation over the approximately
800 years indicated by radiocarbon dates. Certainly over this
period from about 1,500 BC to perhaps 700 BC the village
continually changed in details of area, configuration, architecture, and use. After about 500 BC when sea level began to drop
and the shoreline commenced its seaward migration, the zone

of stilt-houses was gradually shifted to keep them over open water, as the abandoned posts of former dwellings were swallowed up by the accumulating sands. Eventually, the village was abandoned entirely, although its occupants merely shifted their habitations to other parts of Eloaua Island, and the organically-enriched midden soils of the beach terrace became prime yam-planting grounds. These yam gardens, however, have retained in local toponyms a hint of their former residential function: Talepakemalai, "under the *malai* tree," echoes yet across a gulf of time.

Nenumbo (Reef Islands)

The warm, salty water splashed about us as Lawrence Foanaota, curator of the Solomon Islands Museum, and I waded thigh-deep across the sand and sea-grass covered reef flat between Nananiembuli and Ngangaua Islands on a humid April morning in 1977. En route to Nendö from Vanikoro Island, we had decided to visit Roger Green's Nenumbo site on Ngangaua Island, while the *Bona* loaded copra in Mohawk Bay. I had visited the site briefly in 1971, not long after Roger had completed his first season of excavations, and was certain I could locate it again. As we strode up the coral sand beach of Ngangaua Island toward the small cluster of houses with raised floors perched on stilts and located on the beach terrace under shading coconuts and *Calophyllum* trees, I pondered how different this modern landscape may have been to that which had enmeshed the little Lapita hamlet now labeled RF-2 in the Solomon Islands Museum register.

The higher sea level in the western Pacific during the second millennium BC certainly would have affected the reef-lagoon environment, a major food resource zone for the Nenumbo Lapita people, and this is borne out by studies of the fish and shellfish content of the site itself.[13] Extensive mangrove swamps that fringe the Reef Islands today were then absent, and the modern sand and sea grass flats were probably active coral reefs (not yet tidally exposed), supporting a much higher diversity and biomass of marine life. While Ngangaua is a small island of only about 3 km², its slightly upraised interior is blanketed in fertile soil now greatly enriched by volcanic ash falls from nearby Tinakula volcano. With a rich marine environment extending out from their beach, and a fertile plateau suitable to tree and root cropping in the island's interior, the Lapita people who built their cluster of houses at Nenumbo sometime between 1,187–926 BC had chosen a location quite similar to that of their Mussau "relatives" at Talepakemalai.[14] More than 2,000 km from their ancestral homeland in the Bismarck Archipelago, they sought the familiar landscape of small offshore islets and rich reefs in which to situate their *landnam*.[15] The large rainforest-clad island of Nendö (Santa Cruz) could be seen looming darkly on the southern horizon, where other small Lapita communities – with whom the Nenumbo people were in regular contact via exchange relations – had been established on similar offshore coral islets around the coast.[16]

Roger Green's careful field strategy of intensive surface collection and plotting of potsherds, obsidian flakes, and other artifacts over the entire Nenumbo site, followed by extensive areal excavations totaling 153.5 m^2, provided the necessary data for a detailed spatial analysis of this Lapita hamlet.[17] Based on the scatter of surface sherds, Nenumbo covered not much more than 1,000 m^2, or an area about 55 m long by 26 m wide, placing it near the small end of the Lapita site range. Both the artifact distribution pattern, and the subsurface post molds, pits, ovens, and other features exposed by excavation reveal the presence of a rectangular structure in the approximate center of the site (figure 6.2). This house had dimensions of about 7 by 10 m with large posts supporting a central ridgepole. The high concentration of midden and trash within the building space, and the presence of small posts that may have been "stages for storage or supports for a raised floor," suggest a wooden floor elevated above the ground surface. Such an elevated floor evokes the possibility of a continuation of the original Lapita stilt-house architectural design, as at the Talepakemalai and Apalo sites. South of this main, central house are a series of overlapping concentrations of artifacts, along with many small post molds that Sheppard and Green suggest "are the result of a palimpsest of small, comparatively impermanent structures." Also in this part of the site were found stone-filled earth ovens, and a large deep pit that was probably a well tapping the islet's fresh-water lens.[18] A sharp,

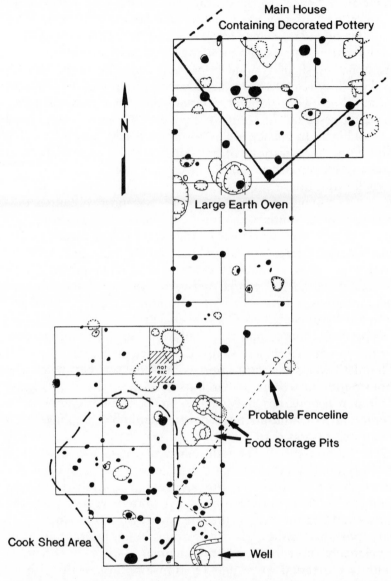

Figure 6.2   Plan of the Nenumbo site excavations, showing the inferred location of the main dwelling structure and other features. (After Sheppard and Green 1991)

right-angle "edge" to the artifact distribution along the south-eastern part of the site suggests the presence of a fence or wooden boundary demarcating this area. Interpretation of these architectural data is enhanced by detailed spatial analyses of fishbone and shellfish midden, pottery, and stone tools. The fish and mollusk remains are concentrated primarily in the southern zone, along with globular pots and jars that were probably cooking vessels.[19] In contrast, the central house is associated with a higher frequency of flat-bottomed dishes (serving vessels), and with concentrations of both obsidian and chert flakes and cores (both retouched/utilized pieces, and debitage). Thus, the large central house was a focus of food consumption, and perhaps some limited food preparation,[20] but most cooking activities took place south of the house, in the smaller, impermanent sheds or structures with their earth ovens. Most activities requiring the use of stone tools, such as gravers and utilized flakes, took place in or around the central house. Nenumbo displays a classic spatial differential between residential and cooking activity areas, a pervasive pattern among a great many ethnographically-documented Oceanic societies.

The Nenumbo community could only have been a fraction of the size of that which occupied Talepakemalai, and the term "hamlet" seems the most appropriate label for the single large house and cluster of smaller huts or sheds on this southeast Solomon Islands beach. Whereas Talepakemalai comprised a community of multiple households, Nenumbo may have been inhabited by less than a score of people, perhaps just a single extended household. The tight clustering of radiocarbon dates from Nenumbo suggests that the settlement's duration was not more than one or two centuries, a few generations in human terms. Careful reconstruction of the pottery vessels from the excavated central part of the site reveal a total of about 105 jars, pots, and dishes, also conforming to an interpretation of a relatively short-lived and small hamlet. Aspects of this community's external exchange relationships are dealt with in chapter 8.

Lolokoka (Niuatoputapu Island)

Our third community in this selected sampling of Lapita sites takes us to the eastern margins of the Lapita world, where at the close of the second millennium BC one group of ocean voyagers hauled their canoes up on the leeward, western beach of Niuatoputapu Island. At a place that would come to be called Lolokoka, "under the *koka* (*Bischofia javanica*) tree," one of the most remote and distant Lapita outposts was established.[21] This was a different kind of beach from those at Takepakemalai and Nenumbo, for it did not front an offshore coral islet. Behind the beach at Lolokoka – and the narrow sandy terrace – rose the rugged volcanic ridge of Niuatoputapu itself. Originally this ridge was heavily forested, prime land for shifting cultivations. Here, in the Eastern Lapita world beyond the vast ocean gap separating Fiji and the eastern Solomons, there were no prior inhabitants, no "land people" with prior claims to the fertile lands behind the beach. On Niuatoputapu, as with contemporaneous settlements at Mulifanua and To'aga (Samoa), Asipani (Futuna), and in the Tongan archipelago, the Lapita colonists were truly "sea people" and "land people" in one. In these Samoan and Tongan archipelagoes, the Lapita descendants would establish patterns of interior land use ultimately setting Polynesian agricultural practices off quite distinctly from those in most of Melanesia.

The local environment of Lolokoka has changed dramatically with sea-level lowering, and with the cumulative effects of three millennia of intensive human land use. Niuatoputapu lies on the edge of the Tonga Trench, the tectonically-active boundary between the Fijian and Pacific Plates. In Niuatoputapu, the effect of a lowered sea-level after about 2,000 years BP was compounded by tectonic uplift, so that the extensive reef flats and sandy lagoon floors of Lapita times now form a large apron of low-lying terrain, in places two km wide.[22] It is relatively easy to locate the older shoreline, with its dense concentration of pottery-bearing shell middens immediately inland on the older beach terrace. When the Lapita colonists first arrived at the close of the second millennium BC, the island's land area was much smaller than today (about 4.9 as opposed to 15.2 km²), consisting of the volcanic ridge, surrounded by a narrow calcareous beach terrace upon which their dwellings were erected (figure 6.3). Conversely, the area of productive reef and lagoon was far more extensive in Lapita times, about 21.5 km² opposed to the roughly 10.5 km² of inshore marine habitats exploitable today.

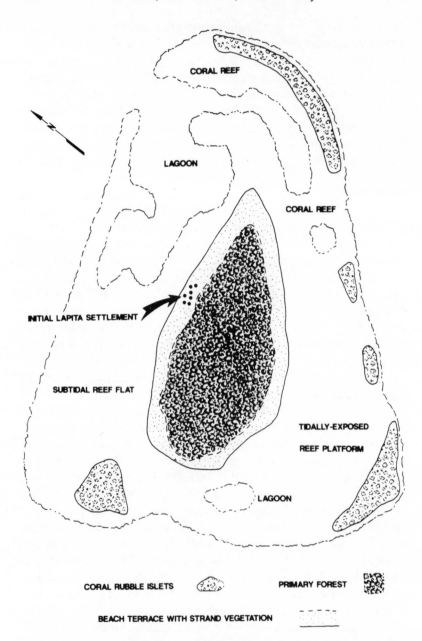

Figure 6.3   Reconstructed paleogeographic map of Niuatoputapu Island, showing the location of the initial Lapita colonization site, Lolokoka. (After Kirch 1988a)

Although pottery-bearing middens completely encircle the volcanic interior of Niuatoputapu, most of these occupations date to the later Polynesian Plain Ware phase which developed out of Lapita. The island's founding settlement, indicated by the presence of classic dentate-stamped pottery, was at Lolokoka, in many respects the most ecologically favorable locality on the island.[23] Situated mid-way along the protected lee shore, the Lapita community at Lolokoka looked out over a wide expanse of reefs and a lagoon teeming with fish and shellfish, while the volcanic hillslopes rising immediately inland of the village were ideal for both tree and root crops.

The Lolokoka site, along with the later plain ware pottery middens of the elevated beach terrace, exemplify a common phenomenon of Lapita sites throughout the southwestern Pacific: extensive disturbance and reworking through later gardening activities. Several centuries of midden dumping, charcoal rakeouts from earth ovens, and other human activities here transformed the calcareous soil of the beach terrace into a rich, organic loam, highly suited to the cultivation of yams (particularly the Lesser Yam, *Dioscorea esculenta*), elephant ear taro (*Alocasia macrorrhiza*), and bananas. In the last two thousand years, as the island's shoreline prograded and occupations were shifted seaward, the old Lapita village sites with their anthropogenically-enriched soils became prime gardening lands. The Niuatoputapu people call this zone of dark gray organic loam the *fasifasi'ifeo*, after the numerous fingers of branch coral and shell midden littering the surface (along with potsherds). For the archaeologist, this transformation of land use has major consequences, for the relatively shallow Lapita deposits are heavily reworked and disturbed due to the repeated penetration and churning of the soil by digging sticks used to plant and harvest yam and aroid root crops. At the Lolokoka site, much of the primary deposit has been reworked in this manner, and intact cultural features are found only when these were deep enough to penetrate the basal sandy terrace, and thus escape later disturbance (plate 6.5).

Excavating at the Lolokoka site in 1976, we used a combined archaeological strategy of stratified random sampling to first define the extent and distribution of Early Eastern Lapita ceramics over the site, followed by expanded excavations in

Plate 6.5   Excavations in progress at the Lolokoka Lapita site on Niuatoputapu Island, in 1976. Intact features were exposed where they extended into the underlying, undisturbed sands of the beach terrace, beneath the extensively-reworked upper garden zone. (Photo by P. V. Kirch)

areas where undisturbed basal features were best preserved. This included an areal block of 24 m² in the area of highest concentration of dentate-stamped pottery.

The initial occupation at Lolokoka probably covered an area of about 3,000 m², three times the size of the Nenumbo hamlet, but still within the smaller size range of Lapita sites. Although the internal structure of Lolokoka is not as clear as that of Nenumbo, a similar division into residential and cooking activity spaces is suggested by the patterns of artifact distribution. Obsidian flakes and decorated potsherds are concentrated in a seaward zone, suggesting that several dwelling houses (two post molds indicate the presence of structures) may have been aligned parallel to the beach, with a zone of cookhouses inland.

Behind the putative dwelling-house zone one of our excavations exposed a deep pit, which seems to have been a well dug in order to tap the fresh-water lens, just as at Nenumbo. This well was surrounded by a high concentration of potsherds of a distinctive type of narrow-necked, globular jar with handles, probably for carrying and storing water.[24] Other features that escaped the later ravages of gardening at Lolokoka, and were exposed by our excavations, included several earth ovens filled with fire-cracked rock, and trash pits including one containing the partial skeleton of a pig.

From the evidence unearthed at Lolokoka, this far Eastern Lapita outpost was not unlike its contemporaneous sister site of Nenumbo in the Reef Islands. Both were small hamlets, constructed on low beach terraces nestled between reefs providing fish and shellfish, and fertile agricultural soils. In both cases, the occupants solved the problem of a lack of streams by digging shallow wells into the beach terrace to reach the brackish but drinkable aquifer under their feet. That the Lapita people knew of the Ghyben-Herzberg aquifer and how to tap it is significant, for this would be a key in the cultural armory required to settle the atolls of Remote Oceania.[25] The Nenumbo and Lolokoka people also organized their settlements into discrete activity zones, separating cooking from other residential functions in a manner that is widely reflected in many ethnographic Oceanic societies. In both communities, their meals were cooked in earth ovens using volcanic oven stones, a practice with implications for their culinary complex (see chapter 7).

The Proto Oceanic House and its Transformations[26]

The three communities just described illustrate not only the range of variation within Lapita settlements, they encapsulate a major change in the nature of settlements associated with the Lapita diaspora into Remote Oceania. Villages made up of stilt-houses constructed over shallow tidal flats – as with Talepakemalai – seem to have been the earlier form of Lapita settlement, and thus far are known only from the Far Western region.[27] In addition to Talepakemalai, such stilt-house settlements have been uncovered in the Arawe Islands, where Chris Gosden excavated similar waterlogged deposits with preserved post bases (Gosden and Webb 1994). Moreover, dense scatters of Lapita pottery on exposed reef flats at Kreslo (Specht 1991), and off the coast of Buka Island in the Solomons (Wickler 1990:145) apparently also derive from such stilt-house occupations.[28] It is probable that some of the other Lapita sites in the Bismarcks, which are today situated in low-lying, sandy cay depositional environments (such as Boduna Island near Talasea [Ambrose and Gosden 1991], and sites in the Duke of York Islands [Lilley 1991a]) were also stilt-house occupations.[29]

As the Nenumbo and Lolokoka sites indicate, however, the Far Western Lapita pattern of stilt-house settlements did not carry over into the Western and Eastern Lapita regions. Likewise, sites in New Caledonia are dry-land occupations. Thus, a pattern of occupation on beach ridges seems to have developed as Lapita people expanded into the previously-unoccupied islands of Remote Oceania. At least two factors may have influenced this change in settlement patterns. First, as I observed in chapter 4, constructing houses over reef flats and away from the mosquito-ridden jungle may have been one strategy for avoiding the deleterious effects of malaria. Second, as the Lapita people expanded in Remote Oceania they encountered islands with no indigenous human occupants to claim the land – or the beach – as their own. Thus, Lapita colonizers could establish hamlets and villages unchallenged on the land itself.

While our archaeological data on Lapita settlements are indeed rich, we can also benefit from a careful consideration of Proto Austronesian and Proto Oceanic house terms, as provided by Green and Pawley (in press), for these provide important clues as to the kinds of houses and their functions in early Austronesian and Oceanic societies. In a classic article on the methods of semantic reconstruction, Robert Blust (1987) demonstrated that early Austronesian peoples had at least five terms relating to houses or settlements. (1) Proto Austronesian *Rumaq*, with reflexes in all of the main subgroups of Austronesian languages, probably referred to the main "dwelling house." (2) *Balay*, a Proto Malayo-Polynesian innovation,[30] whose reflexes in modern Austronesian languages sometimes refer to dwellings (as in certain Philippine languages, and in Fijian and Polynesian languages), but may also refer to yam storage sheds, garden sheds, or public meeting houses. Blust thought that *balay originally referred to a public "meeting house," but Green and Pawley (in press) convincingly argue that its original meaning was that of an "open sided building," whose functions may have been various. (3) *KamaliR, another Proto Malayo-Polynesian innovation, referring to granaries or storehouses in the Philippines, but to "men's houses" in the Oceanic region. Given the evidence for early rice cultivation among Austronesian peoples, an original gloss of "granary" seems well supported (see Fox 1993:12). (4) *Lepaw, a Proto Austronesian term, has occasioned some controversy over its original meaning, although Fox (1993:11) suggests that it may have subsumed "the notion of an 'alternative dwelling,' one that could be used for a variety of purposes such as hunting, gardening, marketing, and even fishing." This term, however, dropped out of the speech of those Austronesian people who moved into the Near Oceanic region, and has no Oceanic language reflexes. (5) The final term, *banua, also a Proto Malayo-Polynesian innovation, has reflexes throughout the modern Oceanic languages. It seems best glossed not as a specific kind of structure, but rather as "village, settlement, or inhabited territory."

If we look more closely at the distribution of the four terms that are reflected among modern Oceanic languages, we find some significant patterns. Throughout most of Austronesian-speaking Melanesia, and in Micronesia, the term for main "dwelling house" is a reflex of *Rumaq (e.g., Arosi *ruma*, Pohnpei *ihmw*). Moreover, as Blust has discussed, there is a strong association between *Rumaq and posts (Proto Austronesian *turu). It is not unreasonable, then, to suppose that the Proto Oceanic speakers who occupied the early Far Western Lapita settlements such as Talepakemalai called their stilt-house dwellings by the Proto Oceanic term *Rumaq. In Fiji, Rotuma, and Polynesian, however, reflexes of Proto Oceanic *Rumaq are lacking, and are replaced by reflexes of Proto Oceanic *pale (from Proto Malayo-Polynesian *balay, see above). Examples are Fijian *vale*, Samoan *fale*, and Hawaiian *hale*, all meaning the principal dwelling house. This major semantic shift can only be explained as an innovation among the early

Eastern Lapita settlers of the Fiji-Tonga-Samoa region, and may well correlate with the change in settlement pattern from stilt-houses over tidal reef flats, to on-land beach ridge settlements. In other words, the Lapita colonizers of Fiji and nearby islands abandoned the practice of building stilt houses as their main dwellings, instead constructing houses with sand or gravel-paved floors directly on the beach terraces.[31] This new house form was an adaptation of the older Proto Oceanic *pale*, or open-sided shed, and hence this term came to be applied to dwelling houses.

The Proto Malayo-Polynesian terms *lepaw* and *kamaliR* also display significant distributions with respect to Oceanic languages. *Lepaw* simply dropped out of use prior to the Oceanic expansion into Near Oceania, for it has no reflexes in this branch of Austronesian. *KamaliR* which, like *lepaw*, may in Proto Malayo-Polynesian have denoted some form of granary or storehouse, was part of the Proto Oceanic vocabulary of house terms, and has witnesses in only a limited number of Melanesian languages (e.g., Titan *kamal*, Banks Islands *gamal*, S. E. Ambrym *nemel*). In these Oceanic languages, the word invariably refers to some kind of "men's house" or "clubhouse," suggesting that there was an important semantic shift in the meaning of Proto Oceanic *kamaliR* from its older usage as a granary. The shift is surely explained in part by the abandonment of rice or other cereal cultivation by the early Oceanic peoples (see chapter 7). Jim Fox (1993:12), as well as Green and Pawley (in press), speculate that one function of the *kamaliR* granary or storehouse was as a men's gathering place.[32] As Green and Pawley argue, "unlike [Proto Malayo-Polynesian] speakers, the [Proto Oceanic] speech community did not cultivate grain crops and it is possible that in [Proto Oceanic] the social function of *kamaliR* became central."

The final term in Blust's list (Proto Malayo-Polynesian *banua*) is widely attested in Oceanic languages, and can be firmly reconstructed to Proto Oceanic, *panua*. The semantic values attached to Oceanic reflexes of *panua* vary considerably, but generally focus on the notion of "land, country, place," and of the people associated with such geographic spaces. To the Lapita people *panua* probably invoked an image of the inhabited territory surrounding and encompassing a settlement, one's "native land".

Table 6.1 Proto Oceanic house terminology

Proto Oceanic term	Probable meaning
*bou	large cross-beam or center-post, supporting the roof
*dridri	post
*kataman	doorway, doorpost
*kaso	rafter
*so(g,k)a(ng)	crossbeam
*pupung-an	ridgepole
*qatop	sago leaf thatch
*raun	thatch
*saja(q)	prepare thatching materials; begin to thatch a roof
*kapit	secure thatch with battens
*gabʷari(n)	area underneath a house
*patar	platform or stage within a house
*para	rack or shelf above hearth for storing or smoking food
*tete	bridge or ladder leading into a house
*rapu(R)	hearth or fireplace
*qumun	oven made with hot stones; earth oven
*giRu or *guRi	pit or well
*lua(ng)	pit, for cooking, food storage, or refuse disposal
*ba(l,R)a	fence, wall, enclosure
*bai	fence, boundary marker

Source: R. Green and A. Pawley (in press)

In addition to these general terms for kinds of houses and settlements, there is a rich vocabulary of Proto Oceanic terms for the structural components of houses, and for associated features of settlements. Some of these are listed in table 6.1. These reconstructed terms help us to flesh out those parts of the early Lapita houses which are not evident in the archaeological record, such as the complex wooden superstructures of posts, crossbeams, rafters, and ridgepole, covered over with thatch made of sago palm or other leaves. Climbing over a narrow walkway or up a ladder to enter a Lapita stilt-house, we would doubtless have seen shelves or platforms within, for sleeping and storage. A hearth for light and some kinds of cooking often had a rack suspended above in which fish or nuts could be smoked (as is still done in many Oceanic societies today). Earth ovens, pits, wells, and fences are among the auxiliary features associated with these early settlements.

Houses with Ancestors: Lapita Social Landscapes

From both archaeological and linguistic data we can achieve a richly-textured portrait of Lapita settlement patterns, in terms of the range of physical structures and how they were constructed, and of their functions. But as anthropologists from Bourdieu to Lévi-Strauss have increasingly recognized, the "built environment" does not merely provide shelter from the elements. The architectonic arrangement of space in human societies is fundamental to the way people construct their social lives, providing the *habitus* in which the practices of everyday life are played out.[33] A discussion of Lapita architecture and spatial organization should, thus, naturally lead us to ask more difficult questions concerning the Lapita social world. How did the people who occupied these houses categorize themselves as social beings? What was their system of kinship terminology, and how (if at all) did they reckon descent? Were they hierarchically organized? Did they have a moiety structure? Questions such as these are exceedingly difficult (if not impossible) to address on strictly archaeological evidence, but are not necessarily intractable to the methods of historical linguistics, combined with careful comparative ethnography. I will end this chapter by briefly considering some evidence for Proto Oceanic kinship and social organization. We must be cautious, of course, for research in these domains is new and the methods need refinement, but we can at least outline some hypotheses that may help to drive future research.

Kinship is fundamental to understanding any social organization, and there have been several efforts to reconstruct and interpret early Austronesian kinship terminologies (Blust 1980, 1994; Fox 1988, 1994; Marshall 1984). Most scholars agree that from at least Proto Malayo-Polynesian times, distinctions within Ego's generation were made through a set of eight kinship terms (Fox 1994:130). These terms, which consist of related pairs, encoded important distinctions between gender, age, and affinity (marriage). Of particular note is the distinction between older and younger siblings (in the Proto Malayo-Polynesian contrast set *kaka/*huaji), an aspect of kinship that is quite pervasive among the Oceanic-speaking societies today. From this evidence, we may hypothesize that birth order was an important social criterion among Lapita peoples. Above and below Ego's generation we also have reconstructed Proto Austronesian or Proto Malayo-Polynesian terms for father, father's brother, father's sister, mother, for grandmother and grandfather, for child, and for grandchild (Zorc 1994:559–60).

In one of the first attempts to reconstruct Proto Oceanic terms for social categories, Andrew Pawley (1982) proposed that there were two terms for hereditary chiefship. Subsequent work by Frantisek Lichtenberk (1986) has slightly modified Pawley's original reconstructions, but still supports the notion of two key terms: Proto Oceanic *tala(m)pat, meaning "big, great person," and *qa adiki meaning "oldest child."[34] As Lichtenberk observes, "oldest children enjoy a privileged position" in numerous Oceanic societies, an aspect of Austronesian social organization with presumably ancient roots, given the birth-order distinction noted earlier. In the formalization of the terms *tala(m)pat and *qa adiki in Proto Oceanic society, however, we may be witnessing an early form of hereditary leadership, in which rank or authority was passed from one generation to the senior offspring of the next. It would be an over-interpretation to say that this is evidence for chiefship in Lapita society, but some of the underlying concepts of later Oceanic chiefdoms (such as differential access to *mana* or spiritual power, according to birth order and succession) may well have been developing at this time.[35]

Most importantly, can we say anything of the way that Proto Oceanic or Lapita people organized themselves into groups? Social anthropologists have long been aware that Oceanic peoples do not organize themselves into strict unilinear descent groups, but rather tend to have more flexible, cognatic (sometimes called "ambilinear" or "non-unilinear") systems of descent reckoning (Goodenough 1955; Davenport 1959). Only recently, however, has anthropological attention been focused on the fact that for many Austronesian-speaking societies, the indigenous term for a such a cognatic kin group is often the same as the term for "house." Following an innovative proposal by Claude Lévi-Strauss (1982) that certain ethnographic regions could be characterized as "*sociétés à maison*,"[36] Austronesianists have now begun to explore the concept of "house societies," finding it highly productive as an organizing principle for Austronesian social organization (Carsten and Hugh-Jones 1995; Fox 1993; Waterson 1990, 1993, 1995). Fox summarizes the importance of "houses" among Austronesian peoples as follows:

> Throughout the Austronesian-speaking world, houses are given great prominence. . . . Although a house has a physical referent, the category of "house" may be used abstractly to distinguish, not just households, but social groups of varying sizes. The "house" in this sense is a cultural category of fundamental importance. It defines a social group, which is not necessarily the same as the house's residential group. (1993:1)

Fox goes on to note that most Austronesian houses possess what he terms a "ritual attractor," part of the structure of the house itself (often a principal post or beam), which is the ritual focus of the "house" as a social group. The Austronesian "house" can thus be thought of as a structure that endures through time, with people affiliating to it often through birth to members of the "house," but also through marriage or even adoption. The "house" often carries a proper name, has its own rituals, and is associated with a specific "estate" or area of land.[37] Fox stresses that the "house" has a history, which is bound up in a frequently botanical metaphor of origin (1993: 17). Thus, rather than thinking in terms of "descent", the members of a "house" think of their origins as the "base" or "trunk" of a tree.

Just as a "house" has origins, so it has ancestors. The concept is old in Austronesian society, for the term *ta(m)pu*, "ancestor" can be reconstructed to Proto Malayo-Polynesian (Zorc 1994: 559). House rituals, physically focused on the ritual attractor of the house, generally honor these ancestors. As Roxana

Waterson writes, "the ancestors and spirits are typically accorded the place of honour within the house, and are kept informed of the doings of their descendants" (1990:227). Old houses, which have become weighty with the history of many departed ancestors (and often the disposal place of their bones) may become temples.[38]

Given the pervasiveness of the "house" as a social concept of fundamental organizing significance throughout the Austronesian-speaking world, it seems plausible that the Lapita peoples also ordered their world along these lines. For the early Lapita colonizers in the Bismarcks, the *Rumaq* was probably not just a physical dwelling, but also the basic social unit with which they affiliated. Moreover, the great importance accorded representations of human faces on their elaborately-decorated pottery (see chapter 5) may well be unerstandable in terms of ancestor rituals.[39] We have seen that ceramics bearing these anthropomorphic faces are discretely-distributed in Lapita sites, associated in Talepakemalai with the over-water stilt-houses, or in Nenumbo with the main dwelling house. They may have been principal accoutrements of the "ritual attractors" within these Lapita houses.

Conservative prehistorians may argue that I have gone too far in my interpretation of Lapita as a "house society," urging that we stick closely to the archaeological data of post molds and fire pits. But I – like my colleagues Roger Green, Jim Fox, and Andrew Pawley – am convinced that a cultural history that draws not only upon the material evidence of archaeology, but also on careful lexical and semantic reconstructions, and on comparative ethnology, has far greater power to inform us about the social lives of Lapita and other ancient peoples. Certainly our current vision of this social world is a fuzzy and incomplete one, for our methods need refinement and our databases enlarging. Only by daring to envision this world, however, can we ever bring it to light.

Lapita Economy and the Ecology of Islands

In spite of decreasing diversity in flora and fauna from west to east, the large islands of the Bismarck and Solomon archipelagoes provided sufficient natural food resources to sustain the small hunting-and-gathering human populations which began to expand out from Sahul during the late Pleistocene, some 40,000 years ago, or perhaps even earlier. Indigenous and endemic species of marsupials (such as bandicoots, cuscuses, and other phalangers), rats (in such genera as *Uromys* and *Melomys*), reptiles, large fruit bats, and many kinds of land and sea birds provided terrestrial protein sources, matched or perhaps exceeded by the shellfish and fish of the mangrove swamps, inshore reefs, and lagoons. Tubers, seeds, fruits, and nuts of various wild plants also contributed significantly to the diet of these early people. Beyond the eastern end of the Solomon Islands, however, the island ecosystems of Remote Oceania become significantly impoverished in the range and diversity of naturally-occurring plants and animals that could provide food sources for colonizing human populations. Marsupials and rats are not naturally distributed in Remote Oceania, and the diversity of reptiles and fruit bats declines markedly. Likewise, many of the useful wild food plants rapidly reach their limits of distribution in the Solomons-Vanuatu region. Of course, the islands of Remote Oceania did harbor rich avifaunas, as well as bountiful inshore marine resources (although the diversity of fish and mollusks also decreases as one moves from west to east in the Pacific). But in the absence of significant plant foods, these alone would have been insufficient to support human populations dependent solely upon a hunting-and-gathering mode of economy.

Indeed, in their natural or pristine state, most of the island ecosystems of Remote Oceania were poor environments for sustained human settlement, and certainly would not have permitted the growth of large populations. Essential to the human colonization of Remote Oceania – in addition to the maritime technology which allowed for long-distance voyaging – was a developed *system of food production*, as well of marine resource exploitation. Among the numerous ethnographically-documented cultures of Oceania which are the ultimate legacy of the Lapita diaspora, it was such horticultural, arboricultural, and agricultural production systems[1] that sustained often large and dense populations, and that underwrote frequently complex and hierarchical political economies.[2] It has long been known that the crop plants on which these production systems were based – such as the major starch staples of taro, yam, breadfruit, and banana – were ultimately of Southeast Asian or New Guinean origin. (As we have seen in chapter 2, some of these crops were probably brought under domestication in the Near Oceanic region during the early Holocene.) What has proved more difficult is unraveling the history of agricultural systems in the Pacific Islands. How and when were the crop plants and agronomic knowledge needed to cultivate them transferred to the islands of Remote Oceania, there to be further adapted and modified by successive generations of island gardeners? Through recent advances in archaeological methods of studying prehistoric agriculture, it has become clear that the Lapita peoples played a title role in this as yet imperfectly recorded saga, one of the great chapters in the history of world agriculture.

Reconstructing Lapita Economies

It was not always appreciated that the Lapita peoples were key participants in the dispersal of agricultural systems to the islands of Remote Oceania, or that they even practiced any plant cultivation at all. As recently as 1971, in an otherwise brilliant synthesis of the Tongan archaeological record, Les Groube advanced the hypothesis that the Lapita colonizers of Fiji and

Tonga were "Oceanic strandloopers" with a "restricted mari-
time/lagoonal economy," who "expanded ahead of colonization by agriculturalists" (1971:312). Groube was influenced by
the rich shell middens associated with Early Eastern Lapita
pottery in Tonga, and by the apparent absence of pig bone
from these sites (pig being commonly linked to agricultural
production systems in Oceania). Unfortunately, negative evidence often proves to be a weak or erroneous basis for hypothesis development. In the humid tropics of Oceania, where fruits
and tubers rarely preserve in archaeological contexts, evidence
for prehistoric agriculture can be difficult to obtain. (This is in
marked contrast, for example, to the situation in arid regions
where seed crops provided the dominant basis of subsistence,
such as the Near East or the highlands of Mesoamerica. In
such areas abundant and well-preserved archaeobotanical evidence readily permits reconstructions of prehistoric agricultural
systems.) In his 1979 synthesis of Lapita, Roger Green adduced
several lines of indirect archaeological evidence to strongly refute
Groube's hypothesis. Finding that pig bones – while scarce –
were indeed present in Lapita contexts, along with those of the
chicken, implied a production base linked to animal husbandry.
Green also argued persuasively from other lines of evidence:

> The need for horticulture is supported by the location of many
> Lapita sites. They are in situations that otherwise would require
> a far stronger commitment by the occupants than is evident to
> exploitation of marine resources or to hunting of birds and sea
> animals. Settlement size also demands that the residents must
> have maintained an economy in which horticulture was a main-
> stay. One very likely interpretation of the pits is in fact their use
> for storage of fermented banana, taro, or breadfruit. Finally,
> horticulture fits with the evidence of cooking ovens, pottery,
> cooking vessels, adzes, vegetable scrapers, and peelers in shell,
> and other tools typical of Oceanic societies that utilized tropical
> root and tree crops. (Green 1979a:37)[3]

Since Green's article was published, we have accumulated
more evidence along the lines he outlined; moreover, archaeological methods for the recovery of archaeobotanical remains
in the humid tropics have improved substantially.[4] Thanks to
the waterlogged depositional contexts of several Lapita sites

such as Talepakemalai and Apalo, we now have direct botanical evidence for a large number of Lapita crop plants. Moreover, these closely match the roster of reconstructed Proto Oceanic names for cultivated plants. Thus, archaeological and linguistic evidence can be used to independently cross-check our reconstructions of Lapita subsistence. As Green noted, the technology or artifacts associated with food production and food preparation are also a key component of the archaeological record, and the microscopic analysis of starch residues on such artifacts provides a new direction of inquiry (Fankhauser 1994; Loy 1994).

Understanding the maritime aspects of Lapita economy is perhaps a more straightforward task, because the archaeological record is strong in this respect. Of foremost importance are the extensive collections of fishbones and shellfish remains excavated from Lapita sites. These provide direct evidence for the range of fish and invertebrates taken from the reefs, lagoons, and open seas by Lapita peoples (plate 7.1). The technology of fishing is evidenced, in part, by fishhooks, lures, and net weights, although these testify to only some of the fishing strategies used. As with the reconstruction of cultivation methods, we may turn to the independent evidence of historical linguistics, which provides us with Proto Oceanic word sets pertaining to shellfish, fish, fishing methods, and related terms. In short, it is possible to reconstruct in considerable detail the nature of Lapita food production systems, but the exercise demands a broad inter-disciplinary collaboration that extends beyond traditional archaeological methods.

Fishers and Gatherers: Harvesting the Sea

Being "peoples of the beach," Lapita men and women had an extensive and intimate knowledge of the sea that extended out from the very thresholds of their houses. As children, they grew up among stilt-houses situated over tidal reef flats rich in sand-burrowing bivalves and other edible mollusks. They would have learned from their mothers to discriminate among several kinds of edible seaweeds and seagrasses, and the habitats of

*Plate 7.1   Aerial view of the extensive reef-lagoon ecosystem
exploited by the prehistoric inhabitants of the Talepakemalai site
in the Mussau Islands. Eloaua, location of Talepakemalai, is the
long narrow island in the mid-distance. The large high island of
Mussau looms in the far distance. (Photo by P. V. Kirch)*

numerous shellfish. From their fathers and older brothers, they
learned to name the myriad species of fish from the outer reefs,
lagoons, and the open sea.[5] The "sea" (Proto Oceanic *tasik*),
the rich "reefs" (*sakaRu*) engulfed within it, the calm "lagoon"
(*namo*), and the "ocean" (*sawa*) extending beyond the
horizon were intimate components of their world.[6] Historical
linguists inform us that Proto Oceanic speakers had words
distinguishing many kinds of marine and coastal features
(Pawley 1993), such as coral (*laje*), seaweed (*lumut*), ocean
swells and waves (*ngalu*), surf (*napo*), and low tide (*mamasa*).
Richard Walter (1989) canvasses Proto Oceanic fish
names, while Paul Geraghty (1994) and Robin Hooper (1994),
who have worked on fish names in Proto Central Pacific and
Proto Polynesian languages (slightly lower-order branches derived from Proto Oceanic, and spoken by the Lapita settlers of
the Fiji-Tonga-Samoa region), are able to reconstruct more

than one hundred names referring to about sixty major fish families. Ross Clark (1991) has shown that Proto Oceanic speakers had a contrast set of two terms, *paη oda*, a verb meaning "to gather seafood on the reef," and *pinaη oda*, a noun referring to such "seafood gathered on the reef." Pawley (1993) reconstructs some 44 Proto Oceanic terms for reef and shoreline invertebrate taxa. Among these terms are generic categories for crustacea (*quraη*) and for gastropod mollusks (*sisi[q]*), as well as specific terms for several species important for food and/or artifact manufacture (e.g., *japi*, "pearl shell;" *kima*, "*Tridacna* clam;" and, *game*, "*Trochus niloticus*"). Doubtless the Proto Oceanic vocabulary in these matters was rich, and backed by an extensive ethnobiological knowledge of the habitats, breeding cycles, and behavior of the hundreds of kinds of marine life which the Lapita people regularly captured and harvested for food. A selection of Proto Oceanic terms for fishing and marine exploitation is listed in table 7.1.

The archaeological record of Lapita fishing and marine resource exploitation is extensive. Beginning with Gifford's careful identification of more than 74 species of mollusks occurring in the deposits at Lapita (Site 13) in New Caledonia (Gifford and Shutler 1956:30, tables 23–4), archaeologists have devoted considerable effort to recovering, identifying, and analyzing marine faunal remains from Lapita sites.[7] Since Lapita sites usually consist of calcareous depositional environments, the preservation of bone and shell is generally excellent, and most sites yield substantial quantities of both gastropod and bivalve shells, sea urchin spines and tests, crab carapaces, the teeth and vertebrae of sharks, fish bones and teeth of all sorts, and the bones of other sea creatures such as turtles and porpoises. Through the use of reference collections and careful laboratory work, most of the these remains can be identified to family, and often more precisely to genus and species. An astounding catalog of marine life has resulted, representing virtually every habitat and microenvironment of the Indo-Pacific ocean world. While in most Lapita faunal assemblages a relatively few species are dominant, the diversity is nonetheless remarkable, demonstrating that the Lapita people knew how to exploit the resources of their marine world to the fullest.

Shellfish, and in particular mollusks, provided not only an

Table 7.1 Selected Proto Oceanic terms relating to fishing and marine exploitation

Proto Oceanic Term	Probable meaning	Proto Oceanic Term	Probable meaning
Fishing terms			
		*meRa	parrotfish (Scaridae)
*kau	fishhook	*qume	unicorn fish (*Naso* sp.)
*matau	fishhook	*qawa	milkfish (*Chanos chanos*)
*kupenga	fish net		
*pani	bait or lure		
*bintu(l,r)	fish or crab trap	**Invertebrates**	
*tupa	fish poison		
*ndeke	pocket of seine net	*qurang	crustacea in general
*uto	net float	*qaRimango	mangrove crab
*qapa	net gauge	*sisi(q)	edible gastropods
*pupu	basket trap	*game	*Trochus niloticus*
*mpaya	fishing lure	*lalai	*Trochus* sp. shell
*tail	to catch fish	*qaliling	*Turbo* sp. shell
*pangoda	to gather seafood on reef	*Ranga	spider conch (*Lambis*)
*pinangoda	seafood from the reef	*buli(q)	cowrie shell (*Cypraea*)
		*tapuRi(q)	*Triton* conch
		*kima	*Tridacna* clam
Fish		*japi	Pearl shell (*Pinctada*)
		*kaRi	bivalve (scraper?)
		*kuRita	octopus
*qalu	Barracouda	*sala(ng, n)	sea urchin (*Diadema*)
*paRi	ray, stingray	*saRawaki	sea urchin (*Echinometra*)
*sumu	triggerfish (Balistidae)	*(p,b)ula	sea cucumber
*qatu	bonito	*laje	coral
*wete	goatfish	*limut	seaweed

important source of protein, but also of raw material for the manufacture of artifacts. Large *Trochus* and *Turbo* shells yielded strong shell from which to make fishhooks. Large cone shells (*Conus litteratus* and *C. leopardus*) and *Spondylus* oysters were worked into ornaments and exchange valuables of various kinds. Although many Lapita sites contain dense concentrations of molluscan shell (for example, at Talepakemalai, where the average density of mollusk shells per cubic meter was approximately 30 kilograms), their contribution to the Lapita diet was probably relatively low. Rather, it was the abundant fish stocks of the inshore reef and lagoons that seem to have provided the greater share of meat and protein.

The great ecologist Marston Bates once compared the immense diversity and productivity of the tropical rainforests with that of the coral reefs. Coral reefs are great biological "factories," driven by the photosynthesizing power of such primary producers as coral, algae, and seaweeds, which in turn support a food chain of predators and prey. In contrast, the open ocean beyond the reefs that hug island coasts is a relative "desert." Whereas the inshore reefs and lagoons of the Indo-Pacific support thousands of species of fish, the pelagic zone is limited to a much smaller array, including many prized, carnivorous game fish (such as the tunas, swordfish, and marlin). Not surprisingly, the overwhelming majority of fish bones from Lapita middens derived from inshore fishes, and faunal analyses show that inshore fishing provided Lapita households with most of their daily protein. Among the most common inshore fish represented in Lapita sites are parrotfish (Scaridae), wrasses (Labridae), surgeonfish (Acanthuridae), triggerfish (Balistidae), groupers (Serranidae), jacks (Carangidae), eels (Muraenidae), and emperors (Lethrinidae). The benthic or bottom-dwelling taxa found in deeper waters off the outer reef edge or on offshore banks were also exploited. And although they constitute a small percentage of the total fish catch (usually just one or two percent of Lapita fish bone assemblages), open ocean or pelagic fish such as tuna (Scombridae) are also represented. In addition to bony fishes, sharks and rays are also present in Lapita sites, and their tough and versatile skins may have been used for such purposes as drum timpani[8] or rasps.

The methods used to capture such a wide variety of fishes,

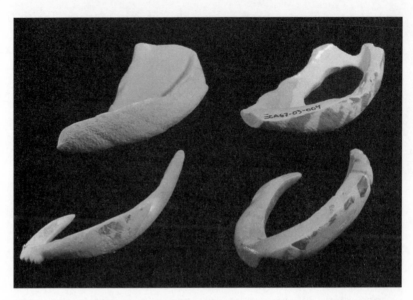

Plate 7.2 Unfinished and completed shell fishhooks from the Talepakemalai site, Mussau Islands. Upper row, roughed out Trochus-shell fishhook tabs; lower row, two forms of one-piece fishhook made from Trochus shell. (Photo by Thérèse Babineau)

including herbivores, carnivores, and omnivores, each with its different microenvironment and habits, must have been highly varied. Unfortunately, most of the fishing tackle and equipment used by traditional Oceanic peoples was manufactured from perishable materials, such as wood, fiber, and line, which rarely preserves in archaeological contexts. Fishhooks, made from several kinds of shell (especially *Turbo* and *Trochus*), are now well documented from a number of Lapita sites, ranging from Talepakemalai (plate 7.2) to Lolokoka. Most of these hooks are fairly large (ca. 5 cm in shank length) and were probably designed for hand-lining from canoes, in order to catch larger benthic species such as groupers. A few hooks are smaller, however, and could have been used for taking smaller species on reefs and along coastlines. We also have evidence for deep-sea trolling, in the form of carefully crafted lures made from *Trochus* shell.[9] These trolling lures (figure 7.1) are streamlined for hydrodynamic lift in the water, and have finely carved

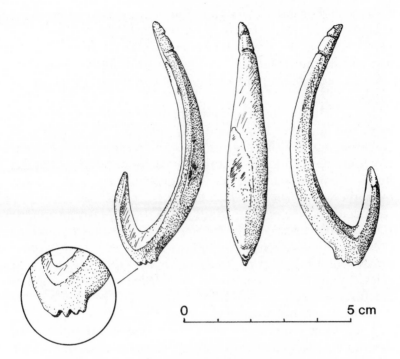

*Figure 7.1   A Trochus-shell trolling lure excavated
from the Talepakemalai site, Mussau Islands.
(Drawing by Margaret Davidson)*

grooves for attaching both the line and hackles (probably feathers or pig bristles) near the recurved point.

Fishhooks and trolling lures cannot account for the full diversity of fishes taken by Lapita people. It seems likely that a wide
range of fishing strategies must have been practiced, including
such methods as spearing, netting, and poisoning. To address
this question, in 1976 Tom Dye and I carried out an ethnoarch-
aeological study of traditional fishing practices on the Tongan
island of Niuatoputapu (location of the Lolokoka Lapita site).
We found that many of the fish represented in the Lolokoka
midden could not have been taken by angling, and other strategies must have been used. Indeed, "the Lapita fishermen must
have been familiar with a range of techniques that included the
use of nets, spears, and plant poisons" (Kirch and Dye 1979:71).

Fishing on the same reef flats and lagoons exploited by the Lapita occupants of the Lolokoka site, the modern Niuatoputapu people obtain the greatest number of fish by using a broad array of netting strategies, along with spearing and poisoning. Angling contributes only a minor amount of fish to the overall catch.[10]

The conclusion that Lapita fishing incorporated diverse strategies and equipment is abundantly supported by linguistic reconstructions of fishing terms in Proto Oceanic (see table 7.1). Not only did the Proto Oceanic speakers have terms for fish-hooks, they also had a variety of words relating to nets. Moreover, the word *tupa* referred to fish poison, which could have been made of one or more kinds of plant (e.g., *Derris trifoliata*, *Barringtonia asiatica*, or *Pittosporum arborescens*), and the presence of basket traps is indicated by the term *pupu*. A portrait of a highly complex, sophisticated set of fishing strategies, founded on an intimate knowledge of the sea and its creatures emerges from the independent evidence of both archaeology and historical linguistics.

A few other aspects of Lapita marine exploitation are worth mentioning. The Green Sea Turtle (*Chelonia mydas*), a species which in modern times has become highly endangered, apparently thrived in southwest Pacific waters at the time of the Lapita dispersal. High frequencies of turtle bones are found in Lapita colonization sites, suggesting that the annually-breeding turtles were easy prey as they returned to their beach locales to lay their egg clutches. The early Polynesians who derived from the Eastern Lapita branch would later develop a highly ritualized feasting pattern based on the annual occurrence of sea turtles, with the first turtles reserved for chiefs.[11] Such practices may well have their roots in the preceding Lapita culture. Other air-breathing creatures of the sea with whom Lapita people were familiar included cetaceans, such as dolphins and porpoises (Odontoceti). For many modern Oceanic peoples, porpoises are regarded as special sea spirits, often respected or revered.[12] While porpoise bones found in the Talepakemalai site suggest that these creatures were hunted, they may also have had a spiritual significance to the Lapita people. From the Talepakemalai sands we excavated in 1985 a small, exquisitely-carved figurine (see frontispiece) made from the heavy, dense bone of a porpoise. Was this the embodiment or representation of a sea-deity, invoked perhaps to insure the bounty of reef and sea, or the safety of kinsmen voyaging to other islands? Unanswerable questions, these, that humble us in how little we understand of that distant world.

Gardens in the Forest: Lapita Horticulture

As important as the sea was to Lapita life, it by no means provided their sole basis for existence. Inland of the beach, the rank tropical rainforests offered another vast array of resources. There were natural forest products to be hunted or gathered, such as the large coconut robber crab (*Birgus latro*), birds and marsupials along with wild fruits and nuts that (in the Bismarcks at least) offered some variation in daily diet. The rainforest also supplied plant fibers such as lianas and rattan, bamboo, and other materials essential for manufacturing fishing nets, baskets, and other artifacts. But most important, the forest offered a fertile landscape for the establishment of gardens, in which the starch staples so essential to permanent settlements could be grown.[13] Using the practices of "swidden" gardening or "shifting cultivation," in which gardens are cut from forest in a cycle of fallow rotation, Lapita peoples transformed Oceanic rainforests into a landscape of high productivity.

Direct archaeobotanical evidence for horticulture, in the form of preserved plant remains, largely eluded prior generations of Oceanic archaeologists. A few sites had yielded carbonized endocarps of coconut and of *Canarium* almond nut shell, but little else. Then, during the 1986 excavation season at the waterlogged Talepakemalai site in the Mussau Islands, we were suddenly confronted with an unprecedented array of well-preserved (non-carbonized) plant remains. Sealed in an anaerobic, wet environment, the literally thousands of seed cases, endocarps, husks, syncarps, and other plant materials, along with wood (including adzed wood chips) opened up a new window on Lapita relations to the plant world (figure 7.2).[14] Subsequently, a similar assemblage of preserved plant parts was also recovered by Chris Gosden (1992a) at his Arawe Island sites. The plant parts preserved in the Mussau and Arawe Islands sites are primarily

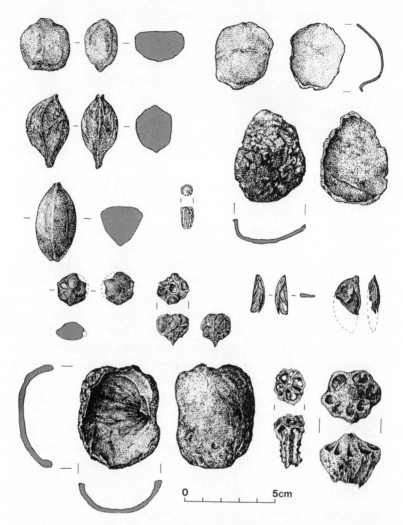

Figure 7.2   Anaerobically-preserved plant remains from the waterlogged deposits at the Talepakemalai site, Mussau Islands, provided direct evidence for extensive arboriculture. The remains shown here include candlenut (Aleurites moluccana), cycads (Cycas circinalis), Corynocarpus cribbeanus, Pangium edule, Canarium almond, Dracontomelon dao, Cordia subcordata, Burckella obovata, Tahitian chestnut (Inocarpus fagiferus), Vi Apple (Spondias dulcis), and screwpine (Pandanus sp.). (Drawing by Margaret Davidson)

woody or fibrous, such as seed cases, fibrous husks, and wood. Soft, fleshy materials such as tubers or the soft flesh of fruits have not survived. Consequently, we have an excellent record of more than twenty kinds of fruits and nuts, but almost no evidence for root or tuber crops. Clearly, this is an artifact of the depositional environment and, therefore, reflects a kind of "sampling error" in the archaeological record.

We can flesh out the record of Lapita crops and cultigens by turning to the independent evidence provided by linguistic reconstructions of Proto Oceanic plant terms. Several scholars, including French-Wright (1983) and Ross (1993), have scrutinized the Oceanic languages for evidence of Proto Oceanic cultivated plants. Table 7.2 lists the major reconstructed terms for these plants, along with their common English and scientific names; also indicated are those plants for which direct archaeological confirmation has been obtained through the excavations at Talepakemalai or other sites. Out of a total of 28 economic plants for which we have Proto Oceanic terms, no less than 15 are now attested by archaeobotanical remains. The main absences are the tuber and root crops, and a few fruits that lack woody seeds or fibrous husks (especially banana and breadfruit), and hence were not preserved in the wet deposits. In my view, the strong confirmation between the linguistic and archaeological evidence leaves little doubt that the full list given in table 7.2 was indeed part of the Lapita economic plant repertoire. New techniques and methods for the identification of carbonized starchy plant parts ("parenchyma") such as those developed by Jon Hather (1994), or the identification of pollen or opal phytoliths, will in all likelihood yield direct archaeological confirmation of such plants as taro, yam, breadfruit, and banana from future Lapita excavations.

As a perusal of table 7.2 indicates, the roster of Lapita or Proto Oceanic cultivated plants includes a wide array of different economic products. Important starch staples included several kinds of aroids (taro, giant taro, and swamp taro), and yams (the Greater Yam, and probably also several other species), which throughout Oceania form the basis of most cultivation systems. Important contributors of staple starch would also have been bananas and breadfruit, the latter a seasonal product. Sago starch, derived from the pith of several species of

Table 7.2 Lapita and Proto Oceanic food plants

Name	Proto Oceanic term[a]	Food type or part eaten	Archaeobotanical evidence
Taro, *Colocasia esculenta*	*talo(s)	corm, leaves	
Giant taro, *Alocasia macrorrhiza*	*piRaq	tuber	
Swamp taro, *Cyrtosperma chamissonis*	*bulaka	tuber	
Greater yam, *Dioscorea alata*	*qupi	tuber	
Banana, *Musa* hybrids	*pudi	fruit	
Banana, *Australimusa* type	*joRaga	fruit	
Breadfruit, *Artocarpus altilis*	*kuluR	fruit	
Sago, *Metroxylon* spp.	*Rabia	pith (starch)	
Cycad, *Cycas circinalis*	*bai-bai(t)	seed	X
Abelmoschus manihot	*bele	leaves	
Coconut, *Cocos nucifera*	*niuR	fruit	X
Screwpine, *Pandanus tectorius*	*padran	fruit	X
Pandanus dubius	*pakum	fruit	X
Vi Apple, *Spondias dulcis*	*quRis	fruit	X
Malay apple, *Eugenia* sp.	*kapika	fruit	

Indian mulberry, *Morinda citrifolia*	*ñoñum	fruit (medicinal)	X
Pometia pinnata	*tawan	fruit	X
Burckella obovata	*ñatu(q)	fruit	X
New Guinea walnut, *Dracontomelon dao*	*raqu(p)	fruit	X
Cut nut, *Barringtonia* sp.	*(wv)ele	nut	?
Canarium almond, *Canarium indicum*	*[ka]ngaRi	nut	X
Indian almond, *Terminalia catappa*	*talise	nut	X
Corynocarpus cribbeanus		fruit	X
Tahitian chestnut, *Inocarpus fagiferus*	*(q)ipi	nut	X
Pangium edule		Seed	X
Turmeric, *Curcuma longa*	*yango	root	
Sugar cane, *Saccharum officinarum*	*topu	stalk	
Kava, *Piper* sp.	*kava ?	Root (infusion)	X

[a] *Source* for Proto Oceanic reconstructions: primarily Ross (1993)

large palms (*Metroxylon* spp.) indigenous to the Indo-Pacific humid tropics, was also known to Lapita peoples. Quite remarkable is the broad array of fruit and nut-bearing trees, including not only coconut, but such soft-fleshed fruit as the Vi-apple and *Corynocarpus*, and the delicious hard-shelled *Canarium* and *Terminalia* nuts. Of special interest is turmeric, which supplied not only an edible ingredient, but a rich orange-red pigment for which a Proto Eastern-Oceanic term (**reng[w]a*) can be reconstructed. Turmeric pigment is of ritual significance in many Oceanic societies, and its origin likely began with Lapita.

How was this array of economically-important plants cultivated? At least two major kinds of cultivation systems are suggested by the crop plants themselves, for these divide into annually-yielding species such as taro and yams that are typically grown as field crops, and perennial species such as the nut- and fruit-yielding trees. The main tuber crops (taro, yams) along with bananas, sugarcane, turmeric, and certain others, were probably cultivated using the methods of shifting cultivation. In fact, our Proto Oceanic reconstructions provide a list of sixteen words pertaining to gardening, and strongly support the interpretation of a shifting cultivation pattern of horticulture (table 7.3). This reconstructed vocabulary allows us to infer a horticultural cycle of clearing new gardens in the forest (either primary rainforest or secondary regrowth), of using digging sticks to plant field crops such as taro and yams, of planting yams in mounds (necessary for good drainage), of regular weeding, and finally of harvesting as weeds and fallow begin to invade the old garden plot. This kind of shifting cultivation forms the basis for most Oceanic horticultural systems throughout the southwest Pacific as recorded ethnographically.[15]

The long-lived nut- and fruit-bearing tree crops on the other hand, would not have been cultivated in shifting cultivations, but rather in permanent "orchard gardens," very likely in relative close proximity to settlements. Throughout island Melanesia today, this kind of village arboriculture is highly typical, and has probably been practiced since Lapita times.[16] Not only did these tree crops yield various edible seeds, nuts, and fruit, but also several other important products. The Putty-Nut tree (*Parinarium*), for example, produces a sticky substance very much like putty which can be used to caulk canoes or other

Table 7.3 Proto Oceanic terms relating to horticulture

Proto Oceanic term	Probable meaning
*poki	to clear a garden
*kokoda	to prepare a garden
*nsada	to clear
*quma	a garden, especially a swidden or shifting cultivation
*wa(a)so	digging stick
*ko(n)so	a digging or husking stick
*koti	to cut taro tops for planting
*upe	taro top (corm apex-petiole cluster, used for vegetative reproduction)
*(m)pula(m)pula	seed yams, used for planting
*pa(n)si	to plant
*(n)suki	to transplant
*ta(m)puki	a yam mound
*papo	to weed
*topa	cultivated land
*talu	fallow or weedy growth
*(pu)put-i	to harvest tubers

Source of Proto Oceanic reconstructions: French-Wright (1983)

wooden artifacts. Leaves from the screwpine (*Pandanus* spp.) provide a source of thatch, but are also woven into mats, and even the sails of canoes.

The most useful of all tree crops, of course, has to be the coconut, whose fruit not only provides both liquid and a vitamin-rich meat, but whose leaves can be woven into mats, baskets, or used for thatch.[17] When cleaned, the hard endocarp provides water bottles or, cut in two, drinking cups. Carbonized fragments of coconut shell have been found from many Lapita sites, and at Talepakemalai we recovered well preserved coconut shells, husks, and even wood. Of great interest was a coconut half-shell with the interior surface covered in parallel grooves resulting from the use of a shell scraper to grate the meat, evidence of the widespread Oceanic practice of grating coconut meat to express the cream, which may then be rendered into oil. The Linguists Andrew Pawley and Malcolm Ross (1995, table 3) stress the importance of "coconut culture" in Proto Oceanic society, and they have reconstructed a substantial vocabulary of terms relating to the tree and its products. Proto Oceanic speakers used a six-stage growth sequence to describe the nut as it developed and matured, a lexical system that has been retained (with modifications) in many Oceanic languages today.

One of the presently-unanswerable questions regarding Lapita horticulture concerns its immediate origins. Did Lapita peoples derive their horticultural complex from island Southeast Asia to the west, or did they adopt cultivation practices from the indigenous occupants of New Guinea and the Bismarck Archipelago? As noted in chapter 2, there is increasing evidence that the domestication of taro and other aroids, and of many tree crops such as *Canarium* almond, began during the early Holocene in Near Oceania (Gosden 1995). The initial Austronesian speaking peoples who voyaged eastwards from the Sulawesi-Halmahera region into the Bismarck Archipelago probably found the peoples they encountered already practicing an "Oceanic" mode of horticulture based primarily on aroids, breadfruit, and tree crops. On the other hand, it is also likely that these Austronesians themselves came from a horticultural tradition, although it may have been based on a somewhat different set of crops.

This question is relevant to one of the enigmas of Indo-Pacific ethnobotany: the absence of rice (*Oryza sativa*) cultivation in the islands of the Pacific. Rice seems to have been domesticated by at least 7,000 BC in China, and terms for rice and rice cultivation can be reconstructed for Proto Austronesian language (Blust 1985). If rice was a part of early Austronesian culture – and indeed it may have been a staple crop – why was it not carried out into the Bismarck Archipelago and the Pacific Islands by pre-Oceanic speaking peoples? The question has long puzzled ethnobotanists, and no clear answer is evident. Peter Bellwood (1985:233–41) thinks that early forms of domesticated rice may not have been well adapted to the humid tropics, having been developed in monsoon climates with seasonal variations in day length and sunshine incidence. Such ecological factors may indeed have been critical. Social factors may also have played a significant role. If the early Austronesian speakers who began expanding eastwards along the northern New Guinea coast and into the Bismarcks were primarily (at least at first) in search of trade or exchange opportunities, they may not have been concerned with transferring in toto their agricultural systems. Finding the local inhabitants already practicing a well-adapted system of horticulture and arboriculture, they may simply have integrated components of their own system with the local system, especially as permanent settlement and inter-marriage between Oceanic and Papuan-speaking communities began. Certainly, these are questions and issues that will require much more thought and research.

Not only did rice fail to move with the Austronesian expansion into Oceania, there is also no evidence for the spread of pondfield irrigation during this early period.[18] Complex, terraced pondfield cultivation of *Colocasia* taro did develop later in several of the island groups colonized by Lapita peoples or their descendants, as in New Caledonia, Fiji, Futuna, Rapa, and Hawai'i. However, archaeological and linguistic evidence examined by Kirch and Lepofsky (1993) strongly suggests that these were independent, convergent developments, and in most cases were responses to the growth of large and dense human populations considerably after the phase of initial island settlement. What the Lapita peoples probably did have was a good understanding that *Colocasia* taro could be grown in either wet or dry field conditions. As with the giant swamp taro, *Cyrtosperma*, they may have cultivated stands of both species in naturally swampy swales behind the beach terraces where they made their homes.

We need to mention one other aspect of Lapita production systems – the domestic animals – of which pigs and chickens seem to have been the most important. Bones of both these animals are found in Lapita sites, although pigs seem in most cases not to have been numerous. In the Talepakemalai site, for example, only 18 pig bones out of a total of 14,148 vertebrate faunal remains were recovered from the large Area B excavation. Pig may have been present in New Guinea by about 5,000 BP, prior to the Lapita period, and it is possible that in the early Far Western Lapita phase in the Bismarcks, pigs were obtained as prestige items through exchange with indigenous populations. Drilled or faceted pig tusk pendants from Talepakemalai, Nenumbo, and Malo hint at such a prestige value for these animals. However, pigs must have been raised by the later Lapita people who voyaged eastwards into the Fiji-Tonga-Samoa region, for pig bones appear in colonization sites of that region. As intensive agricultural economies developed on the larger high islands of eastern Melanesia and Polynesia, pigs would become increasingly important, both as sources of food and as items of prestige feasting and exchange.

Archaeogastronomy: Reconstructing Lapita Cuisine

The basic constituents of the Lapita diet can be inferred from the above discussion of the extraction of sea resources, and cultivation of edible plant products on the land. The staple carbohydrate core of the diet was comprised surely of such swidden crops as taro, yams, and bananas, supplemented seasonally by breadfruit. A wide range of nuts and fruits grown in orchard gardens – as well as green leaves – added variety to the diet, and doubtless provided excellent sources of vitamins. For meat and protein, the Lapita peoples depended heavily upon the sea which offered up countless varieties of fish and shellfish, as well as octopus, sea urchins, crabs, crayfish, and seaweeds. More rarely these seafoods were alternated with birds, or (especially in the Far Western Lapita region) forest game such as cuscus, large lizards, or coconut robber crabs.

It is one thing to enumerate the foodstuffs that comprised the diet of a people, and quite another to comprehend their "cuisine." As Claude Lévi-Strauss taught us, the distinction between the raw and the cooked is the difference between nature and culture. The gastronomic arts are one of the essential traits that distinguish cultures and ethnicities. All too frequently ignored or overlooked among the world's major cuisinary traditions,[19] the Oceanic-speaking peoples possess highly distinctive food patterns. Characteristic of Oceanic cuisine, for example, is the "pudding complex" of starchy (often taro-based) puddings, pounded or mashed and incorporating

coconut cream or oil as an emollient.[20] Also highly typical of
Oceanic cooking is the use of an earth oven, a steaming method
that yields distinctive flavors to vegetable foods and meat. To
what extent can we trace the history of this Oceanic cuisinary
pattern back to ancestral roots in the Lapita culture? Archaeo-
gastronomy is not a well developed field, at least not for the
non-Western archaeological record, but by again employing
the collaborative power of archaeological and linguistic evidence, we can make some informed hypotheses as to the essentials
of Lapita cooking.

Certainly the use of the earth oven is abundantly attested in
the Lapita archaeological record. In the earliest Far Western
Lapita sites, however, such as Talepakemalai, cooking fires
involving the use of coral heating stones seem to have been lit
within the stilt-platform houses, very likely in wooden, earth-
filled "boxes" as used in some southeast Asian cultures today.[21] The transference of this technique to actual underground
pits, as is typical throughout most of Oceania today, may have
been influenced by the practices of indigenous Bismarck Archipelago peoples whom the early Oceanic speakers encountered,
for typical earth ovens have been exposed in early-to-mid
Holocene contexts in the limestone cave sites of New Ireland.[22]
In any event, prehistoric ovens consisting of a shallow pit in
which a hot fire (often ignited with coconut shells) was lit to
heat stones, the latter then retaining sufficient heat to steam
the food, have been excavated at many Lapita sites.[23] These
features were presumably called by the Proto Oceanic term
qumun, whose modern reflexes in various Oceanic languages
are extensive (e.g., Marshallese *um*, Hawaiian *imu*).

Archaeological evidence also informs us regarding some of
the methods used to prepare and process foods in Lapita
cooksheds. Several kinds of peeling knives and scrapers are
well represented (figure 7.3). A common form was made from
the dorsum or "cap" of a large cowry shell (*Cypraea* sp.), with
a carefully ground, curved slicing edge. These cowry shell implements were most likely used to scrape or peel away the outer
rind of breadfruits, prior to cooking. Another form of peeler
found at the Talepakemalai site consists of whole valves of pearl
shell (*Pinctada* sp.), with the ventral edges ground to a fine,
sharp bevel. When held in one hand used with a slicing motion

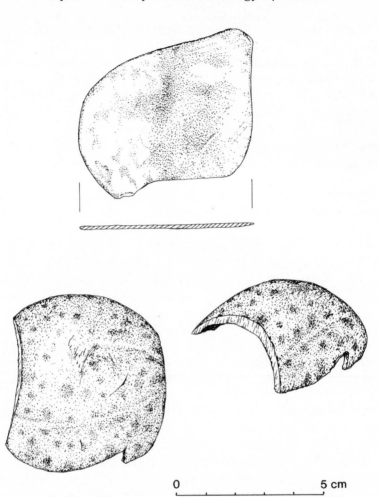

*Figure 7.3   Peeling knives of pearl shell and scrapers of cowrie
shell were used by the Lapita occupants of the Talepakemalai
site to prepare tubers, roots, and certain fruit for cooking.
(Drawing by Margaret Davidson)*

away from the body, these are highly effective for removing
the tough and inedible skins of taro or yam tubers.[24] Parallel
sets of incisions on the inside of a coconut shell from Talepakemalai also attest to the use of shells (probably the naturally
serrated edge of an *Arca* or *Cardium* shell) to grate and re-
move coconut meat. The grated meat could then be squeezed

through a fibrous substance (often shredded bark) to express the cream. When heated stones are dropped into a wooden bowl containing coconut cream, coconut oil is produced.

Extensive linguistic reconstructions by Frantisek Lichtenberk (1994) amplify the food preparation techniques suggested by archaeologically-recovered artifacts. The scraping of tubers is indicated by such Proto Oceanic words as *karis* and *karas* ("to scrape tubers"). Peeling likewise is attested by several other terms (e.g., *kulit*, *sisi*, *pili*). The grating of coconut meat has its own particular terms (*ko[r/R0i]s*) and *ko[r/R]as*), and the squeezing of the grated meat to render cream is lexically indexed as well (*pisak*, *poRos*, *pirik*). The pounding of food such as taro tubers was essential to making puddings, and the Proto Oceanic word *tutuk* doubtless referred to this common culinary task. Although no wooden bowls or bowl fragments have yet been recovered from Lapita archaeological sites, their presence is strongly indicated by the term *kumete*.

Once prepared for cooking, foods might be either placed uncovered in the earth oven (or roasted whole over embers), but more commonly would be wrapped, especially in leaves such as those of banana or the giant swamp taro. The Proto Oceanic terms *apu* and *kopu* both refer to such wrappings. And while baking in the earth oven was obviously important, it was not the sole method for cooking food. Roasting (*tunu*) may have been commonly used for fish or other meats, while steaming (*napu*) and boiling (*nasu*) are also indicated by linguistic reconstructions.

In the humid tropics, food that is not quickly cooked and consumed is liable to rot and become inedible. In some seasons, it may be possible to dry or smoke fish or some starch foods, and sago flour can be stored in clay pots or other containers. In general, however, food storage is a difficult problem, and given the considerable seasonality of food production in Oceanic agricultural systems,[25] this can result in periods of food shortage and even famine. One of the most ingenious solutions to this problem was the invention of semi-subterranean fermentation of starchy foods in pits, especially breadfruit but also bananas, *Burckella* fruit, and other crops. Going under such names as *mar*, *ma*, or *masi* in modern Oceanic languages, these preserved breadfruit pastes can survive in their fermented state for several years, to be drawn upon at times of food shortage. Ethnographically, the technique of pit ensilage and fermentation is found primarily in eastern Melanesia, parts of Micronesia, and central Eastern and Western Polynesia.[26] This practice seems not to have been present in the earliest Far Western Lapita communities, but was invented and developed as Lapita peoples dispersed into the Western and Eastern Lapita regions. A Proto Eastern-Oceanic term, *mara ("be spoiled, foul, preserved breadfruit") can be reconstructed (Ross 1993:20), and reinforces archaeological interpretations of non-cooking pits in Western and Eastern Lapita sites as food fermentation-storage pits.[27] The invention of *mara was certainly one of the major innovations of Oceanic cuisine, one whose importance was later in time greatly elaborated in certain Polynesian cultures (e.g., in the Marquesas Islands).

Finally, it may be germane to mention not only foods of substance, but "foods of the mind," that is to say narcotic or psychoactive plants. Among traditional Oceanic peoples, two such plants are used although they have quite distinct and nearly disjunct geographic distributions: kava (*Piper methysticum*) and betel (*Areca catechu* and associated substances). Indeed, this distribution pattern with kava largely in eastern Melanesia and Polynesia, and betel in western Melanesia attracted considerable attention among such ethnographic pioneers as W. H. R. Rivers (1914) who constructed a whole cultural-historical scenario around it.[28] What can be said on the basis of modern archaeological, linguistic, or ethnobotanical evidence regarding the possible use of either of these plants by the Lapita people? Ethnobotanical and phytochemical studies suggest that the cultivated kava, *Piper methysticum*, originated from the wild (and bitter) species *Piper wichmannii* (Lebot and Lévesque 1989). The latter is naturally distributed throughout Near Oceania, and into the northern Vanuatu Islands, but on a variety of botanical and ethnobotanical grounds, Vincent Lebot argues that the wild form was first brought under domestication and cultivation in Vanuatu. The spotty distribution of kava-drinking societies in Melanesia and Micronesia (as opposed to their wide distribution in Polynesia) is presumed to have resulted from later, and highly selective, introduction of the plant from Vanuatu or other secondary sources.[29]

Lebot's hypothesis has much evidence to support it. However, on strict linguistic grounds it is feasible to reconstruct the
term *kava to Proto Oceanic. Moreover, from the waterogged
deposits at Talepakemalai, we recovered several clearly identifiable stem fragments of a large *Piper* plant, with their characteristic knobby nodes.[30] It therefore seems likely that early Lapita
people in the Bismarck Archipelago may already have been
familiar with the wild form of kava, perhaps for its medicinal
(or even hallucinogenic ?) properties.[31] However, the regular
cultivation of *P. methysticum* and the development of the elaborate social and religious ceremonials surrounding it, were likely
later developments towards the end of the Lapita period, in the
Western and Eastern Lapita regions.

The evidence of the prehistoric use of betel nut is even more
obscure. A well-preserved specimen of *Areca* nut husk was
recovered from waterlogged deposits at the Dongan site on the
lower Ramu River in New Guinea, and has been tentatively
dated to about 5,800 years BP.[32] This would certainly put betel
nut in the Near Oceanic area well before Lapita times. However, we have no current evidence of its use among Lapita
peoples, and the fact that it was not transported to the southern and eastern regions of the Lapita dispersal suggests the
plant was not included within the Lapita repertoire.[33] Its use
in northern Melanesia outside of New Guinea may thus be a
phenomenon of the last two thousand years. In the case of
both kava and betel, however, there is much room here for
further research and interpretations.

Transported Landscapes

As groups of Lapita people began to voyage eastwards down
the arc of the Solomon Islands chain in the mid-second millennium BC, and then expand south, east, and north into the
farther reaches of Remote Oceania, their canoes were loaded
with more than a human cargo. These people quickly learned
that the islands beyond the end of the Solomons held little in
the way of exploitable terrestrial food resources (excepting, of
course, land crabs, birds, and some fruit bats). Thus, an essential part of their strategy for settling new islands would have

to be the transportation and effective introduction of the biological basis for food production, in the form of planting stocks of their tuber, fruit, and nut crops, and of breeding pairs of domestic animals. Using the concept first proposed by economic botanist Edgar Anderson (1952), this transformation of island biotas through the introduction of plants and animals resulted in "transported landscapes." For, having brought these plants and animals to a new island shore, Lapita peoples replicated their familiar cultural world of gardens and orchards surrounding their beach hamlets and villages. In an essential way, the concept of "transported landscape" encompasses not only those biological entities that are physically transferred, but also *cultural concepts* of land use. Of course, the transfer of agricultural plants and domestic animals was not always one hundred percent complete or successful, and as a consequence certain species dropped out of the Lapita crop repertoire at various localities. For example, there is a gradual reduction in the total roster of arboricultural tree crops as one moves from west to east through Melanesia and into the Fiji-Western Polynesian region. Likewise, New Caledonia to the south lacks a number of the tree crops of the tropical, western Melanesian islands.

These transported landscapes, moreover, were the effect of more than just the purposeful movement of crop plants and domestic animals. Human populations everywhere are typically associated with sets of plants and animals that ecologists refer to as "commensal" species, (or, alternatively, "synanthropic," or "anthropophilic" species). Examples range from house-dwelling spiders and cockroaches, to garden weeds, to the parasitic diseases carried within our own bodies and the bodies of our domestic animals. Writing about the biological expansion of European peoples after AD 900, Alfred Crosby (1986) calls the package of such species that accompany humans in their migrations, a "portmanteau biota."

The portmanteau biota of the Lapita peoples – the flora and fauna carried passively or by accident as incidental cargo in their voyaging canoes – is just begining to be catalogued by Pacific archaeologists and natural scientists. Among its most visible members was the Pacific Rat, a small species (*Rattus exulans*) of rodent that first became associated with humans somewhere in the island Southeast Asian region.[34] The Pacific Rat "regularly enters houses and lives in the thatch of native huts" (Tate 1951:322), and must have been dispersed through accidental transport on voyaging canoes. Bones of *Rattus exulans* are common in early Lapita sites throughout the southwest Pacific, while their absence in underlying deposits or fossil contexts proves they were not naturally present prior to human arrival. An innovative and exciting line of research, which is just commencing, uses sequences of DNA in Pacific Rat bones from archaeological contexts as a surrogate or proxy model of human migrations in the Pacific (Matisoo-Smith 1994). Other animals closely associated with human habitations are the ubiquitous house geckos (e.g., *Lepidodactylus* spp. and *Gehyra oceanica*) and skinks (e.g., *Emoia cyanura* and *E. impar*) which were also passively transported in Lapita canoes. Anyone who has spent time in traditional Oceanic villages will be familiar with these small creatures, who dart out across floor mats or dash along thatch-fringed rafters to feed on flies and other household insects.[35]

A rather different component of the Lapita portmanteau biota was not associated with dwellings, but with Lapita gardens. These are several different species of "garden snail," small (ca. 1–8 mm, and, therefore, economically useless to humans) pulmonate gastropods that thrive either on cultivated plants or in the disturbed soil of gardens. When planting stocks and associated soil are transported and transplanted by humans, the snails are inadvertently transferred as well. One species of garden snail, *Lamellaxis gracilis*, with an original homeland in island Southeast Asia, has been identified in early Lapita deposits in Nenumbo, Tikopia, Yanuca, and Niuatoputapu, and was later spread by the Polynesians as far as the Hawaiian Islands.[36] Other widely dispersed garden snails whose range into the central Pacific was presumably extended by Lapita peoples include *Gastrocopta pediculus* and *Lamellidea pusilla*.

There were surely many other species of synanthropic plants and animals, such as garden weeds and insects, that moved along with Lapita peoples as they rapidly expanded into the islands and archipelagoes of the southwest Pacific. Compiling a more extensive inventory of this portmanteau biota will take time and the application of special research methods.[37] What is most important is the realization that with their "transported landscapes," Lapita peoples initiated a process of modification and transformation of Pacific island ecosystems, a process that continues even to the present, and in many cases has radically altered these insular landscapes. The introduction of rats and pigs (the latter frequently becoming feral) on islands that previously had no large terrestrial vertebrates other than birds, could have severe consequences. Pigs uproot, eat, and trample fragile forest understory vegetation, while the Pacific Rat would find the nests and eggs of endemic ground-dwelling rails and other birds easy prey. Of course, the greatest impacts to island environments would come from the activities of humans themselves.

Worlds Transformed

As a consequence of their relative isolation and restricted size, the islands of Remote Oceania are characterized by terrestrial biotas limited in the numbers of high-order (i.e., family-level) taxa, and at the same time marked by high endemicity in lower-order taxa (genus and species-level). That is to say, due to the barriers posed by large ocean distances, only certain kinds of animals and plants were able to disperse to truly oceanic islands, but once there, they often found numerous "empty niches" into which their offspring would speciate and evolve. For this reason, the Remote Oceanic islands generally lack large vertebrates other than birds or bats. These volant groups could naturally disperse to islands, although successive generations of descendants frequently became flightless. Another important consequence of this oceanic isolation was "protection from outside competition and consequent preservation of archaic, bizarre, or possibly ill-adapted forms," and, thus, extreme vulnerability once isolation was broken down.[38] Thus, in the words of the great Pacific naturalist Raymond Fosberg, "the thing that most distinguishes islands, at least oceanic islands . . . is their extreme vulnerability, or susceptibility, to disturbance" (1963b:559).

No species that had arrived on oceanic islands prior to humans created anything remotely approaching the disturbances wrought by canoe-loads of people, carrying with them not only their portmanteau biota, but also cultural concepts of land use that centered around agricultural clearance and gardening.[39] As the Lapita peoples expanded out of the long-inhabited Bismarck and Solomon Archipelagoes of Near Oceania, and out into the far more isolated and ecologically-vulnerable islands of Remote Oceania, they began to disturb, modify, and impact these island ecosystems in myriad ways. Recent archaeological research, in conjunction with collaborative efforts in such natural sciences as palynology and avian paleontology, has begun to provide empirical evidence of these ecological transformations.

As horticulturalists who needed to establish gardens and orchards in order to effectively colonize a new island, Lapita peoples naturally needed to begin some degree of forest clearance within the initial phase of settlement. At first, the impact of such clearance might be restricted to a small zone surrounding the beach habitation zone. The practices of shifting cultivation, however, are by their nature areally extensive, since new gardens are cut into the forest each year. Thus, within even a few generations we can anticipate that Lapita populations would have modified fairly extensive tracts of rainforest, transforming them into mosaics of secondary growth. Forest clearance, even when there is regeneration, exposes the soil to increased rates of erosion and runoff, especially on the steep hillsides characteristic of many oceanic islands. Moreover, on some of the geologically-older islands and in drier, leeward regions, the rainforests were supported on thin, organic soils highly susceptible to erosion; these soils in turn were underlain by deeply laterized oxisols. Once the thin organic soil had been exposed to erosion through one or more cycles of forest clearance, the exposed laterite was frequently resistant to the regeneration of forest species. These lands became terminal grasslands or fernlands, dominated by such species as swordgrass (*Miscanthus floridulus*) and staghorn fern (*Dicranopteris linearis*).

The impacts of forest clearance through shifting cultivation and other cultural practices (such as burning for other reasons, like hunting) are not merely hypothetical; they have been empirically documented through palynological and geomorphological studies on several islands initially colonized by the Lapita peoples. One of the first pollen sequences to be examined was obtained from a coastal swamp on the island of Aneityum in Vanuatu.[40] At around 2,900 years ago, coincident with the presumed Lapita settlement of this archipelago, a radical change occurred in the vegetation on the slopes draining into this swamp. The previously-existing forest (dominated by dicotyledonous trees such as *Podocarpus, Celtis, Eugenia,* and *Acacia*) was drastically reduced, with fire as the main agent. The swamp deposits contained no charcoal particles in the pre-2,900 BP levels, but such particles surged to high concentrations in the deposits immediately after this date. The result was that forest trees and shrubs declined precipitously, while a disturbed vegetation dominated by ground ferns and grasses developed. In the Fijian archipelago, colonized by Eastern Lapita peoples perhaps by 1,200 BC, pollen cores from the main island of Viti Levu, and from the smaller island of Lakeba also reveal similar effects of forest clearance and fire on the vegetation.[41] On Lakeba Island, removal of original forest vegetation through burning during the Lapita period (i.e., the first millennium BC) transformed much of the interior landscape into a pyrophytic (fire-adapted plant) *Miscanthus-Dicranopteris* vegetation called by the modern Fijians *talasiga.*

At the Paligmete Site on Pililo Island off New Britain, Chris Gosden and John Webb identified a brown clay unit containing Lapita pottery, and dating to 2870 ± 70 BP, which accumulated at the base of a cliff. This thick accumulation of clay, derived by erosion from the island's interior, provided evidence to Gosden and Webb that "clearance for gardening was occurring on the upper parts of Pililo Island" (1994:46). A similar clay layer also occurs on nearby Kumbun Island (1994: 41). Yet another example of the dramatic effects of Lapita-introduced shifting cultivation practices on oceanic islands comes from Futuna, also settled during the Early Eastern Lapita phase. Here Lapita-period sites on the coastal plains at Tavai and Asipani were subsequently buried under two to three meters of erosional debris, the result of several centuries of shifting cultivation and consequent erosion of the steep, interior mountain slopes.[42]

The impacts of Lapita colonizers on the island ecosystems of Remote Oceania were not limited to the plant world. Through both direct predation for meat and feathers, and indirectly through habitat destruction resulting from forest clearance, many of the endemic and indigenous bird populations of these islands began to suffer precipitous declines immediately after human arrival. In many cases, these impacts led to extinction or extirpation within a few decades or centuries after Lapita colonization.[43] Particularly vulnerable were flightless, ground-dwelling birds such as rails, although other species such as pigeons, parrots, and fruit-doves were also heavily affected (Steadman 1989, 1995). One group of birds that was especially hard hit by Lapita hunters were the megapodes, a genus of galliform birds whose modern range (of three species) is highly disjunct in the Pacific islands. Prior to human settlement of the southwest Pacific, the distribution of megapodes was far more extensive, and several species of *Megapodius* have become extinct. As large, chicken or bush-turkey sized birds, these would have made easy targets for human hunters, especially as the birds would have had no prior knowledge or experience with large vertebrate predators. Extinct or extirpated species of megapodes have now been identified from archaeological remains in early Lapita contexts in Tikopia, Fiji, Tonga, Samoa, and New Caledonia.[44] In all of these cases, megapode bones occur only in the earliest archaeological deposits, and were, therefore, evidently quickly exterminated. Other large terrestrial fauna, although rare in Remote Oceania, was subject to human predation when present. An example is the former existence of an iguanid lizard, today known only from Fiji but which formerly also inhabited at least some of the Tongan Islands. Bones of this lizard were recovered by Tom Dye in excavations at the Tongoleleka site on Lifuka Island (Pregill and Dye 1989).

One of the most dramatic cases of the impact of Lapita peoples on an island environment is New Caledonia. This long, narrow and geologically ancient island has a highly unique biota that formerly included many endemic birds, the bones of which have begun to be recovered from archaeological contexts (Balouet and Olson 1989). The most bizarre of these was a giant megapode, *Sylviornis neocaledoniae*, with a height of about one meter (figure 7.4). The discovery of this extinct bird, whose bones are found only in the earliest Lapita deposits, presumably explains the long-standing mystery of large earthen

Figure 7.4   Reconstruction of the extinct, giant ground-dwelling megapode Sylviornis neocaledoniae, *and the extinct terrestrial crocodile* Mekosuchus inexpectatus, *from the island of New Caledonia. (After Balouet 1987)*

mounds or "tumuli" that some prehistorians had taken as evidence for a pre-Lapita human occupation of the island. Instead, these mounds are most likely the incubation nests of the *Sylviornis*, given the common behavior of these birds to lay their eggs "in big scratched-together heaps of decaying leaves and forest litter" (Mayr 1945:56).[45] Also disappearing soon after the arrival of Lapita people on New Caledonia was a large terrestrial crocodile (*Mekosuchus inexpectatus*). While the direct pressure of hunting surely contributed to the extinction of these bizarre animals, extensive forest clearance through fire (which in the arid New Caledonian landscape may have been unusually rapid and severe) probably also removed substantial areas of their natural habitat. Stratigraphic and palynological studies by Stevenson and Dodson (1995:40) at Saint Louis Lac situated 9 km east of Noumea reveal abrupt increases in grass pollen, fern spores, and microscopic charcoal particle influx at about 3,000 BP, followed by "sustained environmental disturbance." Future interdisciplinary work on the history of human impacts to the New Caledonian environment should prove particularly fruitful.

While human impacts on the terrestrial floral and fauna of Remote Oceanic islands were the most lasting and visible in the archaeological record, there were also effects on the reefs and lagoons, and their biota. Indeed, coral reefs are highly fragile environments, as modern marine conversation biologists have learned. Unfortunately, for the marine environment we do not have access to the same kinds of depositional records of environmental change that are preserved in coastal swamps or alluvial sediments. Archaeologists must infer the effects of human predation on marine fauna indirectly, from changes in the marine faunal materials excavated from habitation sites. One marine animal that was unquestionably heavily impacted by Lapita predation was the Green Sea Turtle (*Chelonia mydas*). In the Tikopia archaeological sequence, for example, the Lapita phase colonization site (TK-4) yielded an average of 59 turtle bones per cubic meter of deposit, whereas later phases typically had less than 10 bones per cubic meter (Kirch and Yen 1982:284–5, table 40). Similar patterns of high turtle bone concentrations in early sites have been reported from other Lapita contexts, and it seems that the large, annually-nesting populations of sea turtles were easy prey for Lapita people. It is also likely that on many islands, the arrival of humans resulted in reductions in the naturally-occurring levels of fish and mollusk populations. The Tikopia case again demonstrates significant reductions in overall concentrations of both fishbones and mollusk shells in the archaeological deposits over time.[46] Unlike the fragile terrestrial fauna, however, these marine animals did not suffer the same kinds of impact, and we have no evidence of the extinction or extirpation of marine taxa. However, for some islands, a temporal decrease in the sizes of marine mollusk shells has been observed, and this has been attributed to a heavy degree of human harvesting.[47]

To sum up, that the Lapita peoples were able to extend

significantly the range of human habitation in the Pacific, beyond the limits of Near Oceania where humans had been confined since the Pleistocene, and out into the dispersed islands
of Remote Oceania, testifies to their remarkable adaptability.
Fundamentally, three technological developments permitted this
unprecedented expansion into oceanic space: first, their posses-
sion of sophisticated maritime voyaging technology; second,
their horticultural economy and ability to transfer cultivation
systems to islands which otherwise had low terrestrial food
potential; and third, their extensive knowledge and ability to
exploit the rich resources of reef, lagoon, and sea. Thus armed
culturally and technologically, the Lapita peoples expanded
their territory within a mere four centuries from the Bismarck
Archipelago as far east as the Tongan and Samoan islands,
and south to New Caledonia. In the process, they encountered
biological worlds that had been isolated for millions of years,
worlds inhabited by flightless megapodes, terrestrial crocodiles,
and iguanas, and cloaked with fragile rainforests (Flannery
1995). Though their intentions were doubtless simply those
of any humans – to create a secure and comfortable home on
these newly discovered islands – the very technologies that
enabled the Lapita people to colonize also had an inevitable
impact. Just as through their food processing techniques and
earth ovens the Lapita people transformed raw tubers to cooked
food, so their shifting cultivations and fires converted natural
ecosystems to cultural landscapes. Oceania was now brought
within the fold of *Homo sapiens*, the species Tim Flannery
(1995) calls the "future eaters."

8

Systems of Exchange

Oceanic-speaking societies – and most particularly those in Melanesia, Western Polynesia, and central Micronesia – are noted among anthropologists for the diversity and complexity of their systems of *external* exchange.[1] The significance of such exchange networks was catapulted into anthropological consciousness with the 1922 publication of Bronislaw Malinowski's *Argonauts of the Western Pacific*. The "*kula* ring," which had been the focus of Malinowski's pioneering fieldwork (and the subject of much continuing ethnographic study), involves opposing circuits of complex ceremonial or "gift" exchange, along with more mundane but frequently voluminous transfers of perishable commodities such as foodstuffs. But the *kula* is only one of many such complex inter-community and inter-island exchange networks documented by ethnographers of Oceanic societies. Among other well-described systems are those of the Siassi region between New Guinea and New Britain, the *hiri* trade of the Papuan coast, the red-feather money exchange of the Santa Cruz Islands, the exchange maintained by the Tongan "maritime empire," and that of the "Yapese empire."[2] Given the pervasiveness of external exchange among the Oceanic-speaking peoples, it should come as no surprise that a hallmark of the Lapita archaeological record is abundant evidence for the movement of many kinds of materials between Lapita communities in the past.

Ever since Wal Ambrose and Roger Green (1972) first demonstrated the long-distance transport of obsidian and other materials into Lapita sites of the Santa Cruz group, the analysis and modeling of exchange systems has been an important aspect of Lapita research. The archaeologist, however, must approach the study of external exchange from a radically different perspective than that of the ethnographer. The latter observes exchanges in action, but only over very brief time spans. The archaeologist cannot observe the process of exchange, only the material residue resulting from a succession of repeated exchange transactions; he or she has, however, the advantage of studying the long-term history of exchange systems. Ethnographers have tended to emphasize the social context and symbolic meaning of exchange transactions, rather than the material objects that underwrite those transactions. For the archaeologist, such social contexts can only be modeled through a careful analysis of the material record of exchanged objects.

In the following pages, I summarize what we have learned about external exchange among Lapita peoples, beginning with an account of the varied kinds of material objects that were transported and moved between Lapita communities. I then turn to some models of Lapita exchange networks, of which our privileged communities of Talepakemalai, Nenumbo, and Lolokoka will offer substantive examples. Finally, I will address some possible explanatory models for the "function" of external exchange among Lapita peoples, and raise the question of whether the ethnographically-documented external exchange systems of Oceania ultimately derived from Lapita prototypes.

Archaeological Evidence for Lapita Exchange

In 1970, Roger Green began excavations at the Nenumbo Lapita site in the Reef Islands. In their sifting screens, Green's workers found hundreds of small flakes and cores of obsidian, the glassy volcanic rock prized by pre-metal using peoples around the world for its razor-sharp edges. Obsidian has a restricted natural distribution within the southwestern Pacific, and none occurs locally within the Santa Cruz Islands. The closest possible source where the Lapita occupants of Nenumbo might have secured the obsidian recovered in Green's excavations would have been the Banks Islands, roughly 400 km to the south. But when the excavated obsidian flakes were analyzed by emission spectrography in order to determine the relative concentrations of nine key elements, it turned out that the probable source was not the Banks Islands, but Talasea on the Willaumez Peninsula of New Britain, a straight-line distance of roughly 2,000 km (Ambrose and Green 1972). Concurrent analyses of obsidian from the Ambitle site off New Ireland likewise indicated a Talasea source. These striking results were the first empirical demonstration that Lapita peoples had maintained long-distance communication over vast spans of the southwest Pacific.

In the quarter-century since that pioneering research, the methods and techniques in the archaeometric armory have been significantly improved and expanded.[3] Various methods of physical and chemical analysis have been applied to a wide range of materials from Lapita sites, including not only obsidian, but also chert, metavolcanic rocks, and pottery. From these analyses we can begin to outline the sources, paths of movement, and complexity of networks within the broad fabric of Lapita external exchange systems. Detailed treatments of the methods and results obtained from them have been extensively published elsewhere,[4] and need not be repeated here. However, some comments on the main kinds of materials that archaeologists have determined were transported between Lapita communities are given below.

First, however, it is essential to note the distinction, made by archaeologists who study prehistoric exchange, between *characterization* and *sourcing*.[5] Using various mineralogical, chemical, and physical tests or analyses, it is possible to characterize distinctive attributes of particular kinds of material objects found in archaeological sites. Attributing such objects to a particular *source* involves precise matching of the archaeological and source (control) materials from known localities where the material occurs in nature. But often the full range of potential sources for some kind of material may not be known. For example, an obsidian flow mined three thousand years ago may have been covered by subsequent flows. Or, in the case of potting clays, the sheer number and extent of potential sources may exceed current abilities to map and define them. When we say an artifact has been "sourced," we mean that it has been definitively matched with a control sample from the source locality. Often, archaeologists must be content with simply *characterizing*, in precise chemical or physical terms, the range of materials contained within a particular archaeological site or assemblage. Characterization can still provide valuable information, especially if the materials so characterized are known *not* to occur in the vicinity or region of the site (i.e., are "exotic"). Thus, while we might not be able to precisely pinpoint the source of origin for a kind of ceramic clay, we can often state definitively that the clay or pot from which it was made was an import.

Obsidian

Because it has a highly restricted distribution within the Pacific Islands, obsidian is an ideal material for tracing prehistoric exchange routes and networks (map 8.1). Obsidian from each of the known source areas has a distinct chemical "signature" identifiable through one of several analytical techniques. The two primary sources exploited by Lapita peoples are located on the Willaumez Peninsula of New Britain (the Talasea area), and on Lou and Pam Islands in the Manus (Admiralty) group (Allen and Bell 1988).[6] Another source is located at Cape Hoskins in New Britain, while obsidian from sources in the Fergusson Island of the D'Entrecasteaux group appear to have only rarely entered Lapita exchange networks.[7] In Remote Oceania, within the sphere of Lapita distribution, obsidian sources are also found in northern Vanuatu (Vanua Lava and Gaua in the Banks Islands), and on Tanna, as well as on the small island of Tafahi in northern Tonga, and in American Samoa.

The New Britain obsidian sources were initially exploited long before Lapita times, and there is archaeological evidence for the movement of obsidian from New Britain to New Ireland as long ago as 18–20,000 years ago (see chapter 2). When pre-Oceanic speakers first entered the Bismarck Archipelago, they probably "tapped into" an existing exchange network for this highly useful material. Lapita peoples also began exploiting the Lou-Pam sources in Manus, and the volume of obsidian moving around between islands in the Bismarck Sea began to increase dramatically.

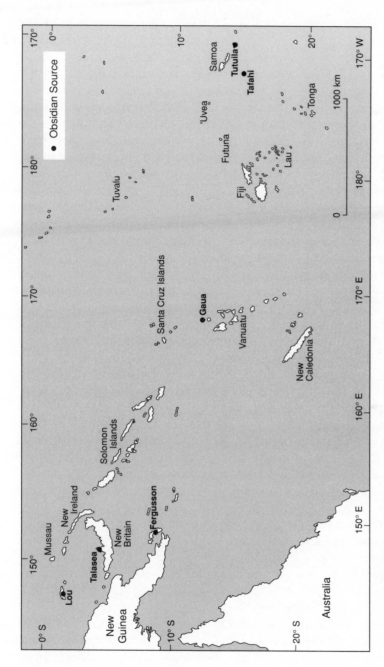

Map 8.1   The location of southwestern Pacific obsidian sources exploited by the Lapita peoples.

With ready sources at hand, obsidian is plentiful in most Far Western Lapita sites in the Bismarck region. At Talepakemalai, we recovered thousands of flakes and cores, with densities as high as 101 obsidian artifacts per cubic meter in the Area B excavation. With the expansion of Lapita peoples into the southeast Solomon Islands, obsidian had to be transported down the Solomons chain some 2,000 km to reach settlements such as Nenumbo. As a consequence, Green and Sheppard have argued that obsidian, although used in a utilitarian manner, also represented something of a symbollically and socially important commodity ("prestige good") in that region. Although the Nenumbo and other Santa Cruz Island Lapita communities quickly discovered, and began to use, the closer Vanua Lava and Gaua sources, they still continued to import New Britain obsidian for several hundred years.

In the Southern and Eastern Lapita regions, obsidian (or its equivalent, volcanic glass) played a much less important role, doubtless due to the absence of ready sources. The Tafahi source in northern Tonga did supply considerable quantities of obsidian to the nearby Niuatoputapu Island communities (e.g., the Lolokoka site), and some of this material moved far afield to Tongatapu and down into the Lau Islands. Quite remarkably, two flakes of New Britain (Talasea) obsidian were recovered from the early Naigani site in Fiji (Best 1987), a straight-line distance from the source of 4,500 km! However, these two flakes were most likely carried on one of the voyaging canoes that brought Lapita explorers eastwards from the Santa Cruz group or Vanuatu, and do not necessarily evidence regular long-distance exchange between Fiji and islands to the west.

Obsidian from Lapita sites has been more intensively studied and analyzed than any other kind of material that was moved about in Lapita exchange networks. A variety of analytical techniques have been applied, including emission spectrography and density-sorting in heavy liquids,[8] but the most powerful and successful have been the use of proton-induced gamma-ray emission (PIGME) and proton-induced X-ray emission (PIXE) methods.[9] At the Lucas Heights facility of the Australian Atomic Energy Commission, several thousand obsidian artifacts from Lapita sites – submitted by a variety of excavators – have now been analyzed by these methods, resulting in a substantial catalog of obsidian data.

Chert

Chert is a term covering a broad range of siliceous rocks, with different geological origins. Like obsidian, chert also provided a good-quality material for expedient flake tools, although it does not hold as sharp an edge. In the southwest Pacific, cherts typically occur in tectonically-uplifted limestones, often of deep marine origin. There are doubtless many highly localized sources, and few of these have as yet been identified or well characterized. However, major sources of marine cherts are known to occur on Ulawa and Malaita Islands in the Solomons, where in late prehistory there was intensive exploitation and manufacture of chert adzes (Ward 1976). These Solomon Island sources also provided chert that was imported to the Lapita sites of the Reef-Santa Cruz group, and perhaps elsewhere (Sheppard 1992, 1993). Another kind of chert, of coralline origin, occurs in the Duff Islands and was also imported to the Nenumbo site (Sheppard 1993). Other as yet unidentified sources exploited by Lapita peoples occur in Fiji or Western Polynesia, and flakes from these sources have been excavated at sites on Futuna and Niuatoputapu (Kirch 1981, 1988a).

Attempts to characterize and source chert have not yet met with the same success as for obsidian. Early efforts by Ward and Smith (1974) were inconclusive, but more recent work by Peter Sheppard that incorporates microscopic identification of foraminifera and other structures, as well as chemical analysis, shows greater promise. For the present, we are often limited to merely identifying chert artifacts in Lapita sites as imports, without being able to tie these to particular source localities.

There have been several technological studies of both obsidian and chert flake assemblages from Lapita sites.[10] With some exceptions, Lapita knappers usually did not modify or "retouch" flakes or cores into formal tools. Rather, a simple bipolar percussion technique was used to produce a variety of flakes with sharp edges, which evidently were simply used as "expedient" tools, probably for a variety of tasks.

Clay, temper, and pottery

Pottery, along with its constituent raw materials – clay and temper – has the greatest potential to reveal external exchange relationships between prehistoric Lapita communities. Since many Lapita sites are found on small coralline islets lacking natural clay deposits, it is obvious that the pottery found in these sites could not have been manufactured without at least importing the necessary clay, and often the volcaniclastic temper as well. Some communities may have specialized in the manufacture of pottery, trading or exchanging ceramic vessels to nearby or more distant communities. The ethnographic record for Oceanic societies provides many examples of such specialized pottery production.[11]

During the 1970s and 1980s most efforts at identifying and characterizing potentially exotic pottery in Lapita and other Oceanic archaeological sites utilized the method of petrographic analysis of temper (Dickinson and Shutler 1979; Hunt 1988). Since the "temper suites" found in particular ceramic fabrics can potentially be traced to one of several distinctive "petrographic provinces" in the southwestern Pacific, it was felt that this method offered the best approach to tracing the movement of ceramics through exchange networks. While several cases of pottery importing and movement were identified, this approach had a number of drawbacks. For one, precise sourcing to a specific locality (as opposed to a broad petrographic province) is rarely possible.

More recently, archaeologists have experimented with the use of microprobe methods (such as energy-dispersive X-ray microanalysis) that permit chemical (elemental) characterization of tempers, clays, or both. The microprobe technique was applied by Terry Hunt (1989) to a large sample of ceramic sherds excavated by me at Talepakemalai and other Mussau Lapita sites. In the Mussau Islands, where the basal geology is largely made up of old, upraised marine limestones, natural clay deposits are rare, as are sources of volcaniclastic temper. Hunt demonstrated that the early Lapita pottery in Talepakemalai included as many as 12 different compositional groups of clay, and that only one or two of these had a local Mussau origin. One of the "exotic" clay types could be sourced to a known clay deposit in the Manus Islands, while the other types could not be definitively located as to point of origin. Hunt's analyses were significant in demonstrating that a large part of the Mussau ceramic assemblage was not locally manufactured, but had been imported to the islands.

While it is clear that considerable amounts of pottery did move between Lapita communities – especially those in the Far Western and Western provinces – it would be wrong to think that *all* Lapita pottery was "trade ware." Even for sites such as Mussau where exotic pottery appears to dominate, there is a component of locally-manufactured ceramics. Moreover, in the Eastern Lapita province, there is very little evidence for inter-island movement of pottery and most ceramics appear to have been locally made (Kirch 1988a; Dickinson et al., in press). Likewise, Galipaud's (1990, 1992) work in New Caledonia suggests some movement of pottery between sites on this large island, but also much local manufacture. The view put forward by Terrell (1989) that Lapita pottery throughout Melanesia consists of a "trade ware," thus, does not appear to stand up to the empirical archaeological record. Such trade wares, marked by high-volume specialist production of ceramics for long-distance commodity exchange with non-ceramic producing groups are indeed known for certain Pacific locales in later time periods, such as Mailu on the south Papuan coast. This is not, however, a model suitable to the Lapita evidence.

Oven stones

Another resource, frequently absent from coral islands and beach terraces, preferred by the Lapita peoples for their hamlet and village sites was volcanic rocks that could be used as heating stones in their earth ovens (see chapter 7). Excavating at Nenumbo in the early 1970s, Roger Green (1976:260) found fire-altered oven stones that had been imported from the nearby islands of Nendö or Tinakula, some 26–52 km distant. In the Talepakemalai Lapita site, I also found numerous volcanic and metavolcanic oven stones that had been imported from several different source areas. Some of these clearly came from the large high island of Mussau, but others more likely derived from the Tabar Islands, New Hanover, or parts of New Ireland.

Other objects

While obsidian, chert, pottery, and oven stones are the most common types of exotic or imported objects occurring in Lapita sites, other materials also extend the catalog of items that were moved between Lapita communities. Among these are finished stone adzes made from different kind of volcanic or meta-volcanic stones, which may have been quite valuable "prestige goods." One of the more bizarre objects was recovered by Green (1976) at the Nenumbo site, and consists of a small piece of soft, muscovite-garnet-schist whose glitter-like properties may have provided face paint or pigment. This object most likely originated somewhere in the D'Entrecasteaux Island group in the Massim region.

Shell "valuables"

All of the materials described above can be unambiguously identified as imports to the Lapita sites in which they are found (even if their sources cannot be precisely defined), because they do not naturally occur in the vicinities of these sites. However, there is yet another broad class of objects that we have good reason to believe were key components in Lapita exchange transactions, namely various kinds of shell 'valuables' (plate 8.1). These include rings, discs, beads, and worked rectangular sections made from several species of marine shell, especially from large cone shells (*Conus leopardus* and *C. litteratus*), *Spondylus* oysters, *Tridacna* clam shells, and *Trochus* shells. Similar kinds of shell objects are virtually a hallmark of many of the ethnographically-documented exchange networks of Oceania, including the classic *kula* ring described by Malinowski, with its *mwali* and *soulava* valuables.[12] In these networks, shell valuables constitute what have been called "inalienable possessions," objects with personal histories that in theory circulate endlessly between sets of exchange partners (Weiner

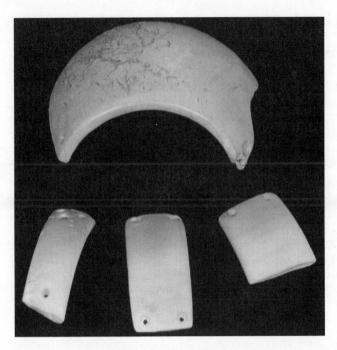

Plate 8.1   *Exchange valuables made from large species of* Conus
shell, excavated from the Talepakemalai site, Mussau Islands.
The carefully worked plaques of shell have drilled holes at
each corner for attachment or suspension with cords.
(Photo by Thérèse Babineau)

1992). Because the species of mollusks from which these objects were made are widely distributed throughout the southwestern Pacific reefs and lagoons, however, demonstrating that
such objects were moved between Lapita communities is a
more difficult matter than with obsidian or pottery.

In a comprehensive analysis of the distribution of such shell
valuables in ten Lapita assemblages, I was able to demonstrate
that while *finished* (or broken parts of finished) valuables were
fairly widespread, unfinished rejects, manufacture debris, and
tools were restricted to only a few sites (Kirch 1988c). This
discovery led me to argue that certain Lapita communities had
specialized production industries for making such valuables,
which they then exchanged for other imported commodities.

Plate 8.2　Two species of large Conus *shell were used to manufacture finely-polished rings. The stages of shell ring manufacture are illustrated here with excavated specimens from the Talepakemalai site; a finished ring is shown in the center foreground. (Photo by Thérèse Babineau)*

One such specialized production locale was clearly the Talepakemalai site, which contains large quantities of manufacture debris and unfinished rejects of *Conus* shell discs and rings (plate 8.2). More rarely, large shell rings made from the valves of the giant *Tridacna* clam are evidenced by detritus and manufacture rejects (plate 8.3). The Talepakemalai people were also manufacturing large numbers of *Trochus* shell fishhooks, and these may also have been objects of export. Within the Eastern Lapita region, the sites of Lakeba and Naigani in Fiji seem to have similarly specialized in the production of shell objects that were then moved out into an exchange network that incorporated Lapita communities in Tonga, Samoa, and other islands.

The missing record of exchange

Despite considerable success in identifying a range of transported, exchanged, or traded materials between Lapita communities, we must always be cognisant of the incompleteness of the archaeological record. There can be no doubt that many

Plate 8.3   Stages in the manufacture of large shell rings made from the giant Tridacna *clam. The specimens illustrated here were all excavated from the Talepakemalai site, Mussau Islands. (Photo by Thérèse Babineau)*

other classes of material were moved between Lapita sites, some of them quite likely in significant volumes. Mats and barkcloth – or materials for their manufacture – are a likely possibility, as are quantities of foodstuffs (taro or yam tubers, for example, or dried sago flour). (The large globular, plain ware ceramic jars so common in some Lapita sites may well have been used for the storage and transport of sago flour.) Such materials, being perishable, have not survived to become part of the archaeological record of prehistoric exchange.

Modeling Lapita Exchange

External exchange among Lapita communities was both complex and dynamic. How then, do we proceed from merely cataloging varied materials moved between sites – often over remarkable distances – to actually modeling the complex structure of external exchange, and its changing configurations over time and space? We cannot simply impose ethnographic models of Oceanic exchange on the archaeological evidence for Lapita. For one thing, the geographic scale of Lapita external exchange was far greater than any ethnographically-documented system in Oceania. Moreover, because social anthropologists and archaeologists deal with entirely different kinds of data (social transactions in the first case, and material objects in the second), and with wholly different time scales (years or perhaps a few decades for the ethnographer, versus centuries and millennia for the archaeologist), the concepts, categories, and models that ethnographers have developed for Oceanic exchange are of little use to the archaeologist. For example, beginning with Mauss (1925) and on to Sahlins (1972), Weiner (1992), and Thomas (1991), social anthropologists have debated theories of exchange *value*. But the relative value of a prehistoric object, or its permutation in a series of transactions in the past, are not accessible to the prehistorian.

Archaeologists need to model prehistoric exchange in terms appropriate both to our data and to the time scales at which we work, always remembering as well that what is evidenced in the archaeological record is likely to be incomplete, partial. Fred Plog, whose pioneering work on prehistoric exchange in the American Southwest was one of the first to articulate such an explicitly archaeological approach to exchange, rightly observed that the elements of our models cannot be individual people or social groups, but spatial *loci*: "sites, rooms on a site, activity areas on a site," (Plog 1977:128) and the like. In the current state of Lapita archaeological research, such loci will generally be specific sites, from which we have been able to identify – and better yet quantify – one or more classes of imported objects.[13] If the site is stratified, we may be able to trace changes in the variety and quantities of such imported materials being received and discarded over time. In addition to imports, our sites may yield information on localized and often specialized production of materials for export. Such is the case with specialized production of shell artifacts at Talepakemalai and at several other Lapita sites.

Once these data have been accumulated for a number of such loci or nodes within a particular geographic region, it is possible to model the prehistoric interactions between these nodes, in terms of a number of variables.[14] These include: (1)

the *content* of the network, that is the kinds or range of materials being exchanged; (2) the *magnitude* of the network; (3) the *diversity* of materials, including measures of richness and evenness; (4) the geographic *size* of the network; (5) the *time span* or temporal dimension; (6) the *directionality* of exchange, in terms of the flow(s) of materials; (7) the *symmetry* or *asymmetry* of exchange between loci; (8) *centralization* or *decentralization* of the network; and (9) the overall *complexity*, a combination of symmetry, directionality, centralization, and diversity. Analysis of exchange networks using these variables may be qualitative or quantitative, and can benefit from the application of various kinds of matrix and graph-theoretic analyses (Hage and Harary 1991).

Over the course of their millennium-long existence, Lapita external exchange networks or systems were highly dynamic, fluid structures. Despite the remarkable discovery of Talasea obsidian flakes as far east as Fiji, it is highly unlikely that there was ever a single, integrated "Lapita exchange network" that spanned the entire geographic region in which Lapita sites are found.[15] At most, it seems that the Far Western and Western Lapita provinces were for some time connected by regular communication links, over distances of roughly 2,000 km. Once the Fiji-Tonga-Samoa region had been colonized, a separate exchange network was established within the Eastern Lapita province. The 850 km ocean gap between Fiji and the southeast Solomons was simply too great, and the risks of voyaging too high, for regular communication to be maintained. The large island of New Caledonia, once settled, also became disconnected from the rest of the Lapita world, at least in any regular sense.

For these reasons, it is necessary to look at Lapita exchange in terms of several principal areas or "provinces" that we have defined (see chapter 3). In the following paragraphs, I turn again to the three principal sites upon which I have repeatedly focused in this book (Talepakemalai, Nenumbo, and Lolokoka) to illustrate the nature and transformation of Lapita exchange. Talepakemalai exemplifies well a major node in the early, highly complex Far Western exchange network, as well as later transformations of that network. Nenumbo was one node at or near the terminus of Lapita long-distance exchange at its farthest extension, and thus illuminates exchange relations between the Far Western and Western communities once the Lapita expansion into Remote Oceania had commenced. Lolokoka, however, was never connected to these ancestral networks, but rather played a role in the new Eastern Lapita network that linked communities in the Fiji, Tonga, and Samoa archipelagoes.

Talepakemalai and the Far Western exchange network

The islands of the Bismarck Archipelago – home of the earliest Far Western Lapita assemblages yet documented archaeologically – are arrayed in an oval-shaped configuration around the Bismarck Sea, a region roughly 500 by 800 km across. Most of these islands are inter-visible, with only Mussau and Manus in the northwest requiring slightly more risky voyages out of sight of land.[16] At least 20 Lapita sites have now been identified around this ring of islands, and future fieldwork will doubtless reveal many more. Among the important resources entering into the regional exchange network was obsidian, obtained from the two main sources at Talasea and in Manus. Various kinds of geographic network models allow us to pose a number of hypotheses regarding prehistoric exchange networks in the region. Such models can be used to assess the probable effect of geography on any transport or communication network.[17] For example, we find that the Mussau Islands are especially well situated with regard to connectivity within the Bismarck Archipelago network. That is, in a graph-theoretic sense, Mussau has high centrality within the Bismarck Archipelago geographic network. This finding should lead us to hypothesize that Lapita communities situated in the Mussau Islands might be expected to have played a significant role in regional exchange.

Ideally, one would use actual Lapita site locations as the nodes in these network models, rather than idealized geographic spaces. Unfortunately, until further field research has filled in many of the gaps in our knowledge of Bismarck Archipelago prehistory, this will not be possible. That is, we are not yet in a position to model the actual shape and configuration of the early Far Western Lapita exchange network based on empirical knowledge of its specific nodes. What we can do, is assess something of the *complexity* of the overall system as reflected at one or more specific nodes or sites that have been well studied. One of the most thoroughly researched of these nodes is Mussau, with the early Talepakemalai (ECA) and Etapakengaroasa (EHB) sites, as well as later sites and deposits that span the entire Lapita period in the Bismarcks. In our field and laboratory research in Mussau, we emphasized characterization and sourcing of all exotic materials recovered through our excavations, including obsidian, chert, pottery, oven stones, and other materials. As much as possible, we have tried to obtain quantitative measures of changing flows of these materials into Mussau, as measured by the proxy indices of rates of deposition in the archaeological record.[18]

Table 8.1 uses the modeling variables outlined by Plog (1977) to define and contrast the position of Mussau in the larger Far Western Lapita exchange network at three points in time. We may think of these three temporal points as "snapshots" taken of a dynamic system at different times. At the beginning of the Far Western period, as it is currently known archaeologically by the evidence from Mussau, Lapita exchange was already highly complex. The *content* and *diversity* of the system were greater than at any subsequent times. Obsidian was being imported from both the Talasea and Manus sources, in roughly equal quantity, while chert was also being imported from an unknown source or sources. More remarkably, the ceramics at Talepakemalai and other early Mussau sites derive from at least 12 different clay sources, as determined by Terry Hunt's microprobe analysis of the clay. One of these sources was very probably in Manus, and another one or two sources were on the main high island of Mussau, but the others remain unknown as to geographic provenance. However, there is significant diversity in both clay composition and in temper suites to indicate that pottery was being manufactured at several different communities, and subsequently exchanged or traded over a complex set of communication paths. Oven stones were also coming into the Mussau Islands from several sources, most probably in the Tabar Islands, New Hanover, or New Ireland. Other low frequency imports included finished stone adzes. At the same time that this diversity of materials was flowing into

Table 8.1 Far Western Lapita exchange viewed from the Talepakemalai node: formal characteristics

Variable	Early phase (1,400 BC)	Late phase (500 BC)	Post-Lapita phase (AD 1,200)
Content: Imports	Pottery: 12 groups Obsidian: 2 sources Oven stones, chert, metavolcanic adzes	Pottery: 6 groups Obsidian: 2 sources (1 dominant) Oven stones	Pottery: 3 groups, low frequency Obsidian: 1 source
Content: Exports	Shell valuables and fishhooks	?	?
Magnitude	High volumes of pottery and obsidian imported; high volumes of shell artifacts exported	Greatly reduced volumes of imports; export volume low or nonexistent	Very small quantities of materials imported; exports unknown
Diversity	Greatest	Reduced	Least
Network Size	Large number of participating nodes	Reduced number of nodes	Restricted to Manus and New Ireland
Directionality	Multiple flows both in and out of Mussau	Reduced directionality	Restricted flow from Manus to Mussau
Centralization	Not centralized	Not centralized	Highly focused on Mussau
Complexity	High	Reduced	Simple

Modified after Kirch (1990, table 2)

the Mussau Lapita communities, there was a substantial outward flow of finished shell artifacts, including *Conus* shell rings and discs, and *Trochus* shell fishhooks. That such objects were being manufactured and exported out of Mussau is shown by the differential quantities of finished artifacts versus rejects and detritus in the local sites. In short, the early Lapita communities in Mussau were highly connected with a significant number of other communities dispersed around the Bismarck Sea, with access to a variety of different resources. Mussau itself may have been an important node in the movement of Manus obsidian to other, more distant parts of the Archipelago, and certainly was the place of origin of large numbers of shell artifacts.

If we "fast forward" ahead in time to the late Far Western Lapita phase (the middle column in table 8.1) we see that the situation had changed considerably, and that overall there had been a substantial decrease in system complexity. First of all, the content of the system had been reduced. The overall quantity of obsidian coming into Mussau had now dropped off significantly, and most of this was originating at the geographically closer Manus source. Likewise, ceramic diversity had declined from the original twelve groups down to only six, with two of these being local and at least one in Manus. The manufacture of shell artifacts for export had also declined. These quantitative measures indicate that the number of external nodes with which the Mussau communities were connected had declined markedly, and there seems to be a greater emphasis on geographically more proximal connections (e.g., with Manus and New Ireland).

What we are witnessing in the archaeological record of dynamic exchange flows in the Bismarck Archipelago over some 1,000 years is the gradual *regionalization* and *localized specialization* of what initially began as a very extensive and highly connected network. As local populations increased and local resource bases developed, there was less interest in keeping the larger network intact, and communities began to focus more on external exchanges with their near geographic partners. Over time, the original network was breaking down into several regional systems. Remarkably, such a model fits well with the linguistic evidence for the breakup of an early Proto Oceanic dialect chain into several regionally-focused primary subgroups (Ross 1988; Pawley and Ross 1995), as we have seen in chapter 4. The Western Oceanic languages can be divided into three main subgroups or clusters: the North New Guinea Cluster (which spans the Vitiaz Strait and includes southwestern New Britain), the Meso-Melanesian Cluster (northeast New Britain, New Ireland, and the west-central Solomons), and the Papuan Tip Cluster (the Papua and Massim areas). The Manus and Mussau groups also form distinct high-order subgroups. The geographically extensive and nodally-complex early Far Western Lapita exchange network would have helped to maintain and facilitate linguistic (as well as economic and social) communication through the Bismarck-Solomons region, thus resulting in a complex dialect chain. However, as exchange became regionally focused, so the dialect chain would be broken in places, to create sets of smaller chains. These in turn would form the basis for the higher order subgroups or "clusters" of Oceanic languages recognized today.[19]

We can also trace the continued transformation of external exchange in Mussau after the end of the Lapita period (column three in table 8.1). Our third "snapshot" indicates a radically different kind of external exchange system, with only infrequent and minimal links to Manus and New Ireland. In its place, the Mussau people had come to place much greater emphasis on *internal* exchange between local communities, in which competitive pig feasting seems to have played a major role. But this is another story, the legacy of Lapita in Near Oceania.

"Down-the-line" to Nenumbo

The first significant expansion of Lapita peoples beyond the intervisible archipelagoes of Near Oceania (the Bismarcks and Solomons) was across a 450 km ocean gap to the islands of the Santa Cruz group. There they discovered and settled a number of ecologically-diverse islands, including the coral islets of the Reef Islands, the larger island of Nendö, and slightly later in time such remote volcanic islands as Tikopia and Anuta.[20] Roger Green's extensive excavations at three sites in the Reefs/ Santa Cruz Islands provide important data relating to external exchange in this region over a time span of about 500 years.[21] The oldest site in this sequence is Nanggu (SZ-8), which probably dates to about 1,200 BC. Nenumbo (RF-2) was settled soon after, and may have been occupied until about 900 BC, while Ngamanie (RF-6) ends the sequence at about 650 BC (Green 1991c). As with the Mussau case, we may take the data from this series of three sites to represent a set of temporal "snapshots" of changing patterns of external exchange in the Western Lapita region.

For various reasons, exchange among the communities who settled the Reef-Santa Cruz group differed somewhat from that of their immediate ancestors in the Far Western Lapita region. Not only were inter-island distances greater, but these were pioneering communities, initially at least on the edge of the (to them) known world. There would have been strong reasons to maintain ties with the ancestral or homeland communities from whence they (and in later generations, their ancestors) had come. Thus, the Reefs/Santa Cruz Lapita communities were at "the end of the line" of a chain of regular exchange connections extending back into the homeland region of the Solomons and Bismarcks.

Such extended, linear exchange networks are well known to prehistorians in various parts of the world. They are likely to be characterized by what Colin Renfrew (1984) termed "down-the-line" patterns of exchange, where materials are passed along through a series of transactions, often gaining commodity value as they progress along the chain. Such systems display "drop off" curves in the total quantity of materials as one progresses farther and farther from the source (such as the Talasea obsidian source). These curves are typically negatively exponential, and behave according to Renfrew's "law of monotonic decrement."

From his work at Nenumbo (RF-2), Green was able to identify a surprising range of imported or exotic materials. Indeed, in Green's view "it was importing alone that made possible the continuance in the Reef-Santa Cruz area of a cultural adaptation more in keeping with the physical resources of the larger continental islands to the west than with the rather limited resources available on raised atolls" (1976:258). Green identified pottery, obsidian, chert, oven stones, and a variety of stone

Table 8.2   Changing densities (grams/cubic meter) of
obsidian and chert in three Reef-Santa Cruz Islands sites

Material	Nanggu, SZ-8 (ca. 1,100 BC)	Nenumbo, RF-2 (ca. 1,000 BC)	Ngamanie, RF-6 (ca. 650 BC)
Obsidian	34.6	17.36	6.12
Chert	23.4	23.1	10.5

Data from Sheppard (1993)

artifacts as imports to Nenumbo and other Reef Island sites. In
subsequent analyses, he and Peter Sheppard have concentrated
on the obsidian and chert assemblages as providing the best
evidence for changing patterns of exchange.

Green (1987:246; in press) classifies the range of imported
materials into four "distance based modes" of exchange. The
first consists of *direct access* to materials (such as oven stones)
that derived from localities close to the sites, between 26–56
km distant. The second mode involved *local reciprocity* with
neighboring communities located 46–100 km distant. The third
mode is characterized by materials (such as obsidian from the
Vanua Lava and Gaua sources, chert, and meta-volcanic adzes)
with sources at about 3–400 km distant. Obtaining these items
presumably involved *one-stop reciprocity*. Finally, there was
down-the-line exchange involving materials with sources at
2,000 km or more. In the latter category are obsidian from
Talasea, Lou, and West Fergusson, and small quantities of
some peculiar rocks such as muscovite-garnet-schist and meta-
morphosed sandstone.

A quantitative index of changing volumes or rates of flow of
materials into the Reef-Santa Cruz Lapita sites over a 500-year
period can be obtained by looking at the densities of obsidian
and chert artifacts in the three sites (table 8.2).[22] The earliest
site, Nanggu, shows the highest densities of these imports, as
we would expect in the case of an initial pioneering community
that maintained close links to its immediate homeland. Slightly
later in time (perhaps only 100 years later), the Nenumbo site
shows a significant decrease in the quantity of obsidian obtained

through down-the-line exchange, but no appreciable drop in chert, which was obtained at a closer distance through one-stop reciprocity. By the end of this 500-year period, represented by the Ngamanie site, however, both obsidian and chert importing had decreased substantially below their initial levels. Nonetheless, in the Reef-Santa Cruz Islands external exchange continued unabated for a period of at least five centuries.

Green, and Peter Sheppard who has studied the lithic technology associated with the Reef-Santa Cruz obsidian and chert assemblages, have both speculated on the exchange *value* of these materials. Even though once on site the obsidian that had traveled some 2,000 km to reach Nenumbo was put to utilitarian uses, Green argued that it must have had considerable value as a "luxury item and status import" (1987:246). He opined that "people used this obsidian because they had learned to use it in their homeland, and they wished to maintain 'ties' with their relatives there by importing a luxury and status-maintaining item with social and ideological significance, rather than depend on, for example, a slightly inferior and less prestigious replacement import from a non-homeland community much closer to hand [the Vanua Lava and Gaua obsidian]" (1987:246).[23] While obsidian may well have been a status-enhancing or "prestige" good, it was not treated as such through any maximizing use-patterns, as Sheppard's analyses show. As Sheppard points out, the commodity value of obsidian may have been maximized "in social terms at points in its history where it may be a concrete symbol of exchange" (1993:135). At these times, the value of obsidian was not likely to have been assessed in strictly utilitarian terms, and subsequent to the socially-meaningful exchange transactions the glassy rock may have been consumed "according to another set of commodity (utilitarian) values."

Finally, just as exchange in the Far Western homeland ultimately segmented into a series of regionalized systems or networks, so the Reef-Santa Cruz Islands eventually became disengaged from down-the-line exchange. There are indications in the archaeological record from the Santa Cruz Group[24] that immediately following the Lapita period, external exchange focused primarily on linkages with communities in northern Vanuatu (the Banks Islands). At the time of early European

contact (the so-called "ethnographic present") the various islands of Santa Cruz Group were linked by a complex, regional
exchange network sometimes referred to as the "red feather
money" trading network (Davenport 1962, 1964). The linkages
themselves were maintained by seafaring and canoe-building
people from Taumako (Duff Islands), who facilitated a complex
set of transactions involving women, food, red feathers and
feather currency, shell discs, and other materials.

Lolokoka: recreating social worlds

Sometime late in the second millennium BC, one group of Lapita
people made the then-unprecedented voyaging leap across 850
km of open Pacific Ocean to discover the large, fertile islands
of the Fiji Archipelago. Soon after, these or others who had
received the news of extensive possibilities for island colonization, fanned out to reconnoiter and settle not only Fiji and the
Lau Group, but the north-south trending Tongan chain, the
tropical Samoan group, and several more isolated islands including Futuna, 'Uvea, and Niuatoputapu. By about 1,000 BC
Lapita communities had been established throughout this region;
their archaeological assemblages constitute the Early Eastern
Lapita phase.

Although the wide and turbulent ocean gap between the
southeast Solomons-Vanuatu and Fiji was doubtless crossed
more than once, it was significantly daunting so as to preclude
two-way voyaging on any regular basis. Although there are a
few scraps of materials from Early Eastern Lapita sites that
originated in the Western Lapita homeland (such as the two
flakes of Talasea obsidian from the Naigani site, Best [1987]),
the archaeological evidence overwhelmingly suggests that once
settled, the Eastern Lapita region became effectively isolated
and separated from ancestral communities to the west. Rather
than maintaining their ties to homelands at great risk of life,
the Eastern Lapita peoples recreated their social world in the
islands of the Fiji-Tonga-Samoa archipelagoes. This involved
the establishment of a new external exchange network linking
these Eastern Lapita communities.

Although at least 30 Lapita sites have now been identified

within the Eastern Lapita province, it would be premature to claim that we could in any precise way model the exchange system linking these communities. As with the Far Western network, however, some insights can be gained both from an examination of graph-theoretic models and by examining the input and output flows at particular locales or nodes. One such node is that of Lolokoka, an Early Eastern Lapita site on Niuatoputapu Island. Although Niuatoputapu is a geographic isolate – lying mid-way between the Tongan and Samoan archipelagoes – it occupies a position of high *centrality* in the "topologic structure" of this region (Kirch 1988a:255, figure 136, table 49). A short-path connectivity matrix for the Eastern Lapita region yields a second-order rank for Niuatoputapu, primarily because it would have been the most likely point for voyaging connections between Samoa and Tonga, and also to 'Uvea and Futuna.[25] Moreover, Niuatoputapu Island and the Lolokoka people were ideally situated to control the source of obsidian on Tafahi Island (only 6 km distant), the largest and best-quality source within the Eastern Lapita region.

That Lolokoka was connected into a larger external exchange network is archaeologically evidenced by the presence of chert or chalcedony flakes of non-local origin (Kirch 1988a:254). We also know that the Lolokoka people were exporting Tafahi obsidian, for flakes of this material have been found in the Lau Islands and Tongatapu (Green, in press). Other materials that seem to have been circulating among the Eastern Lapita communities include finished adzes of basalt and other volcanic rock. Interestingly – and in striking contrast with exchange among Far Western communities – pottery was not an imported item at Lolokoka. Our analyses of the Lolokoka ceramics indicate local manufacture, with the exception that a small quantity of pottery was moving locally between Niuatoputapu and Tafahi.

At Lolokoka, however, we do find small numbers of finished (often broken, hence discarded) shell valuables, such as rings and discs. Within the Eastern Lapita region, only the sites of Naigani and – particularly so – Lakeba have yielded good evidence for the manufacture or specialized production of such shell objects. I suspect that the location of these centers for shell exchange valuable production in Fiji was more than coincidence. Having been the first islands within the Eastern Lapita region to be settled, Fiji came to represent what was old and "ancestral" within this social world now isolated by great ocean distances from the true ancestral homelands in the southeast Solomons and beyond. In the "socio-logics" of Eastern Lapita exchange, the Fijian communities would be higher ranked, and thus the proper point of origin for high-value, prestige goods such as shell valuables.

Although the Niuatoputapu sites were not sufficiently-well stratified to yield a series of temporal "snapshots" of changing exchange patterns, regionalization also set in within the Eastern Lapita network after the first few centuries.[26] The somewhat later ceramic sites on Niuatoputapu (e.g., sites NT-100 and –93) do not contain exotic chert or shell valuables, suggesting increased isolation or breakdown of the early network. This fits well with linguistic evidence (Geraghty 1983) that an early, widespread dialect chain (Proto Central-Pacific) quickly segmented into geographically localized dialect networks, focused respectively on Fiji-Lau, Tonga-'Eua-Ha'apai, and Samoa-Futuna-'Uvea.[27]

As in the two cases examined above, external exchange networks in the Fiji-Tonga-Samoa region continued to evolve during the post-Lapita period. Archaeological evidence for much of this time span is lacking or minimal, although we do know that basalt adzes from Samoan sources were widely traded (Best et al. 1992). At the time of European contact, however, a well-documented external exchange network operated between Fiji, Tonga, and Samoa, with the Tongans as the main voyaging facilitators of exchange. Referred to as the "Tongan maritime empire" (Guiart 1963), this system moved valuables such as whale's teeth to Fiji, sandalwood and feathers to Tonga and Samoa, and from the social point of view most significantly, involved the marital exchange of chiefly spouses (Kirch 1984:232–42).

Understanding Lapita Exchange

Having looked at Lapita external exchange from several different geographic and temporal perspectives, is it possible to reach any deeper understanding of the significance or import of this aspect of the Lapita social world? Certainly we should not expect to "explain" Lapita exchange activities in any absolute sense, for these complex transactions must have had a panoply of different values and meanings at different times and places. Likewise, it seems futile to interpret Lapita exchange in simple functionalist or ecological terms. Although these networks did have the useful "function" of moving scarce or discretely-distributed resources among communities that were often situated on resource-poor islands, a strictly utilitarian explanation will not hold. For example, Talepakemalai need not have been accorded a monopoly on the specialized production of shell valuables, for the raw materials (*Conus, Trochus,* and other mollusks) were widely available throughout the Far Western and Western Lapita regions. And for the occupants of the Nenumbo site, there is no reason to think that the much closer Vanua Lava and Gaua sources of obsidian were in any functional or utilitarian ways inferior to the Talasea glass that they continued to import from five times the distance for more than half a millennium.

Rather, understanding Lapita exchange must take us into the realm of the social, for as Marshall Sahlins put it, "every transaction, as we already know, is necessarily a social strategy" (1972:303). Yet this poses the greatest challenge to archaeology, for as I observed earlier, ethnographic models of exchange are couched in terms of data and time spans not easily appropriated to prehistory. One kind of "social strategy" that may have been critical to the success of the Lapita peoples – as they began their unprecedented expansion into Remote Oceania – was the maintenance of formal social ties between pioneering and established homeland communities. I outlined this model of Lapita exchange several years ago, in the following words:

> The importance of exchange for Lapita communities did not lie in assuring access to certain material resources such as obsidian or temper, but as a formal mechanism assuring a "lifeline" back to larger and securely established homeland communities. In the formative period of a new settlement, such linkages could be crucial in the event of unpredictable environmental hazards (drought or cyclone), or to augment demographically small and

unstable groups with suitable marriage partners. The ability to
draw upon the total range of social and demographic, as well
as material, resources of a homeland community could have
meant the difference between survival and extinction. A formal
exchange system centering on the status-enhancing acquisition
of prestige goods (shell valuables, high-quality obsidian, adzes,
etc.) provided the social mechanism for maintaining what was
in effect an essential component of the Lapita dispersal and
colonization strategy. (Kirch 1988c:113–4)

It now seems to me that the demographic aspects of this model
should not be underestimated. Beyond the Solomons, Lapita
people were moving for the first time into previously uninhabited regions, where recruitment of marriage partners from pre-
existing local groups was not possible. In the critical stages of
pioneer expansion, exchange networks may been essential for
assuring access to larger pools of eligible marriage partners in
the homeland communities.

Some years ago Jonathan Friedman (1981) outlined a transformational model for the development of the varied social
forms found throughout the Oceanic region today. Friedman
noted that there was linguistic and comparative ethnographic
evidence to support the interpretation of early Austronesian
societies as having generalized exchange (matrilateral cross-
cousin marriage) as well as some kind of asymmetric dualism.
Combined with the then-emerging evidence for long-distance
transport of obsidian and other material items in early Melanesian archaeological sites, Friedman hypothesized that, in the
earlier time periods, systems of "prestige-good" exchange were
essential to the social formations found in Oceania. Friedman
traced two possible transformational trajectories from this
ancestral condition: one, involving increasing trade density led
to a breakdown of hierarchy and the development of "big man"
social systems. The other saw a "collapse of trade," increased
internal competition and agricultural intensification, leading to
the classic chiefdom societies of Eastern Polynesia.

Friedman's model is highly provocative in its attempt to
account for the spectrum of Oceanic social formations in terms
of the properties and systems of social reproduction; three such
fundamental systems are recognized: "prestige-good," "big-
man," and "theocratic feudalism." Archaeological studies of

external exchange among Lapita communities since the time that Friedman's model was advanced have now significantly expanded our understanding of "prestige-good" exchange among the early Oceanic-speaking communities of the Pacific. However, the subsequent transformation of these systems may have been even more complex than Friedman envisioned, and tracing these social changes through the Pacific archaeological record will doubtless provide many challenges for future generations of prehistorians.

9

Epilogue: The Lapita Legacy

Human beings are voyagers to islands ... They might land naked on an empty beach, but in their minds, their languages, their relationships they bring a world with them.
Greg Dening, *Islands and Beaches*

Rather than conclude with a recapitulation of main themes, I prefer to let the preceding chapters speak for themselves as to current evidence and interpretations of Lapita archaeology and cultural history. Instead, I will briefly address some larger issues pertaining to the practice of prehistory in the Pacific Islands, and to how such practice affects our historical constructions of Lapita, and of the myriad societies that descended from Lapita. I am concerned about several aspects of this practice. On the one hand there has been a growing tendency toward academic specialization and its corollary, ignorance about and mistrust of other disciplines and lines of evidence that also have a legitimate claim to knowledge about the past. "Prehistory" is not the sole purview of archaeology, although one might think that many current archaeological practitioners hold such a view, to judge from their stated positions on what evidence they hold as admissible. The rise of specialist departments of archaeology or prehistory, isolated from other social sciences or even from history, has doubtless encouraged this trend. On the other hand, I remain firmly committed to the stance that the most powerful and compelling constructions of past societies and cultures are those which result from integrative research by archaeologists working in consort with historical

linguists, biological anthropologists, ethnobotanists, comparative ethnographers, or any number of others whose data are
relevant to historical problems.[1]

A second concern revolves around the uses to which our
historical endeavors are put in the contemporary world. For
whom do we labor to reconstruct the world of those people
who made, used, and discarded Lapita pottery? Surely a partial
answer is, for ourselves: to satisfy innate curiosity, and perhaps
less altruistically, to secure academic recognition. But such can
only be a partial answer and one that is not wholly satisfying.
The practice of archaeology has become politically and culturally charged throughout the world, as debates rage over "who
owns the past." The past is not merely comprised of those
potsherds and obsidian flakes and myriad other remains that
make up what we call "the archaeological record." It consists
as well in the *constructions* we put on that record, constructions that may be highly meaningful and even politically charged
to those contemporary peoples who identify with some segment of the past (e.g., Trask 1993:161–78).

In this context I am disturbed by the narrow disciplinary
perspectives of some Pacific archaeologists, especially those who
wish to deny the possibility of any cultural construction for
that segment of the archaeological record that we label "Lapita."
By insisting that Lapita sites and artifacts can *never* be correlated with an ethno-linguistic category such as Proto Oceanic,
these scholars exercise a subtle but nonetheless insidious form
of academic hegemony over the past: excluded from being the
cultural patrimony of the modern Oceanic-speaking peoples,
Lapita thus becomes strictly an academic "object." Thus, for
example, appropriate models for the interpretation and understanding of Lapita archaeological remains – which may be
derived from careful historical comparison of ethnographically
and linguistically-attested Oceanic cultural patterns – might be
replaced by an ill-defined paradigm of "human biogeography"
(e.g., Terrell 1986). Or, to cite a more extreme example of this
practice, the entire concept of a Lapita cultural complex or
Lapita expansion is relegated to the trash heap of discarded
scientific paradigms, in favor of a nameless and unspecified
"process for which an archaeological pattern is emerging for the
Pacific islands in general" (Smith 1995:375).[2] Thus prehistory

ceases to be about understanding the real lives of culturally-contexted actors in the past, cultural agency is reified to unspecified "processes," and the archaeological record becomes mere grist for the academic theory mill.

On Archaeology, Prehistory, and Historical Anthropology

Many contemporary practitioners use the term "prehistory" as if it were unproblematic. In academic and anthropological parlance, of course, the term arose in opposition to history classically constructed on the basis of written texts (documents), and eventually came to signify that branch of archaeology that studied past cultures lacking written histories, or prior to the adoption of writing. In the Pacific, the latter generally coincides with the expansion of the West and the modern World System, through the agency of explorers, missionaries, and entrepreneurs. This act of scholarly naming – of marking *prehistory* as somehow qualitatively different from *history* – tends to set up a chain of distinctions, intended or unintended. Thus, historians study texts while prehistorians study material culture; historians are concerned with personal agency while prehistorians search for process; historians are humanists while prehistorians practice science. Archaeology is itself torn apart by these distinctions into such specializations as classical archaeology, historical archaeology, and prehistoric archaeology.

In the Pacific, prehistoric archaeology was originally practiced within the larger context of a holistic anthropology in the North American tradition, in which other branches or subdisciplines of the field were also regarded as having legitimate claims to historical knowledge and research agendas that included historical reconstruction. Thus, in the earlier part of this century, comparative ethnography was the approach to historical reconstruction favored for the most part over archaeology (e.g., Buck 1938). Only with the rise of structural-functionalism within social anthropology, with the critique of extreme diffusionist models, and at mid-century the development of radiocarbon dating, did prehistoric archaeology eventually become the main avenue for investigating the "pre-contact" histories of Pacific island cultures. However, in the past few decades the practice of archaeology in the Pacific has shifted away from holistic departments of anthropology to specialized departments of archaeology or prehistory, and in certain regions of rapid economic growth such as Hawai'i and New Zealand, to commercial archaeological firms (e.g., "cultural-resource management" or "contract" archaeology). With this shift has come a decline in the appreciation that some archaeologists have for other means of knowing the past, and a distancing between ethnography and archaeology. Most Pacific archaeologists do not speak an indigenous Pacific island language, nor have they been trained in the comparative ethnography of the region, and in any event would probably regard such skills as extraneous to their mission. Effectively distanced from the very people whose histories they purport to write, it should perhaps come as no surprise that these archaeologists are uncomfortable applying any notion of ethnicity or culture in the past.

This ceaseless trend towards specialization of intellectual inquiry may be inevitable in the contemporary academic world of exponentially-expanding "information," but it does not necessarily make for good history or good science (if, indeed, there is any fundamental difference between these two). It may be worthwhile revisiting the proposal of one of the early founders of holistic anthropology, Edward Sapir (1916), who saw no utility in drawing distinctions between historical approaches based solely on the kinds of data they used. Rather, Sapir envisioned a historical anthropology in which comparative ethnology, archaeology, linguistics, and physical anthropology all contributed to a key problem: "metaphorically defined as the translation of a two-dimensional photographic picture of reality into the three-dimensional picture which lies back of it" (1916:2). In Sapir's day, archaeological method and theory were still primitive, and he not surprisingly put greater emphasis on evidence obtained from comparative ethnography and linguistics. But the essential concept of a historical anthropology was well developed in Sapir's framework. This framework would later be elaborated by those like Eggan (1954), Romney (1957), and especially Vogt (1964) who also recognized the power that multiple lines of ethnographic, linguistic, archaeological, and

biological evidence could bring to historical analysis of cultur-
ally-defined regions. Flannery and Marcus (1983) demonstrated
how such an approach could be applied in their brilliant
comparative study of the Zapotec and Mixtec civilizations,
prompting Green and myself to formally outline the use of a
"phylogenetic model" for the diversification of the Polynesian
cultures (Kirch and Green 1987).

Some have resisted this phylogenetic approach, mistakenly
thinking that its application requires adherence to a notion of
"isolation" between cultures once colonization has been ef-
fected. This is certainly not the case, for although isolation was
a major factor in the diversification of many of the Eastern Polynesian societies because inter-archipelago distances are extreme
(for example, Easter Island and Hawai'i), the phylogenetic model
or approach is perfectly capable of dealing with contact and
cultural borrowing as well. It is thus heartening to see that
some scholars recognize the power of comparative methods
and the phylogenetic approach for historical study of large
culturally-related segments of the world. Bellwood et al. (1995:3)
recently asserted that not just the Polynesians, but the entire
Austronesian world, may be conceived of as a phylogenetic
unit, "albeit on a much larger scale in both time and space."
In a parallel vein, Pawley and Ross assert that the Austronesian-
speaking region "offers exceptionally favorable conditions" for
practicing an interdisciplinary culture history in which con-
stant comparisons between the data and models generated by
each discipline "are necessary in order to evaluate competing
hypotheses within disciplines and to gain a more complete
picture of the past than any single method can provide" (1993:
426). Regrettably, there will always be those whose academic
insecurities or willful ignorance of the methods and evidence of
scholars in fields not their own keep them from joining in such
interdisciplinary enterprises. But the promise of a truly integrative historical anthropology envisioned long ago by Sapir
is now more than ever within our grasp, as the methods and
theories of its respective components have gradually improved.
The Pacific Islands truly offer a magnificent arena in which to
go beyond the narrow confines of a strictly material "prehistory," to lengthen the questionnaire, to construct history as rich
in cultural breadth as it is scientific rigor.

On Lapita and Oceanic Cultural History

This book is an essay, of sorts, in the kind of historical anthropology just outlined. One of its central arguments has been that a distinctive cultural phenomenon – the archaeological manifestation of which is the Lapita horizon – can be identified and historically situated in time and space, for the southwestern Pacific. Moreover, by applying multiple lines of evidence that derive only partly from archaeology, one may argue that this Lapita cultural complex and the people who fundamentally were responsible for it, were ultimately ancestral to the several hundred modern cultures of the Pacific Islands whose members speak languages belonging to the Oceanic subgroup of Austronesian. This does *not* mean, as Gosden asserts, that "ancestor and present outcome" are merged, "leaving no sense that any period of the past was radically different from the present" (1994:22). Quite the contrary, contextualizing Lapita within the broad historical narrative framework for the Oceanic-speaking peoples as a whole allows the historical anthropologist to understand with ever so much more clarity just how much change has occurred in the three-and-one-half millennia since these Lapita ancestors began their rapid expansion out of the Bismarck Archipelago into the uninhabited world of Remote Oceania. A great deal of change – social as well as material – occurred within the thousand years bracketed by the "Lapita period" and substantially more would continue to transform the Oceanic cultures that descended from the dispersed and diversified Lapita peoples. Yet there is much that remains held in common by these Oceanic descendants of the Lapita peoples, not the least of which are the similarities in language and in ways of naming and thinking about the world as structured by language.

Indeed, the second half of the twentieth-century has witnessed remarkable advances in our ability to conceive of and reconstruct various facets of the history of the Oceanic-speaking peoples. Two major developments have been essential to these advances. The first was the archaeological discovery of the Lapita complex itself, which in spanning the long-held ethnographic divide separating Melanesia from Polynesia, ultimately forced a thorough rethinking of those ingrained typological categories. The second has been the cumulative knowledge of modern Oceanic languages and their historical relationships, painstakingly acquired by several generations of linguists beginning with the foundation researches of Otto Dempwolff. It is difficult to think of any other major cultural region of the world where archaeological and historical linguistic studies have had such a fruitful collaboration, although the potential for such interdisciplinary history is obviously present in many other regions.

All of this is merely to say that Oceanic scholars have finally constructed an intellectual space in which it will now be possible to begin to address some of the most important and fascinating questions of the region's culture history. Far from having gone "too far, too fast . . . before we have even thought up satisfactory questions," as Gosden (1991b:262) asserts, I would argue that the path to our present understanding of the Lapita peoples as ancestors of the Oceanic-speaking world has been long and at times difficult, built on the cumulative research of several generations of scholars. Yet thanks to these efforts, we have no dearth of "satisfactory questions" if only were are prepared to shrive ourselves of narrow academic territoriality. Such questions concern the very nature of Oceanic societies themselves – their structures of reproduction, their modes of economic livelihood, their world views – and how these have been changed and transformed over some three-and-one-half millennia to result in the diversity of cultural forms spread today from Mussau to Easter Island, from New Caledonia to Pohnpei. Nor can such questions be based on an unthinking retrodiction of the present onto the past, for such in fact is anathema to any kind of sound comparative method.[3] No, let us be clear: the modern descendants of the Lapita peoples are owed a far more sophisticated construction of their history.

Appendix: Gazetteer of Major Lapita Sites

Roughly one hundred sites containing at least some quantity of dentate-stamped, Lapita style pottery have now been recorded between the Bismarck Archipelago in the west, throughout the intervening archipelagoes of island Melanesia, and as far east as Tonga and Samoa in Western Polynesia. Green (1979a:49–57, Appendix) provided the first compendium of Lapita sites, while Kirch and Hunt (1988a:11–14, table 2.1) tabulated 79 sites giving data on site type, area, kind of excavation, excavated area, ^{14}C dates, and bibliographic citations. Eighteen sites discovered and/or investigated during the 1985–6 Lapita Homeland Project are reported in Gosden et al. (1989:565–71, table 2), while preliminary reports on the investigation of many of these sites are provided in the volume edited by Allen and Gosden (1991). In this gazetteer, I summarize basic data on some 32 sites – or roughly one-third of those known – focussing on those localities which have had significant excavation (more than a single test pit), radiocarbon dating, or have yielded information critical to the present synthesis. For the remaining two-thirds of the site inventory, very little is known indeed; this, in itself, is a commentary on how much more basic field research remains to be carried out. Only selected radiocarbon ages are cited herein; for the most comprehensive listing of radiocarbon age determinations from Lapita sites, see Spriggs (1990a; see also Kirch and Hunt 1988a).

Bismarck Archipelago

Talepakemalai

Code: ECA *Location*: Mussau Islands, Papua New Guinea
Probably the largest Lapita site known (with an area in excess
of 82,000 m²), Talepakemalai is situated on Eloaua Island in
the Mussau group northwest of New Ireland. The site incorporates a calcareous beach terrace (ca. 2 m above present sea
level), and an area of prograded sands only 1 m above sea
level, the latter containing a waterlogged component. The waterlogged deposits have anaerobically preserved both the wooden
bases of a former stilt-house village originally constructed over
the reef flat, and large numbers of seeds and nuts of economically important tree crops. Extensive excavations in 1985, 1986,
and 1988 yielded a large assemblage of pottery, spanning a
temporal sequence beginning with elaborately dentate-stamped
ceramics and ending with incised forms. Thirty radiocarbon
dates from the site indicate a calibrated occupation span from
about 1,600 BC to perhaps 500 BC. *References*: Kirch (1987,
1988b); Kirch et al. (1991); Kirch and Hunt (1988b).

Etakosarai

Code: ECB *Location*: Mussau Islands, Papua New Guinea
Also situated on Eloaua Island, the Etakosarai site represents
a small hamlet-type occupation, possibly also of stilt-houses
although no anaerobically-preserved architecture was uncovered. The relatively shallow deposits have been heavily disturbed by post-Lapita agricultural activities. The site was tested
by Kirch, and subsequently excavated by means of systematic
transect sampling method by T. L. Hunt. ECB yielded both
early dentate-stamped and later, incised forms of pottery. *References*: Kirch (1987); Kirch et al. (1991).

Etapakengaroasa

Code: EHB *Location*: Mussau Islands, Papua New Guinea
This is the third Lapita site in the Mussau group, situated on
the east coast of Emananus Island, across the lagoon from

Eloaua Island. The site occupies a narrow, calcareous coastal beach terrace (currently behind a mangrove swamp) which may have been sub- or inter-tidal at the time of Lapita habitation. Limited test excavations by Kirch and Hunt yielded a small assemblage of classic Lapita ceramics, obsidian, and other artifacts and midden. Two radiocarbon dates indicate that the site was occupied relatively early in the local Mussau sequence, probably around 1,400 BC. *References*: Kirch (1987); Kirch et al. (1991).

Epakapaka

Code: EKQ *Location*: Mussau Islands, Papua New Guinea
Epakapaka is a rockshelter on the northwest coast of Mussau Island, about 2 km north of Pomanai Village. Marshall Weisler excavated two 1 m^2 test pits during the 1986 phase of the Mussau Project, exposing four cultural strata extending to a depth of 2.6 m below surface. Ceramic sherds were plentiful, with more than 12,000 sherds recovered. The pottery dates to the later part of the Mussau Lapita sequence. Radiocarbon dates suggest an occupation span for the basal strata of between ca. 1,100–800 BC. *Reference*: Kirch et al. (1991:150-1, table 2, figures 4, 7).

Watom

Codes: FAC, SDI, SAC, SAD *Location*: Watom Island, New Britain, Papua New Guinea
The site where Father Otto Meyer first discovered Lapita pottery in 1908; sherds collected by Meyer remain in the collection of the Musée de l'Homme (Paris). J. Specht reinvestigated this site for his doctoral dissertation. During the 1985 Lapita Homeland Project, R. C. Green and D. Anson carried out greatly expanded excavations at Watom, in several areas of the site, which are coded as separated site localities. Among the significant materials uncovered by them were nine subfloor burials of Lapita age (eight adults and a two-year old child), all associated with a single habitation site (SAC). Radiocarbon dates indicate an age span of around the third to fourth

centuries BC for many of the localities, although some earlier occupation is not precluded. *References*: Meyer (1909, 1910); Specht (1968); Green and Anson (1987, 1991); Green et al. (1989).

Ambitle (Malekolon)

Code: EAQ *Location*: Ambitle Island, New Ireland, Papua New Guinea

This site, initially reported by White and Specht (1971), yielded intricately decorated, dentate-stamped ceramics stylistically similar to the earliest pottery at the Talepakemalai (ECA) site in Mussau. Ambrose excavated 19 m^2 of the site in four separate areas (Green 1979a:51). Unfortunately, these materials have yet to be fully analyzed or published. Green (1979a:51) reports that "augering to a depth of 2 m at a grid interval of 20 m indicated that there was at least 4,000 m^2 of deposit containing an estimated 12 tons of pottery." The main occupation deposits are said to lie about 500 m inland, and at about 3 m above present sea level. *References*: White and Specht (1971).

Apalo

Code: FOJ *Location*: Kumbun, Arawe Islands

The Apalo site was discovered by C. Gosden and J. Specht during the 1985 Lapita Homeland Project, and later investigated more intensively by Gosden in 1987–8 and 1989–90. Situated in a low-lying beach and swamp area on Kumbun Island, the Apalo site contains a waterlogged sandy deposit, with well-preserved wood and plant remains, similar to that at Talepakemalai (ECA). This sandy deposit, which yielded high densities of Lapita pottery, evidently represents a phase of stilt-house occupation during a higher period of sea level. A radiocarbon age of 3,680 ± 50 BP, from anaerobically-preserved wooden posts, indicates that the site belongs to the earliest phase in the Far Western Lapita region. *References*: Gosden (1989, 1991a); Gosden and Webb (1994).

Southeastern Solomon Islands

Nenumbo

Code: RF-2 *Location*: Reef Islands, Santa Cruz Group, Solomon Islands
This is one of six Lapita sites in the main Reef Islands of the Santa Cruz group, discovered and investigated by R. C. Green. The Nenumbo site was the object of systematic surface collections and extensive areal excavations by Green, making it one of the most thoroughly studied Lapita sites. As described in chapter 6, RF-2 can best be characterized as a small hamlet. Spatial analysis indicates a primary division of the site into a main dwelling house area, and a cooking area with impermanent structures and ovens. Radiocarbon ages span the time period 1,200–900 BC (calibrated). *References*: Green (1974, 1976, 1978), Parker (1981), Donovan (1973), Sheppard and Green (1991), and Sheppard (1992, 1993).

Ngamanie

Code: RF-6 *Location*: Ngambelipa Island, Reef Islands
This is the latest of three principal sites excavated by R. C. Green in the Reef-Santa Cruz Islands. Ngamanie is estimated to cover about 2,400 m², of which 20 m were excavated by Green in 1971–2. Two radiocarbon dates suggest that the site was occupied sometime between 800 and 500 BC (calibrated). *References*: Green (1976, 1991c).

Nanggu

Code: SZ-8 *Location*: Tömotu Noi, Nendö, Santa Cruz Islands
This site, on Tömotu Noi Island off the southeast coast of Nendö Is. (Santa Cruz), was discovered by R. C. Green, who excavated 51 m² out of an estimated total site area of 14,000 m². The site lies 468 m inland of the present beach, and has "one and perhaps two raised beaches in between" (Green

1979a:51). Green observes that "charcoal-stained occupation deposits in the coral sand soil reached depths of 60 cm before coral limestone was struck; the surface deposits have been intensively gardened, and those at lower levels sufficiently disturbed so that few features were recorded" (1979a:52). Radiocarbon dates from Nanggu indicate this is one of the earliest sites to have been occupied in the Santa Cruz group, probably between around 1,200–1,100 BC. *References*: Green (1976, 1991c); Donovan (1973); Parker (1981).

Malu and Bianga Mepala

Code: SZ-23, and –45 *Location*: Tö Motu Neo Island, Santa Cruz Group

These two sites are about 300 m apart, separated by a channel between Tö Motu Neo and a small islet called Wia; they may originally have constituted a single Lapita community. Excavations at both localities, by P. McCoy and P. Cleghorn in 1977–8, yielded collections of pottery similar to those from the RF-2 site in the nearby Reef Islands. Although no radiocarbon dates were obtained, the ceramic similarities suggest an occupation date of approximately 1,200–1,100 BC. *Reference*: McCoy and Cleghorn (1988).

Kiki

Code: TK-4 *Location*: Tikopia Island, Solomon Islands

This is the earliest site in the Tikopia cultural sequence, and probably the locality first settled by the island's Lapita colonizers. It lies on an elevated, old beach terrace associated with a higher sea level stand (about 340 m inland of the present beach). Excavations carried out by Kirch in 1977–8 exposed 47 m^2. Only a small amount of dentate-stamped Lapita pottery was present, along with abundant plain ware. Imported objects include Talasea obsidian, chert, and meta-volcanic adzes, indicating that the initial colonizers were connected with the Western Lapita external exchange network. A radiocarbon age of 2,680 ± 90 BP (UCR-964) indicates occupation in the first or second centuries of the first millennium BC. *Reference*: Kirch and Yen (1982).

Vanuatu

Malo

Code: NHMa-7, –8 *Location*: Vicinity of Avunatari Village, Malo Island

Two site numbers (NHMa-7 and 8) were given by John Hedrick to two Lapita sherd distributions within the Naone Plantation on Malo Island (lying to the south of the larger Espiritu Santo Island). These sites, which may in fact be part of a more continuous zone of Lapita pottery distribution, lie on an emerged beach terrace several hundred meters inland of the present coastline. Excavations carried out by Hedrick were only incompletely published. Two radiocarbon dates are reported for site NHMa-8, the oldest being 3,150 ± 70 BP (ANU-1135), giving a calibrated range of between 3,015–2,839 BP. *Reference*: Hedrick (1971); Spriggs (1990a).

Erueti

Code: – *Location*: Efate Island

The Erueti site lies 400 m inland of the present beach, overlying a coral platform of Pleistocene age. Garanger excavated 38 m², out of a total site area about 250 m in diameter. The Lapita deposit was shallow (ca. 80 cm deep) and heavily disturbed. A charcoal sample was radiocarbon dated to 2,300 ± 95 BP (GX-1145), suggesting a rather late Lapita occupation (which seems to be in keeping with the fairly simple dentate-stamped designs). *Reference*: Garanger (1972).

New Caledonia

Lapita

Code: Site 13 *Location*: Lapita, Foué Peninsula

This is the site which gave "Lapita" its name, being a beach locality on the west coast of central New Caledonia. In 1956 E. W. Gifford and R. Shutler, Jr. excavated at two separate localities, 400 m apart (sites 13 and 13A). These excavations yielded a large collection of dentate-stamped sherds, as well as paddle-impressed sherds (called by Gifford and Shutler "ribbed relief"). The site has been reinvestigated by Daniel Frimigacci, and by Christophe Sand (personal communication, 1995). Charcoal from "Location 1" was some of the first to be submitted for radiocarbon dating in the Pacific, yielding ages of 2,800 ± 350 (M-341) and 2,435 ± 400 BP (M-336). *References*: Gifford and Shutler (1956); Frimigacci (1975).

Boirra (Koumac)

Code: – *Location*: Koumac
Situated on an embayment along the northwest coast of New Caledonia near the village of Koumac, the Lapita deposits occur in sand dunes on a Holocene marine terrace, 1.8 m above present sea level. An interesting feature of the this site is the co-occurence of classic, dentate-stamped Lapita pottery along with ceramics decorated with paddle-impressing. *Reference*: Frimigacci (1975).

Vatcha

Code: – *Location*: Vao, Île des Pins
Vatcha, on the Île des Pins off the southeast tip of New Caledonia, was investigated by Daniel Frimigacci between 1969–70. The archaeological deposits in this coastal terrace are situated directly on old marine sands, which were subsequently covered with a dune deposit. The site has an uncalibrated radiocarbon date of 2,855 ± 165 BP (ANU-262). The decorated ceramics include a number of examples of highly stylized anthropomorphic faces. *References*: Frimigacci (1974, 1975).

Fiji

Natunuku

Code: VL1/1 *Location*: North coast of Viti Levu, Fiji
A coastal site near Natunuku Village, Viti Levu, VL1/1 was excavated by E. Shaw (Hinds) in 1967. The stratigraphy shows considerable disturbance in the upper layers, but Layer 6 yielded

abundant dentate-stamped sherds; upper layers contain later types of Fijian pottery and evidently post-date the Lapita occupation. Decorated sherds constitute about 40 percent of the pottery assemblage from Layer 6, and include several vessel forms (flat-bottomed dish, globular pot, restricted-neck jar, shouldered vessel, and straight-sided bowl). Few other artifacts were recovered. Flecks of charcoal from Layer 6 yielded a single radiocarbon age of 3,240 ± 100 BP (GaK-1218). *References*: Mead et al. (1975); Davidson et al. (1990); Davidson and Leach (1993).

Yanuca Rockshelter

Code: VL16/81 *Location*: South Coast, Viti Levu
Yanuca is a small islet off the south coast of Viti Levu, and the rockshelter site consists of an overhang in the upraised reef limestone, facing the shallow channel between Yanuca and the main island. Lawrence and Helen Birks excavated 55 m² of deposit at the western end of the shelter, revealing rich cultural deposits to a depth of 1.8 m. The site was later reinvestigated by Terry Hunt. Classic, dentate-stamped Lapita sherds are found in the base deposits. These Lapita sherds are associated with a radiocarbon date of 2,980 ± 90 BP (GaK-1226). *References*: Birks and Birks (1967); Hunt (1980, 1981, 1986).

Sigatoka

Code: VL16/1 *Location*: Sigatoka Valley, Viti Levu
At the mouth of the Sigatoka River which drains much of central Viti Levu, erosion of massive sand dunes has exposed three distinct strata of humus-rich paleosols, each associated with a short-term prehistoric occupation. The oldest of these occupation surfaces dates to the Late Eastern Lapita phase. Sherds from Sigatoka were originally collected by L. Verrier and sent to Prof. Gifford at Berkeley. Green, in revising the Fijian sequence, reasoned that this phase must predate Gifford's other ceramic periods, an interpretation confirmed by the major excavations at Sigatoka carried out by L. Birks. Birks exposed more than 938 m², recovering a marvellous collection of pottery, including many whole or reconstructable vessels. Only

one radiocarbon date is currently available, with an age of 2,460 ± 90 BP (GaK-946). Renewed investigations, carried out by members of the Department of Anthropology, University of Auckland, in recent years should add considerably more information on this site in the near future (R. Green, personal communication, 1995). *Reference:* Birks (1973).

Naigani

Code: VL21/5 *Location*: Naigani Island
A small island in the Lomaiviti Group east of Viti Levu, Naigani is the setting for one of the earliest known Eastern Lapita sites. The site was investigated in 1981 by Simon Best, who excavated 83.5 m^2; Kay later analyzed the finds. The Lapita deposits are situated in an old dune system about 100 m inland of the present beach. In addition to the dentate-stamped pottery, the site yielded a wide array of non-ceramic objects, including stone and shell adzes, and a variety of worked shell artifacts. Four radiocarbon dates on shell were processed, the oldest being 3,152 ± 50 BP (NZ-5616). *Reference:* Kay (1984).

Qaranipuqa

Code: 101/7/197 *Location*: Lakeba Island
This is a large rockshelter, situated in limestone cliffs on the northwest coast of Lakeba Island. Best excavated a 2 by 5.5 m unit to depths of 4.7 m, revealing a complex stratigraphic sequence. Fourteeen radiocarbon dates indicate that the rockshelter was occupied from as early as 1,100 BC up until about AD 1,600. Lapita pottery was present in the lower deposits; the oldest radiocarbon date associated with Lapita pottery was 2,876 ± 70 BP (NZ-4594). *Reference:* Best (1984).

Tongatapu

Moala's Mound

Code: To. 2 *Location*: Nukuleka, Tongatapu
This mound site lies at the southern end of Nukuleka Village, on a small peninsula at the eastern side of the Tongatapu

lagoon entrance. A 1 by 15 m trench was excavated by Jens Poulsen in 1964. A shell midden horizon at the base of the site yielded abundant dentate-stamped Lapita pottery and other non-ceramic objects. Based on analysis of the Tongatapu ceramics, site To. 2 seems to be the oldest known Lapita occupation on the island. It has an associated radiocarbon age of 3,090 ± 95 BP (ANU-541), which, however, may not necessarily date the earliest occupation on the site. *References*: Poulsen (1968, 1983, 1987).

Pe'a

Code: To. 1 *Location*: Pea Village, Tongatapu
A low-lying midden site situated above 2 m above present sea level, along the shoreline of the island's central lagoon. Jens Poulsen excavated 67.5 m² of this site in 1963–4. The two shell-midden strata contained several hearths, ovens, postmolds, and numerous pits. The earlier Horizon I probably dates to fairly early in the Tongan sequence, and has a radiocarbon date on shell of 3,180 ± 100 BP (K-904). The later Horizon II materials appear to date from a later time period (Poulsen's "Middle horizon"). *References*: Poulsen (1968, 1983, 1987).

Ha'apai Islands

Tongoleleka

Code: – *Location*: Lifuka Island
First discovered by Les Groube, the Tongoleleka site lies on the southwestern coast of Lifuka Island. In 1984 Tom Dye carried out stratigraphic excavations revealing four main depositional units, with Early Eastern Lapita ceramics in the basal cultural deposit (Zone III). Aside from ceramics and other portable artifacts, the site is noteworthy for its vertebrate faunal assemblage, which included several species now either extinct or extirpated. These include a giant iguana, two species of flightless megapode, and three pigeon species. Turtle bones from Zone III yielded uncalibrated radiocarbon ages of 3,660 ± 190 BP, 2,960 ± 120 BP, and 2,960 ± 60 BP. *References*: Dye (1988, 1989); Pregill and Dye (1989); Shutler et al. (1994).

Faleloa

Code: – *Location*: Foa Island

Faleloa lies on the northwest coast of Foa Island, and like Tongoleleka, has an Early Eastern Lapita component. It was excavated from 1991–2 by David Burley and associates, who recovered a ceramic assemblage totalling more than 20,000 sherds. No detailed report has yet been published, but the dentate-stamped decorations are said to "closely correspond" with those from Tongoleleka. An age for the initial occupation of this site is given by a radiocarbon sample from Zone III of 2,940 ± 60 BP. *Reference*: Shutler et al. (1994).

Niuatoputapu

Lolokoka

Code: NT-90 *Location*: Niuatoputapu Island, Tonga

A beach-terrace midden site in the Vaipoa area, situated within the principal belt of anthropogenic soils (*fasifasi'ifeo*) deriving from the ceramic-period occupation of the island. The site is consequently heavily disturbed by yam gardening activities, with only remnants of in situ stratigraphy and features at the basal contact with underlying beach sands. Covering about 3,000 m², Lolokoka contains dentate-stamped ceramics of classic Early Eastern Lapita style, exotic chert flakes, obsidian, and a range of portable artifacts in stone and shell. First reported and tested by G. Rogers, and extensively sampled by stratified random testing and areal excavations by Kirch. *References*: Kirch (1978, 1988a); Rogers (1974).

Samoa

Mulifanua

Code: – *Location*: 'Upolu Island, Western Samoa

A completely submerged Lapita deposit, situated under the subtidal reef flat off the coast at Mulifanua, near the international airport. Mulifanua was discovered accidently as a result of dredging operations to extend the inter-island ferry berth, when potsherds were observed in the dredge tailings by a New Zealand engineer. The deposit, which contains dentate-stamped sherds in Early Eastern Lapita motifs, is capped by 0.9 m of cemented coral and shell, and submerged under 1.8 m of water. It is unclear whether this site was originally situated upon a supra-tidal beach terrace, or whether it represents a stilt-house occupation over subtidal reef flat; in either case, tectonic subsidence of the coastline must have played a role in the submergence of the archaeological deposit. *Reference*: Green and Davidson (1974).

To'aga

Code: AS-13-1 *Location*: Ofu Island, Manua Group, American Samoa

The To'aga site occupies a long, narrow coastal terrace along the southern side of Ofu Island. Investigations by Kirch and Hunt over three field seasons from 1986–9 revealed deeply buried cultural strata containing ceramics and other artifacts spanning most of the first millennium BC. No dentate-stamped Lapita was recovered, but the earliest deposits are of the same age as the Mulifanua site in 'Upolu, and contain thin, fine-tempered Lapita plain ware. The calcareous sandy deposits preserved a large assemblage of faunal materials, as well as shell artifacts such as *Turbo*-shell fishhooks. *Reference*: Kirch and Hunt, eds (1993).

Futuna

Asipani

Code: WF-F-SI-001A *Location*: Fiua, Futuna Island

The Asipani site deposits were exposed in an erosional cut along a small stream at Fiua, on the southwest coast of Futuna. Excavations totalling 6 m² were carried out in 1986 by Christophe Sand. The basal strata yielded dentate-stamped as well as paddle-impressed pottery of Early to Late Eastern Lapita type, and chert flakes. Bed 12 yielded a radiocarbon date of 2,400 ± 80 BP (Gif-8068). *Reference*: Sand (1993b).

Tavai

Code: FU-11 *Location*: Tavai, Futuna Island

Site FU-11 is a Late Eastern Lapita occupation situated in the coastal plain at Tavai, on the northwestern side of Futuna. Discovered and excavated by Kirch in 1975, FU-11 is deeply buried by colluvial sediments, and was exposed by a small streamlet that cut through it. A 6 m² excavation produced a large collection of ceramics, along with stone adzes of plano-convex cross-section (Type V), chert flakes, and a probable nut-cracking stone. A radiocarbon age of 2,120 ± 80 BP (I-8355) indicates that FU-11 was occupied toward the end of the Lapita period. *Reference*: Kirch (1981).

Notes

Chapter 1

1   The Austronesian language family, which spans a geographic range from Madagascar to Easter Island and includes about 1,200 modern languages (Tryon 1995), counts as its members all of the Polynesian and Micronesian languages, and most of those spoken in lowland or coastal Melanesia (Pawley and Ross 1993). The Papuan languages (also called Non-Austronesian) include some 1,500 modern languages belonging to several families, and spoken primarily in New Guinea and immediately adjacent islands (Foley 1986). The significance of these language distribution patterns for Lapita prehistory is discussed in detail in chapter 4.

2   Near Oceania encompasses New Guinea, the Bismarcks, and the Solomon Islands. Its biogeographic and anthropological significance is explained in chapter 2.

3   Some aspects of regional biogeography will be discussed in later chapters. Suffice it to note here that marsupials, for example, do not extend in their natural distributions beyond the Solomon Islands, as is also the case with various genera of indigenous rats, and many kinds of plants.

4   The geological structure of the western Pacific, and the evolution of its island-arcs, are the subject of various contributions to the volume edited by P. J. Coleman (1973); Pacific Plate islands are well treated by Menard (1986). For an overview of the Melanesian environment, one can do no better than Brookfield with Hart (1971); the relationship of indigenous Melanesian peoples to their environment is treated in Winslow (ed. 1977). Merrill's (1945) treatise on Pacific flora remains a highly-readable and informative classic. On human impacts to Pacific island environments, see the volumes edited by Dodson (1992), and by Kirch and Hunt (1996).

5 The long, narrow island of New Caledonia, however, is a fragment of the ancient supercontinent of Gondwana (Flannery 1995:42).

6 On the biogeography of the Indo-Pacific region, see Stoddart (1992).

7 The following section is based on my "Brief History of Lapita Archaeology" (Kirch 1988d), which contains a more comprehensive review of scholarly research than can be summarized here.

8 The French geologist Maurice Piroutet (1917) had also discovered dentate-stamped pottery at Foué on New Caledonia, but this report was likewise missed by McKern.

9 The tripartite division of Oceania into Melanesia, Polynesia, and Micronesia dates from the French explorer Dumont D'Urville (1832), and has exercised a kind of intellectual stranglehold on anthropological thinking about the Pacific (see Thomas 1989).

10 Avias (1950) drew on Lenormand's (1948) finds from the Île des Pins. It is ironic that Gifford, whose later expeditions (Gifford 1951; Gifford and Shutler 1956) launched the modern era of systematic archaeology in the Pacific, was McKern's coworker on the 1920 Tongan Expedition.

11 The term BP refers to radiocarbon years "before present" and is standardized at AD 1950.

12 Gifford himself did not use the term "Lapita" to refer to the larger ceramic complex he identified, and indeed the origin of this usage is obscure. By the late 1960s the term "Lapita pottery" was in general use among Pacific archaeologists (see Kirch 1988a:1, n. 1).

13 Smart's work was never published, although some of his data were incorporated into Green and Mitchell's revision of the New Caledonian sequence (1983).

14 Golson's use of the term "ceramic series" derived from Rouse and Cruxet (1963).

15 The Southeast Solomon Islands Culture History Program, directed jointly by Roger Green and Douglas Yen, remains a textbook case for the successful integration of archaeology, ethnobotany, and historical linguistics in prehistoric research. The project spawned a host of important papers and monographs, including Green and Cresswell (1976), Yen and Gordon (1973), and Kirch and Yen (1982).

16 Green's excavations at these and other Lapita sites in the Reef-Santa Cruz Islands are reported in a continuing series of papers, of which the foundation ones are Green (1974, 1976).

17 The "Lapita cultural complex" was formally defined and later elaborated by Green (1979a, 1982), partly in response to a critique by Clark and Terrell (1978).

18 Mead's formal system for analyzing Lapita pottery, based on Fijian materials, was later amplified by Donovan (1973) and others (see Green 1990 for a discussion of the history of Lapita pottery studies).

19 These tests were carried out by Egloff (1975; Bafmatuk et al. 1980). White and Specht (1971) had also reported the Ambitle site.

20 The theoretical underpinnings of the Lapita Homeland Project were spelled out by Allen (1984). A summary of the main results of the 1985 season is provided in Allen and Gosden (1991), as well as in a host of other papers by other participants (see, for example, Gosden et al. 1989 on Lapita sites).

21 In the Bismarcks, the major Lapita excavations have been led by Kirch (1987, 1988b; Kirch et al. 1991) in the Mussau Islands, by Gosden (1991a) in the Arawe Islands, and by Green and Anson (1987, 1991) in Watom. In New Caledonia, Frimigacci (1975), Galipaud (1988), and Sand (1994) have added much to our knowledge of the local ceramic sequence. Other important work has been carried out in Futuna and 'Uvea (Sand 1991, 1993b), in Niuatoputapu (Kirch 1988a), in the Ha'apai group (Dye 1988; Shutler et al. 1994), and in Tongatapu (Spennemann 1989).

22 For current overviews of the Austronesian language family and its subgrouping, see Pawley and Ross (1993, 1995) and Tryon (1995).

23 Not all prehistorians agree, however. The most vociferous detractor from this view is John Terrell (1986, 1989). Others, such as Smith (1995:374) flatly state that "archaeological evidence is not capable of supporting or refuting linguistic models," a viewpoint which I reject.

24 To a certain extent, I am thus using "Lapita" in the way that anthropologists typically use the cover term "Polynesian" to refer to the many individual peoples and societies that speak languages descended from a common ancestral tongue, Proto Polynesian.

25 By "combined methods of historical anthropology," I mean the application of the array of methods and procedures used by biological anthropologists, historical linguists, archaeologists, and comparative ethnographers. The phylogenetic model outlined by Kirch and Green (1987) drew upon earlier efforts by Eggan (1954) and Romney (1957), and especially upon the work of Evon Vogt (1964) with the Maya.

Chapter 2

1 For an overview of the Pleistocene sites of Australia and New Guinea, see Smith and Sharp (1993) .

2 I am using the term "Old Melanesia" somewhat cautiously here, to refer to the coastal and island parts of Near Oceania which were originally occupied by the original ancestors of Papuan-speaking peoples in the late Pleistocene period. This is quite distinct from W. W. Howells' use of the term (1973:177, *passim*) which included the vast region from Sunda to Sahul.

3 For a discussion of the history of Wallace's Line and its emerging significance during nineteenth-century biogeography, see Camerini (1994).

4 Some Australian archaeologists use the term "Greater Australia." White and O'Connell (1982:6–16) provide much useful geographic background information on Sahul.

5 On these Gondwana connections, see Flannery (1995). Yen (1991b, 1993) explores some of the implications of the shared ancient Gondwana flora for early plant utilization and domestication among the indigenous peoples of Sahul.

6 For detailed discussions of Pleistocene sea-level curves see Chappell (1993) and additional references cited therein.

7 Smith and Sharp (1993) provide a comprehensive listing of Pleistocene sites in Sahul; see also Lourandos (1993) for a review of short- and long-term trends in Australian prehistory, including adjacent islands.

8 The exception is the harsh, desertic "dead heart" of the continent, which may not have been occupied until ca. 25,000 years ago.

9 See Roberts, Jones, and Smith (1990) on the thermoluminescence (TL) dating, and Groube et al. (1986) on the Huon Peninsula finds.

10 For a response to Allen's critique, see Roberts et al. (1995).

11 On possible routes of entry for humans into Sahul see Irwin (1991a, 1993).

12 The Huon finds are reported in Groube et al. (1986). It has been speculated that the large waisted axes might have been used for forest clearance, to open up patches in order to encourage the growth of plants such as *Pandanus*, whose seeds and fruit would have provided important food sources.

13 The concepts of Near Oceania and its counterpart Remote Oceania are discussed in a seminal article by Roger Green (1991a).

14 These counts are based on modern biological surveys, and do not take into account reductions in taxa due to extinction during the Pleistocene or Holocene. For example, extinct rats are now recorded for New Ireland (Flannery and White 1991; Flannery et al. 1988) and Steadman (personal communication, 1994) has identified extinct birds from New Ireland cave sites.

15 For details on the New Ireland sites, see Allen et al. (1989), White et al. (1991), Marshall and Allen (1991), and Allen (1993). For the Misisil site on New Britain, see Specht et al. (1981).

16 A preliminary report on the Pamwak excavations appears in Fredericksen et al. (1993).

17 Obsidian also occurs in the Pamwak rockshelter on Manus from the late Pleistocene levels, but this was presumably obtained at the closer Lou Island source within the Admiralty Islands.

18 Carter et al. (1945:25). See Flannery and White (1991) for a detailed discussion of the recent archaeological evidence on the translocation of *Phalanger orientalis* in Near Oceania.

19 The great comparative ethnographers A. C. Haddon and James Hornell (1936–8), in a massive survey of Oceanic watercraft concluded that the earliest occupants of New Guinea and Near Oceania ("the Papuans" in their terms) "were acquainted only with the raft and the simple dugout. . . . If their dugouts were fitted with a sail it may have been a makeshift one of interplaited palm leaves, a vertical oblong sail rigged without a mast" (1938:75).

20 On the possibilities of Pleistocene voyaging in Oceania, see Irwin (1991a; 1992:18–30).

21 I use the term "horticulture" here advisedly, in terms of its connotation of "gardening," given the putative emphasis in this region on a complex of largely vegetatively-reproduced, root/tuber and tree crops.

22 Among his most important contributions to the history of plant domestication in Oceania, see Barrau (1965).

23 Douglas Yen has played an immensely important role in advancing the field of Pacific archaeobotany, drawing not only upon new botanical methodologies (e.g., cytological and morphological studies of plant variation), but innovative techniques of field archaeology in the investigation of prehistoric agricultural systems, and the direct identification of plant remains from archaeological sites. Among his key works on agricultural origins in the New Guinea-Melanesian region are Yen (1973, 1991a, 1993).

24 Golson's Kuk studies have been summarized in a large number of papers (e.g., Golson 1990, 1991; Hope and Golson 1995; Golson and Gardner 1990), although we still await a definitive site monograph.

25 In this regard, we must note the report by Loy et al. (1992) of *Colocasia* starch grains preserved on stone tools from the 28,000-year old Kilu site on Buka. Spriggs (1993a) interprets this as evidence for taro as a "major staple food" for these Pleistocene people.

26 See Matthews (1991) and Yen (1991a).

27 Yen (1991a:77) summarizes the recent genetic evidence. See also Coates et al. (1988).

28 The residue analysis of the Balof 2 implements is presented in Barton and White (1993), who notably did not find evidence for *Colocasia* starch (see Loy et al. 1992).

29 Two important ethnobotanical reports on Melanesian tree cropping are those of Yen (1974) on Santa Cruz, and Lepofsky (1992) on the Mussau Islands. These studies illustrate the range of tree crops found in indigenous Melanesian arboricultural systems.

30 Marshall and Allen (1991:88); Fredericksen et al. (1993:147).

31 Gosden (1995) provides the most recent summary of evidence and argument in favor of indigenous agriculture and arboriculture in Near Oceania.

32 Swadling et al. (1991) provide a preliminary report on the Dongan excavations, and a set of excellent color photos of the site. Some finds are presented in Swadling et al. (1988:14–17).

33 The near exclusive distribution of the two main Oceanic psychoactive plants – betel and kava (*Piper methysticum*) – has long intrigued anthropologists and ethnobotanists. The betel is extensively chewed throughout Melanesia, while kava is used primarily in Fiji and Polynesia; some overlap occurs in Vanuatu. This curious distribution pattern led some early anthropologists, such as Rivers (1914), to view the older inhabitants of Melanesia as the "betel nut people," with the "kava people" as later arrivals. There may yet prove to be some truth in Rivers' observations.

Chapter 3

1 For more comprehensive overviews of the archaeology of southeast Asia, see van Heekeren (1972), Higham (1989), and Bellwood (1985).
2 The date for initial appearance of pigs in New Guinea is a matter of continuing controversy. White and O'Connell (1982:187–9, table 6.5) summarize evidence from Highlands sites suggesting that the pig was present by ca. 5,000 BP, with equivocal evidence for older dates. However, Spriggs (1995:115) reports that direct AMS (accelerator mass spectrometry) dates on pig bone from reputed early contexts have produced more recent age estimates, although details are not provided. At present, it seems advisable to exercise caution with regard to pigs in pre-Lapita contexts.
3 Gifford and Shutler (1956:94–5) drew specific parallels between the pottery of Lapita (New Caledonia) and that recovered by van Stein Callenfels at the Karama River site in Sulawesi (see van Heekeren 1972:185–9), and also noted resemblances between New Caledonian "lenticular" adzes and those of Beyer's "Early Neolithic" type from the Philippines.
4 Among Bellwood's key writings on Lapita are sections in *Man's Conquest of the Pacific* (1979:244–58), and in *Prehistory of the Indo-Malaysian Archipelago* (1985:250–3), as well as several articles (1992, 1993).
5 J. M. Diamond (1988) cited Kirch's then recently published Mussau Island finds as evidence in support of an "express train" model, "in which Lapita arrived from the west and spread rapidly eastwards without measurable pause." Jim Allen (1984:186) had also used the metaphor of a "fast train to Polynesia."
6 Bellwood (personal communication, 1995) notes that he developed his views on Lapita after having done fieldwork in *both* Polynesia and Indonesia. In contrast, most of those who have advocated the IMO model have no field experience in Indonesia, and little in Polynesia. Bellwood believes that such field experiences exercise subtle but important influences on archaeological theory.

7 See also Allen and White (1989:141–3). Terrell (1989) advocates an extreme variant of the IMO model, in which there is no such thing as a Lapita cultural complex at all, the dentate-stamped pottery simply being a "trade ware."

8 The notion that Austronesian-speaking peoples both influenced the indigenous Melanesian populations with whom they came in contact, and at the same time borrowed aspects of culture from the latter, is not new. Pioneer linguist Otto Dempwolff (1904, 1934–8) made just such a proposal: "Wo er eine dunkelfarbige Bevolkerung antraf, hat er sie mit seiner Kultur und Sprache beeinflußt und auch von ihrer Kultur und Sprache vieles aufgenommen" (1937:193).

9 Dening's model of "the beach" was applied in his own writings to the multifaceted encounters between indigenous Pacific peoples and Europeans (Dening 1980, 1992), but it serves equally well for the kinds of cultural encounters that occurred in Near Oceania in the second millennium BC.

10 Detailed assessments of the specific Southeast Asian archaeological assemblages that can be considered precursors to Lapita are presented by Kirch (1995) and Spriggs (in press). Bellwood (1985) provides the most comprehensive survey of island Southeast Asian archaeology. A reconsideration of the radiocarbon dating evidence for the island Southeast Asian Neolithic is provided by Spriggs (1989).

11 See Chang (1969) and Blust (1985) regarding archaeological and linguistic interpretations of Taiwan as the putative Austronesian "homeland."

12 The Cagayan Valley sites are reported in part by Aoyagi and his associates (Aoyagi and Tanaka 1985; Aoyagi et al. 1986, 1991) and by Thiel (1985, 1986).

13 A preliminary report on Uattamdi is provided in Bellwood (1992). I thank Peter Bellwood for showing me slides of the site and excavated finds, and discussing the implications of these materials, during a visit to Berkeley in 1992.

14 The similarities in pottery are not simply my own assessments, because Bellwood was able to examine my Mussau collections at Berkeley after his Uattamdi excavations, and concurs that the assemblages are virtually identical.

15 See Kirch and Hunt (1988a) for this catalog and a discussion of Lapita distribution in space and time. An earlier listing of Lapita sites was provided by Green (1979a).

16 In the main Solomon Islands, Reeve (1989) reports on a similar reef-flat pottery site named Panaivili, in the Roviana Lagoon. The Panaivili pottery is not Lapita *sensu strictu* (it lacks dentate-stamping), but is probably a late variant or derivative of Lapita. This suggests that earlier Lapita reef-flat sites may yet be discovered through further archaeological survey in the Solomon Islands.

17   In a general review of migrations in archaeology, David Anthony (1990:902) refers to the frequent practice of "leapfrogging" in inter-regional migrations, "a recurrent pattern in the expansion of pioneer farming communities." The gap in Lapita sites in the Solomons may have been due to such leapfrogging.

18   Green (1976, personal communication, 1995) believes on geological criteria that certain finished adzes from the Reef-Santa Cruz Island sites were imported from a source on Guadalcanal. Also, some sherds may have come from the Nggela group of islands in the central Solomons.

19   The only region within the modern political state of The Solomon Islands which has been intensively studied archaeologically, and for which it might be supposed that we have a reasonably complete prehistoric cultural sequence, is the Eastern Outer Islands District, including Nendö, the Reef Islands, Vanikoro, Taumako, Tikopia, and Anuta (Green and Cresswell, eds 1976; Kirch and Yen 1982).

20   Kirch and Hunt (1988a) questioned whether the Lapita distribution might extend further eastwards into the Cook or Society Islands, where tectonic subsidence on Pacific Plate islands could create site visibility problems in the coastal zone. More recent palynological work on Mangaia Island in the southern Cook Islands does indicate the likelihood of initial human colonization by ca. 2,400 BP (Kirch and Ellison 1994) although no archaeological deposits per se have been identified.

21   On the prehistoric sequences of the Papuan and Massim regions, and their possible connections to Lapita, see Allen (1972), Irwin (1985, 1991b), Vanderwal (1978), and Egloff (1975, 1979).

22   One of the major problems confronting the development of an "absolute" or calendrical chronology for Lapita has been that of calibrating dates obtained from varying sample materials. In particular, samples which originally grew in a marine envronment (such as shell or turtle bone) typically give ages somewhat older than those from terrestrial environments (charcoal, wood, mammal bone). This is due to a "reservoir effect" whereby the world's oceans contain higher proportions of old carbon (Stuiver et al. 1986). Unfortunately, this reservoir effect is not globally uniform, and local corrections must be made using a Δ-R factor; establishing a suitable Δ-R factor has been a matter of some disagreement among Lapita archaeologists (see Kirch and Hunt 1988a, 1988b, and Spriggs 1990a for further details).

23   Anson (1986) had suggested that Lapita settlement in the Bismarcks had a time depth of nearly 2,000 BC, based on a radiocarbon sample obtained by Brian Egloff (Bafmatuk et al. 1980) at the ECA site in the Mussau Islands. Extensive re-dating of the ECA site, however, demonstrated that this date was anomalous (Kirch and Hunt

1988b), and that ECA and other sites in the Mussau group were first occupied around 1,500 BC.

24 In assessing the probable age of first settlement for each of the four main Lapita "provinces" I have recalibrated all of the relevant radiocarbon dates presented in Spriggs (1990a) using the OXCAL calibration program developed by the Radiocarbon Laboratory of Oxford University. This calibration program allows the application of a Bayesian statistical approach.

25 Spriggs (1990a:20) suggests that the Lapita horizon in the Bismarcks could date as far back as 3,850 BP, based on a single ^{14}C date from Kohin Cave in Manus. However, applying Spriggs' own methods of "chronometric hygiene" (Spriggs 1989, 1990a) this date must be rejected, as being from uncertain stratigraphic association with a very limited sample of dentate-stamped sherds. Until the Kohin Cave site is either adequately published, or better-still re-excavated, this single date cannot be accepted.

26 That the radiocarbon dates for the Eastern Lapita region are slightly earlier than the Western region provides strong inferential support for the notion that the initial colonization phase in the Western (Santa Cruz Islands) region has not yet been adequately dated.

27 On the European agricultural diffusion see Ammerman and Cavalli-Sforza (1984).

28 See Pianka (1974) and Hutchinson (1978) for general discussion of the concept. The terms r and K are derived from the famous Verhulst-Pearl logistic equations for population growth, r being the term for the intrinsic rate of population increase, and K the term for carrying capacity.

29 Among those who have used this concept in anthropological demography are Hassan (1981) and Kirch (1984).

30 Another intriguing indication of such contacts, toward the end of the Lapita phase at ca. 2,300–2,100 BP, was the discovery of a small piece of bronze from a site in the Manus Islands (Ambrose 1988).

31 Certainly in later time periods, both Bird-of-Paradise feathers and birds' nests promoted such trade relations, marked archaeologically by the occasional presence of bronze artifacts in New Guinea and the Admiralty Islands.

32 Such reconstructions of prehistoric social organization are, of course, tenuous and must be based more on historical linguistic and comparative ethnographic evidence than on direct archaeological evidence. Such hierarchical "house societies," however, are characteristic of Austronesian-speaking cultures generally, as discussed further in chapter 6.

33 See Luomala (1949) for a detailed account of Maui in his various manifestations throughout Polynesia, as well as in eastern Micronesia

and Vanuatu. The widespread distribution of the Maui mythic cycle among Oceanic-speaking peoples suggests considerable antiquity and, in my opinion, it is quite conceivable that the Maui saga originated with Lapita voyagers in the late second millennium BC.

34 See Buck (1938). The theoretical underpinnings of historical anthropology in this era were those of the "diffusionist school," which employed culture-trait comparisons to draw putative linkages between various cultural regions. A classic example of this approach in Polynesia is the work of E. S. C. Handy (1930), one of the main ethnographers active in Polynesia during the 1920s and 1930s. Buck's (1938) synthesis is of particular note in emphasizing a "Mcronesian route" for the putative Polynesian migrations, in part it is to avoid associating the lighter-skinned Polynesians with darker-skinned Melanesians which is not surprising given the strongly racist contexts within which Buck worked.

35 See Green (1967, 1968) for two important contemporary discussions of the emerging archaeological sequences of Western Polynesia and Fiji, and their significance for Polynesian origins.

36 See, for example, Kirch (1988a) on the Niuatoputapu Island sequence, Poulsen (1987) on the Tongatapu Island sequence, Shutler et al. (1994) on early Lapita sites in Ha'apai, and Kirch (1981) and Sand (1990, 1992, 1993b) on the sequences from Futuna and 'Uvea.

37 See Kirch (1984) and Kirch and Green (1987) for a discussion of Ancestral Polynesian Culture and of the "phylogenetic model" of Polynesian cultural development and differentiation.

38 Here I must correct the mis-statement of my model of Ancestral Polynesian Society and its relationship to Lapita, as presented by Chris Gosden (1994:21–2, 26). Gosden conflates Ancestral Polynesian Society with the *entire* Lapita Cultural Complex, and then uses this conflation of some 1,500 years of continuous cultural variation to suggest that my view of Pacific prehistory is "a peculiarly timeless form of movement [lacking a] sense that any period of the past was radically different from the present." This is nonsense. In the work that Gosden quotes, I make it clear that Ancestral Polynesian Society *developed out of* Late Eastern Lapita in the Western Polynesian region (primarily the Tonga-Samoa archipelagoes) around 500 BC (Kirch 1984:52). Moreover, Ancestral Polynesian Society is a stage that can be recognized only because of certain material changes in the archaeological record.

39 The Polynesian expansion out of the Western Polynesian "homeland" region originally settled by Lapita people did not occur until after this transition. The exact chronology of Polynesian dispersal and expansion into Eastern Polynesia (e.g., the Cook, Society, Austral, Tuamotu, and Marquesas archipelagoes), and beyond to the marginal extremes of the Polynesian Triangle (e.g., Hawai'i, Easter

Island, and New Zealand), is still under debate but certainly did not begin until at least 500 BC, and was completed by about AD 1,000.

40 Anson's analysis is presented in his dissertation (Anson 1983) and is summarized in Anson (1986). Kirch et al. (1987) critiqued certain aspects of Anson's analysis, noting that his minute sample sizes for certain assemblages posed serious constraints on his statistical analyses, and questioning the reliance on a single early radiocarbon date from the ECA site to infer that the "Far Western" Lapita style phase in the Bismarcks significantly pre-dated an eastwards expansion. Further excavations at ECA have clarified these problems (see Kirch 1987, 1988b; Kirch et al. 1991).

41 The units "Far Western" and "Western" were originally defined strictly in stylistic terms (Green 1978; Anson 1983, 1986) without regard to geography. I am here explicitly redefining these in geographical terms, with the understanding that there are regional sequences of stylistic change. Thus it will be necessary to differentiate between, for example, earlier and later phases of Far Western Lapita ceramics.

42 This observation needs to be qualified, for some communities evidently did become rapidly disengaged from the widespread long-distance exchange networks. A prime example is Tikopia, which was settled around 900 BC by people within the Lapita tradition. The earliest settlement site (TK-4, Kiki) contains exotic imports, including Talasea obsidian, but these quickly disappear from the later archaeological strata, suggesting a rapid onset of isolation (Kirch and Yen 1982).

43 See Gifford and Shutler (1956). Green and Mitchell (1983) reanalyzed Gifford and Shutler's collections and presented a new synthesis of the New Caledonian sequence. Substantial advances have now been made by several French researchers, including Frimigacci (1975), Galipaud (1989), and Sand (1994). Additional reanalyses of the Gifford and Shutler collections are presented in Kirch and Weisler (in press).

44 Green's arguments (1988) are not accepted by all archaeologists, although I find them convincing; see Stone (1989) and Bailey et al. (1994) for a similar debate regarding mounds which may or may not be scrubfowl incubation nests in Australia. On the extinct avifauna of New Caledonia, including the *Sylviornis* finds, see Balouet (1987), and Balouet and Olson (1989)

45 Among the most interesting work in this regard has been Galipaud's demonstration (1988, 1990) that classic Lapita pottery (i.e., dentate-stamped ware) on New Caledonia is marked by a highly distinctive temper containing "spinelle chromifère" which appears to be geologically restricted to the northern part of the island, especially between Koumac and Koné.

46   On paddle-impressing in Fijian and Western Polynesian Lapita assemblages, see Hunt (1980, 1986), Kirch (1981), and Sand (1990, 1992).

47   See Green (in press) for a thorough review of the evidence for Early Eastern Lapita exchange.

48   This is not to deny the existence of contact between the western and central-eastern areas within Micronesia, for indeed such contacts are well documented ethnohistorically, and doubtless led to considerable linguistic borrowing, as well as cultural and genetic flows. This is especially so for Yap Island which lies at the interface between Palau and the Carolines, and had important voyaging and exchange relationships in both directions.

49   Recent overviews of Micronesian archaeology are provided by Cordy (1982), Craib (1983), Rainbird (1994), and in the various contributions to the volume edited by Hunter-Anderson (1990).

50   The Marianas ceramics were initially described by Spoehr, who illustrated a sample of the lime-infilled sherds (1957:120, figure 56), and who later discovered the Sanga Sanga site in the Philippines (Spoehr 1973:184–91).

51   The Fefan Island finds are reported by Shutler et al. (1978) [n.d.]. Among the late Lapita ceramics which are highly similar to the Fefan assemblage, are various plain wares from Talepakemalai, and the Kiki Ware from Tikopia (Kirch and Yen 1982).

52   See also Athens (1990b). Ayres (1990:203) concurs as to a Lapita derivation for the initial settlement of Pohnpei. On the central Micronesian pottery assemblages, see also Bryson (1989) and Intoh (1992).

53   In large part, the atolls of Micronesia (and indeed throughout most of the tropical Pacific) were probably still reefs awash until about 2,000 BP, when the +1–1.5 m mid-Holocene sea level stand dropped to its modern level.

54   Spriggs (1992) has catalogued some of the varied processes that changed Lapita culture throughout this vast area, including the contraction and increased specialization of trading systems, local adaptations, sociopolitical transformation, the absorption of local populations, and secondary migrations.

55   This is an important point, since the transformation from Lapita to Polynesian in this case was marked by ceramic changes but not by the abandonment of ceramics entirely, a change that did not take place until early in the first millennium AD.

Chapter 4

1   Of course, in situations where historical texts are extant, linguists do have access to properly diachronic evidence, but such is not the

case in Oceania. Likewise, skeletal remains excavated from dated archaeological contexts can provide diachronic evidence for changes in population morphology (and, using the PCR technique of DNA amplification, in genotype as well). Lapita skeletal remains do exist, although the sample sizes are extremely small, and the remains fragmentary.

2 George Grace, one of the pioneers whose work was essential in putting comparative Austronesian linguistics on its modern footing, succinctly observed that: "Historical facts are not directly discoverable by any method. What we must in fact seek to discover is the pattern of historical relations which would produce the known facts with the greatest probability" (1961:362).

3 The historical linguistic work which has been done on the Austronesian family has largely applied the *genetic comparative approach* (with a few exceptions, such as Dyen [1965], who used a lexicostatistical analysis). In other parts of the world (e.g., Mesoamerica or California) there is a heavy reliance on cruder statistical approaches, such as lexicostatistics, which may not yield accurate or robust subgrouping models. This has unfortunately led to considerable confusion, misuse, and even distrust of linguistic reconstructions on the part of prehistorians.

4 The most ambitious project of this genre is the world-wide study of *The History and Geography of Human Genes* by Cavalli-Sforza et al. (1994).

5 Although most archaeologists working the Pacific region are well attuned to the proper uses of historical linguistic and biological data in historical reconstruction, a few have preferred to ignore the evidence of these sister disciplines. This is regrettable, for limiting oneself to strictly archaeological data tends to lead to accepting as plausible certain hypotheses that are clearly found to be unwarranted when linguistic and biological evidence is also taken into account. Such is the case, for example, with some of the more extreme positions for wholly indigenous Melanesian origins of Lapita (e.g., White et al. 1988), or for the view that Lapita represents nothing more than a "trade ware" in Melanesia (Terrell 1989; Welsch et al. 1992).

6 Dempwolff's "Proto Austronesian" turns out to be equivalent to the interstage called Proto Malayo-Polynesian by Blust (1985). This was because Dempwolff did not include any Formosan languages in his comparative study, no doubt due to the lack of available data (A. Pawley, personal communication, 1995).

7 The most recent general overviews of Austronesian historical linguistics from the culture-historical viewpoint are by Pawley and Ross (1993, 1995). See also Blust (1985), Dyen (1965), Grace (1961), Pawley (1972), Ross (1988, 1989), Shutler and Marck (1975), Tryon

(1984, 1995), and Wurm (1967) for key discussions of Austronesian subgrouping in relation to culture-historical problems.

8 Taking a conservative view, Foley (1986) lists as many as 60 Papuan language families, but Andrew Pawley (personal communication, 1995) informs me that most linguists expect that future comparative studies will reduce the number of valid family groupings to something of the order of 12.

9 The languages of the Reefs/Santa Cruz group in the southeast Solomon Islands may also be Non-Austronesian, although this is an unresolved issue (see Dutton 1995:201).

10 The one likely exception is the Trans-New Guinea Phylum which may well represent a major linguistic expansion within the last 6–10,000 years (Pawley 1995, and personal communication, 1995).

11 This reluctance (Pawley and Green 1973:49–50) required them to propose the unlikely hypotheses that either some Oceanic speakers in Vanuatu "adopted a Lapita culture," or that "an immigrant Lapita community adopted" an Oceanic language in this region.

12 My viewpoint is shared by several prominent culture historians, as demonstrated by commentaries to the article by Roberts et al. (1995); these commentators include Peter Bellwood, R. C. Green, Joyce Marcus, and Kent Flannery.

13 The literature on the Oceanic languages and their relationships is far too extensive to reference here, but some of the key contributions are those of Grace (1959), Pawley (1972), and most recently, Ross (1988).

14 It is probably significant, in a historical sense, that these "clusters" are not subgroups in the usual sense of having resulted from a period of initial unity followed by subsequent isolation. Rather, they seem to have resulted from *dialect chains*. Indeed, there are hints in the emerging archaeological evidence from Western Melanesia that these dialect chain clusters closely match several regional Lapita exchange networks (see chapter 8).

15 Paul Geraghty's *The History of the Fijian Languages* (1983) provides an excellent case study of the use of a "network-breaking model" (rather than a classic tree model) for linguistic diversification in a region of the Pacific.

16 Sidney Ray used the term "Melanesian" to refer to these "hybrid" languages which were "superimposed on more primitive Papuan languages" (1926:25). Ray went on to state that "the Papuan element is aboriginal, the Melanesian is immigrant. The suggestion . . . is that the immigrants were Indonesians" (1926:25). In contemporary terms, we would say that they were Austronesian.

17 See Dutton (1995) for a detailed discussion of the kinds of processes and interactions that have influenced language contact and change in the Melanesian region.

18 Douglas Oliver (1989:53) describes a first-hand case of the replacement of an Austronesian by Papuan language in one village on Bougainville, as a result of extensive intermarriage.

19 For a provocative discussion of the potential significance of cultural difference among Sepik region peoples, see Filer (1990).

20 See also Moore and Romney (1995), and Roberts et al. (1995).

21 See Hunt (1987) for a case study of the correlation between dialect variation and geographic distance in Fiji.

22 In an important methodological paper, Blust (1987) distinguished between "lexical reconstruction" and "semantic reconstruction," the latter involving the application of a carefully-controlled *contrastive* analysis of the entire semantic field for a set of cognates pertaining to reconstructed etyma. More recently some linguistics, such as Pawley and Ross (1993) use the term *lexical reconstruction* in Blust's second sense, which is also my definition here as explained in further detail below.

23 On the concept of *mentalités* in history and historical anthropology, see J. Le Goff (1980).

24 This work has been vigorously carried out by a small group of scholars chiefly based at the Australian National University, Auckland University, and the University of Hawai'i (see Pawley and Ross 1993:441). The first fruits of the Proto Oceanic reconstruction project are attested in the volume edited by Pawley and Ross (1994).

25 Green (1994) provides an extended discussion of the importance of focusing on rigorous semantic as opposed to lexical reconstruction, with regard to the reconstruction of rank, social status, and social organization in Ancestral Polynesian Society.

26 See Pawley and Ross (eds 1994). Andrew Pawley and Roger Green are currently engaged in a project involving both linguistic and archaeological evidence for the reconstruction of Proto Oceanic culture, while Green and this author are collaborating on a similar project for Ancestral Polynesian Society (see also Kirch and Green 1987).

27 See also Pawley and Green (1984, table 1).

28 The classic early comparative work is that of Haddon and Hornell (1936–8). Recently, Horridge (1986, 1995) has reconstructed the probable form of the early Austronesian canoe on such comparative observations.

29 See Green (1986) and Kirch and Green (1987) for further details and discussion of the "triangulation approach" in historical anthropology.

30 With very few exceptions (such as the Watom site), the Lapita people appear not have buried their dead in their hamlet or village sites, so the likelihood of recovering a large sample of skeletal remains seems remote.

31 For an example of such "racial" classification applied to Melanesia,

see Howells (1943), a paper of interest now only for its historical perspective.

32 Some of the (now amusing) academic perambulations necessitated by this taxonomic approach can be glimpsed in Buck's account of the Polynesians (1938:12–18).

33 For example, Keesing (1946:17–21).

34 The literature on human biological variation in the Pacific is vast, but a useful overview of much of the older material can be found in W. Howells (1973).

35 See, for example, Howells (1970, 1973), Howells and Schwidetsky (1981), and Pietrusewsky (1970, 1983, 1984, 1990).

36 For a classic study of the range of human variation within even a single Melanesian Island (Bougainville) see Friedlaender (1975).

37 To say that Polynesians are phenotypically homogenous is, of course, a *relative* statement made in contrast to Melanesian heterogeneity, and is not to deny some variation within the Polynesian group as a whole.

38 See Brace (1981), Brace et al. (1990), and Turner II (1986). The craniofacial study by Brace et al. (1990) supports a linkage between Polynesian and certain Asian populations, although their proposal of a direct link between Polynesia and Jomon is an over-interpretation, in my view stemming from a failure to include samples from early Neolithic Taiwan or coastal China in their analysis.

39 For a concise review of these developments in relation to the study of human genetic variation, see Cavalli-Sforza et al. (1994:3–22).

40 The contributors to the Hill and Serjeantson (eds 1989) volume provide a comprehensive and excellent overview of various polymorphic systems in the Pacific, and assess these data with specific reference to historical issues of origins and migrations. Likewise, Cavalli-Sforza et al. (1994) in their massive work on *The History and Geography of Human Genes* devote a chapter to Australia, New Guinea, and the Pacific Islands. See also Hill et al. (1985), Lum et al. (in press), Serjeantson et al. (1982), and Serjeantson and Gao (1995).

41 See Pietrusewsky (1985, 1989a, 1994), and Houghton (1989a, 1989b).

42 For additional comments on the Watom sample, in particular their size and stature, see Houghton (1991:181–82).

43 A sample from the Talepakemalai site in Mussau was also provided by the author, but failed to yield DNA.

44 Serjeantson and Gao (1995) disagree with the Kelly and Clark theory, citing good genetic evidence for the presence of malaria-selected mutations in pre-Austronesian populations.

45 I made several visits to Taumako in the 1970s, and each time was amazed that whereas the village islet was free of mosquitoes, as soon as one approached within a few meters of the beach on the

main island, hordes of mosquitoes could be seen flying out of the vegetation to attack and bite ceaselessly. I counted as many of forty mosquitoes biting my exposed hands at one time. However, Roger Green (personal communication, 1995) informs me that the fiercely-biting daytime mosquitoes are of the genus *Culix* which are not malarial vectors. The *Anopheles* mosquitoes that carry malaria are nocturnal and do fly over water. Thus, the offshore islets may have provided more relief from the severe bites of *Culix* species than from malaria itself.

Chapter 5

1   The only real problems in this regard, as discussed later in this chapter, arise in the case of sites yielding strictly plain wares, such as the so-called Podtanéan tradition of New Caledonia.
2   The re-firing experiments were conducted in the Berkeley archaeology labs by Emily Dean.
3   In 1982 I was able to observe such a firing sequence in the Sigatoka Valley, Fiji. Two vessels were placed on a bed of dried coconut endocarps and then covered with a "teepee" like arrangement of dried coconut fronds. An intense, hot, but short-lived burn was produced in which both vessels were fired within less than 20 minutes (see Kirch 1988a:155, figure 93). See also Irwin (1985) on traditional firing methods in Mailu.
4   Roger Green (personal communication, 1995) points out that plotting the distribution of vessel forms within sites and carefully assessing the correlation of specific forms with structural features and distribution patterns of other artifact classes, as he and Peter Sheppard have done for the Nenumbo site, may also help to determine further vessel functions.
5   This is in clear contrast to late prehistoric pottery in both New Caledonia and Fiji (Gifford collections in the P. A. Hearst Museum, University of California at Berkeley), where such attributes are well represented.
6   This is a critical point, because it has sometimes mistakenly been stated that dentate-stamping is an essential defining characteristic of Lapita pottery. Rather, it is the distinctive *formal design system* which defines the ceramic series.
7   The use of dentate-stamps in and of itself would not constitute a strong case for defining a Lapita ceramic series. Indeed, the technique is not unique to Lapita, being found in other, unrelated ceramic traditions ranging from Africa and Europe (e.g., the LBK culture) to the Americas.
8   Golson (1971:75); the reference was to terms defined by Willey and Phillips (1958:29–39).

9   The term was proposed by Rouse and Cruxent (1963) who dealt with similarly complex, related regional traditions in Latin America. They suggest using the suffix "-oid" to demarcate such ceramic series, as in the term "Lapitoid." While some (e.g., Kirch 1981) have scrupulously applied the term Lapitoid in the broad sense of a series, others have not, leading to some confusion.

10 The Far Western tradition was proposed by Anson (1983, 1986). A Southern tradition is evident from the work of Frimigacci (1975), Galipaud (1989), Sand (1993a), and others.

11 See Green (1979b) for an extended argument regarding cultural continuities in Lapita and Polynesian art forms.

12 Mead et al. (1975). A prior effort at formal analysis of Lapita designs was that of Poulsen (1972) which, however, used a rather different methodology.

13 See Green (1990) for a discussion of the history of this approach.

14 See Donovan (1973), Kay (1984), Kirch (1988a), and Sharp (1988) for examples.

15 Leroi-Gourhan's system (1982), developed for European Paleolithic cave art, posits four "figurative states," ranging from *pure geometric* (signs) at one extreme, to *analytical figurative* motifs (in which natural objects such as animals are portrayed with near accuracy of their morphology). In between these lie the *geometric figurative* (where elements are signs, but these are relatively identifiable) and the *synthetic figurative* (in which essentials of form are depicted, but without the attention to detail of the analytical figurative).

16 These objects are cylindrical, with flaring bases open at the bottom, and with vertical, unelaborated rims. Being open at top and bottom, they are not "vessels" in the normal sense. That the rims are plain and flat hints that they could have been used as stands to support large bowls or dishes. Typically, these cylinder stands are elaborately decorated with a combination of raised bands, detailed dentate-stamped and carved motifs, the latter being lime in-filled. Since all known examples carry anthropomorphic face designs, it is also conceivable that they functioned as a form of figurine.

17 I cannot resist again issuing the caveat that we desperately need archaeological data from the northern coastal regions of New Guinea (especially in Irian Jaya), and from the offshore islands. When fieldwork has been carried out in this vast region, our knowledge of the geographic range of Lapita may be considerably modified.

18 Both kinds of materials have been rarely preserved in some later Polynesian contexts, such as mummified skin with tattoo designs from Hawai'i, and fragments of decorated barkcloth from Hawai'i and the Marquesas. While the chances of finding such preserved materials in Lapita sites are slim, it might be possible in special depositional circumstances, such as the anaerobic deposits at the Talepakemalai site.

19 The term "temper" usually implies sand, grit, or other materials purposively added to the clay body by the potter to enhance the workability and strength of the fabric. In Oceanic ceramics, these tempers or non-plastic inclusions are usually some form of sand, either calcareous sand derived from beaches or volcani-clastic sands including such minerals as pyroxine, biotite, basaltic lithic fragments, and so forth. In some cases, these sands are clearly manual additions to the clay, but in other cases they may have been natural inclusions in colluvial clay deposits (e.g., "self-tempered" clays).

20 In most Lapita sites, post-depositional disturbance has made vessel reconstruction virtually impossible, and ceramic analyses must be conducted with the *sherd* as the basic unit of study. Given that many kinds of vessels were only partially covered in decorations, a certain number of "plain" sherds also derive from decorated vessels. Even taking this into account, however, the majority of sherds in most assemblages still derive from plain or non-decorated vessels.

21 A parallel situation obtains in nearby Anuta Island, settled at about the same time as Tikopia (see Kirch and Rosendahl 1973).

22 Three major contributions to New Caledonian prehistory are the doctoral dissertations of Frimigacci (1975), Galipaud (1988), and Sand (1994).

23 I refer here to Bourdieu's (1977) concept. The whole issue of how Lapita ceramics were used to help define and negotiate social roles in the construction of everyday life is a topic of research that will require many years of research, with greatly expanded areal excavations and careful analysis. It may well be worth the effort.

24 These distinctions are so evident that at one stage in the analysis of our 1986 Talepakemalai assemblage, we coined the phrase "all style and no substance" for the dentate-stamped ware.

25 This female-based tradition presumably could be traced back into island Southeast Asia, where the plain wares at sites like Uattamdi in Halmahera are essentially identical with Lapita plain ware.

26 Indeed, this is a project well worth the energies of some enterprising scholar, particularly given the vastly expanded samples of pottery now available as a result of excavations conducted in the past decade.

27 Detailed analysis of this large collection is still in process, but preliminary accounts may be found in Kirch (1987, 1988b) and in Kirch et al. (1991).

28 These plain, red-slipped jars are strikingly similar in every aspect to the ceramic assemblage recently excavated by Bellwood and Irwin at the Uattamdi site on Kayoa Island in Halmahera.

29 Initial comments on the pottery made by Green (1976) were later elaborated in his matrix-analysis study of Lapita decoration at several Western and Eastern Lapita sites (Green 1978). An exhaustive study of the decorated pottery from the three Reef/Santa Cruz sites was carried out by Donovan (1973) using the Mead system (Mead

et al. 1975). Parker (1981) analyzed the vessel and rim forms from these sites, and her data are utilized by Sheppard and Green (1991) in their study of spatial distribution within the RF-2 site. Green (1991c) also provides additional comments on the ceramic sequence from SZ-8, RF-2, and RF-6.

30 On the basis of radiocarbon dates alone, SZ-8 and RF-2 might be considered contemporaneous.

31 Face motifs from the SZ-8 and RF-2 sites are illustrated in Green (1979b, figures 1–3 and 1–4).

32 The Niuatoputapu ceramic assemblages are described and analyzed in detail in Kirch (1988a); see also Kirch (1978).

33 On "cooking without pots" in Polynesia, see H. Leach (1982). The possible role of cuisine in the loss of pottery in Polynesia is explored by Le Moine (1987).

Chapter 6

1   Of the 79 Lapita sites catalogued by Kirch and Hunt (1988a), 65 (82 percent) are situated on beach terraces. The remaining six are caves or rockshelters.

2   Detailed geomorphological data on the Niuatoputapu and Tikopia sites are provided in Kirch (1988a) and Kirch and Yen (1982), respectively. Another instance of 3,000 years BP deposits situated within such a beach terrace is the To'aga site on Ofu Island, American Samoa, which has been the subject of intensive geomorphological, archaeological, sedimentological, and radiometric analyses (Kirch and Hunt, eds 1993).

3   The geomorphological evidence supporting this interpretation of a +1–1.5 m high stand between 4–2,000 BP is far too extensive to cite in full here. A few of the many key studies are Nunn (1990), and Miyata et al. (1990) for Fiji, Ash (1987) for Viti Levu Island, Dickinson et al. (1994) for the Ha'apai group in Tonga, Yonekura et al. (1988) for the southern Cooks, and Pirazzoli and Montaggioni (1986, 1988; Montaggioni and Pirazzoli 1984) for various islands in French Polynesia. Kirch (1993) reviews this evidence with regard to the To'aga site in American Samoa. See also Clark and Lingle (1979), Clark et al. (1978), Mitrovica and Peltier (1991), Nakada and Lambeck (1989), and Tushingham and Peltier (1991) for theoretical analyses of the Holocene geoid and the implications for a mid-Holocene high stand.

4   For a further discussion of the morphodynamics of Pacific Island coastal environments, see Menard (1986) with regard to controlling geological processes, and Chappell (1982) for a discussion of sediment budgets.

5   See Kirch and Hunt (1988a, table 2.1), Gosden et al. (1989, table

2), and Sheppard and Green (1991, figure 18) for data on Lapita site area.

6   Because no complete Lapita houses have yet been excavated, we are uncertain of how large these may have been. A partially excavated house floor in the RF-2 site is interpreted as being about 7 by 10 meters. In the absence of firm data on Lapita house sizes, we must turn to ethnographic analogies from documented Oceanic houses. See, for example, the size ranges of historic and prehistoric Samoan house foundations reported by Davidson (1974:232–6, figure 89, table 27).

7   Until Green's 1970–1 excavations in the eastern Solomons (Green 1976), little attention was paid to site structure and most excavation strategies consisted of limited testing to obtain ceramic assemblages. Green's innovations included the application of random and systematic sampling procedures, methods which have been followed up by other investigators such as Kirch (1988a) on Niuatoputapu, Kirch and Yen (1982) on Tikopia, and Kirch (1987, 1988b) on Mussau, Frimigacci (1975) in New Caledonia, and Best (1984) on Lakeba. It is still the case, however, that few Lapita sites have been excavated in such a manner that details of their internal spatial structures are interpretable.

8   The Talepakemalai or ECA site was first tested by Egloff (1975; Bafmatuk et al. 1980). The present interpretations are based on my own extensive excavations carried out in 1985, 1986, and 1988, and reported in part in Kirch (1987, 1988b; Kirch et al. 1991). A detailed monograph on the Talepakemalai excavations is in progress.

9   The name, of course, is ethnographically-recorded and its antiquity is unknowable, although the practice of naming households after economic trees is very widespread in the southwestern Pacific, and therefore arguably ancient (see the discussion of the Lolokoka site, below). The ECA site actually incorporates several modern land names, and Talepakemalai is that on which the main excavations were concentrated.

10 The ECB or Etakosarai site was excavated by Kirch in 1985 (Kirch 1987) and by Hunt in 1986 (Kirch et al. 1991).

11 Talepakemalai was occupied for several hundred years, during which time the shoreline commenced its progradation northward. As the shoreline prograded, the zone of stilt-houses was also shifted seaward, so that there is a "horizontal stratification" of the waterlogged, stilt-house portion of the site.

12 The detailed analysis of Lapita pottery composition and importing at the Talepakemalai site is reported by Hunt (1989) in his doctoral dissertation, and is also discussed by Kirch (1990a, 1991).

13 Maps showing the environmental context of the RF-2 site were published by Green (1976, figure 73) and by Lepofsky (1988, figure

3.2). Green (1986) and Swadling (1986) provide analyses of the fishbone and shellfish midden, including their implications for changes in the inshore marine environment.

14　The age range of 1,187–926 cal BC represents the pooled mean of four ^{14}C dates from RF-2, all on charcoal, which have been further calibrated to calendar years (Green 1991c).

15　This Scandinavian term refers to a virgin settlement landscape, and was applied by Jens Poulsen (1968, 1987) to lands colonized by the Lapita people.

16　Lapita sites are found on offshore islets of Tömotu Neo and Tömotu Noi adjacent to Nendö, and are reported in Green (1976), and in McCoy and Cleghorn (1988).

17　The spatial analysis of RF-2, which I have drawn freely upon in this section, was published jointly by Sheppard and Green (1991), and is a laudable example of how distributional data can be effectively utilized for interpreting internal site function and activity differentiation.

18　The permeable sands of coral islets typically contain a thin lens of slightly brackish, but potable, water floating on top of salt water, termed the Ghyben-Herzberg Aquifer (Wiens 1962).

19　Sheppard and Green (1991) provide an overview of the pottery distribution within the Nenumbo site, based on the detailed study of ceramic vessel forms by Parker (1981).

20　One large earth oven was situated just south of the house corner.

21　There is no way of knowing whether the name Lolokoka is of great antiquity, possibly even deriving from the Lapita settlement period on Niuatoputapu. But it is significant – from the comparative perspective of Oceanic naming patterns – that "under the *koka* tree" replicates a practice seen as far west as Mussau, with "under the *malai* tree" (Talepakemalai). Having dwelt in the Futunan household of Lalotilo ("under the *tilo* [*Calophyllum*] tree"), as well as excavated at the ancestral dwelling-cum-temple site of Raropuka ("under the *puka* tree") along the Tikopian lake shore, the pervasiveness of naming hamlets and houses by their associated trees is to me striking. I think there is every reason to believe that this practice of naming settlement locations after their associated economic trees is very old in Oceania, and probably dates back to Lapita times.

22　Details of the geomorphic context of the Niuatoputapu Lapita sites are reported in Rogers (1974), and in Kirch (1978, 1988a).

23　That Lolokoka, and the Vaipoa area in general, is the most desirable habitation locality on the island is suggested not only by the presence of the NT-90 Lapita site, but by its status as the ancestral seat of the island's paramount chiefly line, Ma'atu (see Kirch 1988a).

24　This is Vessel Form 10 of the Niuatoputapu ceramic typology, see Kirch (1988a:166).

25 On atolls, such wells not only provide the main source of potable liquid (the other being coconuts), but larger pits excavated to expose the brackish lens and mulched with vegetable matter permitted the intensive cultivation of taro (*Colocasia esculenta*) and pulaka, the giant swamp taro (*Cyrtosperma chamissonis*).

26 I am much indebted to Roger Green for supplying me with an early draft of his important paper with Andrew Pawley (in press), in which they correlate archaeological and linguistic reconstructions for Proto Oceanic and Lapita houses. Access to their innovative ideas on this topic greatly stimulated my own thinking as this chapter was in progress.

27 Hauser-Schaublin (1989:618), who has made a comprehensive study of New Guinea men's houses, regards the "hut on piles" as an Austronesian cultural introduction to Near Oceania. She believes that the Papuan-speaking peoples of the Middle Sepik adopted this construction technique from Austronesian-speaking peoples who settled the north coast of New Guinea.

28 The difference between the Talepakemalai and Arawe sites on the one hand, and the Kreslo and Buka sites on the other, has to do with local geomorphological conditions which favored the accumulation of reef-derived sediments in the former sites thus burying and preserving the archaeological deposits which had accumulated under the stilt-houses.

29 The apparent absence of Lapita sites in the main Solomon Islands (southeast of Buka) may well be due to a continuation of the stilt-house settlement pattern through these islands, and the failure of archaeologists to conduct surveys in the coastal environments (including open reef flats) where these would occur. Future site surveys in the Solomons would do well to consider the possibilities of such site distributions.

30 Because *balay* has no known reflexes in any of the Formosan languages of Taiwan, it is presumed to be a Proto Malayo-Polynesian innovation, rather than a part of the Proto Austronesian vocabulary.

31 An innovation that may well go along with this architectural shift is the term for gravel paving, *kirikiri*, certainly reconstructable to Proto Polynesian, if not also Proto Central Pacific. See Green (1986) for a dicussion of Proto Polynesian house terms.

32 Fox (1993:12) suggests that the 'men's house' aspect of *kamaliR* was borrowed from Non-Austronesian speaking peoples in the Oceanic area, a view to which Green and Pawley (in press) give some support.

33 On the concept of *habitus*, see Bourdieu (1977).

34 Etymologically, these terms are interesting. *Tala(m)pat* is bimorphemic, *ta-* being a bound variant of *tau*, "person." *Qa* is a personal/proper article that preceded the kinship term *adiki* (Lichtenberk 1986:353).

35 Green (1994) argues that such development of rank and status terms in Fiji and Western Polynesia can be traced for late Eastern Lapita and the subsequent Polynesian Plain Ware period.

36 In his brief proposal, based on a reconsideration of Boas' treatment of Kwakiutl kin groups, Lévi-Strauss referred to the following properties of "house societies": "a corporate body holding an estate made up of both material and immaterial wealth, which perpetuates itself through the transmission of its name, its goods, and its titles down a real or imaginary line, considered legitimate as long as this continuity can express itself in the language of kinship or of affinity and, most often, of both" (1982:174).

37 A classic ethnographic example of the "house" as a primary social group within an Oceanic-speaking culture is Firth's discussion of the *paito* in Tikopia (Firth 1936). See also Kirch (in press).

38 A classic example is Tikopia, where the principal temples along the lake shore in Uta were formerly residences (Firth 1936; Kirch, in press).

39 In her discussion of houses of the dead in island Southeast Asia, Waterson (1990) gives many visual examples of anthropomorphic face representations of ancestors, some with remarkable similarity to Lapita face designs (see, in particular, figures 169, 189, 190, 191, and 192). One cannot but think that in these varied ethnographic representations of ancestors as carved faces, is the modern reflection of a very old Austronesian practice.

Chapter 7

1 I use the term horticulture for classic mixed gardening systems, such as the swidden or shifting cultivation systems typical of much of Melanesia and even central Polynesia. Equally important was arboriculture, tree cropping, or orchard gardening, involving a diverse suite of fruit and nut-bearing trees. In some islands, such as Hawai'i, intensive field agriculture involving "landesque capital intensification" also developed, and sustained some of the highest population densities in Oceania.

2 Excellent overviews of the indigenous horticultural and agricultural systems of Oceanic cultures may be found in Barrau (1965) and Yen (1973, 1990, 1991a, 1993). Kirch (1994a) provides a detailed account of the complex agricultural production system of Futuna Island, and extends this case to an argument concening the relative significant of "wet" and "dry" agricultural production throughout Polynesia.

3 The question of Lapita agriculture and of the various lines of evidence potentially relevant to refuting Groube's hypothesis were also discussed in Kirch (1979).

4 For a recent summary of methodological advancements, including specific examples from the Pacific Islands, see Hather (1994).

5 The implied gender distinctions in my characterization of Lapita sea-knowledge are of course speculative, but are based on widespread cultural practices among contemporary Oceanic peoples. Typically in Oceanic societies, the harvesting of mollusks, seaweeds, and other reef-flat invertebrates, and some kinds of inshore fishing, are the work of women and younger children. Offshore fishing, on the other hand (especially that involving the use of canoes), tends to be associated with juvenile and adult men. It is probable that such a gender differentiation was also characteristic of the Lapita people from whom most of these Oceanic societies have descended.

6 I take these and certain other Proto Oceanic reconstructions of marine phenomena from Marck (1994). All Proto Oceanic reconstructed terms that follow in this chapter are indicated with an initial asterisk.

7 Important syntheses of Lapita fishbone data and of Lapita shellfish data were prepared by Butler (1988) and Nagaoka (1988), respectively. See also Butler (1994) for a more recent comparative analysis of fishbone assemblages from several key Lapita sites. Green (1986) and Swadling (1986) present detailed studies of fishbone and shellfish assemblages from the Nenumbo (RF-2) Lapita site. For the Kiki site (TK-4) on Tikopia, see Kirch and Yen (1982).

8 At Talepakemalai, we excavated a large, heavy ceramic "ring" which if it had a shark or ray-skin stretched across it would readily have functioned as a drum.

9 These early Lapita *Trochus* shell lures appear to be the proto-types for the later pearl-shell trolling lures commonly found in Polynesian and Micronesian archaeological sites.

10 For a more extensive description of the Niuatoputapu fishing strategies, see Dye (1983). Green (1986) also argued that angling was unimportant in the fishing strategies practiced by people occupying the Nenumbo site.

11 See Kirch (1994b:283–5) for further discussion of the evidence for early and widespread turtle feasting in Polynesia.

12 See, for example, Firth's (1967) discussion of Tikopia beliefs regarding sea creatures. Cetaceans, in particular, are regarded as embodiments of spirits.

13 One of the most important lines of indirect evidence invoked by Green (1979a) to support his hypothesis that Lapita economy incorporated horticulture, was the size and duration of Lapita settlements. He rightly inferred that such communities could not have been supported by a hunting-and-gathering economy alone.

14 A summary of the plant remains excavated from Talepakemalai during the 1986 field season is provided in Kirch (1989). Additional

plant materials recovered in 1988, including several other species, will be reported in detail by Kirch and Lepofsky.

15 See Kirch (1994a) for a detailed description of shifting cultivation as practiced on the Western Polynesian island of Futuna, which was originally settled by Eastern Lapita people.

16 For ethnographic descriptions of village arboriculture in Melanesia, see Yen (1974) on Nendö Island, and Lepofsky (1992) on Eloaua, Mussau.

17 Coconut shells preserved in swamps, and coconut pollen identified from pollen cores in several islands, indicate that the plant was naturally distributed as far east as the Cook Islands (and probably also the Society Islands) prior to human dispersal in the Pacific. However, the naturally-distributed coconuts may have had rather small-cavitied fruit. Early Oceanic peoples certainly selected certain clones with larger fruit, and also with long fibers suitable for making sennit cordage, and transported these into the central and eastern Pacific.

18 Bellwood (1985:241) and Spriggs (1982), among others, had suggested that complex techniques of pondfield irrigation were diffused into Oceania via initial Austronesian expansion.

19 In her monumental and otherwise well-informed *A History of Food*, Maguelonne Toussaint-Samat (1992) gives only marginal and passing treatment of the great tuber crops of the Indo-Pacific, taro and yams, and that in her chapter on hunting and gathering!

20 See Su'a (1987) for a highly innovative study of the Polynesian "pudding complex" that draws upon ethnographic, linguistic, and archaeological evidence.

21 In the Talepakemalai excavations, burned-coral heating stones were ubiquitous in the deposits, having doubtless been disposed of periodically from the stilt-houses. However, no in situ oven pits were exposed, lending additional support to the notion of these ovens being inside the elevated stilt-houses.

22 Green and Pawley (in press) suggest that the earth oven with heated stones was not present in Proto Malayo-Polynesian times, but rather was borrowed by the Proto Oceanic speakers from people already present in Near Oceania.

23 In my experience excavating in southwest Pacific sites, most earth oven features contain traces of carbonized coconut endocarp. The very hot, intense ignition of these dried shells is still the preferred method of lighting earth ovens throughout most of tropical Oceania.

24 Precisely identical taro peeling knives of pearl shell are made and used by the people of Eloaua Island today, who call them *gaulu*.

25 This seasonality is largely the result of the cropping cycle of yams, and of the short fruit-bearing periods of breadfruit, which are two of the major staple crops. Other nuts and fruits also have highly

seasonal periods of yield. For ethnographic accounts of such food production cycles, and the implications for famine see Firth (1939) and Kirch (1994a).

26 See Yen (1975) and Cox (1980) for further discussions of pit fermentation and preservation of breadfruit and other crops; also Kirch (1984:133–5).

27 See Kirch (1984, figure 15) for an illustration of such a pit on Niuatoputapu Island. Such pits have also been noted for the Nenumbo site and in Lapita sites on Tongatapu.

28 Rivers' use of the terms "kava-people" and "betel-people" to characterize two different periods of migration into Oceania shows the importance he accorded the disjunct distribution of these plants. Rivers' discussion of the origins of these narcotic substances is quite well informed, and presages some current debates, especially with regard to kava (Rivers 1914:243–57).

29 Vincent Lebot's arguments are set out in Lebot and Lévesque (1989) and in Lebot et al. (1992), and his model is largely accepted by Crowley (1994). An alternative view, harking back to Rivers' original ideas, is presented by Brunton (1989). Ambrose (1991) presents a scenario involving the use of stone mortars to prepare strong kava concoctions in parts of western Melanesia.

30 Because the taxonomy of these plants is based on floral parts, the identification of these stems to species level is not possible. On morphological grounds they are more likely to be *P. wichmannii*, however, which reportedly has a harder tissue and, therefore, would be more amenable to preservation in the ECA site conditions.

31 Ambrose (1991) has suggested that stone mortars found in Manus and elsewhere in the Bismarcks might have been used for kava preparation.

32 The find and associated dates are reported by Swadling et al. (1991), and the betel specimen itself is illustrated in Swadling et al. (1988, plate 38 inset).

33 There is linguistic evidence, however, that betel was known to early Austronesian-speaking peoples. Zorc (1994:565) gives a PAN reconstruction (*buáq*) for the nut.

34 On the Pacific Rat and its distribution, see Tate (1951) and Roberts (1991).

35 For accounts of the distribution, behavior, and ecology of these and other geckos and skinks, see Zug (1991).

36 On the transport of terrestrial gastropods by indigenous Pacific peoples, see Cooke (1926). The archaeologically-recovered terrestrial non-marine mollusk fauna of Tikopia is reported by Christensen and Kirch (1981); that from Yanuca is reported by Hunt (1981), and from Niuatoputapu by Kirch (1988a).

37 The recovery of microscopic fauna, such as diminutive land snails

or the faunal remains of geckos and skinks, requires very fine sieving (e.g., 0.5 mm mesh) that is not often applied in archaeological excavations. The newly-developing field of archaeo-entomology has also hardly begun to be applied in the Pacific.

38 The quote is from Fosberg (1963a:5), whose succinct discussion of island ecosystems remains a classic.

39 Two recent volumes provide extensive accounts of the impacts of prehistoric, indigenous peoples to the environments of Australia and Oceania: Dodson, (ed. 1992), and Kirch and Hunt, (eds 1996).

40 This study is reported by Hope and Spriggs (1982).

41 For Viti Levu, see Southern (1986). The Lakeba sequences were originally reported by Hughes et al. (1979), and are summarized in an insightful discussion of the evolution by island landscapes by Bayliss-Smith et al. (1988:16–43).

42 The sequence of environmental change on Futuna is discussed in detail by Kirch (1994a:215–27).

43 The term "extirpation" refers to the elimination of a species from a particular island, while "extinction" refers to the global elimination of a species.

44 See Kirch and Yen (1982) for the Tikopia case, Steadman (1993) for Samoa and Tonga, and Balouet and Olsen (1989) for New Caledonia.

45 For further discussion of the New Caledonian tumuli debate, see Green and Mitchell (1983), Green (1988), and Sand (1994). The *Placostylus* shells incorporated within the tumuli, which yielded radiocarbon dates predating Lapita and extending back as far as 10,000 BP, are a forest-litter dwelling species that would readily have been scratched up by these giant megapodes into their incubation mounds.

46 Similar cases of reductions in marine fauna have been reported for Lapita sites in Tongatapu (Poulsen 1987; Spennemann 1987) and Lakeba (Best 1984).

47 See Spennemann (1987) for a case study of human predation effects on shellfish resources in Tongatapu.

Chapter 8

1 The distinction here, which follows Oliver (1989:799, n. 1), is between exchange that takes places within a social unit or community (internal exchange), and inter-community exchange (external exchange). In Oceania, the latter often links multiple social and cultural units at considerable geographic distance, and crosses linguistic boundaries as well.

2 For a superb overview of the diversity of ethnographically documented exchange system in Oceania see Oliver (1989:501–89).

3   An overview and extensive bibliography of archaeological studies of prehistoric exchange in Western Melanesia is provided in Kirch (1991), while Green (in press) canvasses the situation in Remote Oceania.

4   For overviews of Lapita exchange, and extensive bibliographic references to literature dealing with prehistoric exchange in Melanesia and Western Polynesia, see Kirch and Hunt, eds (1988), Kirch (1991), Green (in press), and Kirch and Weisler (1994).

5   For further discussion of these terms, and of the methods and principles involved in the study of prehistoric exchange, see the various papers in Earle and Ericson (eds 1977) and Ericson and Earle (eds 1982). Renfrew (1984) also provides an important discussion of the problems associated with modeling prehistoric exchange.

6   Both of these sources have numerous "subsources" such as specific flow deposits, which minor but detectable differences in chemical composition.

7   Green (1987; Green and Bird 1989) expended considerable time and energy on the problem of a probable Fergusson Island obsidian flake excavated from his Reef Island site.

8   The density-sorting method was first applied to Lapita obsidian assemblages by Roger Green (1987) and later extended by Kirch et al. (1991); Torrence and Victor (1995) confirm the usefulness of this method within its known limitations.

9   See Bird et al. (1978) and Duerden et al. (1979, 1980) for details of these techniques as initially applied to Melanesian obsidians. A recent application of PIXE-PIGME analysis to archaeological obsidian from several sites in West New Britain is provided by Summerhayes et al. (in press).

10   See Allen and Bell (1988) for an overview; also Sheppard (1993).

11   Among these are the Mailu and other Motu-speaking peoples of the south Papuan coast, who produced large quantities of ceramics for trade with the peoples of the Papuan Gulf (Irwin 1985). Similarly, in the Massim region, the Amphlett islanders specialized in the production of ceramic vessels that were exchanged with the Trobriand islanders, in the famous *kula* ring.

12   Such ethnographic analogies with historic-period Oceanic exchange systems do not prove that the prehistoric Lapita shell objects were used as exchange valuables, but they do provide the basis for proposing this as a reasonable hypothesis, subject to archaeological testing.

13   I cannot overstress the importance of careful and rigorous quantification, for the modeling of exchange flows and their temporal changes demand such numeric data. Roger Green is to be applauded for his efforts to quantify such materials as obsidian and chert in his Reef/Santa Cruz Islands sites.

14 The variables listed here are based on Plog (1977:129).

15 For a detailed review of the varied Lapita exchange networks within Remote Oceania, see Green (in press).

16 I was told by the islanders that Mussau is visible in clear weather from the higher elevations of New Hanover Island, whereas Manus cannot be seen from other islands in the Bismarcks.

17 In this model, small islands are represented by a single node, while large islands are represented by nodes at the ends and the mid-point. See Hunt (1988) and Hage and Harary (1991) for further discussion of these and other graphic-theoretic models and the matrix analyses derived from them.

18 Preliminary reports providing more details on the results of our Mussau Project with regard to prehistoric exchange include Kirch (1987, 1988b 1988c, 1990a), Kirch et al. (1991), and Hunt (1989).

19 It is noteworthy that these high-order subgroups of Oceanic do correspond fairly well with ethnographically-documented exchange networks. This is particularly the case with the North New Guinea Cluster, which incorporates the region linked in modern times by the famous Vitiaz Straits exchange network (see Lilley 1991b).

20 It is probable that Lapita settlements will also be found on Vanikoro and Utupua Islands, once more intensive archaeological exploration has been carried out there.

21 No comprehensive site report for the Reefs/Santa Cruz sites has been published, but data relevant to prehistoric exchange can be found in Green (1976, 1978, 1987) and in Sheppard (1993).

22 These data may appear deceptively simple, but they represent an appreciable field and laboratory effort to obtain. Only because Green excavated his sites according to a rigorous sampling strategy (Green 1976) has he been able to provide density estimates that are reliable and meaningful.

23 From a functional or utilitarian point of view, it is doubtful that the Vanua Lava and Gaua volcanic glass is "inferior" to that from Talasea.

24 The archaeological record for these islands is still spotty and incomplete, but see McCoy and Cleghorn (1988), Kirch (1983), and Kirch and Yen (1982) for data relevant to this discussion.

25 It may be significant that the first-rank is held by Lakeba Island, in the Lau group, locus of an important Lapita community and probable manufacturing center for shell exchange valuables.

26 A similar pattern of increasing regionalization of exchange has been documented by Best (1984) for the Lakeba, Fiji, sequence.

27 This kind of increasing regionalization over time is also attested to by the archaeological ceramic assemblages, with a distinctive set of northern traits indicated (Kirch 1988a:188, figure 114).

Chapter 9

1 In recent years a considerable debate has fomented around the question of whether so-called "four-field" or "holistic" anthropology still has a future in the academy. Certainly such a broad, integrating paradigm for anthropology has become endangered by the trend toward specialization, and many prominent anthropology departments in North American universities no longer represent all of the traditional four-field branches (i.e., archaeology, physical anthropology, linguistic anthropology, and socio-cultural anthropology).

2 Smith's position seems to reflect that of her mentor, Chris Gosden, who has himself proposed that Lapita assemblages may be explained in these unenlightening terms: "structures of reference bring about patterns of action which create pattern in the archaeological evidence" (1994:35).

3 I refer here to the comment of Gosden (1991b:262) who appears not fully to have understood the phylogenetic model proposed by Kirch and Green (1987). Merely because Lapita is (rightly) "seen as ancestral to various social groups which exist in the Pacific today" in no way implies a methodology of retrodictively supplying the features of Lapita society from modern social groups, "through the medium of historical linguistics" (1991b:262). Such comments do not reflect an understanding of the methods of historical linguistics, such as semantic reconstruction, or of comparative methods in anthropology.

References

Allen, J. 1972. Nebira 4: An early Austronesian site in central Papua. *Archaeology and Physical Anthropology in Oceania* 7:92–124.

——. 1977. Sea traffic, trade, and expanding horizons. In J. Allen, J. Golson, and R. Jones, eds, *Sunda and Sahul: Prehistoric Studies in Southeast Asia, Melanesia and Australia*, pp. 387–417. London: Academic Press.

——. 1984. In search of the Lapita homeland. *Journal of Pacific History* 19:186–201.

——. 1993. Notions of the Pleistocene in Greater Australia. In M. A. Smith, M. Spriggs, and B. Fankhauser, eds, *Sahul in Review: Pleistocene Archaeology in Australia, New Guinea and Island Melanesia*, pp. 139–51. *Occasional Papers in Prehistory*, No. 24. Canberra: Department of Prehistory, Australian National University.

——. 1994. Radiocarbon determinations, luminescence dating and Australian archaeology. *Antiquity* 68:339–43.

Allen, J. and C. Gosden, eds 1991. *Report of the Lapita Homeland Project*. *Occasional Papers in Prehistory*, No. 20. Canberra: Department of Prehistory, Australian National University.

Allen, J., C. Gosden, and J. P. White, 1989. Human Pleistocene adaptations in the tropical island Pacific. *Antiquity* 63:548–61.

Allen, J. and S. Holdaway, 1995. The contamination of Pleistocene radiocarbon determinations in Australia. *Antiquity* 69:101–12.

Allen, J. and P. White, 1989. The Lapita homeland: Some new data and an interpretation. *Journal of the Polynesian Society* 98:129–46.

Allen, M. S. and G. Bell, 1988. Lapita flaked stone assemblages: Sourcing, technological, and functional studies. In P. V. Kirch and T. L. Hunt, eds, *Archaeology of the Lapita Cultural Complex: A Critical Review*, pp. 83–98. Seattle: The Burke Museum.

Ambrose, W. 1988. An early bronze artefact from Papua New Guinea. *Antiquity* 62:483–91.

——. 1991. Manus, mortars, and the kava connection. In A. Pawley, ed, *Man and a Half: Essays in Pacific Anthropology and Ethnobiology in Honour of Ralph Bulmer*, pp. 461–69. Auckland: The Polynesian Society.

Ambrose, W. R. and C. Gosden, 1991. Investigations on Boduna Island. In J. Allen and C. Gosden, eds, *Report of the Lapita Homeland Project*, pp. 182–88. *Occasional Papers in Prehistory*, No. 20. Canberra: Department of Prehistory, Australian National University.

Ambrose, W. R. and R. C. Green, 1972. First millennium BC transport of obsidian from New Britain to the Solomon Islands. *Nature* 237:31.

Ammerman, A. J. and L. L. Cavalli-Sforza, 1984. *The Neolithic Transition and the Genetics of Populations in Europe*. Princeton: Princeton University Press.

Anderson, E. 1952. *Plants, Man, and Life*. Berkeley: University of California Press.

Anson, D. 1983. Lapita Pottery of the Bismarck Archipelago and its Affinities. Unpublished Ph.D. Dissertation. University of Sydney, Australia.

——. 1986. Lapita pottery of the Bismarck Archipelago and its affinities. *Archaeology in Oceania* 21:157–65.

Anthony, D. W. 1990. Migration in archaeology: The baby and the bathwater. *American Anthropologist* 92:895–914.

Aoyagi Y., M. L. Aguilera, Jr., H. Ogawa, and K. Tanaka, 1986. The shell midden in the lower reaches of the Cagayan River. *The Journal of Sophia Asian Studies* 4:45–89.

Aoyagi, Y., M. L. Aguilera, Jr., H. Ogawa, and K. Tanaka, 1991. Excavations at Lal-lo shell middens (3). *The Journal of Sophia Asian Studies* 9:49–137.

Aoyagi, Y. and K. Tanaka, 1985. Some problems of the shell mound potteries found in the lower reaches of Cagayan River, Northern Luzon, Philippines. *The Journal of Sophia Asian Studies* 3:81–129.

Ash, J. 1987. Holocene sea levels in northern Viti Levu, Fiji. *New Zealand Journal of Geology and Geophysics* 30:431–5.

Athens, J. S. 1990a. Nan Madol pottery, Pohnpei. *Micronesica* Supplement 2:17–32.

——. 1990b. Kosrae pottery, clay, and early settlement. *Micronesica* Supplement 2:171–86.

Avias, J. 1950. Poteries canaques et poteries préhistorique en Nouvelle-Calédonie. *Journal de la Société des Océanistes* 6:111–40.

Ayres, W. S. 1990. Pohnpei's position in eastern Micronesian prehistory. *Micronesica* Supplement 2:187–212.

Bafmatuk, R., B. Egloff, and R. Kaiku, 1980. Islanders: Past and present. *Hemisphere* 25:77–81.

Bailey, G., J. Chappell, and R. Cribb, 1994. The origin of *Anadara* shell mounds at Weipa, North Queensland, Australia. *Archaeology in Oceania* 29:69–80.

Balouet, J. C. 1987. Extinctions des vertébrés terrestres de Nouvelle-Calédonie. *Mémoires de la Société Géologique de France* 150:177–83.

Balouet, J. C. and S. L. Olson, 1989. *Fossil Birds from Late Quaternary Deposits in New Caledonia*. Smithsonian Contributions to Zoology 469. Washington D.C.: Smithsonian Institution.

Barrau, J. 1965. Histoire et préhistoire horticole de l'Océanie tropical. *Journal de la Société des Océanistes* 21:55–78.

Bath, J. E. and J. S. Athens, 1990. Prehistoric social complexity on Pohnpei: The Saudeleur to Nahnmwarki transformation. *Micronesica* Supplement 2:275–90.

Barton, H. and J. P. White, 1993. Use of stone and shell artifacts at Balof 2, New Ireland, Papua New Guinea. *Asian Perspectives* 32:169–83.

Bayliss-Smith, T. P., R. Bedford, H. Brookfield, and M. Latham, 1988. *Islands, Islanders, and the World: The Colonial and Post-Colonial Experience of Eastern Fiji*. Cambridge: Cambridge University Press.

Bellwood, P. 1976. Archaeological research in Minahasa and the Talaud Islands, northeastern Indonesia. *Asian Perspectives* 19:240–88.

——. 1979. *Man's Conquest of the Pacific: The Prehistory of Southeast Asia and Oceania*. New York: Oxford University Press.

——. 1985. *Prehistory of the Indo-Malaysian Archipelago*. Sydney: Academic Press.

——. 1987. The prehistory of island southeast Asia: A multidisciplinary review of recent research. *Journal of World Prehistory* 1:171–224.

——. 1992. New discoveries in Southeast Asia relevant for Melanesian (especially Lapita) prehistory. In J. C. Galipaud, ed., *Poterie Lapita et Peuplement, Actes du Colloque LAPITA*, pp. 49–66. Noumea: ORSTOM.

——. 1993. Crossing the Wallace Line – with style. In M. A. Smith, M. Spriggs, and B. Fankhauser, eds, *Sahul in Review: Pleistocene Archaeology in Australia, New Guinea and Island Melanesia*, pp. 152–63. *Occasional Papers in Prehistory*, No. 24. Canberra: Department of Prehistory, Australian National University.

——. 1995. Austronesian prehistory in southeast Asia: Homeland, expansion, and transformation. In P. Bellwood, J. J. Fox, and D. Tryon, eds, *The Austronesians: Historical and Comparative Perspectives*, pp. 75–95. Canberra: Australian National University.

——. ed., 1988. *Archaeological Research in South-eastern Sabah.* Sabah Museum Monograph 2.

Bellwood, P., J. J. Fox, and D. Tryon, 1995. The Austronesians in history: Common origins and diverse transformations. In P. Bellwood, J. J. Fox, and D. Tryon, eds, *The Austronesians: Historical and Comparative Perspectives*, pp. 1–16. Canberra: Australian National University.

Bellwood, P. and P. Koon, 1989. Lapita colonists leave boats unburned! The question of Lapita links with Island Southeast Asia. *Antiquity* 63:613–22.

Best, S. 1984. Lakeba: The Prehistory of a Fijian Island. Unpublished Ph.D. Dissertation, University of Auckland, New Zealand.

——. 1987. Long-distance obsidian travel and possible implications for the settlement of Fiji. *Archaeology in Oceania* 22:31–2.

Best, S., P. Sheppard, R. Green, and R. Parker, 1992. Necromancing the stone: Archaeologsts and adzes in Samoa. *Journal of the Polynesian Society* 101:45–85.

Bird, J. R., L. H. Russell, and M. D. Scott, 1978. Obsidian characterization with elemental analysis by proton induced gamma-ray emission. *Analytical Chemistry* 50:2,082–4.

Birks, L. 1973. *Archaeological Excavations at Sigatoka Dune Site, Fiji.* Bulletin of the Fiji Museum No. 1. Suva: The Fiji Museum.

Birks, L. and H. Birks, 1967. A brief report on excavations at Sigatoka, Fiji. *New Zealand Archaeological Association Newsletter* 10:16–25.

Blust, R. 1980. Early Austronesian social organization: The evidence of language. *Current Anthropology* 21:205–26, 237–44.

——. 1985. The Austronesian homeland: A linguistic perspective. *Asian Perspectives* 26:45–67.

——. 1987. Lexical reconstruction and semantic reconstruction: The case of Austronesian "house" words. *Diachronica* 4(1–2):79–106.

——. 1994. Austronesian sibling terms and culture history. In A. K. Pawley and M. D. Ross, eds, *Austronesian Terminologies: Continuity and Change*, pp. 31–72. Pacific Linguistics, Series C-127. Canberra: Australian National University.

Bonhomme, T. and J. Craib, 1987. Radiocarbon dates from Unai Bapot, Saipan: Implications for the prehistory of the Marianas Islands. *Journal of the Polynesian Society* 96:95–106.

Bourdieu, P. 1977. *Outline of a Theory of Practice.* Cambridge: Cambridge University Press.

Brace, C. L. 1981. Oceanic tooth-size variation as a reflection of biological and cultural mixing. *Current Anthropology* 22:549–69.

Brace, C. L., M. L. Brace, Y. Dodo, K. D. Hunt, W. R. Leonard, Y. Li, S. Sangviehien, X. Shao, and Z. Zhang, 1990. Micronesians, Asians, Thais, and relations: A craniofacial and odontometric perspective. *Micronesica*, Supplement 2:323–48.

Brookfield, H. C., with D. Hart, 1971. *Melanesia: A Geographical Interpretation of an Island World*. London: Methuen & Co.

Brunton, R. 1989. *The Abandoned Narcotic: Kava and Cultural Instability in Melanesia*. Cambridge: Cambridge University Press.

Bryson, R. U. 1989. Ceramics and Spatial Archaeology at Nan Madol, Pohnpei. Unpublished Ph.D. Dissertation, University of Oregon. Ann Arbor: University Microfilms.

Buck, P. H. 1938. *Vikings of the Sunrise*. Philadelphia: J. B. Lippincott Co.

Butler, V. L. 1988. Lapita fishing strategies: The faunal evidence. In P. V. Kirch and T. L. Hunt, eds, *Archaeology of the Lapita Cultural Complex: A Critical Review*, pp. 99–116. Seattle: The Burke Museum.

———. 1994. Fishing feeding behavior and fish capture: The case for variation in Lapita fishing strategies. *Archaeology in Oceania* 29:81–90.

Camerini, J. R. 1994. Evolution, biogeography, and maps: An early history of Wallace's Line. In R. MacLeod and R. F. Rehbock, eds, *Darwin's Laboratory: Evolutionary Theory and Natural History in the Pacific*, pp. 70–109. Honolulu: University of Hawaii Press.

Capell, A. 1943. *The Linguistic Position of Southeast Papua*. Sydney: Australasian Medical Publishing Co.

Carsten, J. and S. Hugh-Jones, 1995. Introduction. In J. Carsten and S. Hugh-Jones, eds, *About the House: Lévi-Strauss and Beyond*, pp. 1–46. Cambridge: Cambridge University Press.

Carter, T. D., J. E. Hill, and G. H. H. Tate, 1945. *Mammals of the Pacific World*. New York: The MacMillan Co.

Cavalli-Sforza, L. L., P. Menozzi, and A. Piazza, 1994. *The History and Geography of Human Genes*. Princeton: Princeton University Press.

Chang, K. C. 1969. *Fengpitou, Tapenkeng, and the Prehistory of Taiwan*. Yale University Publications in Anthropology No. 73. New Haven.

Chappell, J. 1982. Sea levels and sediments: Some features of the context of coastal archaeological sites in the tropics. *Archaeology in Oceania* 17:69–78.

———. 1993. Late Pleistocene coasts and human migrations in the

Austral Region. In M. Spriggs, D. E. Yen, W. Ambrose, R. Jones, A. Thorne, and A. Andrews, eds, *A Community of Culture: The People and Prehistory of the Pacific*, pp. 43–8. *Occasional Papers in Prehistory*, No. 21. Canberra: Department of Prehistory, Australian National University.

Chen, C.-L. 1968. *Material Culture of the Formosan Aborigines.* Taipei: Southern Materials Cente, Inc.

Chiang, B. 1992. House in Paiwan society. In P. J.-K. Li, C.-H. Tsang, and Y.-K. Huang, eds, *Papers for International Symposium on Austronesian Studies Relating to Taiwan*, pp. 94–161. Taipei: Academia Sinica.

Christensen, C. C. and P. V. Kirch, 1981. Nonmarine mollusks from archaeological sites on Tikopia, Southeastern Solomon Islands. *Pacific Science* 35:75–88.

Clark, J. A., W. E. Farrell, and W. R. Peltier, 1978. Global changes in postglacial sea level: A numerical calculation. *Quaternary Research* 9:265–87.

Clark, J. A. and C. S. Lingle, 1979. Predicted relative sea-level changes (18,000 years BP to present) caused by late-glacial retreat of the Antarctic ice sheet. *Quaternary Research* 11:279–98.

Clark, J. T. and K. M. Kelly, 1993. Human genetics, paleoenvironments, and malaria: Relationships and implications for the settlement of Oceania. *American Anthropologist* 95:612–30.

Clark, J. T. and J. Terrell, 1978. Archaeology in Oceania. *Annual Review of Anthropology* 7:293–319.

Clark, R. 1991. Fingota/Fangota: Shellfish and fishing in Polynesia. In A. Pawley, ed., *Man and a Half: Essays in Pacific Anthropology and Ethnobiology in Honour of Ralph Bulmer*, pp. 78–83. Auckland: The Polynesian Society.

Coates, D. J., D. E. Yen, and P. M. Gaffey, 1988. Chromosome variation in taro, *Colocasia esculenta*: Implications for origin in the Pacific. *Cytologia* 55:551–60.

Coleman, P. J., ed., 1973. *The Western Pacific: Island Arcs, Marginal Seas, Geochemistry.* Nedlands: University of Western Australia Press.

Cooke, C. M., Jr. 1926. Notes on Pacific land snails. *Proceedings of the Third Pan-Pacific Science Congress*, pp. 2,276–84. Tokyo.

Cordy, R. 1982. A summary of archaeological research in Micronesia since 1977. *Indo-Pacific Prehistory Association Bulletin* 3:118–28.

Cox, P. A. 1980. *Masi* and *tanu 'eli*: Ancient Polynesian technologies for the preservation and concealment of food. *Pacific Tropical Botanical Garden Bulletin* 10:81–93.

Craib, J. 1983. Micronesian prehistory: An archaeological overview. *Science* 219:922–7.

Crosby, A. W. 1986. *Ecological Imperialism: The Biological Expansion of Europe, 900–1900*. Cambridge: Cambridge University Press.

Crowley, T. 1994. Proto who drank kava? In A. K. Pawley and M. D. Ross, eds, *Austronesian Terminologies: Continuity and Change*, pp. 87–100. Pacific Linguistics, Series C-127. Canberra: Australian National University.

Davenport, W. H. 1959. Non-unilinear descent and descent groups. *American Anthropologist* 61:557–72.

———. 1962. Red feather money. *Scientific American* 206(3):94–103.

———. 1964. Notes on Santa Cruz voyaging. *Journal of the Polynesian Society* 73:134–42.

Davidson, J. M. 1974. Samoan structural remains and settlement patterns. In R. C. Green and J. M. Davidson, eds, *Archaeology in Western Samoa*, Volume II, pp. 225–44. Auckland Institute and Museum Bulletin 7.

Davidson, J. M., E. Hinds, S. Holdaway, and F. Leach, 1990. The Lapita site of Natunuku, Fiji. *New Zealand Journal of Archaeology* 12:121–55.

Davidson, J. M. and F. Leach, 1993. The chronology of the Natunuku site, Fiji. *New Zealand Journal of Archaeology* 15:99–105.

Dempwolff, O. 1904. Über austterbende Völker. Die Eingeborenen der "Westlichen Inseln" in Deutsch-Neu-Guinea. *Zeitschrift fur Ethnologie* 36:414.

———. 1934. *Vergleichende Lautlehre des Austronesischen Wortshatzes*, Band 1: *Induktiver Aufbau einer Indonesischen Ursprache*. Beihefte zur Zeitschrift für Eingeborenen-Sprachen 15. Berlin: Dietrich Reimer.

———. 1937. *Vergleichende Lautlehre des Austronesischen Wortschatzes*, Band 2: *Deduktive Anwendung des Urindonesischen auf Austronesische Einzelsprachen*. Beihefte zur Zeitschrift für Eingeborenen-Sprachen 17. Berlin: Dietrich Reimer.

———. 1938. *Vergleichende Lautlehre des Austronesischen Wortschatzes*, Band 3: *Austronesisches Worterverzeichnis*. Beihefte zur Zeitschrift für Eingeborenen-Sprachen 19. Berlin: Dietrich Reimer.

Dening, G. 1980. *Islands and Beaches: Discourse on a Silent Land, Marquesas 1774–1880*. Honolulu: University of Hawaii Press.

———. 1992. *Mr Bligh's Bad Language: Passion, Power and Theatre on the Bounty*. Cambridge: Cambridge University Press.

Diamond, J. M. 1988. Express train to Polynesia. *Nature* 336:307–8.

Dickinson, W. R., D. V. Burley, and R. Shutler, Jr., 1994. Impact of hydro-isostatic Holocene sea-level change on the geologic context of island archaeological sites, northern Ha'apai group, Kingdom of Tonga. *Geoarchaeology* 9:85–111.

Dickinson, W. R. and R. Shulter, Jr., 1979. Petrography of sand tempers in Pacific Island potsherds. *Bulletin of the Geological Society of America* 90:993–5, 1,644–1,701.

Dickinson, W. R., R. Shutler, Jr., R. Shortland, D. V. Burley, and T. S. Dye, in press. Significance of sand tempers in indigenous Lapita and Lapitoid Polynesian Plain Ware and imported protohistoric Fijian pottery of Ha'apai (Tonga) for the question of Lapita tradeware.

Dodson, J., ed., 1992. *The Naive Lands: Prehistory and Environmental Change in Australia and the Southwest Pacific*. Melbourne: Longman Cheshire.

Donovan, L. J. 1973. A Study of the Decorative System of the Lapita Potters in Reefs and Santa Cruz Islands. Unpublished M.A. Research Essay, University of Auckland, New Zealand.

Duerden, P., J. R. Bird, M. D. Scott, E. Clayton, and L. H. Russell, 1979. Elemental analysis of thick obsidian samples by proton induced X-ray emission spectrometry. *Analytical Chemistry* 51:2,350–4.

——. 1980. PIXE-PIGME studies of artifacts. *Nuclear Instruments and Methods* 168:447–52.

Dumont D'Urville, J. S. C. 1832. Sur les îles du Grand Océan. *Société de Géographie Bulletin* 17:1–21.

Dutton, T. 1995. Language contact and change in Melanesia. In P. Bellwood, J. J. Fox, and D. Tryon, eds, *The Austronesians: Historical and Comparative Perspectives*, pp. 192–213. Canberra: Australian National University.

Dye, T. S. 1983. Fish and fishing on Niuatoputapu, Tonga. *Oceania* 53:242–71.

——. 1988. Social and Cultural Change in the Prehistory of the Ancestral Polynesian Homeland. Unpublished Ph.D. Dissertation, Yale University, New Haven.

——. 1989. Marine turtle bones from an archaeological site in Polynesia yield reliable age determinations. *Radiocarbon* 32:143–7.

Dyen, I. 1965. *A Lexicostatistical Classification of the Austronesian Languages*. Indiana University Publications in Anthropology and Linguistics, Memoir 19. Bloomington: University of Indiana.

Earle, T. K. and J. E. Ericson, eds, 1977. *Exchange Systems in Prehistory*. New York: Academic Press.

Eggan, F. 1954. Social anthropology and the method of controlled comparison. *American Anthropologist* 56:743–63.

Egloff, B. J. 1971. Archaeological research in the Collingwood Bay area of Papua. *Asian Perspectives* 14:60–4.

——. 1975. Archaeological investigations in the coastal Madang area and on Eloaue Island of the St. Matthias Group. *Records of the Papua New Guinea Museum and Art Gallery* 5:15–31.

———. 1979. *Recent Prehistory in Southeast Papua*. Terra Australis 4. Canberra: Department of Prehistory, Australian National University.

Ericson, J. E. and T. K. Earle, eds, 1982. *Contexts for Prehistoric Exchange*. New York: Academic Press.

Fankhauser, B. 1994. Protein and lipid analysis of food residues. In J. G. Hather, ed., *Tropical Archaeobotany: Applications and New Developments*, pp. 227–50. London: Routledge.

Filer, C. 1990. Diversity of cultures or culture of diversity? In N. Lutkenhaus, et al., eds, *Sepik Heritage: Tradition and Change in Papua New Guinea*, pp. 116–28. Durham: Carolina Academic Press.

Firth, R. 1936. *We, The Tikopia*. London: George Allen and Unwin.

———. 1939. *Primitive Polynesian Economy*. London: Routledge and Kegan Paul.

———. 1967. Sea creatures and spirits in Tikopia belief. In G. A. Highland, R. W. Force, A. Howard, M. Kelly, and Y. H. Sinoto, eds, *Polynesian Culture History: Essays in Honor of Kenneth P. Emory*, pp. 539–64. Honolulu: Bishop Museum Press.

Flannery, K. V. and J. Marcus, eds, 1983. *The Cloud People: Divergent Evolution of the Zapotec and Mixtec Civilizations*. New York: Academic Press.

Flannery, T. F. 1995. *The Future Eaters: An Ecological History of the Australasian Lands and People*. New York: George Braziller.

Flannery, T. F., P. V. Kirch, J. Specht, and M. Spriggs, 1988. Holocene mammal faunas from archaeological sites in island Melanesia. *Archaeology in Oceania* 23:89–94.

Flannery, T. F. and J. P. White, 1991. Animal translocations: Zoogeography of New Ireland mammals. *National Geographic Research and Exploration* 7:96–113.

Foley, W. A. 1986. *The Papuan Languages of New Guinea*. Cambridge: Cambridge University Press.

Fosberg, R. 1963a. The island ecosystem. In R. Fosberg, ed., *Man's Place in the Island Ecosystem: A Symposium*, pp. 1–6. Honolulu: Bishop Museum Press.

———. 1963b. Disturbance in island ecosystems. In J. L. Gressitt, ed., *Pacific Basin Biogeography*, pp. 557–61. Honolulu: Bishop Museum Press.

Fox, J. J. 1988. Possible models of early Austronesian social organization. *Asian Perspectives* 26:35–43.

———. 1993. Comparative perspectives on Austronesian houses: An introductory essay. In J. J. Fox, ed., *Inside Austronesian Houses: Perspectives on Domestic Designs for Living*, pp. 1–29. Canberra: Australian National University.

———. 1994. Who's who in Ego's generation: Probing the semantics of Malayo-Polynesian kinship classification. In A. K. Pawley and M. D. Ross, eds, *Austronesian Terminologies: Continuity and Change*, pp. 127–40. Pacific Linguistics, Series C-127. Canberra: Australian National University.

———. 1995. Austronesian societies and their transformations. In P. Bellwood, J. J. Fox, and D. Tryon, eds, *The Austronesians: Historical and Comparative Perspectives*, pp. 214–28. Canberra: Australian National University.

Fox, R. B. 1970. *The Tabon Caves*. Monograph of the National Museum No. 1. Manila.

Frankel, D. and J. W. Rhoads, eds, 1994. *Archaeology of a Coastal Exchange System: Sites and Ceramics of the Papuan Gulf*. Research Papers in Archaeology and Natural History, No. 25. Canberra: Australian National University.

Fredericksen, C., M. Spriggs, and W. Ambrose, 1993. Pamwak rockshelter: A Pleistocene site on Manus Island, Papua New Guinea. In M. A. Smith, M. Spriggs, and B. Fankhauser, eds, *Sahul in Review: Pleistocene Archaeology in Australia, New Guinea and Island Melanesia*, pp. 144–54. Occasional Papers in Prehistory, No. 24. Canberra: Department of Prehistory, Australian National University.

French-Wright, R. 1983. Proto-Oceanic Horticultural Practices. Unpublished M.A. Thesis, University of Auckland, New Zealand.

Friedlaender, J. S. 1975. *Patterns of Human Variation: The Demography, Genetics, and Phenetics of Bougainville Islanders*. Cambridge: Harvard University Press.

Friedman, J. 1981. Notes on structure and history in Oceanic. *Folk* 23:275–95.

Frimigacci, D. 1974. Les deux niveaux à poterie du site du Vatcha. *Journal de la Société des Océanistes* 30:25–70.

———. 1975. *La Préhistoire Neo-Calédonien*. Thèse de 3e Cycle. Université Paris I. Paris.

———. 1980. Localisation éco-géographique et utlisation de l'espace de quelques sites Lapita de Nouvelle-Calédonie. *Journal de la Société des Océanistes* 36:5–11.

Fullagar, R. 1992. Lithically Lapita: Functional analysis of flaked stone assemblages from West New Britain Province, Papua New Guinea. In J.-C. Galipaud, ed., *Poterie Lapita et Peuplement, Actes du Colloque LAPITA*, pp. 135–44. Noumea: ORSTOM.

Galipaud, J.-C. 1988. *La Poterie Préhistorique Neo-Calédonien et ses Implications dans l'Étude du Processus de Peuplement du Pacifique Occidental*. Thèse de Doctorat. Université Paris I. Paris.

———. 1989. *Préhistoire de la Nouvelle-Calédonie*. Centre Territorial de Recherche et de Documentation Pedagogique. Noumea, New Caledonia.

———. 1990. The physico-chemical analysis of ancient pottery from New Caledonia. In M. Spriggs, ed., *Lapita Design, Form and Composition*, pp. 134–42. *Occasional Papers in Prehistory No. 19*. Canberra: Department of Prehistory, Australian National University.

———. 1992. Un ou plusieurs peuples potiers en Nouvelle-Calédonie? Analyse physico-chimique des poteries préhistoriques de Nouvelle-Calédonie. *Journal de la Société des Océanistes* 95:185–200.

Garanger, J. 1972. *Archéologie des Nouvelles-Hébrides*. Publication de la Société des Océanistes No. 30. Paris.

Geraghty, P. A. 1983. *The History of the Fijian Languages*. Oceanic Linguistics Special Publication No. 19. Honolulu: University of Hawaii Press.

———. 1994. Proto Central Pacific fish names. In A. K. Pawley and M. D. Ross, eds, *Austronesian Terminologies: Continuity and Change*, pp. 141–69. Pacific Linguistics Series C-127. Canberra: Australian National University.

Gifford, E. W. 1951. *Archaeological Excavations in Fiji*. Anthropological Records 13:189–288. Berkeley: University of California Press.

Gifford, E. W. and D. Shutler, Jr. 1956. *Archaeological Excavations in New Caledonia*. Anthropological Records 18:1–125. Berkeley: University of California Press.

Golson, J. 1961. Report on New Zealand, Western Polynesia, New Caledonia, and Fiji. *Asian Perspectives* 5:166–80.

———. 1971. Lapita Ware and its transformations. *Pacific Anthropological Records* 12:67–76. Honolulu: Bishop Museum.

———. 1990. Kuk and the development of agriculture in New Guinea: Retrospection and introspection. In D. E. Yen and J. M. J. Mummery, eds, *Pacific Production Systems: Approaches to Economic Prehistory*, pp. 139–47. *Occasional Papers in Prehistory No. 18*. Canberra: Department of Prehistory, Australian National University.

———. 1991. Bulmer Phase II: Early agriculture in the New Guinea Highlands. In A. Pawley, ed., *Man and a Half: Essays in Pacific Anthropology and Ethnobiology in Honour of Ralph Bulmer*, pp. 484–91. Auckland: The Polynesian Society.

———. 1992. The ceramic sequence from Lasigi. In J.-C. Galipaud, ed., *Poterie Lapita et Peuplement, Actes du Colloque LAPITA*, pp. 155–68. Noumea: ORSTOM.

Golson, J. and D. S. Gardner, 1990. Agriculture and sociopolitical organization in New Guinea Highlands prehistory. *Annual Review of Anthropology* 19:395–417.

Goodenough, W. 1955. A problem in Malayo-Polynesian social organization. *American Anthropologist* 57:71–83.

——. 1982. Ban Chiang in world ethnological perspective. In J. C. White, ed., *Ban Chiang: Discovery of a Lost Bronze Age*, pp. 52–3. Philadelphia: The University Museum.

Gosden, C. 1989. Prehistoric social landscapes of the Arawe Islands, West New Britain Province, Papua New Guinea. *Archaeology in Oceania* 24:45–58.

——. 1991a. Towards an understanding of the regional archaeological record from the Arawe Islands, West New Britain, Papua New Guinea. In J. Allen and C. Gosden, eds, *Report of the Lapita Homeland Project*, pp. 205–16. *Occasional Papers in Prehistory*, No. 20. Canberra: Department of Prehistory, Australian National University.

——. 1991b. Learning about Lapita in the Bismarck Archipelago. In J. Allen and C. Gosden, eds, *Report of the Lapita Homeland Project*, pp. 260–8. *Occasional Papers in Prehistory*, No. 20. Canberra: Department of Prehistory, Australian National University.

——. 1991c. Long-term trends in the colonisation of the Pacific: Putting Lapita in its place. In P. Bellwood, ed., *Indo-Pacific Prehistory 1990: Proceedings of the 14th Congress of the Indo-Pacific Prehistory Association*, pp. 333–8. Canberra: Indo-Pacific Prehistory Association.

——. 1992a. Production systems and the colonization of the Western Pacific. *World Archaeology* 24:55–69.

——. 1992b. Dynamic traditionalism: Lapita as a long term social structure. In J.-C. Galipaud, ed., *Poterie Lapita et Peuplement, Actes du Colloque LAPITA*, pp. 21–6. Noumea: ORSTOM.

——. 1993. Understanding the settlement of Pacific islands in the Pleistocene. In M. A. Smith, M. Spriggs, and B. Fankhauser, eds, *Sahul in Review: Pleistocene Archaeology in Australia, New Guinea and Island Melanesia*, pp. 131–6. *Occasional Papers in Prehistory*, No. 24. Canberra: Department of Prehistory, Australian National University.

——. 1994. *Social Being and Time*. Oxford: Blackwell Publishers.

——. 1995. Arboriculture and agriculture in coastal Papua New Guinea. *Antiquity* 69, Special Number 265:807–17.

Gosden, C., J. Allen, W. Ambrose, D. Anson, J. Golson, R. Green, P. Kirch, I. Lilley, J. Specht, and M. Spriggs, 1989. Lapita sites of the Bismarck Archipelago. *Antiquity* 63:561–86.

Gosden, C. and N. Robertson, 1991. Models for Matenkupkum: Interpreting a late Pleistocene site from Southern New Ireland, Papua New Guinea. In J. Allen and C. Gosden, eds, *Report of the*

Lapita Homeland Project, pp. 20–45. *Occasional Papers in Prehistory,* No. 20. Canberra: Department of Prehistory, Austrlian National University.

Gosden, C. and J. Specht, 1991. Diversity, continuity and change in the Bismarck Archipelago, Papua New Guinea. In P. Bellwood, ed., *Indo-Pacific Prehistory 1990: Proceedings of the 14th Congress of the Indo-Pacific Prehistory Association,* pp. 276–80. Canberra: Indo-Pacific Prehistory Association.

Gosden, C. and J. Webb, 1994. The creation of a Papua New Guinean landscape: Archaeological and geomorphological evidence. *Journal of Field Archaeology* 21:29–51.

Gosden, C., J. Webb, B. Marshall, and G. R. Summerhayes, 1994. Lolmo Cave: A mid-to-late Holocene site, the Arawe Islands, West New Britain Province, Papua New Guinea. *Asian Perspectives* 33: 97–120.

Grace, G. 1959. *The Position of the Polynesian Languages within the Austronesian (Malayo-Polynesian) Language Family.* Indiana University Publications in Anthropology and Linguistics, Memoir 16. Bloomington: University of Indiana.

———. 1961. Austronesian linguistics and culture history. *American Anthropologist* 63:359–68.

Green, R. C. 1967. The immediate origins of the Polynesians. In G. A. Highland, et al., eds, *Polynesian Culture History,* pp. 215–40. Honolulu: Bishop Museum Press.

———. 1968. West Polynesian prehistory. In I. Yawata and Y. H. Sinoto, eds, *Prehistoric Culture in Oceania,* pp. 99–110. Honolulu: Bishop Museum Press.

———. 1974. Sites with Lapita pottery: Importing and voyaging. *Mankind* 9:253–9.

———. 1976. Lapita sites in the Santa Cruz group. In R. C. Green and M. M. Cresswell, eds, *Southeast Solomon Islands Cultural History: A Preliminary Survey,* pp. 245–65. Wellington: The Royal Society of New Zealand.

———. 1978. *New Sites with Lapita Pottery and their Implications for an Understanding of the Settlement of the Western Pacific.* Working Papers in Anthropology No. 51. Department of Anthropology, University of Auckland, New Zealand.

———. 1979a. Lapita. In J. Jennings, ed., *The Prehistory of Polynesia,* pp. 27–60. Cambridge: Harvard University Press.

———. 1979b. Early Lapita art from Polynesia and island Melanesia: Continuities in ceramic, barkcloth, and tattoo decorations. In S. Mead, ed., *Exploring the Visual Art of Oceania,* pp. 13–31. Honolulu: University of Hawaii Press.

———. 1982. Models for the Lapita cultural complex: An evaluation of some proposals. *New Zealand Journal of Archaeology* 4:7–20.

———. 1985. Comment: Spriggs' "The Lapita Cultural Complex." *Journal of Pacific History* 20:220–4.

———. 1986. Lapita fishing: the evidence of site SE-RF-2 from the main Reef Islands, Santa Cruz group, Solomons. In A. Anderson, ed., *Traditional Fishing in the Pacific*, pp. 19–35. *Pacific Anthropological Records* 37. Honolulu: Bernice P. Bishop Museum.

———. 1987. Obsidian results from the Lapita sites of the Reef/Santa Cruz Islands. In W. R. Ambrose and J. M. Mummery, eds, *Archaeometry: Further Australasian Studies*, pp. 239–49. Canberra: Australian National University.

———. 1988. Those mysterious mounds are for the birds. *Newsletter of the New Zealand Archaeological Association* 31:153–8.

———. 1990. Lapita design analysis: The Mead System and its use, a potted history. In M. Spriggs, ed., *Lapita Design, Form and Composition*, pp. 33–52. *Occasional Papers in Prehistory No. 19*. Canberra: Department of Prehistory, Australian National University.

———. 1991a. Near and Remote Oceania: Disestablishing "Melanesia" in culture history. In A. Pawley, ed., *Man and a Half: Essays in Pacific Anthropology and Ethnobiology in Honour of Ralph Bulmer*, pp. 491–502. Auckland: The Polynesian Society.

———. 1991b. The Lapita Cultural Complex: current evidence and proposed models. In P. Bellwood, ed., *Indo-Pacific Prehistory 1990: Proceedings of the 14th Congress of the Indo-Pacific Prehistory Association*, pp. 295–305. Canberra: Indo-Pacific Prehistory Association.

———. 1991c. A reappraisal of the dating for some Lapita sites in the Reef/Santa Cruz Group of the southeast Solomons. *Journal of the Polynesian Society* 100:197–208.

———. 1992. Definitions of the Lapita cultural complex and its non-ceramic component. In J.-C. Galipaud, ed., *Poterie Lapita et Peuplement, Actes du Colloque LAPITA*, pp. 7–20. Noumea: ORSTOM.

———. 1994. Archaeological problems with the use of linguistic evidence in the reconstruction of rank, status and social organization in ancestral Polynesian society. In A. K. Pawley and M. D. Ross, eds, *Austronesian Terminologies: Continuity and Change*, pp. 171–84. Pacific Linguistics, Series C-127. Canberra: Australian National University.

———. in press. Prehistoric transfers of portable items during the Lapita horizon in Remote Oceania: A review. *Indo-Pacific Prehistory Association Bulletin* 15.

Green, R. C. and D. Anson, 1987. The Lapita site of Watom: New evidence from excavations in 1985. *Man and Culture in Oceania* 3:121–32.

Green, R. C. and D. Anson, 1991. The Reber-Rakival Lapita site on Watom. Implications of the 1985 excavations the SAC and SDI localities. In J. Allen and C. Gosden, eds, *Report of the Lapita Homeland Project*, pp. 170–81. *Occasional Papers in Prehistory*, No. 20. Canberra: Department of Prehistory, Australian National University.

Green, R. C., D. Anson, and J. Specht, 1989. The SAC burial ground, Watom Island, Papua New Guinea. *Records of the Australian Museum* 41:215–22.

Green, R. C. and J. R. Bird, 1989. Fergusson Island obsidian from the D'Entrecasteaux group in a Lapita site of the Reef Santa Cruz group. *New Zealand Journal of Archaeology* 11:87–99.

Green, R. C. and M. M. Cresswell, eds, 1976. *Southeast Solomon Islands Cultural History: A Preliminary Survey*. Royal Society of New Zealand Bulletin 11. Wellington: The Royal Society of New Zealand.

Green, R. C. and J. Davidson, 1974. *Archaeology in Western Samoa, Vol. II*. Bulletin of the Auckland Institute and Museum 7. Auckland.

Green, R. C. and J. S. Mitchell, 1983. New Caledonian culture history: A review of the archaeological sequence. *New Zealand Journal of Archaeology* 5:19–68.

Green, R. C. and A. Pawley, in press. Early Oceanic architectural forms and settlement patterns: Linguistic, archaeological and ethnological perspectives. Paper originally presented at the 7th International Conference on Austronesian Linguistics, Leiden, 1994.

Green, R. C. and H. G. Richards, 1975. Lapita pottery and a lower sea level in western Samoa. *Pacific Science* 29:309–15.

Greiner, R. H. 1923. *Polynesian Decorative Designs*. B. P. Bishop Museum Bulletin 7. Honolulu.

Groube, L. 1971. Tonga, Lapita pottery, and Polynesian origins. *Journal of the Polynesian Society* 80:278–316.

——. 1993. Contradictions and malaria in Melanesian and Australian prehistory. In M. A. Smith, M. Spriggs, and B. Fankhauser, eds, *Sahul in Review: Pleistocene Archaeology in Australia, New Guinea and Island Melanesia*, pp. 164–86. *Occasional Papers in Prehistory*, No. 24. Canberra: Department of Prehistory, Australian National University.

Groube, L., J. Chappell, J. Muke, and D. Price, 1986. A 40,000 year-old human occupation site at Huon Peninsula, Papua New Guinea. *Nature* 324:453–5.

Guiart, J. 1963. *Structure de la Chefferie en Mélanésie du Sud*. Travaux et Mémoires de l'Institut d'Ethnologie, LXVI. Paris: Université de Paris.

Haddon, A. C. and J. Hornell, 1936–8. *Canoes of Oceania*. Bernice P. Bishop Museum Special Publications 27, 28, and 29. Honolulu.

Hage, P. and F. Harary, 1991. *Exchange in Oceania: A Graph Theoretic Analysis*. Oxford: Clarendon Press.

Hagelberg, E. and J. B. Clegg, 1993. Genetic polymorphisms in prehistoric Pacific islanders determined by analysis of ancient bone DNA. *Proceedings of the Royal Society of London, Series B*, 252: 163–70.

Hale, H. 1846. *Ethnography and Philology. United States Exploring Expedition, Vol. VI*. Philadelphia: Sherman.

Handy, E. S. C. 1930. The problem of Polynesian origins. *Bernice P. Bishop Museum Occasional Papers* 9(8):1–27.

Hassan, F. 1981. *Demographic Archaeology*. New York: Academic Press.

Hather, J. G., 1994. The identification of charred root and tuber crops from archaeological sites in the Pacific. In J. Hather, ed., *Tropical Archaeobotany: Applications and New Developments*, pp. 51–65. London: Routledge.

Hauser-Schäublin, B. 1989. *Kulthäuser in Nordneuguinea*, 2 vols. Abhandlungen und Berichte des Staatlichen Museums für Volkerkunde Dresden No. 43. Berlin: Akademie-Verlag.

Hedrick, J. D. 1971. Lapita-style pottery from Malo Island. *Journal of the Polynesian Society* 80:15–19.

Hertzberg, M., K. P. N. Mickleson, S. W. Sergjeantson, J. F. Prior, and R. J. Trent, 1989. An Asian-specific 9-bp deletion of mitochondrial DNA is frequently found in Polynesians. *American Journal of Human Genetics* 44:504–10.

Higham, C. 1989. *The Archaeology of Mainland Southeast Asia*. Cambridge: Cambridge University Press.

Hill, A. V. S., D. K. Bowden, R. J. Trent, D. R. Higgs, S. J. Oppenheimer, S. L. Thein, K. N. P. Mickleson, D. J. Weatherall, and J. B. Clegg, 1985. Melanesians and Polynesians share a unique α-Thalassemia mutation. *American Journal of Human Genetics* 37:571–80.

Hill, A. V. S. and S. W. Serjeantson, eds, 1989. *The Colonization of the Pacific: A Genetic Trail*. Oxford: Clarendon Press.

Hill, A. V. S., D. F. O'Shaughnessy, and J. B. Clegg, 1989. Haemoglobin and globin gene variants in the Pacific. In A. V. S. Hill and S. W. Serjeantson, eds, *The Colonization of the Pacific: A Genetic Trail*, pp. 246–85. Oxford: Clarendon Press.

Hooper, R. 1994. Reconstructing Proto Polynesian fish names. In

A. K. Pawley and M. D. Ross, eds, *Austronesian Terminologies: Continuity and Change*, pp. 185–229. Pacific Linguistics Series C-127. Canberra: Australian National University.

Hope, G. S. and J. Golson, 1995. Late Quaternary change in the mountains of New Guinea. *Antiquity* 69, Special Number 265:818–30.

Hope, G. S. and M. J. T. Spriggs, 1982. A preliminary pollen sequence from Aneityum Island, southern Vanuatu. *Indo-Pacific Prehistory Association Bulletin* 3:88–94.

Horridge, A. 1986. The evolution of Pacific canoe rigs. *Journal of Pacific History* 21:83–99.

———. 1995. The Austronesian conquest of the sea – upwind. In P. Bellwood, J. J. Fox, and D. Tryon, eds, *The Austronesians: Historical and Comparative Perspectives*, pp. 134–51. Canberra: Australian National University.

Houghton, P. 1989a. Watom: The people. *Records of the Australian Museum* 41:223–34.

———. 1989b. The Lapita-associated human material from Lakeba, Fiji. *Records of the Australian Museum* 41:327–30.

———. 1991. The early human biology of the Pacific: Some considerations. *Journal of the Polynesian Society* 100:167–96.

Howard, A. 1967. Polynesian origins and migrations: A review of two centuries of speculation and theory. In G. A. Highland, et al., eds, *Polynesian Culture History: Essays in Honor of Kenneth P. Emory*, pp. 45–101. Honolulu: Bishop Museum Press.

Howells, W. W. 1943. The racial elements of Melanesia. *Papers of the Peabody Museum of American Archaeology and Ethnology, Harvard University* 20:38–49.

———. 1970. Anthropometric grouping analysis of Pacific peoples. *Archaeology and Physical Anthropology in Oceania* 5:192–217.

———. 1973. *The Pacific Islanders*. New York: Charles Scribner's Sons.

Howells, W. and I. Schwidetsky, 1981. Oceania. In I. Schwidetsky, ed., *Rassengeschichte der Menschheit. Asien I: Japan, Indonesien, Ozeanien*, pp. 115–66. Munich: Oldenbourg.

Hughes, P., G. Hope, M. Latham, and M. Brookfield, 1979. Prehistoric man-induced degradation of the Lakeba landscape: Evidence from two inland swamps. In H. Brookfield, ed., *Lakeba: Environmental Change, Population Dynamics, and Resource Use*, pp. 93–110. Paris: UNESCO.

Hunt, T. L. 1980. Towards Fiji's Past: Archaeological Research on Southwestern Viti Levu. Unpublished M.A. Thesis, University of Auckland, New Zealand.

———. 1981. New evidence for early horticulture in Fiji. *Journal of the Polynesian Society* 90:259–66.

———. 1986. Conceptual and substantive issues in Fijian prehistory. In P. V. Kirch, ed., *Island Socities: Archaeological Approaches to Evolution and Transformation*, pp. 20–32. Cambridge: Cambridge University Press.

———. 1987. Patterns of human interaction and evolutionary divergence in the Fiji Islands. *Journal of the Polynesian Society* 96:299–334.

———. 1988. Lapita ceramic technological and composition studies: A critical review. In P. V. Kirch and T. L. Hunt, eds, *Archaeology of the Lapita Cultural Complex: A Critical Review*, pp. 49–60. Seattle: The Burke Museum.

———. 1989. Lapita Ceramic Exchange in the Mussau Islands, Papua New Guinea. Unpublished Ph.D. Dissertation, University of Washington, Seattle.

Hunter-Anderson, R. L., ed., 1990. *Recent Advances in Micronesian Archaeology*. *Micronesica*, Supplement No. 2. Mangilao: University of Guam Press.

Hutchinson, G. E. 1978. *An Introduction to Population Biology*. New Haven: Yale University Press.

Intoh, M. 1992. Pottery traditions in Micronesia. In J.-C. Galipaud, ed., *Poterie Lapita et Peuplement, Actes du Colloque LAPITA*, pp. 67–82. Noumea: ORSTOM.

Irwin, G. 1985. *The Emergence of Mailu*. Terra Australis 10. Canberra: Australian National University.

———. 1991a. Pleistocene voyaging and the settlement of Greater Australia and its Near Oceanic neighbors. In J. Allen and C. Gosden, eds, *Report of the Lapita Homeland Project*, pp. 9–19. *Occasional Papers in Prehistory*, No. 20. Canberra: Department of Prehistory, Australian National University.

———. 1991b. Themes in the prehistory of coastal Papua and the Massim. In A. Pawley, ed., *Man and a Half: Essays in Pacific Anthropology and Ethnobiology in Honour of Ralph Bulmer*, pp. 503–10. Auckland: The Polynesian Society.

———. 1992. *The Prehistoric Exploration and Colonisation of the Pacific*. Cambridge: Cambridge University Press.

———. 1993. Voyaging. In M. A. Smith, M. Spriggs, and B. Fankhauser, eds, *Sahul in Review: Pleistocene Archaeology in Australia, New Guinea and Island Melanesia*, pp. 73–87. *Occasional Papers in Prehistory*, No. 24. Canberra: Department of Prehistory, Australian National University.

Ivens, W. G. 1930. *The Island Builders of the Pacific*. London: Seeley, Service & Company.

Kay, R. M. A. 1984. Analysis of Archaeological Material from Naigani. Unpublished M.A. Thesis, University of Auckland, New Zealand.

Keesing, F. M. 1946. *Natives Peoples of the Pacific World.* New York: The MacMillan Company.

Kelly, K. M. 1990. Gm polymorphisms, linguistic affinities, and natural selection in Melanesia. *Current Anthropology* 31:201–19.

Kirch, P. V. 1978. The Lapitoid period in West Polynesia: Excavations and survey in Niuatoputapu, Tonga. *Journal of Field Archaeology* 5:1–13.

———. 1979. Subsistence and ecology. In J. Jennings, ed., *The Prehistory of Polynesia*, pp. 286–307. Cambridge: Harvard University Press.

———. 1981. Lapitoid settlements of Futuna and Alofi, Western Polynesia. *Archaeology in Oceania* 16:127–43.

———. 1983. An archaeological exploration of Vanikoro, Santa Cruz Islands, Eastern Melanesia. *New Zealand Journal of Archaeology* 5:69–113.

———. 1984. *The Evolution of the Polynesian Chiefdoms.* Cambridge: Cambridge University Press.

———. 1987. Lapita and Oceanic cultural origins: Excavations in the Mussau Islands, Bismarck Archipelago, 1985. *Journal of Field Archaeology* 14:163–80.

———. 1988a. *Niuatoputapu: The Prehistory of a Polynesian Chiefdom.* Thomas Burke Memorial Washington State Museum Mononograph No. 5. Seattle: The Burke Museum.

———. 1988b. The Talepakemalai site and Oceanic prehistory. *National Geographic Research* 4:328–42.

———. 1988c. Long-distance exchange and island colonisation: The Lapita case. *Norwegian Archaeological Review* 21:103–17.

———. 1988d. A brief history of Lapita archaeology. In P. V. Kirch and T. L. Hunt, eds, *Archaeology of the Lapita Cultural Complex: A Critical Review*, pp. 1–8. Thomas Burke Memorial Washington State Museum Research Report No. 5. Seattle: The Burke Museum.

———. 1989. Second millennium BC arboriculture in Melanesia: Archaeological evidence from the Mussau Islands. *Economic Botany* 43:225–40.

———. 1990a. Specialization and exchange in the Lapita complex of Oceania (1,600–500 BC). *Asian Perspectives* 29:117–33.

———. 1990b. La colonisation du Pacifique. *La Recherche* 21:1,226–35.

———. 1991. Prehistoric exchange in Western Melanesia. *Annual Review of Anthropology* 20:141–65.

———. 1993. The To'aga site. Modelling the morphodynamics of the land-sea interface. In P. V. Kirch and T. L. Hunt, eds, *The To'aga Site: Three Millennia of Polynesia Occupation in the Manu'a Islands,*

American Samoa, pp. 31–42. Contribution No. 51, Archaeological Research Facility. Berkeley: University of California.

——. 1994a. *The Wet and the Dry: Irrigation and Agricultural Intensification in Polynesia*. Chicago: University of Chicago Press.

——. 1994b. The pre-Christian ritual cycle of Futuna, Western Polynesia. *Journal of the Polynesian Society* 103:255–98.

——. 1995. The Lapita culture of western Melanesia in the context of Austronesian origins and dispersals. In *Austronesian Studies*, pp. 255–94. Taipei: Academia Sinica.

——. in press. Lapita and its aftermath: The Austronesian settlement of Oceania. *Transactions of the American Philosophical Society*.

——. in press. Tikopia social space revisited. In J. Davidson, G. Irwin, and A. Pawley, eds, *Pacific Culture History*.

Kirch, P. V., M. S. Allen, V. L. Butler, and T. L. Hunt, 1987. Is there an early far western Lapita province? Sample size effects and new evidence from Eloaua Island. *Archaeology in Oceania* 22:123–27.

Kirch, P. V. and T. S. Dye, 1979. Ethno-archaeology and the development of Polynesian fishing strategies. *Journal of the Polynesian Society* 88:53–76.

Kirch, P. V. and J. E. Ellison, 1994. Paleoenvironmental evidence for human colonization of remote Oceanic islands. *Antiquity* 68:310–21.

Kirch, P. V. and R. C. Green 1987. History, phylogeny, and evolution in Polynesia. *Current Anthropology* 28:431–56.

Kirch, P. V. and T. L. Hunt, 1988a. The spatial and temporal boundaries of Lapita. In P. V. Kirch and T. L. Hunt, eds, *Archaeology of the Lapita Cultural Complex: A Critical Review*, pp. 9–32. Thomas Burke Memorial Washington State Museum Research Report No. 5. Seattle: The Burke Museum.

——. 1988b. Radiocarbon dates from the Mussau Islands and the Lapita colonization of the southwestern Pacific. *Radiocarbon* 30:161–9.

Kirch, P. V. and T. L. Hunt, eds, 1988. *Archaeology of the Lapita Cultural Complex: A Critical Review*. Thomas Burke Memorial Washington State Museum Research Report No. 5. Seattle: The Burke Museum.

——. 1993. *The To'aga Site: Three Millennia of Polynesian Occupation in the Manu'a Islands, American Samoa*. Contribution No. 51, Archaeological Research Facility. Berkeley: University of California.

——. 1996. *Historical Ecology in the Pacific Islands: Prehistoric Landscape and Environmental Change*. New Haven: Yale University Press.

Kirch, P. V., T. L. Hunt, M. Weisler, V. Butler, and M. S. Allen, 1991. Mussau Islands prehistory: Results of the 1985–6 excavations. In J. Allen and C. Gosden, eds, *Report of the Lapita Homeland Project*, pp. 144–63. *Occasional Papers in Prehistory*, No. 20. Canberra: Department of Prehistory, Australian National University.

Kirch, P. V. and D. Lepofsky, 1993. Polynesian irrigation: Archaeological and linguistic evidence for origins and development. *Asian Perspectives* 32:183–204.

Kirch, P. V. and P. H. Rosendahl, 1973. Archaeological investigation of Anuta. *Pacific Anthropological Records* 21:25–108.

Kirch, P. V., D. R. Swindler, and C. G. Turner II, 1989. Human skeletal and dental remains from Lapita sites (1,600–500 BC) in the Mussau Islands, Melanesia. *American Journal of Physical Anthropology* 79:63–76.

Kirch, P. V. and M. I. Weisler, 1994. Archaeology in the Pacific Islands: An appraisal of recent research. *Journal of Archaeological Research* 2:285–328.

Kirch, P. V. and M. I. Weisler, eds, in press. A Reanalysis and Reassessment of E. W. Gifford's Pioneering New Caledonian Excavations. *Kroeber Anthropological Society Papers*.

Kirch, P. V. and D. E. Yen, 1982. *Tikopia: The Prehistory and Ecology of a Polynesian Outlier*. Bernice P. Bishop Museum Bulletin 238. Honolulu.

Kirk, R. L. 1989. Population genetic studies in the Pacific: Red cell antigen, serum protein, and enzyme systems. In A. V. S. Hill and S. W. Serjeantson, eds, *The Colonization of the Pacific: A Genetic Trail*, pp. 60–119. Oxford: Clarendon Press.

Kooijman, S. 1972. *Tapa in Polynesia*. Bernice P. Bishop Museum Bulletin 234. Honolulu.

Leach, H. 1982. Cooking without pots: Aspects of prehistoric and traditional Polynesian cooking. *New Zealand Journal of Archaeology* 4:149–56.

Leach, H. and R. C. Green, 1989. New information for the Ferry Berth Site, Mulifanua, Western Samoa. *Journal of the Polynesian Society* 98:319–30.

Lebot, V. and J. Lévesque, 1989. *The Origin and Distribution of Kava (Piper Methysticum Forst. f., Piperaceae): A Phytochemical Approach*. Allertonia vol. 5(2). Lawai: National Tropical Botanical Garden.

Lebot, V., M. Merlin, and L. Lindstrom, 1992. *Kava: The Pacific Drug*. New Haven: Yale University Press.

Le Goff, J. 1980. *Time, Work, & Culture in the Middle Ages*. Chicago: University of Chicago Press.

Le Moine, G. 1987. The loss of pottery in Polynesia. *New Zealand Journal of Archaeology* 9:25–32.

Lenormand, M. H. 1948. Découvert d'un gisment de poteries à l'île des Pins. *Études Mélanésiennes* 3:54–8.

Lepofsky, D. 1988. The environmental context of Lapita settlement locations. In P. V. Kirch and T. L. Hunt, eds, *Archaeology of the Lapita Cultural Complex: A Critical Review*, pp. 33–48. Thomas Burke Memorial Washington State Museum Research Report No. 5. Seattle: The Burke Museum.

———. 1992. Arboriculture in the Mussau Islands, Bismarck Archipelago. *Economic Botany* 46:192–211.

Leroi-Gourhan, A. 1982. *The Dawn of European Art*. Cambridge: Cambridge University Press.

Lévi-Strauss, C. 1982. *The Way of the Masks*. Trans. by S. Modelski. Seattle: University of Washington Press.

Li, K. C. 1983. *Report of Archaeological Investigations in the O-Luan-Pi Park at the Southern Tip of Taiwan*. Taipei: Department of Anthropology, National Taiwan University.

Lichtenberk, F. 1986. Leadership in Proto-Oceanic society: Linguistic evidence. *Journal of the Polynesian Society* 95:341–56.

———. 1994. The raw and the cooked: Proto Oceanic terms for food preparation. In A. K. Pawley and M. D. Ross, eds, *Austronesian Terminologies: Continuity and Change*, pp. 267–88. Pacific Linguistics Series C-127. Canberra: Australian National University.

Lilley, I. 1988. Prehistoric exchange across the Vitiaz Strait, Papua New Guinea. *Current Anthropology* 20:513–16.

———. 1991a. Lapita sites in the Duke of York Islands. In J. Allen and C. Gosden, eds, *Report of the Lapita Homeland Project*, pp. 164–9. *Occasional Papers in Prehistory*, No. 20. Canberra: Department of Prehistory, Australian National University.

———. 1991b. Lapita and post-Lapita developments in the Vitiaz Straits-West New Britain area. In P. Bellwood, ed., *Indo-Pacific Prehistory 1990: Proceedings of the 14th Congress of the Indo-Pacific Prehistory Association*, pp. 313–22. Canberra: Indo-Pacific Prehistory Association.

Lourandos, H. 1993. Hunter-gatherer cultural dynamics: Long- and short-term trends in Australian prehistory. *Journal of Archaeological Research* 1:67–88.

Loy, T. H. 1994. Methods in the analysis of starch residues on prehistoric stone tools. In J. G. Hather, ed., *Tropical Archaeobotany: Applications and New Developments*, pp. 86–114. London: Routledge.

Loy, T. H., M. Spriggs, and S. Wickler, 1992. Direct evidence for

human use of plants 28,000 years ago: Starch residues on stone artifacts from the northern Solomon Islands. *Antiquity* 66:898–912.

Lum, J. K., O. Rickards, C. Ching, and R. L. Cann, in press. Polynesian
mitochondrial DNAs reveal three deep maternal clades. *American
Journal of Human Genetics*.

Luomala, K. 1949. *Maui-of-a-Thousand-Tricks: His Oceanic and
European Biographers*. Bernice P. Bishop Museum Bulletin 198.
Honolulu.

Lynch, J. and D. T. Tryon, 1985. Central-Eastern Oceanic: A subgrouping hypothesis. *Pacific Linguistics (Series C)* 88:31–52.

Malinowski, B. 1922. *Argonauts of the Western Pacific*. London:
George Routledge and Sons.

Marck, J. 1994. Proto Micronesian terms for the physical environment. In A. K. Pawley and M. D. Ross, eds, *Austronesian Terminologies: Continuity and Change*, pp. 301–28. Pacific Linguistics
Series C-127. Canberra: Australian National University.

Marshall, B. and J. Allen, 1991. Excavations at Panakiwuk Cave,
New Ireland. In J. Allen and C. Gosden, eds, *Report of the Lapita
Homeland Project*, pp. 59–91. *Occasional Papers in Prehistory*,
No. 20. Canberra: Department of Prehistory, Australian National
University.

Marshall, M. 1984. Structural patterns of sibling classification in
island Oceania: Implications for culture history. *Current Anthropology* 25:597–637.

Marshall, Y. 1985. Who made the Lapita pots? A cases study in
gender archaeology. *Journal of the Polynesian Society* 94:205–34.

Masse, B. 1990. Radiocarbon dating, sea-level change and the peopling
of Belau. *Micronesica* Supplement 2:213–30.

Matisoo-Smith, L. 1994. The human colonisation of Polynesia, a
novel approach: Genetic analysis of the Polynesian rat (*Rattus
exulans*). *Journal of the Polynesian Society* 103:75–87.

Matthews, P. 1991. A possible tropical wild type taro: *Colocasia
esculenta* var. *aquatilis*. *Indo-Pacific Prehistory Association Bulletin* 11:69–81.

Mauss, M. 1925. Essai sur le don: Forme et raison de l'échange dans
les sociétés archaïques. *L'Année Sociologique* (N.S.) 1:30–186.

May, P. and M. Tuckson, 1982. *The Traditional Pottery of Papua
New Guinea*. Sydney: Bay Books.

Mayr, E. 1945. *Birds of the Southwest Pacific*. New York: The Macmillan Company.

McCoy, P. C. and P. C. Cleghorn, 1988. Archaeological excavations
on Santa Cruz (Nendö), Southeast Solomon Islands: summary report. *Archaeology in Oceania* 23:104–15.

McKern, W. C. 1929. *Archaeology of Tonga*. Bernice P. Bishop Museum Bulletin 60. Honolulu: The Bishop Museum.

Mead, S. M., L. Birks, H. Birks, and E. Shaw. 1975. *The Lapita Pottery Style of Fiji and its Associations*. Polynesian Society Memoir No. 38. Wellington.

Menard, H. W. 1986. *Islands*. New York: Scientific American Library.

Merrill, E. D. 1945. *Plant Life of the Pacific World*. New York: The Macmillan Company.

Meyer, O. 1909. Funde prähistorischer Töpferei und Steinmesser auf Vuatom, Bismarck Archipel. *Anthropos* 4:215–52, 1,093–5.

———. 1910. Funde von Menschen- und Tierkochen, von prähistorischer Töpferei und Steinwerkzeugen auf Vuatom, Bismarck-Archipel. *Anthropos* 5:1,160–1.

Mitrovica, J. X. and W. R. Peltier, 1991. On postglacial geoid subsidence over the equatorial ocean. *Journal of Geophysical Research* 96:20,053–71.

Miyata, T., Y. Maeda, E. Matsumoto, Y. Matsushima, P. Rodda, A. Sugimura, and H. Kayanne, 1990. Evidence for a Holocene high sea-level stand, Vanua Levu, Fiji. *Quaternary Research* 33:352–359.

Montaggioni, L. F. and P. A. Pirazzoli, 1984. The significance of exposed coral conglomerates from French Polynesia (Pacific Ocean) as indicators of recent relative sea-level changes. *Coral Reefs* 3:29–42.

Moore, C. C. and A. K. Romney, 1994. Material culture, geographic propinquity, and linguistic affiliation on the north coast of New Guinea: A reanalysis of Welsch, Terrell, and Nadloski (1992). *American Anthropologist* 96:370–92.

———. 1995. Commentary on Welsch and Terrell's (1994) reply to Moore and Romney (1994). *Journal of Quantitative Anthropology* 5:75–84.

Nagaoka, L. 1988. Lapita subsistence: The evidence of non-fish archaeofaunal remains. In P. V. Kirch and T. L. Hunt, eds, *Archaeology of the Lapita Cultural Complex: A Critical Review*, pp. 117–34. Seattle: The Burke Museum.

Nakada, M. and K. Lambek, 1989. Late Pleistocene and Holocene sea-level change in the Australian region and mantle rheology. *Geophysical Journal* 96:497–517.

Nevermann, H. 1933. *St. Matthias-Gruppe*. In G. Thilenius, ed., *Ergebnisse der Sudsee-Expedition 1908–1910*. II. *Ethnographie*: A. *Melanesien*, Band 2. Hamburg: Friederichsen, De Gruyter & Co.

Newton, D. 1988. Reflections in bronze: Lapita and Dong-Son art in the Western Pacific. In J. P. Barbier and D. Newton, eds, *Islands and Ancestors: Indigenous Styles of Southeast Asia*, pp. 10–23. Munich: Prestel.

Nunn, P. D. 1990. Coastal processes and landforms of Fiji: Their bearing on Holocene sea-level changes in the south and west Pacific. *Journal of Coastal Research* 6:279–310.

Oliver, D. L. 1989. *Oceania: The Native Cultures of Australia and the Pacific Islands*. 2 vols. Honolulu: University of Hawaii Press.

Palmer, B. 1966. Lapita style potsherds from Fiji. *Journal of the Polynesian Society* 75:373–7.

Parker, V. N. M. 1981. Vessel Forms of the Reef Islands SE-RF-2 Site and their Relationships to Vessel Forms in other Western Lapita Sites of the Reef/Santa Cruz and Island Melanesian Area. Unpublished M.A. Thesis, University of Auckland, New Zealand.

Pavlides, C. and C. Gosden, 1994. 35,000-year-old sites in the rainforests of West New Britain, Papua New Guinea. *Antiquity* 68:604–10.

Pawley, A. 1972. On the internal relationships of Eastern Oceanic languages. *Pacific Anthropological Records* 13:1–142.

——. 1981. Melanesian diversity and Polynesian homogeneity: A unified explanation for language. In J. Hollyman and A. Pawley, eds, *Studies in Pacific Languages and Cultures, in Honour of Bruce Biggs*, pp. 269–309. Auckland: Linguistic Society of New Zealand.

——. 1982. Rubbish-man, commoner, big-man, chief? Linguistic evidence for hereditary chieftainship in Proto-Oceanic society. In J. Siikala, ed., *Oceanic Studies: Essays in Honor of Aarne A. Koskinen*, pp. 33–52. Transactions of the Finnish Anthropological Society, No. 11. Helsinki: Finnish Anthropological Society.

——. 1993. Proto-Oceanic terms for reef and shoreline invertebrates. Paper presented to the First International Conference on Oceanic Linguistics, Port Vila, July 4–9, 1993.

——. 1995. C. L. Voorhoeve and the Trans New Guinea Phylum hypothesis. In C. Baak, M. Bakker, and D. van der Meij, eds, *Tales from a Concave World: Liber Amicorum Bert Voorhoeve*, pp. 83–123. Leiden: Leiden University.

Pawley, A. and R. C. Green, 1973. Dating the dispersal of the Oceanic languages. *Oceanic Linguistics* 12:1–67.

——. and R. C. Green, 1984. The Proto-Oceanic language community. *The Journal of Pacific History* 19:123–46.

Pawley, A. and M. Pawley, 1994. Early Austronesian terms for canoe parts and seafaring. In A. K. Pawley and M. D. Ross, eds, *Austronesian Terminologies: Continuity and Change*, pp. 329–61. Pacific Linguistics Series C-127. Canberra: Australian National University.

Pawley, A. K. and M. Ross, 1993. Austronesian historical linguistics and culture history. *Annual Review of Anthropology* 22:425–59.
——. 1995. The prehistory of Oceanic languages: A current view. In P. Bellwood, J. J. Fox, and D. Tryon, eds, *The Austronesians: Historical and Comparative Perspectives*, pp. 39–74. Canberra: Australian National University.

Pawley, A. K. and M. Ross, eds, 1994. *Austronesian Terminologies: Continuity and Change*. Pacific Linguistics Series C–127. Canberra: Australian National University.

Pianka, E. 1974. *Evolutionary Ecology*. New York: Harper and Row.

Pietrusewsky, M. 1970. An osteological view of indigenous populations in Oceania. *Pacific Anthropological Records* 11:1–12. Honolulu: Bishop Museum.
——. 1983. Multivariate analysis of New Guinea and Melanesian skulls: A review. *Journal of Human Evolution* 12:61–76.
——. 1984. *Metric and Non-Metric Cranial Variation in Australian Aboriginal Populations Compared with Populations from the Pacific and Asia*. Occasional Papers in Human Biology No. 3. Canberra: Australian Institute of Aboriginal Studies.
——. 1989a. A study of skeletal and dental remains from Watom Island and comparisons with other Lapita people. *Records of the Australian Museum* 41:235–92.
——. 1989b. A Lapita-associated skeleton from Natunuku, Fiji. *Records of the Australian Museum* 41:297–326.
——. 1990. Craniometric variation in Micronesia and the Pacific: A multivariate study. *Micronesica*, Supplement 2:373–402.
——. 1994. Lapita origins: An osteological perspective. In P. J. C. Dark and R. G. Rose, eds, *Artistic Heritage in a Changing Pacific*, pp. 15–19. Honolulu: University of Hawaii Press.

Pirazzoli, P. A. and L. F. Montaggioni, 1986. Late Holocene sea-level changes in the northwest Tuamotu Islands, French Polynesia. *Quaternary Research* 25:350–68.
——. 1988. Holocene sea-level changes in French Polynesia. *Paleogeography, Paleoclimatology, Paleoecology* 68:153–75.

Piroutet, M. 1917. *Étude Stratigraphique sur la Nouvelle Calédonie*. Macon: Imprimerie Protat Frères.

Plog, F. 1977. Modeling economic exchange. In T. K. Earle and J. E. Ericson, eds, *Exchange Systems in Prehistory*, pp. 127–40. New York: Academic Press.

Poulsen, J. 1968. Archaeological excavations on Tongatapu. In I. Yawata and Y. H. Sinoto, eds, *Prehistoric Culture in Oceania*, pp. 85–92. Honolulu: The Bishop Museum.

———. 1972. *On the Processing of Pottery Data.* Haandbøger II. Aarhus: Jysk Arkaeologisk Selskab.

———. 1983. The chronology of early Tongan prehistory and the Lapita ware. *Journal de la Société des Océanistes* 76:46–56.

———. 1987. *Early Tongan Prehistory*, 2 vols. *Terra Australis* 12. Canberra: Department of Prehistory, Australian National University.

Pregill, G. K. and T. S. Dye, 1989. Prehistoric extinction of giant iguanas in the South Pacific. *Copeia* 2:505–8.

Rainbird, P. 1994. Prehistory in the northwest tropical Pacific: The Caroline, Mariana, and Marshall Islands. *Journal of World Prehistory* 3:293–349.

Ray, S. 1926. *A Comparative Study of the Melansian Island Languages.* Cambridge: Cambridge University Press.

Reeve, R. 1989. Recent work on the prehistory of the western Solomons, Melanesia. *Indo-Pacific Prehistory Association Bulletin* 9:46–67.

Renfrew, C. 1984. *Approaches to Social Archaeology.* Cambridge: Harvard University Press.

Rivers, W. H. R. 1914. *The History of Melanesian Society.* Cambridge: Cambridge University Press.

Roberts, J. M. Jr., C. C. Moore, and A. K. Romney, 1995. Predicting similarity in material culture among New Guinea villages from propinquity and language: A log-linear approach. *Current Anthropology* 36:769–88.

Roberts, M., 1991. Origin, dispersal routes, and geographic distribution of *Rattus exulans*, with specific reference to New Zealand. *Pacific Science* 45:123–30.

Roberts, R. G., R. Jones, and M. A. Smith, 1990. Thermoluminescence dating of a 50,000 year-old human occupation site in northern Australia. *Nature* 345:153–6.

———. 1995. Beyond the radiocarbon barrier in Australian prehistory. *Antiquity* 68:611–16.

Roe, D. 1992. Investigations into the prehistory of the central Solomons: Some old and some new data from Northwest Guadalcanal. In J.-C. Galipaud, ed., *Poterie Lapita et Peuplement, Actes du Colloque LAPITA*, pp. 91–102. Noumea: ORSTOM.

———. 1993. Prehistory Without Pots: Prehistoric Settlement and Economy of North-west Guadalcanal, Solomon Islands. Unpublished Ph.D. Dissertation, Australian National University.

Rogers, G. 1974. Archaeological discoveries on Niuatoputapu Island, Tonga. *Journal of the Polynesian Society* 83:308–48.

Romney, A. K. 1957. The genetic model and Uto-Aztecan time perspective. *Davidson Journal of Anthropology* 3:35–41.

Ross, M. D. 1988. *Proto Oceanic and the Austronesian Languages of Western Melanesia*. Pacific Linguistics, Series C, No. 98. Canberra: Department of Linguistics, Australian National University.

———. 1989. Early Oceanic linguistic prehistory. *Journal of Pacific History* 24:135–49.

———. 1993. **kanang ma wasa*: Reconstructing food plant terms and associated terminologies in Proto Oceanic. Paper presented to the First International Conference on Oceanic Linguistics, Port Vila, Vanuatu.

Rouse, I. and J. M. Cruxent, 1963. *Venezuelan Archaeology*. New Haven: Yale University Press.

Sahlins, M. 1972. *Stone Age Economics*. Chicago: Aldine-Atherton.

———. 1995. *How "Natives" Think: About Captain Cook, For Example*. Chicago: University of Chicago Press.

Sand, C. 1990. The ceramic chronology of Futuna and Alofi: an overview. In M. Spriggs, ed., *Lapita Design, Form and Composition*, pp. 123–33. *Occasional Papers in Prehistory No. 19*. Canberra: Department of Prehistory, Australian National University.

———. 1992. La differenciation des chronologies ceramiques de Polynésie occidentale a partir d'une tradition culturelle commune issue du complexe culturel Lapita. In J.-C. Galipaud, ed., *Poterie Lapita et Peuplement, Actes du Colloque LAPITA*, pp. 207–18. Noumea: ORSTOM.

———. 1993a. *Archéologie en Nouvelle-Calédonie*. Noumea: Agence de Développement de la Culture Kanak.

———. 1993b. Données archéologiques et géomorphologiques du site ancien d'Asipani (Futuna – Polynésie occidentale). *Journal de la Société des Océanistes* 97:117–44.

———. 1994. La Préhistoire de la Nouvelle-Calédonie. These de Préhistoire, Ethnologie, Anthropologie, Université Paris I (Pantheon-Sorbonne), Paris.

Sand, C. and A. Ouétcho, 1993. Three thousand years of settlement in the South of New Caledonia: Some recent results from the region of Païta. *New Zealand Journal of Archaeology* 15:107–30.

Sapir, E. 1916 *Time Perspective in Aboriginal American Culture: A Study in Method*. Canada, Department of Mines, Geological Survey, Memoir 90 Anthropological Series No. 13. Ottawa: Government Printing Bureau.

Serjeantson, S. W. 1989. HLA genes and antigens. In A. V. S. Hill and S. W. Serjeantson, eds, *The Colonization of the Pacific: A Genetic Trail*, pp. 120–73. Oxford: Clarendon Press.

Serjeantson, S. W. and X. Gao, 1995. *Homo sapiens* is an evolving species: Origins of the Austronesians. In P. Bellwood, J. J. Fox, and

D. Tryon, eds, *The Austronesians: Historical and Comparative Perspectives*, pp. 165–80. Canberra: Australian National University.

Serjeantson, S. W. and A. V. S. Hill, 1989. The colonization of the Pacific: The genetic evidence. In A. V. S. Hill and S. W. Serjeantson, eds, *The Colonization of the Pacific: A Genetic Trail*, pp. 286–94. Oxford: Clarendon Press.

Serjeantson, S. W., D. P. Ryan, and A. R. Thompson, 1982. The colonization of the Pacific: The story according to human leukocyte antigens. *American Journal of Human Genetics* 34:904–18.

Sharp, N. 1988. Style and substance: A reconsideration of the Lapita decorative system. In P. V. Kirch and T. L. Hunt, eds, *Archaeology of the Lapita Cultural Complex: A Critical Review*, pp. 61–82. Thomas Burke Memorial Washington State Museum Research Report No. 5. Seattle.

——. 1991. Lapita as text: The meaning of pottery in Melanesian prehistory. In P. Bellwood, ed., *Indo-Pacific Prehistory 1990: Proceedings of the 14th Congress of the Indo-Pacific Prehistory Association*, pp. 323–32. Canberra: Indo-Pacific Prehistory Association.

Shaw, E. 1975. The decorative system of Natunuku, Fiji. In S. Mead, L. Birks, H. Birks, and E. Shaw, *The Lapita Style of Fiji and Its Associations*, pp. 44–55. Polynesian Society Memoir 38. Wellington.

Sheppard, P. J. 1992. A report on the flaked lithic assemblage from three Southeast Solomons Lapita sites. In J.-C. Galipaud, ed., *Poterie Lapita et Peuplement, Actes du Colloque LAPITA*, pp. 145–54. Noumea: ORSTOM.

——. 1993. Lapita lithics: Trade/exchange and technology. A view from the Reefs/Santa Cruz. *Archaeology in Oceania* 28:121–37.

Sheppard, P. J. and R. C. Green, 1991. Spatial analysis of the Nenumbo (SE-RF-2) Lapita site, Solomon Islands. *Archaeology in Oceania* 26:89–101.

Shutler, R., Jr., D. V. Burley, W. R. Dickinson, E. Nelson, and A. K. Carlson, 1994. Early Lapita sites, the colonisation of Tonga and recent data from northern Ha'apai. *Archaeology in Oceania* 29:53–68.

Shutler, R., Jr. and J. C. Marck, 1975. On the dispersal of the Austronesian horticulturalists. *Archaeology and Physical Anthropology in Oceania* 10:81–113.

Shutler, R., Jr., Y. H. Sinoto, and J. Takayama, n.d. [1978]. Fefan Island Survey and Mitigation Project. Mimeographed report prepared for U. S. National Park Service. Available on microfiche from National Technical Information Service, Washington, D.C.

Siorat, J.-P. 1990. A technological analysis of Lapita pottery decoration. In M. Spriggs, ed., *Lapita Design, Form and Composition,* pp. 59–82. *Occasional Papers in Prehistory No. 19.* Canberra: Department of Prehistory, Australian National University.

——. 1992. Analyse test sur les decors des bandeaux principaux de la poterie Lapita du site WBR001 de Nouvelle-Caledonie. In J.-C. Galipaud, ed., *Poterie Lapita et Peuplement, Actes du Colloque LAPITA,* pp. 193–206. Noumea: ORSTOM.

Smith, A. 1995. The need for Lapita: Explaining change in the Late Holocene Pacific archaeological record. *World Archaeology* 26: 366–79.

Smith, M. A. and N. D. Sharp, 1993. Pleistocene sites in Australia, New Guinea and Island Melanesia: Geographic and temporal structure of the archaeological record. In M. A. Smith, M. Spriggs, and B. Fankhauser, eds, *Sahul in Review: Pleistocene Archaeology in Australia, New Guinea and Island Melanesia,* pp. 37–59. *Occasional Papers in Prehistory,* No. 24. Canberra: Department of Prehistory, Australian National University.

Southern, W. 1986. The Late Quarternary Environmental History of Fiji. Unpublished Ph.D. Thesis, Department of Geography, Australia National University, Canberra.

Specht, J. 1968. Preliminary report on excavations on Watom Island. *Journal of the Polynesian Society* 77:117–34.

——. 1974. Lapita pottery at Talasea, West New Britain, Papua New Guinea. *Antiquity* 48:302–6.

——. 1991. Kreslo: A Lapita pottery site in southwest New Britain, Papua New Guinea. In J. Allen and C. Gosden, eds, *Report of the Lapita Homeland Project,* pp. 189–204. *Occasional Papers in Prehistory,* No. 20. Canberra: Department of Prehistory, Australian National University.

Specht, J., R. Fullagar, and R. Torrence, 1991. What was the significance of Lapita pottery at Talasea? In P. Bellwood, ed., *Indo-Pacific Prehistory 1990: Proceedings of the 14th Congress of the Indo-Pacific Prehistory Association,* pp. 281–94. Canberra: Indo-Pacific Prehistory Association.

Specht, J., I. Lilley, and J. Normu, 1981. Radiocarbon dates from west New Britain, Papua New Guinea. *Australian Archaeology* 12:13–15.

Spennemann, D. H. R. 1987. Availability of shellfish resources on prehistoric Tongatapu, Tonga: Effects of human predation and changing environment. *Archaeology in Oceania* 22:81–96.

——. 1989. 'Ata 'a Tonga mo 'Ata 'o Tonga: Early and Later Prehistory of the Tongan Islands. Unpublished Ph.D. Dissertation, Australian National University, Canberra.

Spoehr, A. 1957. *Marianas Prehistory: Archaeological Survey and*

Excavations on Saipan, Tinian, and Rota. Fieldiana: Anthropology 48. Chicago: Field Museum of Natural History.

———. 1973. *Zamboanga and Sulu: An Archaeological Approach to Ethnic Diversity.* Ethnology Monographs No. 1. Department of Anthropology, University of Pittsburgh.

Spriggs, M. 1982. Taro cropping systems in the Southeast Asian-Pacific region. *Archaeology in Oceania* 17:7–15.

———. 1984. The Lapita Cultural Complex: origins, distribution, contemporaries and successors. *Journal of Pacific History* 19:202–23.

———. 1989. The dating of the Island Southeast Asian Neolithic: An attempt at chronometric hygiene and linguistic correlation. *Antiquity* 63:587–613.

———.1990a. Dating Lapita: Another view. In M. Spriggs, ed., *Lapita Design, Form and Composition*, pp. 6–27. *Occasional Papers in Prehistory, No. 19.* Canberra: Department of Prehistory, Australian National University.

———. 1990b. The changing face of Lapita: Transformation of a design. In M. Spriggs, ed., *Lapita Design, Form and Composition*, pp. 83–122. *Occasional Papers in Prehistory, No. 19.* Canberra: Department of Prehistory, Australian National University.

———. 1991a. Lapita origins, distribution, contemporaries and successors revisited. In P. Bellwood, ed., *Indo-Pacific Prehistory 1990: Proceedings of the 14th Congress of the Indo-Pacific Prehistory Association*, pp. 306–12. Canberra: Indo-Pacific Prehistory Association.

———. 1991b. Nissau, the island in the middle. In J. Allen and C. Gosden, eds, *Report of the Lapita Homeland Project*, pp. 222–43. Occasional Papers in Prehistory, No. 20. Canberra: Department of Prehistory, Australian National University.

———. 1992. What happens to Lapita in Melanesia? In J.-C. Galipaud, ed., *Poterie Lapita et Peuplement, Actes du Colloque LAPITA*, pp. 219–30. Noumea: ORSTOM.

———. 1993a. Pleistocene agriculture in the Pacific: Why not? In M. A. Smith, M. Spriggs, and B. Fankhauser, eds, *Sahul in Review: Pleistocene Archaeology in Australia, New Guinea and Island Melanesia*, pp. 137–43. *Occasional Papers in Prehistory, No. 24.* Canberra: Department of Prehistory, Australian National University.

———. 1993b. Island Melanesia: The last 10,000 years. In M. A. Smith, M. Spriggs, and B. Fankhauser, eds, *Sahul in Review: Pleistocene Archaeology in Australia, New Guinea and Island Melanesia*, pp. 187–205. *Occasional Papers in Prehistory, No. 24.* Canberra: Department of Prehistory, Australian National University.

———. 1993c. How much of the Lapita design system represents the human face? In P. J. C. Dark and R. G. Rose, eds, *Artistic Heritage in a Changing Pacific*, pp. 7–14. Honolulu: University of Hawaii Press.

——. 1995. The Lapita culture and Austronesian prehistory in Oceania. In P. Bellwood, J. J. Fox, and D. Tryon, eds, *The Austronesians: Historical and Comparative Perspectives*, pp. 112–33. Canberra: Australian National University.

——. in press. What is southeast Asian about Lapita? In T. Akazawa and E. Szathmary, eds, *Prehistoric Mongloid Dispersals*. Oxford: Oxford University Press.

Steadman, D. 1989. Extinction of birds in eastern Polynesia: A review of the record, and comparisons with other Pacific island groups. *Journal of Archaeological Science* 16:177–205.

——. 1993. Bird bones from the To'aga Site: Prehistoric loss of seabirds and megapodes. In P. V. Kirch and T. L. Hunt, eds, *The To'aga Site: Three Millennia of Polynesian Occupation in the Manu'a Islands, American Samoa*. ARF Contribution No. 51. Berkeley: University of California.

——. 1995. Prehistoric extinctions of Pacific Island birds: Biodiversity meets zooarchaeology. *Science*: 267:1,123–31.

Stevenson, J. and J. R. Dodson, 1995. Palaeoenvironmental evidence for human settlement of New Caledonia. *Archaeology in Oceania* 30:36–41.

Stoddart, D. R. 1992. Biogeography of the tropical Pacific. *Pacific Science* 46:276–93.

Stone, T. 1989. Origins and environmental significance of shell and earth mounds in Northern Australia. *Archaeology in Oceania* 24:59–64.

Stuiver, M., G. W. Pearson, and T. Braziunas, 1986. Radiocarbon age calibration of marine samples back to 9,000 cal BP. *Radiocarbon* 28(2B):980–1,021.

Su'a, T. I. 1987. Polynesian Pudding Processes in East and West Polynesia. Unpublished M. A. Thesis, University of Auckland, New Zealand.

Summerhayes, G. R., J. R. Bird, R. Fullagar, C. Gosden, J. Specht, and R. Torrence, in press. Application of PIXE-PIGME to obsidian characterization on West New Britain, Papua New Guinea. In S. Shackley, ed., *Method and Theory in Archaeological Volcanic Glass Studies*. New York: Plenum Press.

Summerhayes, G. R., and M. Hotchkis, 1992. Recent advances in Melanesian obsidian sourcing: Results of the 1990 and 1991 PIXE/PIGME analyses. In J.-C. Galipaud, ed., *Poterie Lapita et Peuplement, Actes du Colloque LAPITA*, pp. 127–34. Noumea: ORSTOM.

Swadling, P. 1986. Lapita shellfishing: evidence from sites in the Reef Santa Cruz group, Southeast Solomon Islands. In A. Anderson, ed., *Traditional Fishing in the Pacific*, pp. 137–48. *Pacific Anthropological Records* 37. Honolulu: Bernice P. Bishop Museum.

Swadling, P., N. Araho, and B. Ivuyo, 1991. Settlements associated with the Sepik-Ramu Sea. In P. Bellwood, ed., *Indo-Pacific Prehistory 1990: Proceedings of the 14th Congress of the Indo-Pacific Prehistory Association*, pp. 92–112. Canberra: Indo-Pacific Prehistory Association.

Swadling, P., J. Chappell, G. Francis, N. Araho, and B. Ivuyo, 1989. A Late Quaternary inland sea and early pottery in Papua New Guinea. *Archaeology in Oceania* 24:106–9.

Swadling, P., B. H. Schaublin, P. Gorecki, and F. Tiesler, 1988. *The Sepik-Ramu: An Introduction*. Boroko: National Museum of Papua New Guinea.

Tate, G. 1951. The rodents of Australia and New Guinea. *American Museum of Natural History Bulletin* 97:189–430.

Terrell, J. 1981. Linguistics and the peopling of the Pacific Islands. *Journal of the Polynesian Society* 90:225–58.

———. 1986. *Prehistory in the Pacific Islands*. Cambridge: Cambridge University Press.

———. 1989. What Lapita is and what Lapita isn't. *Antiquity* 63:623–6.

Thiel, B. 1985. Austronesian origins and expansion: The Philippine archaeological data. *Asian Perspectives* 26:119–30.

———. 1986. Excavations at the Lal-lo shell middens, Northeast Luzon, Philippines. *Asian Perspectives* 27:71–94.

Thomas, N. 1989. *Out of Time: History and Evolution in Anthropological Discourse*. Cambridge: Cambridge University Press.

———. 1991. *Entangled Objects: Exchange, Material Culture, and Colonialism in the Pacific*. Cambridge: Harvard University Press.

Torrence, R. and K. Victor, 1995. The relativity of density. *Archaeology in Oceania* 30:121–31.

Toussaint-Samat, M. 1992. *A History of Food*. Translated by A. Bell. Cambridge: Blackwell Publishers.

Trask, H.-K. 1993. *From a Native Daughter: Colonialism and Sovereignty in Hawai'i*. Monroe, Maine: Common Courage Press.

Tryon, D. T. 1984. The peopling of the Pacific: A linguistic appraisal. *The Journal of Pacific History* 19:147–59.

———. 1994. Oceanic plant names. In A. K. Pawley and M. D. Ross, eds, *Austronesian Terminologies: Continuity and Change*, pp. 481–510. Pacific Linguistics Series C-127. Canberra: Australian National University.

——. 1995. Proto-Austronesian and the major Austronesian subgroups. In P. Bellwood, J. J. Fox, and D. Tryon, eds, *The Austronesians: Historical and Comparative Perspectives*, pp. 17–38. Canberra: Australian National University.

Tsang, C.-H. 1992. *Archaeology of the P'eng-Hu Islands*. Institute of History and Philology, Special Publication No. 95. Taipei: Academia Sinica.

Turner II, C. G. 1986. Dentochronological separation estimates for Pacific Rim populations. *Science* 232:1,140–2.

——. 1989. Dentition of Watom Island, Bismarck Archipelago, Melanesia. *Records of the Australian Museum* 41:293–6.

Tushingham, A. M. and W. R. Peltier, 1991. Ice 3G: A new global model of late Pleistocene deglaciation based upon geophysical predictions of post-glacial relative sea-level change. *Journal of Geophysical Research* 96:4,497–523.

Vanderwal, R. L. 1978. Exchange in prehistoric coastal Papua. *Mankind* 11: 416–28.

van Heekeren, H. R. 1972. *The Stone Age of Indonesia*. Verhandelingen van het Koninklijk Instituut voor Taal-, Land- en Volkenkunde 61. The Hague.

Vogt, E. Z. 1964. The genetic model and Maya cultural development. In E. Z. Vogt and A. Ruz. L., eds, *Desarrollo Cultural de los Mayas*, pp. 9–48. México D. F.: Universidad Nacional Autónoma de México.

Wallace, A. R. 1895. *Island Life, or the Phenomena and Causes of Insular Faunas and Floras, including a Revision and Attempted Solution of the Problem of Geological Climates*. Third Edition. London: MacMillan and Co.

Walter, R. 1989. Lapita fishing strategies: A review of the archaeological and linguistic evidence. *Pacific Studies* 31:127–49.

Ward, G. K. 1976. The archaeology of settlements associated with the chert industry of Ulawa. In R. C. Green and M. M. Cressell, eds, *Southeast Solomon Islands Cultural History*, pp. 161–80. Royal Society of New Zealand Bulletin 11. Wellington: The Royal Society of New Zealand.

Ward, G. K. and I. E. Smith, 1974. Characterization of chert as an aid to the identification of patterns of trade, southeast Solomon Islands: A preliminary investigation. *Mankind* 9:281–6.

Waterson, R. 1990. *The Living House: An Anthropology of Architecture in South-East Asia*. Singapore: Oxford University Press.

——. 1993. Houses and the built environment in island southeast Asia: Tracing some shared themes in the uses of space. In J. J. Fox, ed., *Inside Austronesian Houses: Perspectives on Domestic*

Designs for Living, pp. 220–5. Canberra: Australian National University.

——. 1995. Houses and hierarchies in island Southeast Asia. In J. Carsten and S. Hugh-Jones, eds, *About the House: Levi-Strauss and Beyond*, pp. 47–68. Cambridge: Cambridge University Press.

Weiner, A. B. 1992. *Inalienable Possessions: The Paradox of Keeping-While-Giving*. Berkeley: University of California Press.

Welsch, R. L., J. Terrell, and J. A. Nadolski, 1992. Language and culture on the North Coast of New Guinea. *American Anthropologist* 94:568–600.

White, J. P., J. Allen, and J. Specht, 1988. Peopling the Pacific: The Lapita Homeland Project. *Australian Natural History* 22:410–16.

White, J. P., T. F. Flannery, R. O'Brien, R. V. Hancock, and L. Pavlish, 1991. The Balof Shelters, New Ireland. In J. Allen and C. Gosden, eds, *Report of the Lapita Homeland Project*, pp. 46–58. *Occasional Papers in Prehistory*, No. 20. Canberra: Department of Prehistory, Australian National University.

White, J. P. and J. F. O'Connell, 1982. *A Prehistory of Australia, New Guinea and Sahul*. Sydney: Academic Press.

White, J. P. and J. Specht, 1971. Prehistoric pottery from Ambitle Island, Bismarck Archipelago. *Asian Perspectives* 14:88–94.

Wickler, S. 1990. Prehistoric Melanesian exchange and interaction: Recent evidence from the Northern Solomon Islands. *Asian Perspectives* 29:135–54.

Wickler, S. and M. Spriggs, 1988. Pleistocene human occupation of the Solomon Islands, Melanesia. *Antiquity* 62:703–6.

Wiens, H. J. 1962. *Atoll Environment and Ecology*. New Haven: Yale University Press.

Willey, G. R. and P. Phillips, 1958. *Method and Theory in American Archaeology*. Chicago: University of Chicago Press.

Winslow, J. H. ed., 1977. *The Melanesian Environment*. Canberra: Australian National University Press.

Wurm, S. 1967. Linguistics and the prehistory of the south-western Pacific. *The Journal of Pacific History* 2:25–38.

——. 1982. *The Papuan languages of Oceania*. Acta Linguistica 7. Tubingen: Gunter Narr.

Yen, D. E. 1973. The origins of Oceanic agriculture. *Archaeology and Physical Anthropology in Oceania* 8:68–85.

——. 1974. Arboriculture in the subsistence of Santa Cruz, Solomon Islands. *Economic Botany* 28:274–84.

——. 1975. Indigenous food processing in Oceania. In M. Arnott, ed., *Gastronomy: The Anthropology of Food and Food Habits*, pp. 147–68. Chicago: Aldine.

——. 1990. Environment, agriculture and the colonisation of the Pacific. In D. E. Yen and J. M. J. Mummery, eds, *Pacific Production Systems: Approaches to Economic Prehistory*, pp. 258–77. *Occasional Papers in Prehistory* No. 18. Canberra: Department of Prehistory, Australian National University.

——. 1991a. Polynesian cultigens and cultivars: The questions of origin. In P. A. Cox and S. A. Banack, eds, *Islands, Plants, and Polynesians*, pp. 67–96. Portland, Oregon: Dioscorides Press.

——. 1991b. Domestication: The lessons from New Guinea. In A. Pawley, ed., *Man and a Half: Essays in Pacific Anthropology and Ethnobiology in Honour of Ralph Bulmer*, pp. 558–69. Auckland: The Polynesian Society.

——. 1993. Pacific subsistence systems and aspects of cultural evolution. In M. A. Smith, M. Spriggs, and B. Fankhauser, eds, *Sahul in Review: Pleistocene Archaeology in Australia, New Guinea and Island Melanesia*, pp. 88–96. *Occasional Papers in Prehistory*, No. 24. Canberra: Department of Prehistory, Australian National University.

Yen, D. and J. Gordon, eds, 1973. *Anuta: A Polynesian Outlier in the Solomon Islands*. Pacific Anthropological Records 21. Honolulu: Bishop Museum Press.

Yonekura, N., T. Ishii, Y. Saito, Y. Maeda, Y. Matsuhima, E. Matsumoto, and H. Kayanne, 1988. Holocene fringing reefs and sea-level change in Mangaia Island, Southern Cook Islands. *Paleogeography, Paleoclimatology, Paleoecology* 68:177–88.

Zorc, R. D. P. 1994. Austronesian culture history through reconstructed vocabulary. In A. K. Pawley and M. D. Ross, eds, *Austronesian Terminologies: Continuity and Change*, pp. 541–94. Pacific Linguistics, Series C-127. Canberra: Australian National University.

Zug, G. R. 1991. *The Lizards of Fiji: Natural History and Systematics*. Bishop Museum Bulletin in Zoology 2. Honolulu: Bishop Museum Press.

Index